PUBLIC ARCHAEOLOGY

Increasing public interest and participation in archaeology have ensured that the relationship between archaeology, heritage and the public is now studied as a subject in its own right. This volume, written by contributors from the UK, North and South America, Africa, Australia and China, provides a much needed survey of the relationship from an international perspective.

The focus is on two key themes: communication and interpretation, and public stakeholders – the people or organisations who participate in archaeology, from schoolchildren to state bodies. The case studies range from indigenous communities and archaeology, a scheme to bring treasure hunters and archaeologists together, and public archaeology in Brazil and the USA, to involving the public in museum archaeology, and the use of the Internet and the media to reach out to wider audiences.

As one of the first books to concentrate on different aspects of public archaeology around the world, this will be a valuable guide to the issues involved for both students and practitioners in archaeology and heritage.

Nick Merriman is Reader in Museum Studies and Cultural Heritage at the Institute of Archaeology, University College London, and curator of UCL Museums and Collections. His previous publications include *Beyond the Glass Case: The Past, the Heritage and the Public in Britain* (1991, 2000) and *Making Early Histories in Museums* (1999).

PUBLIC ARCHAEOLOGY

Edited by Nick Merriman

Routledge
Taylor & Francis Group

LONDON AND NEW YORK

First published 2004
by Routledge
2 Park Square, Milton Park, Abingdon, Oxon OX14 4RN

Simultaneously published in the USA and Canada
by Routledge
270 Madison Avenue, New York, NY 10016

Reprinted 2005

Routledge is an imprint of the Taylor & Francis Group

Typeset in Garamond by
Keystroke, Jacaranda Lodge, Wolverhampton
Printed and bound in Great Britain by
MPG Books Ltd, Bodmin

British Library Cataloguing in Publication Data
A catalogue record for this book is available from the British Library

Library of Congress Cataloging in Publication Data
has been applied for

ISBN 0–415–25888–x (hbk)
ISBN 0–415–25889–8 (pbk)

FOR CAROLINE

CONTENTS

ILLUSTRATIONS

Figures

Tables

Boxes

CONTRIBUTORS

Neal Ascherson, freelance journalist, c/o Institute of Archaeology, University College London, UK

Roger Bland, British Museum, UK

Denis Byrne, New South Wales National Parks and Wildlife Service, Australia

Tim Copeland, The International Centre for Heritage Education, University of Gloucestershire, Cheltenham, UK

Pedro Paulo A. Funari, Department of History, University of Campinas, Brazil

John H. Jameson Jr., Southeast Archeological Center (SEAC), US National Park Service, Florida, USA

Paul Lane, British Institute in Eastern Africa, Nairobi, Kenya

Carol McDavid, Department of Archaeology, University of Cambridge, UK

Sally MacDonald, Petrie Museum of Egyptian Archaeology, University College London, UK

Bertram Mapunda, Archaeology Unit, Department of History, University of Dar es Salaam, Tanzania

Nick Merriman, Institute of Archaeology, University College London, UK

Mike Parker Pearson, Department of Archaeology, University of Sheffield, UK

Dashu Qin, Department of Archaeology, University of Peking, People's Republic of China

Ramilisonina, Université d'Antananarivo, Madagascar

Tim Schadla-Hall, Institute of Archaeology, University College London, UK

Catherine Shaw, National Children's Bureau, London, UK

Karolyn E. Smardz Frost, Department of History, University of Waterloo, Ontario, Canada

Roger M. Thomas, English Heritage, UK

ACKNOWLEDGEMENTS

This book has its origins in a session organised by myself and Tim Schadla-Hall at the 4th World Archaeological Congress in Cape Town in 1999. Some of the papers delivered at that session were rewritten and updated for the book, and others were specially commissioned to provide wider coverage of some of the issues.

I would like to acknowledge the input of Tim Schadla-Hall in the initial work for this book, and would like to thank the authors of the individual contributions for their patience while the volume has been assembled.

I am grateful to the owners of the copyright for the various illustrations used for permitting their use. They are credited in the list of illustrations.

Finally, I would like to thank my wife Caroline for bearing with me while I have been working on the editing. I dedicate this book to her.

1

INTRODUCTION

Diversity and dissonance in public archaeology

Nick Merriman

What do we mean by 'the public'?

The notion of 'the public' in the sense of a collective body of citizens, and in contrast to the private realm, has been around since at least Roman times (Melton 2001: 1). However, there are two more specific meanings of the term, both of which are central to any discussion of public archaeology. The first is the association of the word 'public' with the state and its institutions (public bodies, public buildings, public office, the public interest), which emerges in the era of intensive state-formation from the Early Modern period onwards (ibid.). As far as archaeology is concerned, the opening of the British Museum in 1753 is probably the first instance of a state creating a public institution which includes the display of archaeological collections as part of its central remit.

The second is the concept of 'the public' as a group of individuals who debate issues and consume cultural products, and whose reactions inform 'public opinion' (ibid.). This notion developed during the Enlightenment, and has received its fullest treatment in Habermas's *The Structural Transformation of the Public Sphere* (1962). For Habermas, the model for an open, critical, participatory democracy was founded in the development of a bourgeois public sphere in the eighteenth century, fuelled by developments in new kinds of public spaces such as coffee houses and salons, and in new forms of communication such as newspapers and novels. Habermas's own model has been criticised for its insufficient attention to gender, for its lack of acknowledgement that only property owners were in practice admitted to the public sphere, and for ignoring the 'plebeian public sphere' often dismissed as 'the mob' (McGuigan 1996: 24–5). However, for our purposes his work is seminal in identifying the specific historical circumstances during which a notion of 'the public' as a critical body external to that of the state, developed.

On the one hand, therefore, we have a notion in which the state assumes the role of speaking on behalf of the public and of acting 'in the public interest'.

This can include the state's provision of public institutions and services such as archaeology, museums, and education. The assumption by the state that it acts in the overall public interest means that minority interests may not be represented effectively, and a high-handed approach by the state can mean that it can lose contact with the wishes of a diverse public. One of the questions for a public archaeology must therefore be how to ensure that the state, when discharging the public interest, takes into account the views of the public, and is held properly accountable to the public for its actions (see Thomas, Chapter 9, this volume).

On the other hand, the second notion of 'the public' encompasses debate and opinion, and is inherently unpredictable and conflictual. The public, particularly when defined as an active and multivalent force rather than the faceless mass portrayed by the critics of mass culture (e.g. Adorno and Horkheimer 1944), can have the power to influence, criticise or subvert the wishes of the state and to bring about change. Indeed the blanket term 'the public' is always unsatisfactory to describe a hugely diverse range of people, with different age, sex, class, ethnicity and religious interests and affiliations, many of which are in conflict with each other. Despite criticism in most texts on, for example, visitor studies, the notion of 'the general public' manages to survive. Its only validity for our purposes comes if it is used as a shorthand term to describe the huge diversity of the population, who do not earn their living as professional archaeologists. It is only their characteristic of not being professional archaeologists that unites 'the public' in our context; by any other measure, 'the public' does not exist. Rather, we should conceive of those who are not professional archaeologists as a shifting set of cross-cutting interest groups which sometimes have a great deal in common, but often have little in common at all.

So, the two notions of 'the public' – the state and the people – have always been potentially in tension. At its starkest, this tension can be reflected in a distant, largely unaccountable state apparatus for archaeology which does not reflect the diversity of views and interests held by the public, and a public which is disenchanted with the archaeology provided by the state, feeling that it does not reflect their interests, and preferring to explore other ways of understanding the past. At best, this tension can be embraced as an inevitable and positive quality of people's relationships with the past. This would entail the state authorities recognising, respecting and working with the great diversity of public attitudes to the heritage and involving communities in the stewardship and interpretation of their pasts. These two slightly different definitions of the public also beg the question of what kind of definition is used by archaeologists. In the literature, most often 'public' archaeology means the archaeology regulated by the state, discharging a generalised public interest, and only occasionally does it mean the archaeology of 'the public', who pursue their own (different and competing) ways of understanding the past.

How is 'public archaeology' defined?

The term 'public archaeology' first entered widespread archaeological use with the publication of McGimsey's volume of the same name in 1972. At this time, the term was associated with the practical exigencies of development-led cultural resource management (CRM), in contrast with academic archaeology and its apparent concern with wider research questions. As Jameson and Smardz Frost (Chapters 2 and 3, this volume) note, the sheer size of the USA and the vastness of its potential archaeological resource led to a realisation that the non-archaeological public had to be co-opted in the service of archaeology, if sites were to be protected or responsibly investigated. CRM was therefore 'public' archaeology because it relied on public support in order to convince legislators and developers that archaeological sites needed protection or mitigation, and often it relied on non-professionals to do the work. Through time, however, as archaeology became more professionalised, the 'public' element of this archaeology came to consist of archaeologists managing cultural resources *on behalf of* the public, rather than entailing a great deal of direct public involvement in the work itself. 'Public archaeology' in these terms in fact signalled the professionalisation of archaeology, and the relative decline of public participation. This situation has been paralleled in the UK.

The increasing professionalisation of archaeology results in a situation where the state and its agents act on behalf of the public through the planned implementation of cultural resource management strategies. Under such strategies, the public interest is generally thought to be served through the preservation of cultural resources, or their careful recording during destruction. In this way, the public interest is served not so much in the present, but more in a vaguely defined future time called 'posterity' when the resources, or the records of them, may be consulted. In such a future-oriented strategy, the public itself, in the sense of the citizens of today, is only served indirectly, and will rarely be involved in the archaeology itself. 'Public interest' elements of public archaeology include, for example, cultural resource management, site stewardship, and combating looting and illicit trade.

Over recent years, as archaeologists have come to realise that the current public's interest in archaeology has been inadequately catered for in the CRM approach, they have begun to develop a closer interest in the public's own interests. I have traced elsewhere the factors that have led to a new 'opening-up' of professional archaeology to embrace the wider public, and to the treatment of the public's relationship with archaeology as a topic of academic interest in its own right (Merriman 2002). These have included the strong influence of archaeological theory, from Marxism to post-modernism, which has led to a recognition of the historical contingency of archaeological work, and the multivalency of interpretation. Change has also been impelled from outside the discipline, following the campaigns by indigenous and other minority peoples to have a say in the study and interpretation of their own pasts, supported by successive World Archaeological Congresses and subsequent publications. From a very different direction, change has been prompted by the fact that many of the outlets for public representations of archaeology (museums, exhibitions, heritage sites) have been forced to compete for visitors in a commercial leisure market, and have been subject to new forms of management which have involved the demonstration of accountability for public funds and value for money.

This 'return to the public' can also be placed within a wider context which has seen the development of the notion of the active citizen, in which choice and participation (particularly expressed through consumerism) is seen to be a major political advance: 'Citizenship is to be active and individualistic rather than passive and dependent. The political subject is henceforth to be an individual whose citizenship is manifested through the free exercise of personal choice among a variety of options' (Rose 1992: 159).

Perhaps in recognition of this problem, in recent years 'public archaeology' in the USA has, for some, grown in meaning to encompass direct public engagement again: 'Public archaeology in America can be understood as encompassing the CRM compliance consequences as well as educational archaeology and public interpretation in public arenas such as schools, parks, and museums' (Jameson, Chapter 2, this volume).

In other parts of the world, an even wider meaning of the term has developed, and it is this which is predominant in this book. Schadla-Hall (1999: 147) has defined it as 'any area of archaeological activity that interacted or had the potential to interact with the public'. Ascherson, in the first editorial for a new *Public Archaeology* journal, has suggested that the issues in public archaeology 'are about the problems which arise when archaeology moves into the real world of economic conflict and political struggle. In other words, they are all about ethics' (Ascherson 2000: 2).

Public archaeology therefore also has to be rooted in the relatively sophisticated debates which have now emerged around heritage in general. This debate has evolved in recent years away from a rather fruitless bipolar argument between the critical 'heritage baiters' and the populists celebrating heritage from below (Samuel 1994) to a more nuanced treatment of issues of identity and conflict, coupled with those of tourism and economics. Graham *et al.* (2000: 22) have usefully defined heritage – and by implication the archaeological heritage – as a duality of both economic and cultural capital, which exist in tension with each other: 'tension and conflict are thus inherent qualities of heritage, whatever its form'. We should not perhaps be surprised that most of the public aspects of archaeology are about conflict, or what Tunbridge and Ashworth (1995) have called 'dissonant heritage', because archaeology is ultimately about the development of cultural identities, and therefore it is inextricably bound up with politics. We see this most clearly in the actual destruction of physical remains in civil war (Layton *et al.* 2001) and in the contestation over the right to own, or interpret archaeological materials (Layton

1989a; Fforde *et al.* 2002; Simpson 1996), but we also see it in local disputes about destruction of sites or rights of access which do not make the national media. The dissonance of archaeological heritage has been most thoroughly explored by Skeates in his volume *Debating the Archaeological Heritage* (2000), which is replete with examples of conflict, debate and negotiation over all aspects of archaeology.

The field of public archaeology is significant because it studies the processes and outcomes whereby the discipline of archaeology becomes part of a wider public culture, where contestation and dissonance are inevitable. In being about ethics and identity, therefore, public archaeology is inevitably about negotiation and conflict over meaning. This broader definition of public archaeology opens up a space in which to discuss not just archaeological products (such as educational programmes, museum displays and site tours) but the processes by which meaning is created from archaeological materials in the public realm. Public archaeology, therefore, embraces the debates which open up between the official provision of archaeology on behalf of the public, and the differing publics which have a stake in archaeology, who will often debate amongst themselves about the meanings and values of archaeological resources.

What is the purpose of engaging with the public?

The deficit model

In examining why professional archaeology has found it important to engage more closely with the public, it is instructive to look at the development of the movement to promote the public understanding of science. The Royal Society's 1985 report, *The Public Understanding of Science*, put forward two main arguments for the importance of better public understanding. The first argued that Britain as a nation would gain economically if its workforce were more familiar with science and technology. The second was that improved public understanding created better citizens, who were more able to make informed democratic decisions in a culture increasingly pervaded by science (see Irwin and Wynne 1996). As MacDonald (2002: 49) notes:

> There was here an implicit casting of the public as deficient and misguided in its present 'lack of uptake' of science – a 'deficit model' of the public, whose failing had to be repaired by getting more science 'out' or 'across' the boundary from a specialised and relatively bounded world into that of the largely ignorant masses.

There is something of this 'deficit model' pervading many of the arguments given for the importance of public archaeology. If we engage with the public, the argument goes, then more people will understand what archaeologists are trying to do, and will support their work more. Public education, it is argued, will attempt to promulgate the message that stewardship of archae-ological resources is important, and 'correct' misapprehensions about the past propagated by the lunatic fringe (see McManamon 2000). To this extent, the 'deficit model' of public archaeology sees the public as needing education in the correct way to appreciate archaeology, and the role of public archaeology as building confidence in the professional work of archaeologists. Public participation is encouraged, of course, but only along lines of approved profes-sional practice. Alternative views are not to be particularly encouraged, except in the case of indigenous belief systems, which occupy a separate category (a point to which I shall return later). This could be called the 'public interest' approach, which is derived from the need for a professional archaeology to separate itself from the non-professionals, and is associated ultimately with authoritative knowledge, taking its model from that of science.

Whilst there are merits to this public interest approach in ensuring for example that sites and records are preserved for the future, there are also some flaws. The prime amongst these is the difficulty of reconciling the 'deficit model' with heritage's inherent property of 'dissonance'. If contestation, debate and conflict form the very essence of heritage, and therefore of archaeology as an element within this, then attempting to 'correct' deficits in knowledge and incorrect beliefs may not be a fruitful approach. Education in such contexts may not be a matter of instilling appropriate facts, but instead of equipping people with a set of tools with which to evaluate different forms of evidence and competing claims, and allowing them to come to their own conclusions, whether or not they conform to some external form of 'truth'. This, in essence, is what the constructivist approaches to museum and heritage interpretation have concluded (Ballantyne 1998; Copeland, Chapter 6, this volume; Hein 1998; and see below).

The multiple perspective model

However, scrutiny of some of the literature on the public understanding of science, and indeed on public archaeology, shows that there is another side to this. The debate on the public understanding of science has been domi-nated by attacks on the deficit model by social scientists, who argue that if public understanding is seen as a problem of public ignorance, 'the problem throws all the critical research attention on the public and the media. The only problems within science are to do with inducing scientists to communicate more clearly and entertainingly in lay terms' (Wynne 1992: 38). Critics have instead concentrated on challenging the authoritative role of science, as one aspect of what have been termed 'the science wars' (Durant 1997).

This criticism can be laid even more convincingly at the door of archaeology, which has even less claim on ultimate truths than the natural sciences. The deficit model in archaeology has been challenged, for example, by Holtdorf (2000) who, in a reply to McManamon's (2000) article, argued for the recognition of multiple perspectives: 'I can see no reason why non-professionals should not be welcomed and indeed be encouraged and supported in their own encounters with archaeology, whether these may closely resemble professional attitudes or not' (Holtdorf 2000: 215).

As Jameson (Chapter 2, this volume) notes, too often in cultural resource management, archaeologists 'lose sight of the real purpose of the compliance process: to provide public enjoyment and appreciation of the rich diversity of past human experiences'. Or, as Smardz (1997: 103) puts it, archaeology should: 'stop taking archaeology to the public for archaeology's sake and start doing it to meet the general public's educational, social, and cultural needs'.

In this 'multiple perspective' model, then, the purpose of engaging the public with archaeology is to encourage self-realisation, to enrich people's lives and stimulate reflection and creativity.

The advantage of this approach to public archaeology is that it recognises the importance of agency: no matter how hard archaeologists try, non-archaeologists will re-appropriate, re-interpret and re-negotiate meanings of archaeological resources to their own personal agendas. It is better, surely, to work actively with this realisation when considering the relationship between archaeology and the non-professional public, rather than to try to force people to follow a single agenda.

The problem with this approach, however, is that it can overbalance into an uncritical celebration of all public engagement with archaeology, no matter what its content or political orientation may be. This is a problem common to archaeology as a whole, where extreme relativism has been argued to presage the destruction of the discipline as a serious undertaking (Yoffee and Sherratt 1993). In practice, very few archaeologists take a position whereby any person's view about the past is as valid as anyone else's. Instead, most who would accept that archaeological interpretations are historically contingent, would subscribe to the 'perspectivist' view of Thomas (1995), which is that within a shared belief system such as western rationality it might be possible to agree on certain core issues, but these themselves will be interpreted from a number of different perspectives. Nevertheless, as Schadla-Hall (Chapter 14, this volume) argues, it is time to distinguish between 'good' and 'bad' public archaeologies, condemning those that denigrate or oppress others, while recognising and celebrating the diversity of other beliefs about the past, while at the same time being clear that archaeologists have strong arguments against the validity of some of them.

There are thus benefits to both the deficit model and the multiple perspective model. Even relativists might view the untrammelled depredation and destruction of archaeological sites with some misgivings, and most people would probably wish for some broad agreement on archaeological terms, chronologies, culture histories and the like to enable communication and debate to take place. By the same token it is surely right that a truly public archaeology also recognise and embrace the huge popular interest in the past in all its diversity, rather than seeing elements of it as a problem that has to be corrected.

Both approaches are followed in this book, and in many papers the two overlap, with it being recognised that a responsible approach to stewardship of basic primary archaeological resources, and a tolerant attitude to the diversity of the public and its interests are both appropriate. This book, it is hoped, represents something of a way forward in showing that the two approaches can exist side by side. This is explored in the two main sections of the book, which cover some, but by no means all, of the major issues in public archaeology today.

Issues in communication and interpretation

Understanding publics

The first section of the book deals with issues relating to communication in its broadest sense. We have already discussed some of the issues in the public understanding of science, and its predominant 'deficit model' of communication. It is most noticeable, however, that work on the public understanding of science is dominated by empirical studies of the understanding of scientific issues and research amongst the non-scientific public. As a result, scientists have built up a good understanding of the preconceptions, misconceptions, 'naïve notions', interests and opinions of their diverse publics. Their self-imposed challenge has then been to use these empirical studies to build effective communication. By contrast, there have been very few published studies of public understanding and attitudes to archaeology. Indeed, it often seems that archaeologists have shown little interest in the audiences for their work, other than that composed of the narrow band of their peers. All sensible models of communication (see for example Hooper-Greenhill 1994) show it to be a two-way process, a transaction or negotiation between the receiver and the transmitter, filtered by a variety of factors. With such a weak knowledge of the attitudes, conceptions and beliefs of the receivers of archaeological information, archaeologists have therefore been communicating blindly to an audience they do not understand, and it is no wonder that so many attempts at communicating archaeology result in boredom or incomprehension. In terms of understanding the public, then, archaeology has a lot to learn from the public understanding of science.

The little work that has been done has mostly been in North America, where for example Feder has undertaken surveys at an interval of ten years on 'cult archaeology' and creationist beliefs amongst students (Feder 1984, 1995) and Pokytolo and his colleagues have surveyed the attitudes of the wider public to archaeological heritage (Pokytolo and Mason 1991; Pokytolo and Guppy 1999). The largest scale study has been that undertaken by Harris Interactive on behalf of the Society for American Archaeology (Ramos and Duganne 2000), which interviewed 1016 American adults. These studies have generally demonstrated the high value placed upon archaeology by the public, and showed variable levels of understanding of what precisely it is that archaeology studies, or of how the discipline of archaeology works in practice. Some of the studies (e.g. those by Feder) have specifically concentrated on the adherence of even well-educated people to 'alternative' beliefs such as astro-archaeology and creationism (see Schadla-Hall, Chapter 14, this volume for a fuller discussion). The framing and the analysis of these surveys has been undertaken within the deficit model of analysis, attempting to understand misconceptions in order to work out how best to correct them.

In general, though, we still do not have a good understanding of the composition of the different audiences for archaeology and its different manifestations, what motivates people to take an interest in archaeology, what causes them to be bored by it, or of how people re-interpret and use the materials that archaeologists provide for them. My own survey undertaken several years ago (Merriman 1991) attempted to be a first step in this direction. It argued that there was a strong relationship between people's beliefs about the past in general and their current circumstances, with attitudes to the past being used as an unspoken commentary or critique of the present. In terms of attitudes specifically to archaeology and its alternatives, the survey suggested that there was a considerable overlap, with people who were interested in mainstream archaeology also sometimes professing 'alternative' beliefs at the same time. It was suggested that:

> Even if everyone were clear as to the established archaeological inter-
> pretation of Stonehenge or the Pyramids, this would not necessarily
> prevent many people from believing in spacemen and power fields,
> simply because these are more exciting explanations than the prosaic
> arguments put forward by archaeologists . . . In an increasingly
> rational and materialistic society the past, especially prehistory,
> may offer a refuge for the creative use of emotion and imagination in
> the construction of a non-rational and non-materialistic past.
>
> (Merriman 1991: 116–17)

This survey took a large-scale quantitative approach and needs to be developed further by more in-depth and qualitative research. An interesting contribution has been made by the research commissioned by English Heritage on attitudes to the historic environment (MORI 2000). Although it focused more broadly than archaeology, it was significant in identifying the fact that significant sectors of the UK's diverse population felt that the country's heritage was not their heritage or made relevant to them, and it also acknowledged that heritage was essentially personal in its meaning. It identified 'the need for meaning' as an important aspect of contemporary life, consequent upon the decline of traditional frameworks of meaning such as the family and religion.

'In a rapidly shifting society, heritage and the historic environment represent something constant and reliable' (MORI 2000). It also identified 'poly-sensuality' as another trend:

> More and more people are relying to a greater extent on their feelings and emotions in their everyday lives, at the expense of the purely rational. Meaning and value will be placed on something if it satisfies an individual in different ways. Not only does this mean that providers will need to consider audio, visual and tactile interpretation techniques, but they will also have to think about how to engage visitors' emotions, if they are to make a lasting impression, and create true value.
>
> (MORI 2000)

Constructing communication

What, then, are the implications of a challenging of the deficit model and an acceptance of the findings of some of the surveys above? The first implication must be that archaeologists must work very much harder at understanding the diversity of their audiences, and the kinds of meanings that people derive from archaeological materials. A great deal more qualitative visitor research needs to be undertaken in order to achieve this. A model for how this kind of work might be undertaken is provided in MacDonald and Shaw's paper (Chapter 5, this volume) where they report on research which, seemingly for the first time, has examined what potential audiences for Egyptian archaeology (including, crucially, people from Egypt itself, and people of African descent) want to know about the subject and what preconceptions they hold. As indicated by the MORI work cited above, what archaeology can say to increasingly mobile and culturally diverse audiences must be one of the most important issues for public archaeology in the near future, and it is essential that this issue be examined sensitively and thoroughly to avoid archaeology being deemed as irrelevant by major sections of the population.

Another implication of a focus on audiences is that archaeologists must recognise communication as a specialised field with its own research and disciplinary framework. Too often, archaeologists have treated communication as if it were a straightforward and transparent exercise. Copeland (Chapter 6, this volume) quotes M.W. Thompson, for example, who distinguished between 'primary interpretation', which is the archaeological interpretation of the evidence, and 'secondary interpretation', which is 'the popular transmission of this account . . . to other people', as if the public were blank sheets of paper on which archaeological interpretations could be written.

As Ascherson (Chapter 7, this volume) shows, when discussing archaeology and the media, we are not dealing with a case of 'translation' or 'dissemination'. Instead, in the representation and reception of archaeology in the media, there is a whole variety of actors and relationships involved, which form a new cultural discourse using the materials given to them.

An alternative is proposed by McDavid in her paper (Chapter 8, this volume) where she uses Rorty's (1989) idea of the 'conversation' between archaeologists and the public, rather than a 'presentation' or 'education'. Copeland's paper (Chapter 6, this volume) takes this further, when he argues that visiting a site is a 'cultural negotiation between the presentation and the visitor'. Criticising the limited work undertaken on visitors to archaeological sites for its concentration on assessing factual knowledge gained (the deficit model), he proposes instead that we should learn from the theories of constructivism, which are increasingly being used by educators as a useful model for the non-classroom environment of the museum or the site. This approach sees meaning as being constructed by the individual from the objects, events and ideas that they encounter, by building on and consolidating previous knowledge:

> Meaning is not necessarily evident within the exhibition material itself. Rather it acquires meaning when visitors relate it to aspects of their own experience and reasons for being there. Learning is not only the accretion of bits of information, but the development and elaboration of a person's understanding and knowledge organisation.
>
> (Ballantyne 1998: 84)

From the point of view of constructivism, what is important is that people derive meaning from an encounter with archaeology by relating it to their own lives, rather than whether it corresponds to current archaeological consensus.

This can also be seen in the ethnographic work of Angela Piccini (1999) on visitors to Iron Age 'constructed sites'. She shows how visitors use the sites essentially as a backdrop or 'theatre' in which to play out contemporary social relations, constantly relating what they are seeing to their present-day concerns.

This does not mean that the content of archaeological communications (books, lectures, site presentations, museums, television programmes) is meaningless. It does mean, however, that archaeologists will have to work *with* rather than *against* the fact that people constantly derive meanings from what is provided by reworking it into something that relates to them personally. In my own paper (Chapter 4, this volume) I suggest that an approach to communication which encourages 'informed imagination' would be a way forward which attempts to reconcile archaeologists' desires to impart correct information with the ways in which research shows people re-use the material given to them.

Challenges in communication and interpretation

However, there are a number of problems or challenges facing the approach to communication and interpretation described above. In her paper (Chapter 8),

McDavid shows in her case study that such an open approach to stimulating the interest of traditional non-participants does not really work, partly perhaps because archaeologists can be over-optimistic about the desire for some members of the public to participate.

For others, an open-ended celebration of 'visitor readings' can lead to a feeling of empowerment which is merely illusory. As I argue, being apparently 'active' and 'participative' in a physical sense can give an illusion of involvement when mental involvement is in fact reduced, just as 'choice' of interpretations can in fact close down options for real choice and engagement (MacDonald 2002).

The core issues in communication and interpretation, then, come down to the role ascribed to agency on the part of the public, and the degree to which expertise is allowed a place to shape and guide public engagement. From a cycle beginning with the 'deficit model' we have moved to a multivalent model which stresses the validity of all interpretations made by the public. It may now be right to insert the expert back into the agenda (Skeates 2000: 122–4).

The stakeholders

Some of the sharpest debates in public archaeology focus around the questions of who has rights to own and interpret the material remains of the past. Unlike issues of communication and interpretation, there has been a good deal published in this area, much of it in the One World Archaeology series, which has highlighted in several of its volumes the need to recognise the interests, for example, of indigenous peoples and other excluded groups (Layton 1989a, b; Stone and Mackenzie 1990).

Thomas, (Chapter 9, this volume), outlines a general model of how the state might respond to the recognition of the diversity of views held about archaeological evidence and the ancient past amongst members of the public. He puts forward the idea of the state as a facilitator in helping communities to come to a sense of their own past, and notes that in the UK some steps are already being taken in this direction by English Heritage, the state agency responsible for archaeology.

A good example of how professional archaeologists might act as facilitators for others in practice is given in Bland's case study (Chapter 15) of the portable antiquities recording scheme in England and Wales where, following decades of mutual suspicion and antagonism, metal detectorists were invited to become involved in a nationwide programme of voluntary recording of finds made by members of the public. The role of the professional experts – the portable antiquities liaison officers – has extended beyond that of simply recording finds, to giving advice about cleaning and conservation, to providing talks for metal detector clubs and school groups, developing exhibitions, and to incorporating metal detectorists into professional archaeological survey work.

Here, however, we are dealing with liaison between two groups both sharing the same cultural background and both ultimately interested in the rescuing and recording of the past (surveys show that few detectorists are motivated in their hobby by financial rewards: Dobinson and Denison 1995). What happens when archaeologists interact with those with very different outlooks?

Qin's paper (Chapter 16) is another example of the experiences of an archaeologically rich country of the global trade in antiquities. Here, he argues that the expansion of archaeology itself has been a direct spur to the expansion of the antiquities trade, as the increase in knowledge draws attention to sites and finds, and high academic value leads to high financial value. Most alarmingly, he shows how in one instance of 'community archaeology' where local people were trained in archaeological techniques to participate in excavations, they returned subsequently to loot the site, and archaeologists were accused of exacerbating the problem by training the looters!

Unfortunately, archaeologists are numerically very small on a national and global scale, and their political lobbying power can be negligible, particularly when it comes up against the interests of big business, other well-organised political lobbies, or the circumstances of war. The weakness of archaeologists in such cases was exposed very clearly, for example, during the third World Archaeological Congress in India, when participants were forced to agree not to discuss the destruction of the mosque at Ayodhya for fear of endangering their own safety (Colley 1995). Funari's paper (Chapter 10) also shows the difficulties faced by some archaeologists in Brazil, a non-western industrialised nation with significant social divisions and indigenous and other minorities, where indigenous people are occasionally set on fire by youths. After the restoration of civilian rule, however, he notes some improvements, notably the rise in interest in indigenous and African/African-Brazilian heritage, in prehistory, and in archaeological education. Such gains, though, can be relatively small and precarious, liable to be swept away in any wider political changes.

The recognition of the political nature of archaeology, and of the political weakness of archaeologists, raises the problem of how archaeologists themselves may be able to recognise a diversity of views about the past without finding themselves politically highjacked. As Hamilakis (1999) has noted, archaeologists may have to become more politically engaged if they embrace diversity of views, and may have to sacrifice notions of neutrality as a result.

One area where this is particularly relevant is in the field of 'alternative archaeology'. Schadla-Hall (Chapter 14) shows that historically, archaeologists have rebutted alternative views. However, while 'the comforts of unreason' can be seductive, he argues, archaeologists have been rather too simplistic in their treatments: some alternative archaeology is an entirely legitimate expression of other perspectives on the past and should be respected; some is inherently racist or demeaning to other social groups and should be challenged. Public archaeology, then, is indeed a matter of ethics.

However, ethics may not be universally applied. Another area where the issue of diversity of views comes particularly into focus is in relation to indigenous archaeology. In westernised countries with indigenous communities at least, it has become the norm for archaeologists to consult and involve these communities in the development and execution of archaeological projects and in the interpretation of the results (e.g. Pokytolo and Brass 1997). However, it is also the norm in such countries to try to 'correct' what are seen as misinterpretations or blatant distortions of the archaeological evidence by 'the lunatic fringe'. But how does one distinguish between 'indigenous beliefs' and 'lunatic fringe'? The dilemma posed by the respect archaeologists wish to show to indigenous archaeology and their desire to correct misinterpretations by all other groups has been powerfully summarised by Tarlow in her discussion of universal codes of ethics (Tarlow 2001). Whilst acknowledging that ethical principles regarding 'indigenous' peoples in places such as North America and Australasia are possible (though accompanied by their own particular issues) she argues that the blanket application of ethics about indigeny is completely misguided when applied to areas such as Europe, where it is the recent immigrants or those without traditional lands (gypsies, Jews) who are discriminated against rather than the 'indigenous' people (however these might be defined). She notes that:

> In theory, far right and neo-Nazi groups could employ the WAC Code of Ethics as legitimating their own racially exclusive and discriminatory political claims. To my knowledge, they have not done so, but the principle that, for example, 'the indigenous cultural heritage rightfully belongs to the indigenous descendants of that heritage' (WAC principle 5) is one which they would certainly recognise and espouse.
>
> (Tarlow 2001: 256)

This point is developed further by Parker Pearson and Ramilisonina (Chapter 12, this volume) when they discuss the complexities and irrationalities of what is termed 'indigenous' and argue for its replacement by the term 'local', as 'within, an increasingly globalized society, everyone is a local somewhere'. Importantly, too, they stress that 'local' archaeology, although important, should not be the sole *raison d'etre*, as the audiences for archaeology are global and dispersed. Mapunda and Lane (Chapter 11) suggest how a locally responsive non-western model for doing archaeology might work in practice. In contrast with much past archaeological practice, which has signally failed to inform or involve local people about the archaeological work undertaken in their area, they suggest a model for future work which involves consultation about research goals, employment of local people as 'ambassadors' as well as labour, an exhibition, a popular publication, and a discussion forum assessing the project.

Perhaps the best expression of the tying together of the indigenous and the local is Byrne's paper (Chapter 13), on the return of Aboriginal remains and artefacts as an 'archaeology in reverse'. He suggests that the movement of these remains and objects represent movements back to *local* spaces, specifically local cemeteries, and argues that Aborigines have resisted European domination through their attachment to local spaces. He shows how the pattern of movements of 'dispersal' of Aborigines to towns are not simply to be seen as movements 'away' but are 'lines of communication that have, in a sense, allowed the local to expand'. People retrace their steps to visit local cemeteries, and huge efforts are made to bury people 'locally'. This attachment to locality is also mirrored in the efforts of the Stolen Generations to return 'home', thus 'reburial and repatriation are not ruptures of a normality but are companions to a whole formation of other homeward movements'. In a global society, it seems, the fundamental unit of a public archaeology must be the local.

Conclusion

This volume, it is hoped, shows something of the wide range of debates that can open up when we move away from a narrow definition of public archaeology as cultural resource management, or away from a deficit model of archaeological education. The papers here show that there is a large amount of unexplored territory concerning, in particular, the perceptions and use of archaeology and archaeological presentations by the vast majority of people who are not professional archaeologists. Many basic questions remained unanswered because archaeologists have until recently not treated their relationship with the public as something which merited their academic attention. It is time now to study that relationship with the same degree of rigour as archaeologists study societies of the past.

Bibliography

Adorno, T. and Horkheimer, M. 1944. *Dialectic of Enlightenment* (English translation 1979). London: New Left Books.

Ascherson, N. 2000. Editorial. *Public Archaeology* 1(1): 1–4.

Ballantyne, R. 1998. Interpreting 'Visions'. Addressing Environmental Education Goals Through Interpretation. In Uzzell, D. and Ballantyne, R. (eds) *Contemporary Issues in Heritage and Environmental Interpretation*. London: Stationery Office.

Colley, S. 1995. What happened at WAC-3? *Antiquity* 69: 15–18.

Dobinson, C. and Denison, S. 1995. *Metal Detecting and Archaeology in England*. London: English Heritage/Council for British Archaeology.

Durant, J. 1997. Editorial. *Public Understanding of Science* 6(4): 1–3

Feder, K. 1984. Irrationality and popular archaeology. *American Antiquity* 49: 525–41.

Feder, K. 1995. Ten years after: surveying misconceptions about the human past. *Cultural Resource Management* 18(3): 10–14.

Fforde, C., Hubert, J. and Turnbull, P. (eds) 2002. *The Dead and their Possessions: Repatriation in Principle, Policy and Practice.* London: Routledge.

Graham, B., Ashworth, G.J. and Tunbridge, J.E. 2000. *A Geography of Heritage. Power, Culture and Economy.* London: Arnold.

Habermas, J. 1962. *The Structural Transformation of the Public Sphere. An Inquiry into a Category of Bourgeois Society* (English translation, 1989). Cambridge: Polity Press.

Hamilakis, Y. 1999. La trahison des archeologues? Archaeological practice as intellectual activity in postmodernity. *Journal of Mediterranean Archaeology* 12(1): 60–79.

Hein, G.1998. *Learning in the Museum.* London: Routledge.

Holtdorf, C. 2000. Engaging with multiple pasts. Reply to Francis McManamon. *Public Archaeology* 1(3): 214–15.

Hooper-Greenhill, E. (ed.) 1994. *The Educational Role of the Museum* (2nd edition). London: Routledge.

Irwin, A. and Wynne, B. (eds) 1996. *Misunderstanding Science? The Public Reconstruction of Science and Technology.* Cambridge: Cambridge University Press.

Layton, R. (ed.) 1989a. *Conflict in the Archaeology of Living Traditions.* London: Unwin Hyman.

Layton, R. (ed.) 1989b. *Who Needs the Past? Indigenous Values and Archaeology.* London: Unwin Hyman.

Layton, R., Stone, P. and Thomas, J. (eds) 2001. *Destruction and Conservation of Cultural Property.* London: Routledge.

MacDonald, S. 2002. *Behind the Scenes at the Science Museum.* Oxford: Berg.

McGimsey, C. R. 1972. *Public Archaeology.* New York: McGraw Hill.

McGuigan, J. 1996. *Culture and the Public Sphere.* London: Routledge.

McManamon, F. 2000. Archaeological messages and messengers. *Public Archaeology* 1(1): 5–20.

Melton, J.V.H. 2001. *The Rise of the Public in Enlightenment Europe.* Cambridge: Cambridge University Press.

Merriman, N. 1991. *Beyond the Glass Case: the Past, the Heritage and the Public in Britain.* Leicester: Leicester University Press.

Merriman, N. 2002. Archaeology, heritage and interpretation. In Cunliffe, B., Davies, W. and Renfrew, C. (eds) *Archaeology. The Widening Debate.* Oxford: Oxford University Press/British Academy.

MORI. 2000. *Attitudes Towards the Heritage. Research Study Conducted for English Heritage July 2000.* Available on English Heritage website.

Piccini, A. 1999. War games and wendy-houses: open-air reconstructions of prehistoric life. In Merriman, N. (ed.) *Making Early Histories in Museums.* Leicester: Leicester University Press.

Pokotylo, D. and Brass, G. 1997. Interpreting Cultural Resources: Hatzic Site. In Jameson, J. (ed.) *Presenting Archaeology to the Public. Digging for Truths.* London: AltaMira Press.

Pokytolo, D. and Guppy, N. 1999. Public opinion and archaeological heritage: views from outside the profession. *American Antiquity* 64: 400–16.

Pokytolo, D. and Mason, A. 1991. Public attitudes towards archaeological resources and their management. In Smith, G. and Ehrenhard, J. (eds) *Protecting the Past.* Baton Rouge, Florida: CRC Press.

Ramos, M. and Duganne, D. 2000. *Exploring Public Perceptions and Attitudes about Archaeology*. Washington, DC: Society for American Archaeology.

Rorty, R. 1989. *Contingency, Irony and Solidarity*. Cambridge: Cambridge University Press.

Rose, S. 1992. Governing the enterprising self. In Heelas, P. and Morris, P. (eds) *The Values of the Enterprise Culture. The Moral Debate*. London: Routledge.

Royal Society. 1985. *The Public Understanding of Science*. London: Royal Society.

Samuel, R. 1994. *Theatres of Memory*. London: Verso.

Schadla-Hall, T. 1999. Editorial: Public Archaeology. *European Journal of Archaeology* 2(2): 147–58.

Simpson, M. 1996. *Making Representations; Museums in the Post-Colonial Era*. London: Routlege.

Skeates, R. 2000. *Debating the Archaeological Heritage*. London: Duckworth.

Smardz, K. 1997. The past through tomorrow: interpreting Toronto's heritage to a multicultural public. In Jameson, J. (ed.), *Presenting Archaeology to the Public. Digging for Truths*. London: AltaMira Press.

Stone, P. and Mackenzie, R. (eds) 1990. *The Excluded Past. Archaeology in Education*. London: Unwin Hyman.

Tarlow, S. 2001. Decoding ethics. *Public Archaeology* 1(4): 245–59.

Thomas, J. 1995: Where are we now? Archaeological theory in the 1990s. In Ucko, P.J. (ed.), *Theory in Archaeology: A World Perspective*. London: Routledge.

Tunbridge, J. E and Ashworth, G. J. 1995. *Dissonant Heritage: the Management of the Past as a Resource in Conflict*. Chichester: John Wiley

Wynne, B. 1992. Public understanding of science research: new horizons or hall of mirrors? *Public Understanding of Science* 1: 37–44.

Yoffee, N. and Sherratt, A. 1993. Introduction: the sources of archaeological theory. In Yoffee, N. and Sherratt, A. (eds) *Archaeological Theory: Who Sets the Agenda?* Cambridge: Cambridge University Press.

Part I

SPREADING THE WORD
Communication and interpretation

2

PUBLIC ARCHAEOLOGY IN THE UNITED STATES

John H. Jameson Jr.

Introduction: what is 'public archaeology' in America?

I should start by stating that this account of public archaeology in America is not in any way intended to be complete or comprehensive. Such a discussion would easily cover several volumes. Rather, this account attempts to outline the major episodes in the development of public archaeology in the United States based on my personal experiences and perceptions. Most of my professional career has been spent in one aspect or another of cultural resources management, in particular archaeological resources management, in three federal agencies.

In the United States, the term 'public archaeology' has become a somewhat ambiguous term. Many equate it with the late twentieth century developments of cultural resource management (CRM) and the astonishingly rapid swell of site information and collected artifacts caused by enforcement of federal and state historic preservation mandates since the 1960s. This definition was used in early accounts of public archaeology (McGimsey 1972; McGimsey and Davis 1977).

For many in the 1980s and 1990s, the term 'public archaeology' took on new meanings as the subfields of 'educational archaeology' (Stone and Molyneaux 1994; Smardz and Smith 2000; Esterhuysen and Smith 1999; Bender and Smith 2000) and 'public interpretation of archaeology' (Jameson 1997) have been articulated, albeit with many overlaps to each other and to the CRM definition. 'Educational archaeology' often refers to formal classroom situations but can also apply to less formal education settings.

For purposes of this discussion, educational archaeology also encompasses 'public interpretation of archaeology,' which focuses on the methods and techniques of conveying archaeological information to the lay public in an engaging, informative, and accurate manner. Public interpretation takes place in schools, park interpretative programs, exhibits, ranger talks, books, brochures, interpretive artworks, and other forms of public presentation. Methods and standards for public interpretation have been developed in response to the accumulation of information and the growing public attention to archaeology in national and

21

state parks, museums, and other public arenas. Approaches to educational archaeology, including public interpretation, serve to empower the public to participate in the critical evaluations of historical and archaeological interpretations that are presented to them and to better understand how and why the past is relevant to the present (Jameson 1997).

In summary, public archaeology in America can be understood as encompassing the CRM compliance consequences as well as educational archaeology and public interpretation in public arenas such as schools, parks, and museums. However, to fully understand what public archaeology is in America, one must look at the sources and developments that led us to the present situation.

Early developments in public recognition

Events of the late eighteenth and nineteenth centuries

We know that the early European explorers and settlers were intrigued by ancient earthen mounds, attributing them to exotic non-American cultures. The great mounds of the Lower Mississippi Valley, for example, were often attributed to wayward ancient Egyptians or non-Indian Asians who pre-dated the Biblical flood (Willey and Sabloff 1993). One reason for this misperception is that the vast pre-Columbian mound building activities had entirely ceased by the time Europeans arrived in America. Surely, the early settlers posited, the great complexes of mounds in America could not have been constructed by the native 'savages.' This belief of non-American origins was common until the end of the nineteenth century.

Many American archaeologists point to the writings of Thomas Jefferson (Figure 2.1) as the earliest documented instance of public exposure to systematic or scientific archaeology in North America. Jefferson carefully recorded in *Notes on the State of Virginia*, written in 1781–82 and published in 1787, his excavation of a section of a prehistoric Indian mound. Jefferson (1787) noted that the site, located on his property in Virginia, contained 'different states of decay in these strata, which seem to indicate a difference in the time of inhumation.' This is the first known observation and description of what we would term 'stratification' in modern archaeological parlance. Jefferson, the third US president and author of the American Declaration of Independence, helped spur public interest in Native American culture by collecting, chronicling, and displaying an impressive array of information and artifacts, many sent back to him during the Lewis and Clark Expedition of 1803–6. Often receiving hundreds of visitors a year at his home at Monticello in Virginia, Jefferson arranged an entrance hall waiting area that was designed to inform as well as inspire, displaying hundreds of artifacts, maps, fossils, and documents stemming from his life-long quest for knowledge about the world.

Figure 2.1   Thomas Jefferson, third president of the United States, is given credit by many for the first recorded observation of archaeological context in the widely read *Notes on the State of Virginia*, first published in 1787. Painting by Charles Willson Peale, Philadelphia, 1791, copyprint of oil on canvas. Courtesy of Independence National Historical Park Collection, Philadelphia (128).

Early investigations stir public interest

The growing public interest in the remains of Native American cultures encouraged the work of the Smithsonian Institution, founded in 1848, to record the lifeways, customs, material culture, and language of native groups. Beginning in 1881, Congress appropriated funds for the Smithsonian's Bureau of American Ethnology to investigate prehistoric Indian mounds, the first publicly-supported archaeology in the United States (National Park Service 1999a).

In the late 1800s, a World's Fair in Chicago and other public events such as the International Centennial Exhibition at Philadelphia in 1876 displayed American Indian artifacts. These events drew tens of millions of visitors. Unfortunately, the growing popular appeal of American archaeology was accompanied by commercial demands for authentic prehistoric antiquities and the looting of artifacts from archaeological sites for private use. In the 1880s and 1890s, scientific investigators visited and reported on the destruction and looting of prominent prehistoric ruins, such as Pecos in New Mexico and Casa Grande in Arizona (Figure 2.2) (National Park Service 1999b). As a result of public and scientific community outcries, the first specified archaeological preserve created by the government was at the ruins of Casa Grande in 1892. The late 1800s was also a period when the preservation of historic landscapes, exemplified by the concern for preserving battlefields of the American Civil War (1861–65), had captured the interest of the public.

In the early twentieth century, as part of the growing public interest spurred by the Conservation Movement, these descriptions and sites were cited in arguments for federal action to protect historical and archaeological sites.

Figure 2.2 A modern open shelter protects the Casa Grande, or 'Big House,' one of the largest and most mysterious prehistoric structures ever built in North America, at Casa Grande National Monument in Arizona. Photo courtesy of National Park Service.

A 'square deal' for archaeology: Teddy Roosevelt and the Conservation Movement

President Theodore Roosevelt (1858–1919), a dynamic leader and fervent nationalist, dramatized the need to conserve both natural and cultural resources and his policies advanced the cause of the Conservation Movement. Arguably the most knowledgeable and intellectual president since Thomas Jefferson, Roosevelt blended science and morality effectively and succeeded in persuading Congress and the states to put the future public interest above the current private interest.

Roosevelt, who was passionately interested in reform and determined to give the people a 'square deal,' initiated his policy of increased government supervision in the enforcement of antitrust laws and protection against unrestrained private development. In 1902, Roosevelt gave his support to the Reclamation Act of 1902 (the Newlands Act), which made possible Federal irrigation projects, resulting in the government-sponsored construction of 30 major irrigation projects, including Roosevelt Dam in Arizona. In the meantime, he vetoed a bill to authorize private development of the Muscle Shoals Area of the Tennessee River, later the heart of the Tennessee Valley Authority (TVA).

In 1905, Roosevelt reorganized the US Forest Service and made Gifford Pinchot its chief. Encouraged by Roosevelt, Pinchot staffed the agency with trained foresters, and, for the first time, development of waterpower sites by private utilities was subjected to enlightened safeguards. Three times as much land (125 million acres, or 50 million hectares) as Roosevelt's three immediate predecessors had assigned to national forests was put into the reserves. The hiring of trained staff specialists provided an important precedent that later greatly aided historical and archaeological protection when the National Park Service was authorized to hire significant numbers of professional historians, historical architects, and archaeologists in the 1930s.

Roosevelt, influenced by the naturalist John Muir and often defying members of Congress, pushed to double the number of national parks, adding five, including Mesa Verde and Crater Lake. He created 16 national monuments such as California's Muir Woods and also established 51 national wildlife refuges. He declared: 'Is there any law that will prevent me from declaring Pelican Island a Federal Bird Reservation? Very well, then I so declare it' (GII 1996).

By the turn of the twentieth century, the work of the Bureau of American Ethnology and others had alerted the scientific community and politicians to the unbridled looting of the Southwest pueblos and many other archaeological sites. Provisions of the Antiquities Act of 1906, enacted during Roosevelt's second term, marked a national recognition of the importance of archaeological resources. It authorized the president to reserve and establish by executive order or proclamation national monuments containing sites and structures of historic or scientific value on public lands. Notably, it required permits to examine or excavate historic or prehistoric ruins and limited permits to recognized scientific institutions. It also prohibited the removal or destruction of any object of antiquity on public lands and provided penalties for violations. For 73 years, until the passage in 1979 of the Archaeological Resources Protection Act (ARPA), the Antiquities Act was the chief archaeological protection authority in the United States.

Roosevelt's rhetoric and powers of persuasion with Congress, the states, and the public at large did much to prepare the way for reform under his successors. Echoes of his influence were seen in the enactment of the National Park Service Organic Act in 1916 that established the National Park Service to protect the nation's natural and cultural gems and later in the 1935 enactment of the Historic Sites Act that authorized the preservation of properties 'of national historic or archaeological significance.'

The 'New Deal' archaeology of the 1930s

The development of significant public funding of archaeology in the United States arose from two major episodes tied to the economic history of the country: the Great Depression of the 1930s; and the post-World War II economic boom that began in the late 1940s and continues today. The former sprang from catastrophic economic recession, the latter from an unprecedented economic expansion.

The Great Depression relief programs

Desperate to lift the spirits as well as the pocketbooks of Americans during the Great Depression of the 1930s, President Franklin Roosevelt initiated what he called a 'New Deal for Americans,' an ambitious program of government relief projects that continued until World War II. These involved a massive infusion of government funds to put people to work. In the name of preservation, a multitude of projects was launched under the auspices of the major New Deal relief programs: the Civil Works Administration (CWA), the Civilian Conservation Corps (CCC), the Tennessee Valley Authority (TVA), the Works Progress Administration (WPA), and many others. Work under these programs was also accomplished for both preservation and interpretation purposes by the National Park Service. Unemployed workers, including skilled artisans such as writers, artists, craftsmen, engineers, and architects, were widely recruited to manage or be crew members for a wide array of projects such as road construction, building large and small reservoirs, constructing and maintaining bridges, improving national park facilities, construction, and adornment of countless public buildings. Oral historians embarked on projects such as interviewing former slaves (National Park Service 1999a).

Archaeology, with its labor-intensive methods, was seen by the relief project administrators as ideal for putting people to work on excavation projects around

Figure 2.3 1930s New Deal relief project: reconstruction of the prehistoric earthlodge at Ocmulgee National Monument, Georgia, Photo courtesy of National Park Service.

the country. Field and laboratory personnel were often large in number, reaching a scale not seen previously in American archaeology and rarely equaled since (Figure 2.3) (SEAC 1998). Large-scale government programs continued for almost a decade until the United States entered World War II (Anderson 1997: 16–18).

The Historic Sites Act of 1935 provided for the preservation of historic sites, buildings, objects, and antiquities of national significance. This legislation made it national policy to preserve significant historic or prehistoric sites for 'the inspiration and benefit of the people.' The Department of the Interior through the National Park Service was charged with securing existing information and conducting further studies, if necessary, to determine the identity and significance of sites. The department was given the authority to acquire such properties, within limitations, for the purpose of their preservation. The department was also authorized to restore or reconstruct or otherwise treat sites with an aim towards preservation and benefit within the purpose of the Act. The Act authorized the creation of the National Park System Advisory Board, to be composed of an interdisciplinary group, including archaeologists. Most germane to the consequences for public archaeology was that the Interior Department was authorized to develop an educational program and service for the purpose of making available to the public facts and information pertaining to significant historic or prehistoric sites (National Park Service 1999a).

During the New Deal, a whole generation of archaeologists concentrated on native and historic period cultures in the United States. This is the basis for modern Americanist specialization of many American university departments today. These archaeologists had learned to manage large scale projects and collections. Examining extensive areas with large crews, the New Deal projects infused masses of data and collections resulting in new knowledge and making the development of new synthesis of data and artifact classification schemes possible. The birth of several major archaeology organizations occurred during this time and occupied the talents of a full generation after the 1930s. Reports from these New Deal projects are still being produced today (Anderson 1997: 16–18).

Although many of these relief projects were located in the American Southeast, the New Deal projects were truly national in scope. Many were noted for their exemplary quality. For example, in excavations in Somerset County, Pennsylvania, the methodology developed and employed was remarkably similar to modern field techniques. As in the case of many of the relief projects, the utility of this information was nonetheless hampered by inadequacies of data collection (Means 1998).

Historic preservation sentiments gain ground

Besides the alarms over looting of Native American sites in the Southwest, other major events and developments, such as the opening of Colonial Williamsburg by the Rockefeller Foundation in 1933 and passage of the Historic Sites Act of 1935, furthered the cause of historic preservation and brought public, private, and professional interest in American archaeology to new heights. The resulting collection of national and state historic sites, monuments, and parks, as well as an abundance of privately administered buildings and sites, became standard fare for an increasingly mobile American public; the public was becoming increasingly enamored of the physical remains (and representations thereof) of its history. By the late 1940s and 1950s, the beginnings of a new historic preservation ethic had entered the mainstream of public consciousness.

The development of cultural resources management (CRM)

The TVA projects

A New Deal relief program, managed by the Tennessee Valley Authority (TVA), established the precedent for later reservoir salvage programs. Created in May 1933, the TVA was charged with developing a series of dams that would provide flood control and electric power, leading, it was hoped, to economic recovery. With the assistance of the Smithsonian Institution, the TVA created its own archaeological program. Much of the archaeological expertise was recruited from the anthropology departments at northern universities such as Harvard. Although the work conducted during this time failed to meet modern standards of investigation, its quality surpassed all previous archaeological research in the area (Anderson *et al.* 2000).

This and subsequent reservoir programs after World War II profoundly affected public and scientific community awareness of the magnitude of archaeological data loss that could occur nationwide. The decade of the 1930s provided a tremendous amount of information that has formed the basis for present-day understanding of archaeology in North America, especially the southeastern United States. These early salvage (rescue) programs paved the way for the broad range of historic preservation programs that emerged in the United States in the 1960s and continue today. Also, they set precedents for new standards of archaeological management and recording that have influenced all subsequent CRM-related work in North America (Anderson *et al.* 2000).

The River Basin Survey of the 1940s to the 1960s

Following World War II, the US began an ambitious construction program for flood control, irrigation, hydroelectric installations, and navigational improvements along its many river basins. Although largely unexplored archaeologically, a few spectacular archaeological sites had been found in these areas and the scientific community faced the likelihood that considerable archaeological and paleontological information would be irretrievably lost. In response, the National Park Service and the Smithsonian Institution, in collaboration with US Bureau of Reclamation and the US Army Corps of Engineers, devised an interagency agreement in 1946 to locate historic and prehistoric sites in threatened areas and to salvage as much information as possible prior to their inundation and destruction. Spurred on largely by the organizational and lobbying efforts of the Society for American Archaeology's Committee for the Recovery of Archaeological Remains (CRAR) (Wendorf and Thompson 2002), work carried out in the late 1940s to early 1960s resulted in the recording of thousands of previously unknown sites. This was the beginning of the phenomenon in America that was termed 'salvage archaeology' and later expressed in the emerging preservation ethic as 'cultural resource management' or CRM. Except for the continuing TVA program, until the middle 1970s, most archaeology projects were limited in scope and budget and carried out by museum staff, university professors, and their students (Anderson *et al.* 2000).

One major post-war program, the River Basin Survey, was run by the Smithsonian Institution's Bureau of American Ethnology. It attained a level of efficiency not possible during the New Deal, when work was conducted under a number of different and competing relief programs. Under this program, a core of archaeologists was hired to conduct or manage work on federally constructed projects. Contracts, grants, and cooperative agreements were also issued with public museums, universities, and colleges. Like their TVA predecessors, the River Basin Survey managers were constrained by the availability of funds and time limitations. In some instances, Native Americans were hired during these projects as field laborers, informants, and consultants (Minthorn 1997). In just the first five years of the program, 213 reservoir areas situated in 28 states were investigated, recording about 2350 archaeological sites and conducting excavations at 36 sites (Anderson *et al.* 2000).

In 1965, the River Basin Survey was disbanded and the responsibility for reservoir salvage archaeology was given to the National Park Service where it remained, under the name of the Interagency Archaeological Salvage Program, until 1974. Many of today's most senior archaeologists in the United States started their careers in the salvage program (Anderson *et al.* 2000).

Mandates with teeth: the federal CRM legislation

The flow of information coming from relief projects of the 1930s, coupled with the ambitious river basin salvage programs of the 1940s to 1960s, alerted the public as well as the scientific community to the magnitude of the resource and potential information loss to unbridled construction and development. The passage of the National Historic Preservation Act (NHPA)(1966), Executive Order 11593 'Protection of the Cultural Environment' (1971), the National Environmental Policy Act (1969), and Archeological and Historic Preservation Act (1974) eventually exerted a transformational effect on the character of archaeological research and preservation and radically changed the way that archaeology was administratively conducted in the United States. The 1966 bill furnished the foundations for a system of resource protection centering upon a National Register of Historic Places, authorized the creation of the President's Advisory Council on Historic Preservation, provided for establishment of National Historic Landmarks, and provided a mechanism for the development of state-level historic preservation programs. The 1974 Act extended the provisions of earlier legislation that had mandated the preservation of historical and prehistoric archaeological data which would otherwise be lost during the construction of federal reservoirs. It applied to all federal construction activities as well as federally licensed or assisted activities which had the potential to destroy archaeological data.

These mandates, together with the broadened coverage of archaeological resource protection from river basins to all federal, federally licensed, and permitted construction and development, provided funding authority for cultural resources mitigation work. The combination of NHPA and Executive Order 11593 in 1971 prompted the National Park Service to take the lead in developing strong, enforceable federal regulations for the identification, evaluation, and protection of significant sites. The resulting rules and regulations, in particular 36 CFR 800, issued by the Advisory Council on Historic

Preservation, greatly improved and expanded cultural resource compliance standards.

Another key law passed in 1966 was the Department of Transportation Act. This law stated that the Secretary of Transportation had to assess the effects of federal highway projects on properties listed or determined eligible for listing in the National Register of Historic Places. Use of federal monies was contingent on an assessment of feasible planning alternatives to affecting historic properties and minimizing damage to historic properties and effected resources. Since the late 1970s, when regulations to enforce this law and the National Historic Preservation Act were finalized, hundreds of millions of dollars have been spent by federal and state governments on highway construction projects for archaeological surveys, testing and evaluation studies, laboratory analysis, and report preparation (Walthall *et al.* 1997).

Prior to 1966, the conduct of salvage archaeology required the participation of the National Park Service, the Smithsonian Institution, the constructing agency, and the archaeologist. Archaeological decisions were made, for the most part, by the project archaeologist. After 1966, a process evolved that required the participation of the responsible (lead) federal agency, the National Park Service, the Advisory Council on Historic Preservation, and the State Historic Preservation Officer to determine if and what archaeological work needed to be done. Once agreement had been reached among the consulting federal and state agencies, contracts to conduct the archaeological work were awarded on a competitive basis (Anderson *et al.* 2000). Competitive contracting for archaeological work began in 1975 (Keel 2001). Standards for archaeological contracting were eventually developed that, by the late 1980s, stressed public education and outreach as recommended outcomes of compliance mitigation activities (Jameson *et al.* 1992).

Another important law passed during this period was the National Environmental Policy Act (NEPA) of 1969 that required all federal agencies to utilize a systematic interdisciplinary approach in planning and decision-making for projects that may have an impact on the environment. It also stated that a significant impact or controversy triggers an Environmental Assessment or Environmental Impact Statement which assesses impacts and unavoidable environmental effects to both natural and cultural resources and establishes alternatives, including 'no-action.'

The Archeological and Historic Preservation Act (Moss-Bennett Act) of 1974 has had major impacts on funding levels. It required federal agencies to provide notice to the Secretary of the Interior of any constructions and other federal undertakings, and, if archaeological resources are found, for recovery or salvage of them. The law applies to any agency whenever it received information that a direct or federally assisted activity could cause irreparable harm to prehistoric, historic, and archaeological data. Most significantly, up to 1 percent of project funds could be used to pay for salvage (data recovery) work. Prior to the passage of the Moss-Bennett bill, federal archaeological expenditures had averaged less than a million dollars a year. By the early 1980s, estimates of annual archaeological expenditures reached 200 million dollars (Anderson *et al*. 2000).

Following the passage of the Archeological and Historic Preservation Act of 1974, the National Park Service eventually relinquished its role as the lead agency in conducting reservoir archaeology as agencies such as the US Army Corps of Engineers, Bureau of Reclamation, and TVA developed their own archaeological programs and staffs. The National Park Service continued to provide assistance through the 1980s and early 1990s when the dam and reservoir construction projects ended (Anderson *et al*. 2000).

A hallmark legislation for resource protection on federal lands was the Archeological Resources Protection Act (ARPA) of 1979. This law provided increased protection of archaeological resources located on public lands and Indian lands. It also exempted information relating to location of archaeological resources from the Freedom of Information Act and established heavy civil and criminal penalties for violation of the act.

The latest major law affecting public archaeology in the twentieth century was the Native American Graves Protection and Repatriation Act (NAGPRA) of 1990. This Act required that museums and agencies that receive federal funding must keep and inventory all human remains, funerary objects, and sacred objects. Federally-recognized Native American Tribes, including Native Hawaiian organizations, can repatriate these items. Part of the rationale for NAGPRA was to curb the illicit traffic in stolen and looted artifacts through a thorough inventory of artifacts. NAGPRA requires a federal agency or tribe to deal with any graves that are inadvertently discovered. They are then required to contact the affiliated Native American group. As is discussed later in this chapter, NAGPRA has had sea change effects on the archaeology of Native American sites since 1990.

State and local protection efforts

Some states have followed the federal lead in passing legislation that protects archaeological sites and provides for impact mitigation. For example, the California Environmental Quality Act (CEQA), enacted in 1970 and patterned after NEPA, requires that before approving most discretionary projects, the lead agency must identify and examine the significant adverse environmental effects which may result from that project. Where a project may adversely affect a unique archaeological resource, the lead agency must treat that effect as a significant environmental effect and prepare an Environmental Impact Report (EIR). When an archaeological resource is listed in, or is eligible to be listed in the California Register of Historical Resources, any substantial adverse effect to that resource is considered a significant environmental effect (GOPR 1994). Another example is from the Commonwealth of Virginia, drawing from ARPA and NAGPRA, where the Virginia Antiquities Act requires that archaeology be conducted with a permit and that an additional permit be obtained before human remains are exhumed.

In general, however, efforts to protect and preserve archaeological sites at the state, county, and local levels have been less successful than at the federal level. State-level versions of the National Historic Preservation Act, the National Environmental Policy Act, and the Archaeological Resources Protection Act have been slow to emerge, although significant progress has been made in many areas. In most cases, states make special allowances for property tax credits, historic building rehabilitation, and creation of historic districts and local protection ordinances.

At the local county or city level, archaeological preservation has often been an up-hill climb, sometimes meeting with political opposition from special interest groups such as bottle and relic collectors. Since most housing and construction development is done on private land with private funding, the federal and state laws do not provide protection. A recent survey of 2,000 local preservation commissions found that 91 percent of the respondents do not in any way consider the impacts of development on archaeological sites (Cushman 1998: 4). There are notable exceptions however, such as in Charleston (South Carolina), Alexandria (Virginia), New York City, and Boston. In these cases, local communities have taken the initiative in historic preservation, educational outreach, and archaeological protection planning. The most successful local archaeological protection programs also embrace pro-active preservation planning that does not rely solely on regulatory review but rather emphasizes broad and long-term identification and preservation goals and public education initiatives to foster a local preservation constituency (Simon and Bell 1998: 5–8).

Major dam construction projects of the 1970s and early 1980s

With the promulgation of regulations to enforce the unprecedented mandates of the 1960s and 1970s, almost overnight, contract archaeology underwent an explosion of activity and contract spending by government agencies and private companies. Sometimes this spending went into the tens and hundreds of thousands of dollars and even reached, in a few instances, to the million-dollar-plus mark (Anderson *et al.* 2000; National Park Service 2000a). Two of the most important and influential of these large budget projects are the Tennessee–Tombigbee Waterway and the Richard B. Russell Reservoir, both located in the southeastern United States.

The Tennessee–Tombigbee Waterway

The Tennessee–Tombigbee Waterway in Alabama, Mississippi, and Tennessee was designed to improve navigation between the Lower Tennessee River and the Gulf of Mexico. It was a multi-year, complex engineering project consisting of several individual dams and locks, a canal, and channel projects.

Bennie C. Keel, chief of the Interagency Archaeological Services Office, Southeast Region, National Park Service during the 1970s, orchestrated a multi-agency cooperative scheme to effectively meet the challenges faced. The US Army Corps of Engineers, the Advisory Council on Historic Preservation, concerned State Historic Preservation Officers, and the staff of the National Register of Historic Places agreed to treat the work as a single mitigation plan rather than separate construction projects. This plan, developed during a week-long planning meeting chaired by Keel, was accomplished by identifying a research framework that included the profession's best formulated research problems in relation to southeastern history and prehistory. Sites were selected for investigation using flow charts that identified research questions and relevant data. Contracts were awarded to educational institutions and private firms, both local and from outside the three-state area. Fieldwork was carried on simultaneously by at least six organizations. In order to fully comply with the pertinent statutes, contracts and agreements were developed with historians, historical architects, and engineers to evaluate, record, and mitigate impacts on a multitude of properties from all time periods. The government required the individual contractors to share information on a timely basis by holding periodic field consultation meetings (Anderson *et al.* 2000).

The Tennessee–Tombigbee mitigation plan became the model for a number of other major dam projects such as the New Melones in California, the Central Arizona project, and the Richard B. Russell project in Georgia and South Carolina (Anderson *et al.* 2000).

The Richard B. Russell Dam and Lake

The Richard B. Russell Cultural Resources Mitigation Program, carried out between 1968 and 1985, was exemplary for many reasons. First, given the sheer magnitude of the field effort, the Russell project area represents one of the most intensively studied regions in the United States. The archaeological and historical investigation reports, collectively called the *Russell Papers*, were of a very high quality and have inspired follow-up research for a more than a generation. Second, the range of investigations undertaken reflected a rare sensitivity and appreciation for the diversity of cultural resources in the area. Sites included large landmark plantations and colonial fortifications as well as small farmsteads, tenant sites, and industrial occupations. Prehistoric sites included large mound complexes and village sites as well as smaller and less spectacular campsites and stone knapping stations (Figures 2.4, 2.5, and 2.6). Archaeology, history, architectural history, and oral history were all applied to the understanding of the region. Complementing the *Russell Papers* technical reports were two standard-setting, widely distributed popular overviews, making the Russell studies collectively one of the most successful regional investigations programs yet to be undertaken under American historic preservation mandates (Anderson *et al.* 2000).

Figure 2.4 Aerial view of excavated area at the Rocker's Bottom archaeological site, Richard B. Russell Reservoir, Georgia. Photo courtesy of National Park Service and US Army Corps of Engineers.

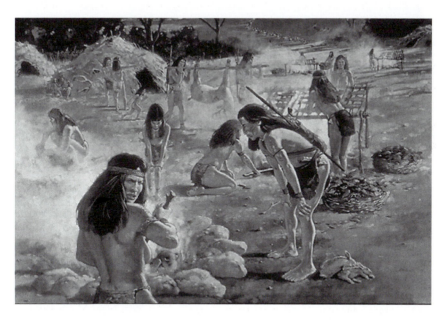

Figure 2.5 Interpretive rendering of a *c.* 7,000 year old Archaic period habitation scene from the *Beneath These Waters* popular history volume. Painting by Martin Pate. Courtesy of Southeast Archeological Center, National Park Service.

Figure 2.6 Archaeological field crew working at the Rocker's Bottom archaeological site, Richard B. Russell Reservoir, Georgia. Photo courtesy of National Park Service and US Army Corps or Engineers.

A flood of compliance-related archaeology

The late 1970s and 1980s saw a virtual flood of compliance-related cultural resource investigations through the United States. Work was especially prolific in the western oil and gas states where construction projects were spurred by fuel shortages in an expanding economy. Studies were conducted in advance of hundreds of thousands of oil and natural gas pipelines, wells, roads, dams, bridges, and other land-disturbing activities. Hundreds of thousands of reports have recorded millions of archaeological and historical sites containing hundreds of millions of cultural objects. Still, less than 5 percent of the public lands in America have been investigated. Thousands of reports have been placed on the table and millions of artifacts on the shelf: the sheer magnitude of this record is overwhelming. Despite some serious setbacks and mistakes, the continuing flow of information, as well as the evolution of field methodologies and recording standards, has sharpened archaeologists' abilities to focus on the important aspects and attributes of a rich and diverse cultural heritage (Jameson 2000a).

An army of several hundred archaeologists was hired to oversee these studies by the chief land managing agencies such as the Bureau of Land Management, the US Forest Service, the Bureau of Reclamation and the US Army Corps of Engineers. Though architectural and oral historians were sometimes members of investigation teams, most of the work was planned and carried out by archaeologists. The investigators were stretched thin, however. The writer was the lone cultural resources specialist in the 1980s for the Bureau of Land Management in an area of Wyoming that encompassed over 6 million acres (2.5 million hectares) of affected public lands. The Bureau of Land Management alone is responsible for 264 million acres of public land, about one-eighth of the land in the United States and about 300 million additional acres of subsurface mineral resources.

Changes in philosophy and methodology

New paradigms for research

In addition to the much more complicated regulatory situation that was in place by the late 1970s, archaeologists both within and outside of the government had to deal with a shift in theoretical emphasis from a classificatory-historical (historical reconstruction) emphasis during the decades before and after World War II to the modern paradigm, beginning about 1960. Before the 1960s, the goal of studies was largely the description of artifacts and chronology (Willey and Sabloff 1993).

Beginning in the 1960s, interpretation as well as descriptions of data become important, firmly establishing archaeology as a technique for recovering anthropological data. With this new approach to research, theories about cultural processes were proposed and tested through generating hypotheses and testing the hypotheses. This philosophical or paradigm shift in emphasis in research from cultural history and environmental concerns to a more scientific or 'processual' approach, in combination with the passage of the CRM laws, transformed the conduct of salvage archaeology from a simple to a complex enterprise.

More recent philosophical developments have produced debates among postprocessualists, who emphasize the political and public aspects of archaeology, and the more traditional logical empiricists. The proponents of the postprocessual 'critical theory' argue that when the past is interpreted and becomes history it tends to become ideology (Leone *et al.* 1987). In this vein, public interpreters realize that the meanings they impose on the past are particular to their own cultural and social background. With this awareness, they can help their audiences appreciate that many, if not all, of their preconceived notions about time and space are actually part of their own, modern, historically-based ideology. Thus, audiences can appreciate that knowledge about the archaeologically-revealed past is useful in giving meaning to the present. However, some American archaeologists, like Stanley South, have reacted to the critical theory approach by calling it an 'anti-science fad.' South (1997) warns archaeologists against going too far in accepting the conclusions of critical theorists, that there are no facts or truths in archaeology, and that the past is not knowable with any integrity. If the past has no integrity, he says, then anyone's interpretation is as good as anyone else's and the interpretation would be open to anyone's political or ideological whims.

The promulgation of professional standards

By the 1970s, with so much work being done by so many people, one of the major issues addressed was the need for the establishment of written standards and a code of ethics for professional archaeologists in both the public and private sectors. This was accomplished with some success with the creation of the Society of Professional Archeologists (SOPA) in 1976. SOPA functioned as a membership society independent of other professional societies. To qualify for SOPA membership, applicants had to demonstrate minimal educational and supervisory research (field and laboratory) experience, and agree to abide by a Code of Ethics and Standards of Research Performance. SOPA also developed institutional standards (minimal standards for office facilities, allocations of space, research libraries, security systems, etc.) and standards for academic archaeological field schools. Members were encouraged to upgrade their listing by expanding their certification to specialties such as museology, underwater archaeology, teaching, and archeometric research. In 1998, the need for higher profile professional sponsorship and registration (as opposed to membership) led to the creation of the Register of Professional Archaeologists, with SOPA transferring its responsibility, authority, and assets to the Register. The hallmark of SOPA (and now the Register) is a formal grievance procedure that allows for the investigation of complaints about the professional conduct of a member. If an allegation of a violation of the code or standards was supported during an investigation, sanctions, including termination of membership certification, can be enforced.

Governmental standards were also developed. In 1983, the Secretary of the Interior's Standards and Guidelines for Archeology and Historic Preservation were issued that provided guidelines for preservation planning, documentation, evaluation, treatment, and minimal qualification standards.

Archaeology and CRM: crises of management

Challenges in site protection

By the 1980s, it was evident to archaeologists in the United States that a tremendous increase in the commercialization of the human prehistoric and historic record had contributed to archaeological sites being looted to the extent that 'if something is not done soon to curb this destruction, there will be little of our collective past left for future generations' (Smith and Ehrenhard 1991). It was also clear to many that agencies lacked adequate staff, training, and resources to enforce ARPA. ARPA was also proving difficult to prosecute. Americans were still generally unaware of the magnitude and destructiveness of site looting and the precise definitions contained in ARPA. As a result, vandals were often prosecuted not with ARPA but with either the 1906 Antiquities Act or theft of government property which were easier for the public (and many judges) to understand.

A 1988 report to Congress estimated that 90 percent of known archaeological sites on public lands in four states in the American Southwest had been looted. In a report prepared by the National Park Service that same year, it was reported that as much as 50 percent of all sites on private and public lands in the United States had been looted. Looting of archaeological sites in the Navajo Reservation alone suffered a 1,000 percent increase from 1980 to 1987. Most looting occurs at night in remote areas using heavy equipment such as trucks, plows, and even aircraft.

The 1988 report estimated that tens of thousands of sites had been affected and that looting and thefts were largely spurred by increasing pressure from the international art market and black market. Objects tend to acquire higher prices the further they travel from their place of origin. One case study in 1993 cited an example of a Native American pot from the American Southwest that would fetch between two hundred and one thousand dollars locally but in Albuquerque could bring up to $45,000, in New York $95,000, and as much as $400,000 in Europe (TED 1993).

Part of the problem stems from the American right of ownership. In the United States, the property owner by law also owns whatever is contained on, or in, that property. This is in contrast to most other areas of the world where objects of antiquity are nationalized and owned by the national government.

An attempt to reconcile the situation was made in late 1990 when President Bush signed NAGPRA into law. One of the purposes of NAGPRA was to reduce the international market by cataloging all artifacts, beginning with museum collections. Furthermore, NAGPRA required repatriation of all sacred objects and human remains still contained within or upon archaeological sites. NAGPRA has assisted in promoting heritage values in archaeological resource management and federal land protection (TED 1993), and increased ethnographic interest and awareness for Native Americans. It has also forced agencies and museums to come to grips with curation problems (Waldbauer 2000).

Contributing to recent optimism is the fact that federal law enforcement officers and the legal profession have become more familiar with both ARPA and NAGPRA, thus permitting the increased prosecution of these laws. Since 1986, agencies have stepped up their public awareness efforts in order to solicit more public support for discouraging looting and enforcing ARPA and NAGPRA. Amendments to ARPA in 1988 significantly enhanced its effectiveness by lowering the felony threshold from $5,000 to $500. Consequently, ARPA has become more attractive to prosecutors as it is much easier to pursue a felony case. Although some attorneys still prefer to use the US Code of Federal Regulations and other regulatory instruments, in the last ten years, the conviction rate under ARPA has increased to about 50 percent to 85 percent, greatly increasing the ability to protect sites through criminal sanctions. NAGPRA received its first conviction in late March 1995. A more comprehensive approach to criminal investigations and prosecutions has been developed by using both ARPA and NAGPRA in conjunction with other criminal statutes against property theft, illegal interstate trafficking, and tax evasion. For the last ten years, one in ten reported violations has been taken to court by prosecutors and federal district attorneys (Waldbauer 2000).

The US Forest Service, Bureau of Land Management, and National Park Service have teamed with the Federal Law Enforcement Training Center (FLETC) to develop training courses for archaeologists, attorneys, and law enforcement officials to more effectively enforce these laws. During the program, students participate in integrated lectures and discussions where advanced and specialized training is offered to both the law enforcement officers and archaeologists in the same classroom setting. At other times, the participants are separated in order to provide more concentrated law enforcement training to the archaeologists and archaeological training to the law enforcement officers. This program identifies the need for a team concept for archaeological resource crime scene investigation. Topics presented to archaeologists include introduction to the Federal Criminal Justice System, testifying in court, and site damage assessment reporting. Topics presented to law enforcement officers include introduction to archaeology, surveillance techniques, and undercover operations (FLETC 2000). The program has trained about 300 persons per year since 1986 (Waldbauer 2000).

More effective enforcement of ARPA and NAGPRA and greater public awareness about looting have helped to stem the pressure from the black market and decrease the destruction of archaeological sites. Nevertheless, looting remains a tremendous problem throughout America.

Abandoned shipwrecks

The Abandoned Shipwreck Act (ASA) of 1988 established protection measures for significant shipwrecks and authorized state management of them. It established United States ownership of all abandoned shipwrecks on submerged state lands that are either embedded in such lands or included in or determined eligible for the National Register of Historic Places. The Act transfers title of these abandoned wrecks to the states except where they are in submerged lands administered by a federal agency or Indian tribe. In cases where these wrecks are embedded in federal lands, the federal lead agency has responsibility for the abandoned shipwreck. The ASA only applies to formally abandoned shipwrecks. Abandonment of a wrecked military vessel requires an act of Congress. Wrecked confederate naval vessels, and the ships and aircraft lost to the US in war, are generally the property of the US government and are not subject to the terms of the Act. Wrecks beyond the boundaries of US waters are not subject to the terms of the Act, but are subject to federal admiralty law.

States vary in how effectively they protect abandoned shipwrecks. In Florida, which has passed some of the strongest protection mandates, problems persist because of a lack of enforcement resources and conflicts with the ancient common law of treasure trove, which awards title of an artifact to the finder, whether he is a looter or an archaeologist. In recent years, however, the majority of federal and state courts have rejected treasure trove and similar common law rationales, fostering legal policies that discourage wanton trespass to real property and give protection to landowners' claims. Rejection of the rules that reward finders at the expense of landowners has also strengthened anti-looting provisions (Cunningham 2000).

The artifact storage and curation crisis

A virtual avalanche of reports and collected artifacts accompanied the CRM explosion starting in the late 1970s. No one could have predicted the magnitude of this vast acceleration of cultural resources work. In previous years, agencies had relied upon agreements with non-federal repositories such as state and university museums to care for their collections. These agreements were often vague and usually did not provide funding or facilities support for housing, accessioning, or conservation of the materials.

A government report in 1986 revealed some shocking facts. It found that a large percentage of excavation reports prior to 1975 had been lost or destroyed. There were no binding standards or criteria to guide agencies in evaluating repositories. Agencies had very poor inventory records; for example, most of the approximately 25 million artifacts stored by the National Park Service had not been cataloged, requiring 50 million dollars to rectify, and 200 million dollars were needed for new and upgraded storage facilities. One-third of all non-federal curation facilities had already run out of storage space. Other government facilities were found to be in similar shape, with poor maintenance practices, inadequate security and fire protection, and inadequate staff (Childs 1995).

Regulations (ref.: 36 CFR 79) for the curation of federally-owned collections were finally issued in 1990, only to be upstaged the same year by the newly enacted NAGPRA. NAGPRA, with its specified deadlines for compliance reporting, forced agencies and museums to focus on NAGPRA compliance to the detriment of the new 36 CFR 79 curation requirements. One positive effect of NAGPRA, however, has been to force agencies to conduct artifact inventories and determine their disposition. Some agencies, such as the US Army Corps of Engineers, have been able to consolidate collections. Overall progress has been slow, however, and the curation crisis will continue well in to the twenty-first century (Childs 1995).

Challenges in data management

The stampede of recorded sites and collected artifacts since the 1970s has also created a crisis of data management among responsible federal and state agencies nationwide. Since the early 1980s, site forms have become more automated as technical advances have facilitated the development of various database systems. Automation of data has facilitated the use of automated land resource distribution tools such as geographic information systems (GIS) in CRM planning among government agencies at federal, state, and local levels. A major challenge among agencies has been to create systems that are mutually compatible. One of the problems has been to create dynamic systems that can evolve along with the rapidly changing technologies.

The National Archaeological Database (NADB) is maintained by the National Park Service and consists of a Reports module and a NAGPRA data module. The Reports module is an expanded bibliographic inventory of approximately 250,000 reports on archaeological investigation and planning, mostly of limited circulation. This 'gray literature' represents a large portion of the primary information available on archaeological sites in the US. It can be searched by state, county, worktype, cultural affiliation, keyword, material, year of publication, title, and author.

This database benefits from the bibliographic records contributed by many partners, particularly State Historic Preservation Offices and federal agencies. In order to help partners access and search their records more directly, subsets of data are provided for some federal agencies and states. Partners may request direct access to their records. The NAGPRA module contains NAGPRA-related documents organized in five major categories: laws and legal mandates, guidance information, Kennewick Man documents, museums and federal agency inventory submissions, public notices, and Review Committee reports (National Park Service 2000b).

The Native American Consultation Database (NACD) is a tool for identifying consultation contacts for each Indian tribe, Alaska Native corporation, and Native Hawaiian organization. The database is not a comprehensive source of information, but it does provide a starting point for the consultation process by identifying tribal leaders and NAGPRA contacts. The NACD is updated semiannually (National Park Service 2000b).

Archaeology and the reconstructions controversy

Another controversial CRM topic since the 1930s has been the debate over the pros and cons of reconstructions versus preservation-in-place. The main focus of discussion for archaeologists has been on the appropriate level of archaeological investigations and knowledge needed prior to on-site reconstructions and whether reconstructions of any nature are appropriate when in situ materials will be damaged or destroyed.

The philosophical arguments for and against the practice of reconstructing historical and archaeological sites in America are rooted in the early developments of the conservation and historic preservation movements of the nineteenth and twentieth centuries (Jameson 2004). Other major events and developments, such as the opening of Colonial Williamsburg by the Rockefeller foundation in 1933, and passage of the Historic Sites Act of 1935, furthered the cause of historic preservation and brought public, private, and professional interest in American archaeology to new heights. At Colonial Williamsburg, a reconstructed historic community of the 1770s was based on detailed historical and limited archaeological research. These reconstructions proved to be immensely popular with the public. The reconstruction technique at Colonial Williamsburg involved recreating over 450 buildings in an effort to completely restore the town. Lack of specific information on a particular building presented no problem to project designers and architects, who relied on architectural precedents and an examination of surviving colonial buildings in the region to invent building types based on general architectural practices of the period. These planners and architects saw life in eighteenth century Virginia as more homogenous and genteel than do historians today. This popular, yet conjectural, technique became the standard applied to hundreds of reconstructions in the United States for decades to come. It pervaded and guided the work of the National Park Service and other federal agencies in scores of New Deal public works projects carried out in the years preceding World War II (Jameson and Hunt 1999).

By the late 1940s and 1950s, historic preservation as the commemoration of sites and structures associated with famous people and events had entered the mainstream of public consciousness. The resulting collection of national and state historic sites, monuments, and parks, as well as an abundance of privately administered buildings and sites, became standard fare for an increasingly mobile American public.

Against this backdrop of a developing preservation ethic, a small but vocal cadre of scholars (architectural historians, historians, and archaeologists) have opposed the broad use of reconstructions (or 're-creations' as some have termed it). Starting in the 1930s, there was a steadily growing outcry in the National Park Service and elsewhere, especially among cultural resource professional staffs, to severely limit, if not abolish altogether, the use of reconstructions as an interpretive device (Pitcaithley 1989). The debate has been between these conservative preservationists and others in the historic preservation field, such as site managers, planners, and professional interpreters, who see the qualified use of reconstructions as sometimes essential to the public's appreciation of the resource.

In the National Park Service, the US government's leading preservation agency, policies for reconstruction have always been a source of controversy among staff professionals. This policy calls for reconstructions to occur only after thorough archaeological investigations have been carried out. Archaeological research provides details of architectural design not available in existing records and contributes further information on the uses and cultural contexts of architectural features and material objects (Jameson and Hunt 1999).

The National Park Service defines 'reconstructions' as measures to preserve any remaining prehistoric or historic materials, features, and spatial relationships. It is based on the accurate duplication of features documented through archaeology, archival research, or physical evidence, rather than on conjectural designs. In most cases, methodology is not restricted to the technology of the period. By inference, reconstructions may include the use of modern materials and tools only if these do not conflict with the purpose of 'replicating its appearance.' Reconstructions differ from restorations in that they involve *new* construction of various components of the cultural landscape, such as buildings, huts, towns or villages, earthworks, living areas, trails, and roads (Figure 2.7). A reconstructed cultural landscape re-creates the appearance of the non-surviving cultural landscape in design, color, textures, and, where possible, materials. Reconstructions have addressed a wide temporal range including sites such as the prehistoric Great Kiva at Aztec Ruins National Monument in New Mexico and a ceremonial earthlodge (Ocmulgee National Monument) in Georgia (Figure 2.3), to historic period buildings, trading posts, and forts of the seventeenth, eighteenth, and nineteenth centuries.

The National Park Service definitions of 'reconstruction' and 'restoration' are used to guide management decisions on whether such actions are justified or warranted. Strictly speaking, however, as Fowler (1999) and others have pointed

Figure 2.7 The reconstructed stockade fort at Ninety Six National Historic Site, South Carolina. Photo courtesy of National Park Service.

out, it is impossible to 'reconstruct' or 're-create' the past in that our modern biases and perceptions take away from getting to the 'truth' of the matter. This does not negate the value of 'reconstructions' as public interpretation tools, however, especially if the presentation encompasses an explanation of these shortcomings so that the public understands their explicative limitations.

In the America as elsewhere, the 'value' of reconstructions often goes beyond any scientific, educational, or conservation considerations to premeditated or desired outcomes that are also influenced by a blend of other factors such as societal morality, politics, local economy, and tourism (Jameson 2004). In a representative democracy such as the United States, the determining factors for creating any given national park unit revolve around these issues (Jameson and Hunt 1999; Stone and Planel 1999; Culleton 1999; Ijureef 1999). Despite agency policies that have generally discouraged the use of reconstructions as public interpretation tools, a wide variance in the National Park Service has developed between sites that have virtually no reconstructions, such as at Jamestown, Virginia, to parks that depend almost entirely on reconstructions in their public programs, such as Fort Vancouver National Historic Site, Washington, which has a reconstructed stockade and five major buildings. At Jamestown, long a 'sacred cow' among preservationists, the preservation purist philosophy has prevailed.

At Fort Vancouver and a number of other sites, *in situ* preservation has been de-emphasized in favor of a comprehensive program of reconstructions based on intensive archaeological and historical research. Archaeological research at the nineteenth century Hudson Bay Company site has been going on inter-mittently for fifty years, supplying detailed information and artifacts for the public interpretation and education programs, including museum displays and living history demonstrations.

Archaeology and ethnicity issues

A new era of Native American archaeology

In the 1990s, the aftermath of the passage and implementation of NAGPRA has forced many archaeologists, historians, and cultural resource managers to rethink fundamental assumptions that traditionally guided the develop-ment of research designs and the interpretation of findings. Archaeologists find that they are no longer the sole proprietors and interpreters of pre-European history. The definition of 'cultural resources' in the archaeological sense has broadened from a focus on objects, features, and architectural elements to less tangible items such as 'place,' or 'setting,' or 'traditional cultural property.' This is due primarily to the effects of new federal mandates that have made Native Americans integral players in cultural resource management, a redefinition of what constitutes 'data,' and who owns or controls the data (Edgar 2000). Archaeologists and cultural resource managers can no longer rely on material culture alone to identify or describe historic and archaeological properties. This change from the traditional definition also means that cultural resources, especially archaeological resources, cannot be identified through traditional investigation procedures (Banks *et al.* 2000).

Just as the concept and context of 'cultural landscape' have been added to the evaluation criteria for National Register eligibility, so has 'traditional cultural property' (TCP). Both terms were outside the boundaries of items traditionally considered by archaeologists until the CRM developments of the late twentieth century. The era of Native American archaeology with its different concepts of cultural resources is here. Many archaeologists as well as Native Americans are looking to these new definitions and concepts to help mend past animosities and provide a bridge for communication and cooperation in their common passion for Native American cultural history (Banks *et al.* 2000).

The Kennewick Man controversy

A recent NAGPRA-related controversy involves the human skeletal remains associated with the 'Kennewick Man', or 'Ancient One.' A nearly complete skeleton was found in July 1996 below the surface of Lake Wallula, a pooled part of the Columbia River behind McNary Dam in Kennewick, Washington. Based on the preliminary 1996 study, the remains were determined to be approximately 9,000 years old, thus qualifying them as 'of, or relating to, a tribe, people, or culture that is indigenous to the United States, including Alaska and Hawaii' and therefore 'Native American' as defined by NAGPRA (McManamon 2000b). The original scientist on the scene retrieved a nearly complete human skeleton, with a long, narrow face suggestive, he thought, of a person of European descent.

Almost immediately, a dispute developed regarding who was responsible for determining what would be done with the remains. Claims were made by Indian tribes, local officials, and some members of the scientific community. The US Army Corps of Engineers, the agency responsible for the land where the remains were recovered, took possession. The Army Corps of Engineers planned to return the remains to a Native American local tribe for reburial, but a group of archaeologists and a local special interest group sued the Corps because they wanted the opportunity to study the remains prior to reburial. In March 1998, the Department of the Interior and National Park Service agreed to assist the Army Corps in resolving some of the issues related to the federal case.

Adding fuel to the controversy were claims by another special interest group, pointing to the 1996 study, that the remains are of European rather than Native American origin. This, they said, raises the question of who came to the Americas first. It also raises a question among some researchers whether the earliest humans in North America arrived via the Bering Land Bridge, a long-held belief, or by boat or some other route. The dispute revolves around the historical connections and whether the definition of 'Native American' under NAGPRA applies to the Kennewick Man skeleton. Another aspect of the dispute is whether the involved scientists, despite NAGPRA definitions and requirements, have a legal right to study the remains.

In 1999, additional carbon-14 dating was successfully carried out on the Kennewick Man bone fragments. Results reported in January 2000 supported earlier carbon-14 findings and interpretations based on soils analysis, geomorphology, and artifact descriptions that the Kennewick Man remains qualify as "Native American" as defined by NAGPRA (McManamon 2000). Having qualified as "Native American" under NAGPRA, the next step was to determine if the remains are affiliated with a modern Native American group. A study to evaluate the feasibility of conducting DNA analysis for tribal affiliation recommended in February 2000 that the amounts of datable organic material and overall conditions of the remains were not adequate for carrying out a reliable DNA test, especially if the intent was to determine tribal or "racial" origins (Tuross and Kolman 2000).

Nonetheless, some researchers pressed the National Park Service to go ahead with the DNA analysis. In April 2000, a team of experts at the Burke Museum of Natural and Cultural History in Seattle, Washington, began to conduct the first steps in the DNA analysis. The scientific team consisted of three physical anthropologists, two experts in bone chemistry and DNA analysis, and two experienced archaeological conservators. The stated purpose of the scientific analyses was to carry out a more thorough study of the skeletal remains in order to learn about the cultural treatment and environmental factors that affected the Kennewick remains post mortem. Some have believed that Kennewick Man may have been intentionally buried soon after death and that red ochre or some kind of staining might have been applied to his body before burial. The post mortem anthropological and taphonomic analyses could aide the team in identifying specimens most likely to provide sufficient collagen protein for DNA analysis. The US Department of the Interior Department hoped that this work would provide conclusive evidence to determine whether or not there is a shared group identity or cultural affiliation between Kennewick Man and modern Indian groups (National Park Service 2000d).

In September 2000, the US Secretary of the Interior concluded that, based on the radiocarbon dates, geographic data, and oral history accounts, the remains were affiliated with Indian tribes of the region and should be return to the Indian tribes as required by NAGPRA (Babbitt 2000). To date, laboratory studies have failed to obtain DNA from tiny bone samples taken from the Kennewick Man remains. The US Department of the Interior has hoped that this work will provide conclusive evidence to determine whether or not there is a shared group identity or cultural affiliation between Kennewick Man and modern Indian groups. Post-mortem anthropological and taphonomic analyses would also aid the team in identifying specimens most likely to provide sufficient collagen protein for DNA analysis (National Park Service 2000d).

Some researchers pressed the National Park Service to go ahead with the DNA analysis. A team of experts at the Burke Museum of Natural and Cultural History in Seattle, Washington, conducted the first steps in the DNA analysis. The scientific team consisted of three physical anthropologists, two experts in bone chemistry and DNA analysis, and two experienced archaeological conservators. The stated purpose of the scientific analyses was to carry out a more thorough study of the skeletal remains in order to learn about the cultural treatment and environmental factors that affected the Kennewick remains post mortem. The 2001 report concluded that the Kennewick Man remains are of a single individual who was interred at the site instead of being left to decompose on the surface of the ground or incorporated into the deposit through some catastrophic hydrologic event. These findings are consistent with the belief by some that Kennewick Man was intentionally buried soon after death and that red ochre or some kind of staining might have been applied to his body before burial. Studies conducted in 2000 and 2001 confirmed previous findings suggesting that there is significant variation in the degrees of intact collagen preservation in different portions of the Kennewick skeleton. Attempts to recover non-contaminated DNA from one or more bones from the skeleton were not successful. From a morphological perspective, the Kennewick specimen appears to be more similar to modern South Asians and Europeans than to modern Native Americans or to contemporary indigenous populations of Northeast Asia. Mitochondrial DNA analyses have been unable to assign the Kennewick skeleton as Asian-specific because no ancient DNA has so far been isolated from the samples of Kennewick bone examined (Taylor 2001).

A lawsuit was filed in Federal court by one of the leading scientists who wanted to delay re-interment to allow for further scientific analysis of the remains. A ruling in February 2004 upheld a lower court decision of August 2002 finding that the remains were not Native American and therefore that NAGPRA did not apply to the remains. The February 2004 ruling allowed the scientific study of the remains to go forward.

The Kennewick Man controversy has heightened the post-NAGPRA debate among archaeologists and Native Americans on who owns, controls, and interprets the artifacts and data. In the new era of Native American archaeology, many American archaeologists are questioning the appropriateness of the privileged access that professionals, especially prehistorians, have long enjoyed. The challenge will be in moving toward a greater reconciliation among divergent cultural perspectives in ways that enhance both the archaeologist's and the public's knowledge and appreciation for the past (Edgar 2000). No doubt, the controversy and litigation surrounding the Kennewick Man issue will be with us for some time to come.

African-American archaeology

Another recent focus in the 'archaeology of ethnicity' in America has been in the realm of African-American studies. An impressive collection of data has accumulated from rural plantation sites as well as urban settings.

As archaeological data on African-American lifeways has accumulated over the last thirty years, archaeologists have taken two basic methodological approaches in carrying out research. One approach seeks to recognize the archaeological patterning of slave sites and using these as signals or markers when sites are discovered. The second, centering on the search for objects with physical or behavioral links to Africa's west coast, has moved beyond the simple transfer of objects and ideas across the Atlantic to a more refined focus which integrates behavior with material culture. The aim of the latter approach is not on direct, unaltered 'transferences,' but rather on how West African cultural traditions, as reflected in the archaeological record, were modified in the face of the new environments, different social groups, and altered power structures in which the slaves in the New World found themselves. No longer having access to the same commodities once at their disposal, West African slaves and their descendants lived in a material world populated largely with goods of English or European manufacture. The assumption is that the slave population thought about and used objects differently than the object manufacturers had originally intended, adapting these new forms of material culture for use within African-American cultural systems (Samford 1994).

Much productive work has been conducted on plantation sites in the southern and mid-Atlantic regions of the United States. At sites such as Mount Vernon, Monticello, and Colonial Williamsburg, new insights to the lives of enslaved African Americans are being revealed. Most importantly, these insights are beginning to make their way into public interpretation programs and exhibits, 'to render significant what has been thought incidental; to make central the important contribution that the common person has made to America's past . . . not simply to add voices to mainstream history, but rather mainstream those voices into history' (Bograd and Singleton 1997).

The largest and probably the most important African-American archaeological site to date in the United States is the eighteenth century African Burial Ground located in Lower Manhattan, New York City. The African Burial Ground, a cemetery located in a potters field outside the eighteenth century fortified walls of the city, was rediscovered by archaeologists in 1991 during pre-construction NHPA-compliant investigations for a new federal office complex. The remains of 427 individuals were eventually removed from the site before the nearly 300 million dollar construction project was halted in the face of local and scientific community protests. The project since 1993 has involved an ambitious program of study and analysis, including curation, anthropomorphic recording, pathological assessment, DNA sampling, chemical isotope analysis, demographic profiles, analysis of burial artifacts and practices, analysis of disease processes, as well as studies focusing on biocultural continuity and change for this population, mostly enslaved persons of African descent (Bruinius 1999; GSA 1999; OPEI 2000).

Over 500 artifacts, mostly from coffins, were analyzed, resulting in the confirmation of a high mortality rate and the harsh realities of slavery. About half of the skeletons were found to be from children aged 12 and under, more than half of whom died in infancy. Among the artifacts is an unusual array of studs hammered into a coffin lid in a complex heart-shaped design. The design is an Ashanti symbol of 'sankofa,' meaning 'Look to the past to inform the future', an ironic phrase considering the history of the site (Coleman 2000). The human remains have been studied at Howard University in Washington, DC. They were returned to New York City and re-interred at the African Burial Ground Memorial Site, designated a National Historic Landmark, on October 4, 2003. The National Park Service was tasked to develop an Interpretive Center within the lobby of 290 Broadway, adjacent to the burial ground. A final archaeological report is expected by 2006.

The emergence of educational archaeology

Educational archaeology in the US and worldwide

Although notable efforts had occurred previously (South 1997), the 1980s and 1990s were a time when many in the archaeology profession in America came to the realization that it could no longer afford to be detached from mechanisms and programs that attempt to convey archaeological information to the lay public. In the face of an increasing public interest and demand for information, archaeologists have collaborated with historians, museum curators, exhibit designers, and other cultural resource specialists to devise the best strategies for translating an explosion of archaeological information for the public. The 1980s and 1990s saw a great proliferation of efforts to meet this demand, with varying degrees of success (Jameson 2000a).

Until recently, forums for discussion and available literature on this topic were scarce and largely obscured in isolated accounts and the gray literature of archaeologists and educators. At the turn of the twenty-first century, many success stories in educational archaeology remain to be publicly discussed or written. However, the 1990s saw significant improvement in the number of public and professional forums and a few notable publications have recently been produced (e.g. Stone and Mackenzie 1990; Stone and Molyneaux 1994; Jameson 1997; McManamon and Hatton 2000; Smardz and Smith 2000; Bender and Smith 2000). Discussions have also taken place at international forums such as the World Archaeological Congress (Esterhuysen and Smith 1999; Jameson 1999a).

In America, professional societies, notably the Society for American Archaeology (SAA), the Archaeological Institute of America (AIA), and the Society for Historical Archaeology (SHA), plus state and local groups, have played important roles in providing leadership and inspiration in educational archaeology (see Smardz Frost, Chapter 3 this volume). An important recent project is SHA's 'Unlocking the Past: Historical Archaeology in North America,' a multi-year public outreach and education initiative. The project is composed of two major components, a World Wide Web site, and a generously illustrated book. Both the Web site and the book introduce general readers to the archaeology of North America's history beginning with the early contacts between Europeans and Native Americans. They take the reader on a journey to significant historical archaeological sites and projects from Canada to the Caribbean, from the early Viking voyages through World War II. They tell the stories of historical archaeologists conducting pioneering work in rural and urban North America, on the land and under water, at forts, shipwrecks, missions, farms, city lots, and sites of industry. They also explain why historical archaeology is important in providing objectively derived context as well as filling information gaps in the historical record. Historical archaeologists share in North America their findings to engage readers and encourage them to join in preserving and studying cultural heritage. The material is designed to appeal to a wide general audience of young readers as well as adults interested in archaeology, North American history, and historic preservation (De Cunzo and Jameson 2000).

Exemplary government programs at federal, state, and local levels have taken the lead in promoting education and outreach (see Smardz Frost, Chapter 3 this volume). At the federal level, the US Bureau of Land Management's Heritage Education Program has made important contributions to archaeology education through the 'Project Archaeology' program. Teacher workshops and the development of quality educational materials such as the *Intrigue of the Past* teacher's guide have been very effective. The Passport in Time (PIT) program of the US Forest Service uses volunteers who work with professional archaeologists and historians on projects such as archaeological excavation, rock art restoration, survey, archival research, historic structure restoration, gathering oral histories, and preparing interpretive brochures. The National Park Service (NPS) has traditionally taken the lead in promoting education and outreach activities at the federal level. A major emphasis has been in promoting partnerships and initiatives both within and outside the government. In recent years, a number of NPS publications have been produced that support archaeology education and outreach. The principal publication is *Common Ground*. This quarterly magazine is distributed to more than 12,000 members of the public as well as archaeologists, land managers, preservation officers, museum professionals, Native Americans, law enforcement agents, and educators. An interdisciplinary course of study was developed by NPS that can be used in cross-training employees in the three career fields of archaeology, interpretation, and education. Specialists in these fields are trained together in the skills and abilities needed to carry out a successful public interpretation program. Among the main precepts of the curriculum are the needs for interdisciplinary communication and for sensitive interpretation to multicultural audiences. The NPS Southeast Archeological Center (SEAC) in Tallahassee, Florida, has provided leadership by promoting the objectives of educational archaeology by helping to develop archaeology-related curricula, both in formal school settings and at more informal settings such as national parks and museums. Activities have included the organization and coordination of public-oriented publications, academic symposia, workshops, and training sessions presented in a variety of professional venues (Jameson 1999b, 2000c).

Many private and public universities, archaeology and anthropology departments, and museums have launched effective outreach programs in recent years. One example is Sonoma State University's Anthropological Studies Center (ASC) which has placed special emphasis on education and outreach in the production of publications and activities for teachers, local civic organizations, archaeology groups, and continuing education programs. ASC's award-winning publications have included public awareness slide shows and videos. A leader and innovator among natural and historical museums is the Chicago Field Museum which provides outstanding public-oriented educational programs. The museum programs focus on cultural diversity as well as the contents of its collections. More than 300,000 students visit the museum annually on organized school field trips.

A large number of private CRM contracting firms have provided leadership in promoting educational opportunities for volunteers and students. An example is the establishment of a full-time public programs division by Statistical Research, Inc. (SRI) in Tucson, Arizona. At SRI, public programs are structured into compliance and non-compliance projects as well as being funded by stand-alone contracts dedicated to public outreach. SRI produces the US Forest Service's 'Passport in Time' *PIT Traveler* publication that advertises nationwide programs and volunteer opportunities.

Archaeology in popular history writing

It is generally accepted today among public archaeologists in America that *both* quality research and the public interpretation of research findings are indispensable outcomes of their work. After all, is not the ultimate value of archaeological studies not only to inform but also ultimately to improve the public's appreciation of the nature and relevance of cultural history? This improved appreciation results in an improved quality of life for Americans.

Exhibits and popular history writing are two of the most effective techniques for public interpretation of archaeology. To be successful, both techniques must not only inform but entertain. The goals are to connect, engage, inform, and inspire, resulting in a lasting and improved appreciation of the resource.

Too often, among the flood of reports and artifacts that have come from CRM studies, archaeologists lose sight of the real purpose of the compliance process: to provide public enjoyment and appreciation for the rich diversity of past human experiences. An important, and some would say the *most* important, outcome of CRM mitigation programs is the production of publications, programs, and exhibits that provide public access to research findings.

For example, an important outcome of the Richard B. Russell (RBR) CRM program was the production of publications and exhibits that would provide public access to the findings of the RBR studies. In 1985, the US Army Corps of Engineers established an on-site public exhibit and brochure derived from the results of the RBR Cultural Resources Mitigation Program. The exhibit continues to be maintained at the Richard B. Russell Project Office near Elberton, Georgia. In the production of the Richard B. Russell popular history volume, *Beneath These Waters*, the National Park Service and the Corps placed heavy emphasis on producing a popular account that is both informative and entertaining. The resulting exhibits and publications, when coupled with the technical work, make the Richard B. Russell Cultural Resources Mitigation Program an exemplary model on a global scale, both in providing high quality research and also public access to research findings.

In preparing *Beneath These Waters*, the National Park Service chose a team of professional writers adept at the art of effectively translating technical information for the lay public. Contract writers Sharyn Kane and Richard Keeton, because they were not formally trained archaeologists or historians and were unfamiliar with the world of federal contracting, faced distinct disadvantages in taking on the task of writing these books. However, as they pored over the various technical archaeology and history reports, they realized that this estrangement from technical know-how had given them an important advantage in writing the RBR popular history: nearly complete objectivity in viewing the overall project and its results, unencumbered by the predictable baggage of professional biases, cultivated styles, and emotions attached to a project of this magnitude and importance. The authors' task was to take the results of these two decades of research, strip them down to the essentials, and reclothe them in a fashion readily acceptable to a general audience without losing the fundamental integrity of the original material (Kane *et al.* 1994). The universal praise of *Beneath These Waters* from the educational, scientific, and local communities attests to the book's success in providing informative access to research findings.

Archaeology as inspiration: art and imagery

Many archaeologists today are not content to rely solely on traditional methodologies and analytical techniques in their attempts to reconstruct human history and bring it to life for the public. They want to venture beyond utilitarian explanations and explore the interpretive potential of cognitive imagery that archaeological information and objects can inspire. They realize the value and power of artistic expression in helping to convey archaeological information to the public. Archaeologists are increasingly concerned with how the past is presented to, and consumed by, non-specialists. They want to examine new ways of communicating archaeological information in educational venues such as national parks, museums, popular literature, film and television, music, and various multimedia formats (Jameson *et al.* 2003).

Archaeology and archaeologically-derived information and objects have inspired a wide variety of artistic expressions ranging from straightforward computer-generated reconstructions and traditional artists' conceptions to other art forms such as poetry and opera. Although some level of conjecture will always be present in these works, they are often no less conjectural than technical interpretations and have the benefit of providing visual and conceptual imagery that can communicate contexts and settings in compelling ways. Two such interpretive formats, two-dimensional paintings and popular history writing, are used by the National Park Service as public interpretation and education tools (Jameson 2000b, 2001).

In order to provide a richer conceptual imagery to the accounts of prehistoric lifeways and to augment the large collection of available photographs, the authors of *Beneath These Waters* made use of original paintings commissioned by the National Park Service from an artist. The two original oil paintings produced as illustrations greatly enhanced the attractiveness of the volume. The paintings depict prehistoric scenes based on published archaeological findings, adding an entertaining, yet informative dimension not commonly seen in government-sponsored popular accounts (Figure 2.5).

Public archaeology in America: past, present, and future

This chapter has described public archaeology in America as being shaped by the historic preservation and conservation movements of the nineteenth and twentieth centuries, the outcomes of post-World War II CRM compliance, and recent developments in educational archaeology. Challenges to management, such as site protection, looting, and the curation crisis will continue to be the focus of government programs for the foreseeable future. Perhaps one measure of the status and maturity of public archaeology in America is its recent turn toward a greater accommodation of Native American values. In this sense, public archaeology and a new and expanded definition of cultural resources have steered the archaeological profession toward a firmer embrace of archaeology as anthropology. Although limitations of manpower and resources continue to be sources of frustration for many public archaeologists in America, we can take some solace in knowing that our efforts in site protection, public education, and interpretation, in the Jeffersonian tradition, are producing a more aware, appreciative, and inspired public.

Bibliography

Anderson, D. G. 1997. A National Commitment to Archaeology. *Common Ground* 2(1): 14–19.

Anderson, D.G., B.C. Keel, J. H. Jameson, J.E. Cobb, and J.W. Joseph, Jr. 2000. Reservoir Construction in the Southeastern United States: The Richard B. Russell Program as an Example of Exemplary Heritage/Cultural Resources Management. Paper presented at the Culture Heritage Management and Dams Workshop, University of Florida, Gainesville.

Babbitt, B. 2000. Letter to Louis Caldera, Secretary of the Army. Washington, DC: US Department of the Interior, (September 21, 2000).

Banks, M. K., M.Giesen, and N. Pearson 2000. Traditional cultural properties vs. traditional cultural resource management. *CRM* 23(1).

Bender, S. J. and G. S. Smith (eds) 2000. *Teaching Archaeology in the Twenty-first Century*. Washington, DC: Society for American Archaeology.

Bograd, M. D. and T. A. Singleton 1997. The interpretation of slavery: Mount Vernon, Monticello, and Colonial Williamsburg. In J. H. Jameson, Jr (ed.) *Presenting Archaeology to the Public: Digging for Truths*. Walnut Creek: AltaMira Press.

Bruinius, H. 1999. African burial ground under New York streets. URL: http://www.csmonitor.com/durable/1999/06/17/p16s1.htm. *The Christian Science Monitor Electronic Edition*, June 17, 1999. Boston, Massachusetts: The Christian Science Publishing Society.

Childs, S. T. 1995. The curation crisis: What's being done? *Federal Archeology* 7(4): 11–15.

Coleman, S. 2000. Personal communication. New York: African Burial Ground Steering Committee, General Services Administration.

Conrad, N., J. H. Jameson, Jr, and C. Van Voorhies 1999. A Partnership for the 21st Century: The Fort Frederica Archaeology Education Workshop. Paper presented at the 1999 National Interpreters Workshop, Syracuse, New York. October.

Culleton, E. 1999. The Origin and Role of the Irish Heritage Park. In P. G. Stone and P. G. Planel (eds) *The Constructed Past: Experimental Archaeology, Education and the Public*. London: Routledge.

Cunningham, R. B. 2000. The slow death of the treasure trove. *Archaeology* online features. URL: http://archaeology.org/online/features/trove/index.html. Archaeological Institute of America (February).

Cushman, D. W. 1998. Public archaeology and local land use law. *CRM* 21(10).

De Cunzo, L. A. and J. H. Jameson, Jr. 2000. 'Unlocking the Past': An SHA Public Awareness and Education Project. Paper presented at the 2000 Society for Historical Archaeology Annual Conference on Historical and Underwater Archaeology, Quebec, Canada (January).

Edgar, B. 2000. Whose past is it, anyway? Review of *Skull Wars* (2000) by David Hurst Thomas. *Scientific American* July 2000:106–7.

Esterhuysen, A. and J. Smith 1999. The Form, Physique And Fitness Of Educational Archaeology; Is It Working Out? Symposium held during the 1999 World Archaeological Congress (WAC 4), Cape Town, South Africa (January 4–10).

FLETC (Federal Law Enforcement Training Center) 2000. Enforcement Techniques Division Archeological Resources Protection Training Program. URL: http://www.ustreas.gov/fletc/etd/etd_home.htm. The Federal Law Enforcement Training Center (March).

Fowler, P. 1999. Bede's world, UK: the monk who made history. In P. G. Stone and P. G. Planel (eds) *The Constructed Past: Experimental Archaeology, Education and the Public*. London: Routledge.

GII (Grolier Interactive, Inc.) 1996. Theodore Roosevelt biography. URL: http://gi.grolier.com/presidents/ea/bios/26proos.html.

GOPR (Governor's Office of Planning and Research) 1994. *CEQA and Archaeological Resources. The CEQA Technical Advice Series*. Sacramento: California Office of Planning and Research (April).

GSA (US General Services Administration) 1999. The African Burial Ground. URL: http://r2.gsa.gov/afrburgro/abg.htm. Washington, DC.

Haas, D. 1995. Education and Public Outreach in Federal Programs. *CRM* 18(3): 13–18.

Ijureef, G. F. 1999. The Reconstruction of Sites in the Archaeological Theme Park. In P. G. Stone and P. G. Planel (eds) *The Constructed Past: Experimental Archaeology, Education and the Public*. London: Routledge.

Jameson, J.H. Jr. (ed.) 1997. *Presenting Archaeology to the Public: Digging for Truths*. Walnut Creek: AltaMira Press.

Jameson, J. H. Jr. (ed.) 1999a. Archaeology and the National Park idea: challenges for management and interpretation. *The George Wright Forum* 16(4).

Jameson, J. H. Jr. 1999b. The NPS Public Interpretation Initiative Program. Online article, URL: http://www.cr.nps.gov/seac/pii.htm.

Jameson, J. H. Jr. 2000a. Public interpretation, education and outreach: the growing predominance in American archaeology. In F. P. McManamon and A. Hatton (eds) *Cultural Resource Management in Contemporary Society*. London: Routledge.

Jameson, J. H., Jr. 2000b. Review of *The Apalachee Indians and Mission San Luis. Historical Archaeology* 34(2): 146–8.

Jameson, J. H. Jr. 2000c. Striking a Balance: the NPS Archaeology-Interpretation Shared Competency Curriculum. Paper presented at the 2000 Society for Historical Archaeology Annual Meeting, Quebec, Canada (January).

Jameson, J. H. Jr. 2001. Using Art as Public Interpretation and Education Tools in Archaeology. Paper presented at the 2001 Society for American Archaeology Annual Conference, New Orleans, Louisiana (April).

Jameson, J. H. Jr. 2004. Introduction in J. H. Jameson Jr. (ed.) *The Reconstructed Past, Reconstructions in the Public Interpretation of Archaeology and History*. Walnut Creek: AltaMira Press.

Jameson, J. H. Jr. and W. J. Hunt 1999. Reconstruction vs. preservation-in-place in the National Park Service. In P. G. Stone and P. G. Planel (eds) *The Constructed Past: Experimental Archaeology, Education and the Public*. London: Routledge.

Jameson, J. H. Jr., J. E. Ehrenhard, and W. M. Husted 1992. Federal Archaeological Contracting: Utilizing the Competitive Procurement Process. Revised from original 1990 publication. *Technical Brief No. 7*. Washington, DC: Archaeological Assistance Program, National Park Service.

Jameson, J. H. Jr., N. Conrad, and C. Van Voorhies 2000. A Colonial Classroom: Fort Frederica National Monument. Paper presented at the 2000 Society for Historical Archaeology Annual Conference on Historical and Underwater Archaeology, Quebec, Canada.

Jameson, J. H. Jr., J. E. Ehrenhard, and C. A. Finn (eds) 2003. *Ancient Muses: Archaeology and the Arts*. Tuscaloosa: University of Alabama Press.

Jefferson, T. 1787. Notes on the State of Virginia. In *Thomas Jefferson Writings*, compiled by Merrill D. Peterson, seventh printing, 1984, p. 225. New York: The Library of America.

Kane, S., R. Keeton, and J. H. Jameson Jr. 1994. Beneath These Waters: A Publication for the Public. Online article, URL: http://www.cr.nps.gov/seac/ beneath.htm.

Keel, B. C. 2001. Personal communication. Tallahassee, Florida: Southeast Archaeological Center, National Park Service.

Leone, M. P., P. B. Potter Jr, and P. A. Shackel 1987. Toward a critical archaeology. *Current Anthropology* 28(3): 251–302.

McManamon, F. P. 2000a. Memorandum: Results of Radiocarbon Dating the Kennewick Human Skeletal Remains (January 13, 2000).

McManamon, F. P. 2000b. The protection of archaeological resources in the United States: reconciling preservation with contemporary society. In F. P. McManamon and A. Hatton (eds) *Cultural Resource Management in Contemporary Society*. London: Routledge.

McManamon, F. P. and A. Hatton (eds) 2000. *Cultural Resource Management in Contemporary Society*. London: Routledge.

McGimsey, C. R. III. 1972. *Public Archeology*. New York: Seminar Press.

McGimsey, C. R. III and H. A. Davis 1977. *The Management of Archaeological Resources: The Airlie House Report*. Washington, DC: Society for American Archaeology.

Means, B. K. 1998. Archaeological past and present: field methodology from 1930s relief excavations in Somerset County, Pennsylvania and its relevance to modern archaeological interpretations. *Journal of Middle Atlantic Archaeology* 14: 39–63.

Minthorn, P. 1997. Native peoples and river basin surveys. *Common Ground* 2(1): 38.

National Park Service. 1998. The power to preserve: public archaeology and local government. *CRM* 21(10).

National Park Service. 1999a. Public Archaeology in the United States Timeline. URL: http://www.cr.nps.gov/aad/timeline/timeline.htm. Washington, DC: National Park Service.

National Park Service. 1999b. Cultural resources and the Interior Department: an Overview. *CRM* 22(4).

National Park Service. 2000a. Dam good archaeology: The Bureau of Reclamation's Cultural Resources Program. *CRM* 23(1).

National Park Service. 2000b. National Archaeological Database. URL: http://www.cr.nps.gov/aad/nadb.htm. Washington, DC: National Park Service.

National Park Service. 2000c. Federal Archaeology Program. URL: http://www.cr.nps.gov/aad/fedarch.htm. Washington, DC: National Park Service.

National Park Service. 2000d. Scientists to Begin Kennewick Man DNA Studies. NPS Press Release, April 21, 2000. Washington, DC: National Park Service.

OPEI (Office of Public Education and Interpretation of the African Burial Ground) 2000. *Update* 3(1), *OPEI Newsletter*, New York: World Trade Center, US Customs House.

Pitcaithley, D. 1989. Pious Frauds: Federal Reconstruction Efforts During the 1930s. Paper delivered at the annual meeting of the Organization of American Historians, St. Louis, Missouri. Copy on file at the Office of the Chief Historian, National Park Service, Washington, DC.

Samford, P. 1994. Searching for West African cultural meanings in the archaeological record. *Newsletter of the African-American Archaeology Network* 12.

SEAC. 1998. *Celebrating 60 Years of Archaeology in the Southeast: 1938–1998*. Commemorative poster. Tallahassee, Florida Southeast Archaeological Center, National Park Service.

Simon, B. G. and E. L. Bell 1998. Community archaeology: working with local governments. *CRM* 21(10).

Smardz, K. and S. Smith (eds) 2000. *Sharing Archaeology with Kids: A Handbook of Strategies, Issues, and Resources in Archaeology Education*. Walnut Creek: AltaMira Press.

Smith, G. S. and J. E. Ehrenhard (eds) 1991. *Protecting the Past*. Boca Raton, Florida: CRC Press.

South, S. 1997. Generalized versus literal interpretation. In J. H. Jameson Jr (ed.) *Presenting Archaeology to the Public: Digging for Truths*. Walnut Creek: AltaMira Press.

Stone, P. G. and R. Mackenzie (eds) 1990. *The Excluded Past: Archaeology in Education*. London: Routledge.

Stone, P. G. and B. L. Molyneaux (eds) 1994. *The Presented Past: Heritage, Museums, and Education*. London: Routledge.

Stone, P. G. and P. G. Planel 1999. Introduction. In P.G. Stone and P.G. Planel (eds) *The Constructed Past: Experimental Archaeology, Education and the Public*. London: Routledge.

Taylor, R. E. 2001. Amino Acid Composition and Stable Carbon Isotope Values on Kennewick Skeleton Bone. Attachment B in *Report on the DNA Testing Results of the Kennewick Human Remains from Columbia Park, Kennewick, Washington*. Washington, DC: National Park Service.

TED (Trade and Environment Database) 1993. TED Case Studies: Artifact Trade, Case No. 216. URL: http://www.american.edu/projects/mandala/TED/ ARTIFACT. HTM. American University, Washington, DC (January).

Tuross, N. and C. J. Kolman. 2000. Potential for DNA Testing of the Human Remains from Columbia Park, Kennewick, Washington. Report to the Department of the Interior and Department of Justice. URL: http://www.cr.nps.gov/aad/kennewick/tuross_kolman.htm. Washington, DC: National Park Service.

Waldbauer, R. 2000. Personal communication. Washington, DC: National Park Service.

Walthall, J., K. Farmsworth, and T. E. Emerson 1997. Constructing {on} the Past: Illinois paves the way for preservation partnerships. *Common Ground* 2(1): 26–33.

Wendorf, F. and R. H. Thompson. 2002. The Committee for the Recovery of Archaeological Remains: three decades of service to the archaeological profession. *American Antiquity* 67(2).

Willey, G. R. and J. A. Sabloff 1993. *A History of American Archaeology* (3rd edition). New York: W.H. Freeman and Company.

3

ARCHAEOLOGY AND PUBLIC EDUCATION IN NORTH AMERICA

View from the beginning of the millennium

Karolyn E. Smardz Frost

The idea of presenting an overview of current public and educational archaeology in North America is daunting. This is even true if one limits, as I do here, the discussion to projects whose focus is primarily educational, and whose explicit objective is enhancing popular interest in matters archaeological. A recent appeal for a description of current programs sent out over the Internet resulted in some 122 e-mails, and there are undoubtedly literally hundreds more educational archaeology projects in operation. Accordingly, I begin here with a discussion of the history, purpose and development of educational archaeology on the North American continent.[1] The latter half of this chapter demonstrates the wide range of educational archaeology programs that are available at the moment. These are divided into general categories based on the venue and intended audience of the program, and are usually direct quotes from the many professionals in the field who so generously responded to my request for information.

Archaeology as a subject has always garnered quite a lot of general interest – witness the many newspaper articles, television programs, videos and Web sites devoted to discoveries all over the globe. And, almost since the birth of the discipline, we have recognized that cultural tourism has both economic and proselytizing benefits, that immense amounts of dirt can be moved by enthusiastic volunteers, and that garnering public support beforehand is essential to ensuring the passage of protective heritage legislation. Cultural research and preservation has always required the support of the well-to-do, be they private patrons or governments. Antiquarian pictures are full of Victorian ladies with parasols on the arms of frock-coated gentlemen, perusing the finds being made at Giza, or Pompeii, or Stonehenge. In

North America, thousands of prehistoric mounds and earthworks have been mapped and recorded over the years by interested travelers, artists and geographers. The Workers Progress Administration of Roosevelt's New Deal sent archaeologists out to supervise unemployed miners and factory workers in the survey and excavation of more sites has ever been investigated at one time before or since. And some of the better known of our early archaeologists were actually amateurs-turned-professional.[2]

(I. Dyke, pers. comm.)

On the institutional side, public education has always been included in the mission statements of museums from coast to coast. For instance, the Royal British Columbia Museum was founded with a petition to the provincial government in 1886. This included a plea for a facility which would raise 'public consciousness about stewardship and educational matters concerning the province's heritage.' The Smithsonian in Washington DC sees itself as 'primarily an institution to increase and diffuse knowledge', and museum education is an acknowledged and highly respected area of specialization within the field of museology (Corley-Smith 1989).

It was clear early on that public interest in, and support for, archaeology were recognized as central to accomplishing the discipline's research and conservation goals. However, it was only in the late 1960s and early 1970s, with the prospect of escalating site destruction looming before us, that the archaeological profession reached the point of developing a full-scale program for what early advocate and influential spokesman for the cause Charles R. McGimsey entitled 'public archaeology' (McGimsey 1972, 1991). According to Hester Davis who took part in many of the early discussions, the term was intended to describe what today we would term 'cultural resource management.' It also encompassed the whole realm of volunteerism, public interpretation and education. In a recent exchange of e-mail on this subject, Davis said:

> CRM is public archeology; field schools are public archeology (because not all those students are going to be professional archeologists); NAGPRA [the Native American Graves Protection and Repatriation Act] consultation is public archeology, etc. I don't consider archeology education, and all the great things that SAA, SHA, AIA, etc are doing in that realm, to be the essence of public archeology – it is one small part of public archeology only. It happens to be the most visible at the moment, certainly the most visibly active, but all the things that archeologists do from open houses at digs to writing reports to talking to 3rd graders to lobbying congress are a part of public archeology.
>
> (H. Davis pers. comm.)

Public and educational archaeology really became priorities when the profession realized that it needed the public to accomplish what it could neither do alone, nor force with the help of legislation – the preservation of the vast quantities of cultural resources which lay both above and below ground across the continent. Exponentially increasing urban, suburban and industrial development, increasingly efficient and destructive extractive and resource acquisition processes, and both enhanced mobility and more leisure time on the part of the general populace, joined with site vandalism and a lucrative and expanding trade in antiquities, to generate site destruction at an unprecedented and entirely alarming rate (G. Smith 1994; Lipe 1994; Fagan 1994). North America is a very big place, and much of the landmass of both Canada and the United States is relatively unpopulated; it was readily apparent that even with very stringent archaeological conservation laws in place, effective enforcement was practically a pipe dream. Public archaeology was perceived as a real and viable solution; if people could be made to feel that the loss of archaeological resources somehow impinged upon their own quality of life, upon their pride in their respective national heritages, and that site stewardship was the responsibility of every citizen, perhaps the tide of cultural resource destruction could be at least slowed (Brown 1991; Davis 1990; McManamon and Smith 1991; Smardz 1990).

Actually, what some archaeologists were trying to do was to bring about a radical attitudinal change in the general populace. Surveys conducted by David Pokotylo of the University of British Columbia in 1985 and 1989, and shortly thereafter by Paul Erickson on behalf of the American Anthropological Association, showed the general public to be overall quite interested and supportive of archaeology and heritage conservation, and that anthropology and archaeology information was indeed being transmitted by a variety of media including in the pre-collegiate classroom. On the other hand, the surveys also demonstrated that the majority of people were woefully ignorant about First Nations and Native American cultural history, confused as to the antiquity of human occupation in their local areas, unaware of archaeological research results, and not generally cognizant of the legislative measures that had already taken place to help preserve cultural resources (Erickson 1990; Pokotylo and Mason 1991; Selig 1991).

It was clear that legislation was not enough to ensure site protection. It was also evident that archaeologists were not themselves sufficiently involved in the development and implementation of programs which would transmit exactly the messages which the discipline wanted ordinary people to hear. As a result, the popular impression of archaeology ranged from something that one could do in one's own backyard, through a profession so skilled and arcane that the only possible public access to its findings could be behind glass in a museum (McManamon and Smith 1991; McManamon 2000).

Progressive and very creative approaches were undertaken by the various federal government agencies in the US which are responsible for resource protection, amongst them the Parks Service, Bureau of Land Management, Forestry Service, and Fish and Wildlife Services. Likewise, public education and interpretation programs at national sites had always been a priority of what is most familiarly known as Parks Canada. The extensive work in historic site restoration done on sites from coast to coast, including many military installations destined to serve as interpretive and living history centers in national parks, has always had a significant public education objective, and frequently in recent years, public involvement as well. The early coordination, material support and both liaison and advisory services provided by agency staff to the cause of educational and public archaeology have been absolutely critical to its success.

Yet, this was a far from pervasive movement throughout the discipline, and one which was often either derided or actively resisted by the archaeological communities at the local level. However, as is often the case with an idea whose time has come, many independent programs and projects were founded in the early to mid-1980s to help meet what their progenitors perceived as a real crisis. There was for some time little coordination between these efforts. Likewise, their degree of both success and longevity varied immensely, largely due to funding difficulties. The leadership and innovative program design of the Arkansas Archaeological Survey dates to this period, as do several of the excellent programs offered through federal government agencies and various State Historic Preservation Offices (Smith and Ehrenhard 1991; Butler 1992; Haas 1995). Stuart Struever, a visionary, a highly respected archaeologist and an immensely practical man with a bent for fund-raising, was the driving force behind the foundation of first the Center for American Archaeology at Kampsville, Illinois, and then Crow Canyon Archaeological Center. Both of these remain privately funded and operated, and are archaeology research and education facilities that enjoy remarkable success on both fronts (Struever 2000). Likewise, the justly admired community–university partnership at the Mississippi Valley Archaeological Center (MVAC) at the University of Wisconsin-La Cross was founded in 1982. MVAC provides 'programs for people of all ages . . . field and laboratory experiences, a lecture series, Archaeology Days, an annual artifact show, and various displays around the community' as well as an ambitious program of courses and workshops directly targeting pre-collegiate teachers (Christensen 1995, 2000, pers. comm. 1999).

Less fortunate were some of the programs dependent upon government funding and political goodwill; witness the much-protested demise of the Archaeological Resource Centre – the Province of Ontario's joint archaeology education venture with the Toronto schools – and the excellent programs developed by Heather Devine, Education Officer of the Archaeological Survey of Alberta. Both were victims of the mid-1990s cash crunch, despite demonstrated popularity amongst students, teachers and the general public, and in the face of strong protest from professional archaeological and educational associations, community groups and parents (Devine 1989a, b, pers. comm. 1994; Jameson 1997; Smardz 1997).

Combined professional and avocational groups such as the Ontario Archaeological Society, and those of Colorado, Illinois, New Mexico, Oklahoma and the Dakotas had long operated programs with a public focus, and conducted a great deal of excellent archaeological research with the help of enthusiastic volunteers. The province-wide archaeological program and the support for the provincial museum in Saskatchewan have traditionally been based on the enthusiasm and backing of the amateur societies, principal amongst them the Saskatchewan Archaeological Society (Johnson and Jones 1999).

Throughout the 1980s, such groups worked to develop more formalized training and education programs aimed not only at interested adults but also at school-aged children and their teachers. The Society for Georgia Archaeology founded the LAMAR Institute expressly for this purpose, offering teachers' education, a wide variety of volunteer opportunities, exhibits, lectures and since 1992 a series of children's experiential programs (Elliott, pers. comm. 1999). Arizona established the 'Archaeology is More than A Dig' program, and initiated one of the first 'Archaeology Week' projects anywhere (Hoffman and Lerner 1988; Ellick 1991). In North Carolina's Underwater Archaeology Unit, Mark Wilde-Ramsing, more recently Chair of the Society for Historical Archaeology's Education Committee, developed both an educational kit and an archaeology 'camp' based on his research, *Hidden Beneath the Waves* (1996/7).

Many other resources were produced during this period: Traveling Suitcase educational kits such as those produced by the Kelsey Museum at Ann Arbor and the Royal Ontario Museum in Toronto (Talalay 1991); lesson plans and instructional media kits like the ones available through the Cataraqui Archaeological Research Foundation at the Kingston Archaeological Centre in Ontario, Canada (Bazeley 1999, and pers. comm.); computer programs aimed at schoolchildren including Doug Price and Gitte Gebauer's *Adventures in Fugawiland!* (1990); free newsletters aimed at teachers and archaeologists interested in teaching such as St. Mary University, Halifax's publication, *Teaching Anthropology Newsletter*, and the Smithsonian's *AnthroNotes*; curriculum guides such as the much admired *Classroom Archaeology* by Nancy Hawkins (1984; revised 1999), in charge of Educational Archaeology for the State of Louisiana; *Clues From the Past: A Resource Book on Archeology* from the Texas Archaeological Society (Wheat and Whorton 1990); and Nan McNutt's privately published *Project Archaeology: Saving Traditions* (1988). An excellent collection of available resources for the classroom teacher was also published by K.C. Smith (1990) as part of her work as Chair of the Society for American Archaeology Educational Resources Forum. It was entitled *Pathways to the Past: An Educator's Guide to Resources in Archaeology*.

While state and provincial government heritage divisions such as those of Louisiana and Arizona, Saskatchewan and Nova Scotia began to hire educational specialists, museums all over the continent established formal programs incorporating the archaeological stewardship message into school and public education curricula and instructional media. Senior archaeologists spoke up to advocate the proper education of undergraduates in archaeological ethics and concepts. These contended that university students were also an important component of the public education initiative, and one for which academics ought to feel themselves responsible (Schuyler 1991). Conferences such as the University of Minnesota's 1987, 1988 and 1989 series entitled 'Presenting the Past' were held to discuss the relative merits of different approaches to public interpretation (Wells 1991). Everywhere, archaeologists began to work with teachers and students, volunteers and government agency staffs to establish educational partnerships.

The profession as a whole began to sit up and take notice. More and more requests from teachers in both the US and Canada for instructional materials, information and guest lecturers were pouring into the offices of archaeologists across the continent. Teachers' journals and educational magazines began to produce articles and lesson plans for classroom use to their membership. Some were excellent. Inevitably, some of them were not at all acceptable to professional archaeologists in terms of the messages that they were sending about heritage conservation. Educational advocates within the archaeological profession lobbied for more direct professional archaeological involvement in program design and delivery to ensure that the public was learning what archaeologists believed they ought to know (Smardz 1990; 1991; Smardz and Smith 2000: 25–53).

Archaeologists were involved with public education on a very broad scale, and clearly, it was having an appreciable effect upon public interest in and perception of what archaeologists were doing, and what they were supposed to be doing, with their time. Inevitably, the need for some leadership from the larger archaeological community, for coordination between programs, and for a forum to discuss not only methods and approaches, but also ethics and standards for archaeological education was thrown into high relief by some of the more negative results of archaeology's newly-minted public profile. There were some unfortunate incidents of outright site destruction when over-enthusiastic amateurs – most often school teachers and local history buffs – tried to operate hands-on 'excavations' for hordes of school children without benefit of either archaeological knowledge or of archaeologists themselves. Indeed, few of us who have been involved in public and educational archaeology do not have such tales to tell. That popular interest, improperly challenged, threatened to actually destroy sites demonstrated to even the less publicly-oriented archaeologists the need for professional involvement in program design. It was clear that some form of constructive educational opportunities had to be developed to serve an appetite for archaeological participation which the archaeologists had, after all, themselves generated and sought.

Senior level leadership on the part of the professional community was needed to both develop and ethically implement archaeology education in North America. Following the 1986 Society for Historical Archaeology meetings in

Savannah, the respected teacher-turned-archaeologist Martha Williams brought to the attention of the Executive the need to establish a Public Education Committee. This committee has provided important leadership, not only in program development but also in the creation of educational material. Indeed, it helped set the standard for the inclusion of a public interpretation component in all archaeological projects operated by the society's membership. Most recently, a very ambitious web, video and print media project entitled *Unlocking the Past* (2000) and aimed at the reading public and professional educators was launched by this active group.

During the same period, the Canadian Archaeological Association (CAA), founded in 1968, appointed Carole Stimmell, first of the University of Toronto and later public relations officer for the Toronto Archaeological Resource Centre, Public Archaeology Chair. Public education was made a priority of the organization in the 1990s, especially during the terms of office of Jane Kelley and then David Pokotylo as CAA Chairs. Beginning in the 1980s, the CAA engaged in a series of discussions whose goals were the development of public and political support for the passage of national archaeological resources protection legislation. Tragically, the legislation has been repeatedly tabled, and it is a national scandal that Canada has to this day no federal laws for heritage resource protection. This remains a matter for provincial and local ordinances, as does both culture and education within this country.

It was also in the 1980s that the American Institute for Archaeology (AIA) began planning a new media approach to the dissemination of archaeological information. This ultimately led to the creation of the excellent 'Archaeology' television series. The objective was to encourage interest and knowledge of archaeological research amongst members of the public unlikely to read the AIA's superb Archaeology Magazine or to attend the organization's public lectures. The latter are offered at AIA chapters all over the continent, and have had a faithful following for decades. Today, AIA continues in this work with the recent foundation of a new magazine, *Archaeology's Dig*, aimed at children and young people, and with the ongoing development of educational materials including an excellent bibliography of pedagogical resource materials with an archaeological focus. It can also be credited with the recent establishment of a North American network of scholars, agency staff, interpreters, museums professionals and cultural resource management personnel willing to provide educational support to the classroom teacher.

Some of the most ambitious and most politically effective work in public archaeology on this continent has come from the prestigious Society for American Archaeology (SAA). This is the largest of the professional societies in North America, and the one to which nearly all the senior professionals who conduct research on Native and American and First Nations archaeology, as well as many others in the field, belong. In the late 1980s, SAA established the 'Save the Past for the Future' project and held a series of conferences and seminars starting with a working conference at Taos, New Mexico, in 1989.

The issue was how to bring about the cessation of looting, vandalism and site destruction in the Americas. Partnerships were sought with federal, state and local agencies, private foundations, universities and special interest groups to help support what was planned as a multi-year program. Included in the 'Action for the '90s' list were seven tasks that SAA believed should be undertaken; these included an enhanced public information program, the development of educational and training outreach programs, the strengthening of legislation, the enhancement of existing protective mechanisms at all levels, the improvement of intergovernmental cooperation relating to heritage conservation and public education, advancement of research into the means and extent of archaeological site destruction, and the development of productive and acceptable alternatives for the public to become involved in archaeological excavation and research under professional supervision (Reinburg 1991).

One of the first steps was the foundation of the SAA's extremely active and productive Public Education Committee. In less than a decade, the group grew to some 11 subcommittees. It produced a whole series of publications, workshops and resource collections for use by pre-collegiate teachers, and was instrumental in supporting a wide range of partnership initiatives with other organizations. These include the new Boy Scouts of America Archaeology Merit Badge program, the Archaeology Network which has designated an archaeological resource person to help teachers implement archaeology education in their classrooms in more than 40 states and provinces, the SAA-sponsored annual workshop for educators of Native American students, and the Public Session and public school teachers' workshops offered at the Society's yearly meetings (B. Smith 1995; K.C. Smith 1995; Clark pers. comm. 1999).

With the support of the professional community, public and educational archaeology came to be more and more in the mainstream. As funding for archaeology and related heritage work dried up during the recession of the early 1990s, gaining the support of a knowledgeable and interested public came to be a major priority of archaeologists everywhere. University programs teaching the method and theory of educational and public archaeology are still few and far between, but the University of South Florida has had a master's degree program available for more than two decades, and a specialist area is available in public archaeology (White 2000, pers. comm.). Likewise, the University of Indiana at Bloomington recently initiated a graduate program in applied anthropology with a public education bent, and there are individual courses available within many North American anthropology departments today (K. A. Pyburn pers. comm.). Syracuse University in Syracuse, New York sponsors annual 'public archaeology' digs to celebrate New York State Archaeology Week which occurs the first week in October (B. Ryan pers. comm.), and the South Carolina Institute of Archaeology and Anthropology at the University of South Carolina is one of the leaders in the establishment of Archaeology Month with help from a state-wide archaeological society. They also offer the public opportunities to participate at the Allendale Paleoindian and Santa Elena archaeological excavations, and the Savannah River Site Archaeological program. The program includes a very innovative approach to underwater archaeological education; there are two heritage trails where visitors can either paddle or scuba dive to see remnants of South Carolina's maritime past (J. Spirek pers. comm.).

Across North America, smaller regional, special interest, and state and provincial organizations have continued to devote a great deal of time and energy to the development and implementation of educational programs in archaeology. This includes highly productive partnerships between universities, federal programs and community groups, such as that operated by the Public Archaeology Facility at the Department of Anthropology, Binghampton University in New York. Nina Versaggi has provided the following synopsis of this very effective community–university effort in archaeology education:

> The Public Archaeology Facility is a research center within the Dept of Anthropology at Binghamton University (State University of New York). We conduct a variety of CRM projects and also incorporate public programs in a lot of what we do. Through the Community Archaeology Program (CAP), for example, we sponsor CAP for Adults, Teachers, and Kids. These are 4-day summer programs that pair non-archaeologists with professionals for one day of lecture/lab/training and three days in the field at a Late Woodland research site that is the dissertation topic of several students. The site will eventually be destroyed by ongoing topsoil mining. The CAP for Kids satisfies some of the requirements for the Boy Scout Merit Badge in Archaeology and we offer follow-up meetings to help complete the badge. Our grad student instructors are certified merit badge counselors. Our staff produced three workbooks for the Adults, Teachers, and Kids. These are descriptive, but also contain sample exercises for use in the classroom. We also have school tours and lectures where we invite 5th/6th grade classes to campus for lab tours and slide presentations. We also go to schools for career days and discussions. Finally there is the Travelling Exhibit: through a grant from the President's office, exhibit designers were contracted to construct an 8-panel exhibit, called *Time and Tradition: The Archaeological History of New York State*. These are offered to local schools, museums, federal agencies, etc. Usually, the teachers from the CAP program request the exhibit for their schools to illustrate things they've learned from the program and incorporate into lesson plans.
>
> (N. Versaggi pers. comm.)

Anne Rogers, a long-time SAA Public Education Committee member, describes the ambitious program of education undertaken by her institution:

Western Carolina University has an on-going project in cooperation with the National Forests in North Carolina (USDA Forest Service) to conduct archaeological research at the Appletree Campground site (31Ma56). The university conducts field courses for students, and the Forest Service has a *Passport in Time* project at the same site. This has been a very successful project that serves both educational and public archaeology initiatives. Our work there began in 1992, and will continue in the summer of 2000 and hopefully beyond. In addition to students from the U.S., we have had exchange students from the University of Glamorgan in Wales working with us. Several participants have been members of the Eastern Band of Cherokee Indians.

(A. Rogers pers. comm.)

Public education programs in archaeology are more and more linked to work of professional educators. This, of course, helps ensure that archaeologists aren't designing programs inappropriate to the age or ability level of the audiences which they wish to reach, and also that the programs will actually be used in North American classrooms (Davis 2000). This is accomplished by matching national, state and local curriculum standards; working directly with school districts; and by incorporating teachers into each stage of the curriculum development process. The American Bureau of Land Management's spectacularly successful program, 'Project Archaeology,' is expressly designed to encourage teacher education of archaeological concepts and ethics.

Archaeologists are also working in partnership on a much broader, official level than had previously been the case, and are taking an intergenerational approach. Groups such as Boy Scouts, Elderhostel, and the Sierra Club have all made commitments to educational archaeology programs. This cooperation developed over years of negotiation by archaeologists and both professional and amateur societies. Educational archaeologists today work closely with museums, historic sites, cultural resource management (CRM) firms, and national, state and local government programs. In all, this broader scope has been very productive, blanketing North America with the stewardship message, and providing a consistent vision. All of this work, of course, is not to supplant older efforts that are still very successful, such as the private institutes for archaeology education, university–community partnerships such as those described above, and also the many wonderful volunteer programs operated by avocational societies in most states and provinces on the continent. Some offer progressive volunteer accreditation in archaeological skills – excavation, mapping, laboratory cataloging and the like. These are provided by such diverse groups as the Arkansas Archaeological Survey, the Fairfax County program in Virginia, and the now-defunct Archaeological Conservancy Opportunity Program of Ontario's culture ministry.

John Jameson's (1997) compendium volume on public archaeology's title, *Presenting Archaeology to the Public: Digging For Truths*, reflects the perspective of many archaeologists today. The slogan 'Saving the Past for the Future' has been adopted by the US Forestry Service, and wholesale by many educationally-oriented North American archaeologists, while the title of the first textbook on educational archaeology, sponsored by the SAA, is a joint Canadian–American production entitled *The Archaeology Education Handbook: Sharing the Past With Kids* (Smardz and Smith 2000). The underlying message seems to be an ending of exclusivity regarding matters archaeological.

A review of current programs

Public archaeology today is alive and well and expanding in the US and to some extent in Canada. Perhaps the best way of illustrating the types of programs on offer is by providing a snapshot of programs operating now in North America. I have divided these into some fairly broad categories so as to demonstrate how these have come into operation, and how they are currently administered and disseminated. I shall begin with North America-wide and national efforts by both professional organizations and government agencies, and then describe successively state and provincial programs; initiatives serving a national audience such as Archaeology Week and the Boy Scout Merit Badge; those offered through specialized foundations, institutions, universities and historic sites; programs specifically designed in cooperation with Native American and Canadian First Nations peoples; ones developed by avocational, professional and combined groups, communities of special interest, school districts and local government; public archaeology as conducted by museums and living history centers; and unusual or innovative programs such as underwater archaeology education programs. The relationship between CRM and educational archaeology will also be included. Some crossover between the categories will, of course, take place because of the growing partnerships between government and independent organization initiatives, for instance.

The US Federal government has taken the lead in the development and implementation of archaeology education programs since the beginning. The US National Park Service (NPS) has been involved in public education initiatives for many years, and has perhaps the most extensive (and best funded) of all the North American programs. NPS maintains the Listing of Education in Archaeological Programs Clearinghouse (LEAP). This computer database contains information about archaeology and education programs collected from various state and federal agencies, museums, private groups, historical societies, and academic institutions. Another excellent program, Teaching with Historic Places, represents a partnership between the National Park Service and the National Trust for Historic Preservation. Sites listed on the National Register of Historic Places provide the focus for a series of lesson plans and instructional media designed to teach about history and archaeology. Local heritage is also emphasized through the Parks as Classrooms program. This

KAROLYN E. SMARDZ FROST

is a special outreach program that seeks to enroll local and regional schools in learning activities using park resources.

NPS also provides an excellent series of publications, including *CRM*, *Common Ground* and the Technical Briefs series. These serve to disseminate information about NPS initiatives to archaeologists, land managers, preservation officers, museum professionals, Native Americans, law enforcement agents, and educators. Canadian professionals in various heritage-related fields also publish in these journals, which are available free-of-charge.

Public interpretation initiatives are a major component of both Canadian and US NPS programming. Ongoing training in interpretation is coupled with the provision of up-to-date information to parks staff, teachers, archaeologists and environmental professionals about scientific and cultural findings relevant to each site's natural and human heritage. The NPS Southeast Archaeological Center (SEAC) has been central to the national development of communications programs, training sessions and symposia to this end. It has also worked hard to establish an archaeology-interpretation shared competency curriculum, where employees in education, interpretation and archaeology work together to develop programs for delivery. Every effort is made to ensure that site-based learning programs meet state and national educational standards, and that multicultural and environmental heritage issues remain at the forefront of educational programming (J. Jameson pers. comm.).

The park services in both the US and Canada have for the past several years been engaged in a continent-wide effort to discover and commemorate sites relevant to the Underground Railroad. This refers to the networks of routes and assistance available to fugitive slaves working their way northwards in the long years before the American Civil War. Both places and people have received national designation status on both sides of the US–Canadian border, and a productive partnership between the two federal parks agencies has developed to facilitate the establishment of accurate and appropriate educational programs relevant to meeting the goals of the Underground Railroad initiative.

In fact, in Canada the single most active organization for public education in archaeology is Parks Canada, an arms-length agency of the Department of Canadian Heritage. Parks Canada has always had a policy of public education at its various sites, many of which were excavated as part of historic site research and restoration projects over the years. Indeed, for many Canadians, the only public education in archaeology they have received has come from visiting such sites as Louisburg in Nova Scotia and Old Fort William in Ontario. Parks Canada has done a great deal of work in cooperation with Native Canadians in the development of programs to conserve Canada's wealth of heritage resources dating to the era prior to the onset of European immigration. For instance, Bill Fox (pers. comm.) cites as very significant the Paulatuk student dig and the community projects in the Keewatin. The latter is described in an article entitled 'Aboriginal peoples, archaeology and Parks Canada' in the 1999 edition of *Plains Anthropologist*. Fox tells us:

70

Last summer, we supported a co-sponsored excavation project on the Tseshaht Nation's origin site at Benson Island in the Broken Group Islands Unit of the Park (Barkley Sound). It involved both Tseshaht and non-aboriginal students, as well as Tseshaht elders.

(Fox 1999: 56)

Returning to federal US government initiatives, Jeanne Moe of the Bureau of Land Management's (BLM) National Heritage Education Program describes her agency's program, which was launched in 1992. She says:

Project Archaeology, a heritage education program, teaches students nationwide the fundamentals of science and math through hands-on exercises using the principles and techniques of archaeology . . . BLM's goal is to educate America's young citizens to value and protect our nation's rich cultural legacy and Project Archaeology, an education program for teachers and their students, has been the program's mainstay. Since 1992 independent Project Archaeology programs have been implemented in 15 states and five states are currently developing new programs. In addition, to Project Archaeology, many BLM archaeologists work directly with teachers, youth group leaders, and other educators to bring archaeology to a broad cross section of the population. This BLM is launching a new initiative called the Young Steward's Club which will bring archaeology education directly to children.

(J. Moe pers. comm.)

The US Forest Service publishes a newsletter called *PIT Traveler: Passport in Time*. It lists opportunities for volunteers to participate in archaeological surveys and excavations. In addition, local historical, archaeological, and genealogical societies, universities, and colleges often need the assistance of volunteers. The Passport in Time programs provide participants with progressive instruction and experience in various field and laboratory skills important in the discovery and conservation of archaeological remains, and has proven a very popular pastime amongst its adherents.

On the other hand, agencies such as the Fish and Wildlife Service do not have large-scale 'initiatives' like Passport in Time. Instead, according to Virginia Parks (pers. comm.), they work on the regional level to develop educational outreach and include the public in resource management. For instance, the agency is working with Earthwatch to preserve and record rock art in the Malheur Marshlands, a program that has been underway for several years with students from around the country. Other programs include cultural heritage festivals, either in conjunction with other federal agencies such as at birding festivals or during Archaeology Weeks. Staff produce a series of technical publications synthesizing archaeological research on refuges and fish hatcheries which are available without cost to the public, as well as a growing series of more general interpretive materials, including an educational resource kit used by teachers in the classroom which focuses on the cultural and natural history of an archaeological site on a refuge in WA (Ridgefield). 'Discover Cathlapotle' includes artifact replicas by a tribal artist, background information with lessons and activities, natural resource samples, and multimedia resources, which explore both the past and present culture of the Chinook people who once lived at this site, one of the largest villages on the Columbia when Lewis and Clark visited in 1805. Several similar kits are underway for other culture areas within the region, including traditional fishing methods on the Columbia River, and native Hawaiian heiaus on Kauai (Virginia Parks pers. comm.).

At the state and provincial level, many programs and projects are currently underway to encourage public involvement in archaeological conservation efforts. Mary Kwas of the Arkansas Archaeological Survey offers the following summary of her agency's very active public archaeology program:

> The Arkansas Archeological Survey provides a variety of educational materials through various sources. Materials for teachers include educational flyers, two books in the Survey's Popular Series, and slide sets, a video, and exhibits on Arkansas archeology that can be borrowed by teachers through the Arkansas Humanities Resource Center. The Survey's web site also features educational information and resources for teachers. The Survey and the Arkansas Archeological Society co-sponsor a summer Training Program and excavation that introduces hands-on methods to amateurs and is part of a larger Certification Program. The Survey and Society also cosponsor the annual Arkansas Archeology Week in October. Recently the Survey has expanded into computer-based education: With funding from NEH, the Survey is part of a team developing a CD-ROM on the Contact Period in the Mississippi Valley. The CD explores the first encounters and interactions of Native Americans and Europeans, and the modules are illustrated with images of artifacts, historic paintings, and maps. A unique feature of the CD is the development of modules in French and Spanish, as well as English, in order to enhance foreign-language learning.
>
> (M. Kwas pers. comm.)

In Iowa, the Office of the State Archaeologist, a research, service, and educational unit of the University of Iowa, sponsors and offers a wide variety of public archaeology programs. Lynn M. Alex has described these programs as follows:

> Many are conducted as collaborative efforts with Area Education Agencies, county conservation boards, and other agencies. A principal

focus is to provide instructional materials and continuing education opportunities to teachers and conservation educators. Each year archaeological awareness is promoted through a week or month long event.

(L. M. Alex pers. comm.)

Maryland is another state with highly effective archaeology education programs in place. The Lost Towns of Anne Arundel Project is a year-round team of archaeologists and historians whose mission is to involve the public in original archaeological, archival and environmental research, focusing on the discovery and exploration of Anne Arundel County's (Maryland) 'lost' colonial towns. As James Gibb of the Lost Towns Project tells us:

> Not every archaeological program has the structure and formal association with a recognized historical organization to admit easy replication. The Lost Towns of Anne Arundel Project in Maryland, USA, is one such program. Sponsored by the Anne Arundel County Department of Planning and Code Enforcement and several non-profit organizations, The Lost Towns Project's team of twelve historians and archaeologists involves the public in original archaeological, archival, and environmental research, focusing on the discovery and exploration of the county's colonial period town sites. Volunteers work alongside professionals in the field, archives, and laboratory during the week and one Saturday each month. School children, under close supervision and after some preliminary instruction, screen soil and learn about historic trash and what scientists learn by studying that material. Much of The Lost Town's public programming occurs at the county-owned London Town historical park, a 23-acre facility in the midst of a suburban residential community just south of Maryland's state capital, Annapolis. Support services offered by the London Town Foundation, park managers, and public facilities provided by the county's Department of Recreation and Parks, make the site an ideal setting for research and public involvement program.
>
> The team reaches wider audiences through an aggressive public outreach program that includes: in-house video productions for local cable television; special spots on public broadcasting and commercial television; a segment on Nickelodeon television's Nick News for children; radio interviews; press releases and interviews with newspaper and magazine journalists; professional quality brochures and booklets; and staff-written articles for magazines, local newspapers, and local historical and archaeological journals. The combination of year-round research and public outreach programs keeps team members and the public engaged in an exciting, publicly-funded enterprise. Streetscape reconstruction on the park grounds will provide a tangible, long-term product that will complement the less tangible,

non-measurable good will created by the efforts of this annually
funded project. Each team member's involvement and responsibilities
keeps the team together in the face of annual budgetary uncertainties.

(J. G. Gibb pers. comm.)

Another program in Maryland is the Jefferson Patterson Park and Museum
in St. Leonard, Maryland, which has run a two-month Public Archaeology
program every summer since 1996. Edward Chaney states that:

> It is designed specifically and solely to allow members of the public
> to participate fully in an actual excavation. We try to conduct the
> program as an informal field school, so that the volunteers don't come
> away from the site thinking that archaeology is just the removal
> of goodies from the ground. We try to make it a learning experience.
> Under the guidance of two professional archaeologists, volunteers have
> had the opportunity to do preliminary survey work, surface collec-
> tions, shovel test pit excavation, feature excavation and mapping,
> and historical research, as well as process artifacts in the new 38,000
> square foot Maryland Archaeological Conservation Laboratory. During
> the first 4 years of the program, we investigated a colonial domestic
> site. Next year we will begin work on a nineteenth-century slave
> quarters, including oral history interviews with descendents of
> the quarters' inhabitants, who will also be helping with the excava-
> tions. Participants in the Public Archaeology program are mostly local
> volunteers, but some have come from as far away as Wisconsin and
> Canada, and have spent up to a week with us. In addition, high school
> students taking part in a program in historical ecology sponsored
> by a local research consortium spend time with us each summer. We
> have also had Boy Scout troops working on their archaeology merit
> badge, and include the archaeology program in a teachers' workshop
> on multiculturalism sponsored by our Museum each summer. After
> the summer, the head of the Public Archaeology program leads
> volunteers in excavations at a variety of Southern Maryland sites on
> one Saturday each month, in conjunction with the Southern Chapter
> of the Archeological Society of Maryland.

(E. Chaney pers. comm.)

Programs in underwater archaeology are growing in both availability and
popularity across North America. For instance, the South Carolina Institute of
Archaeology and Anthropology at the University of South Carolina has several
programs dedicated to public archaeology. Those with an interest in hands-on
experience can participate at the Allendale Paleoindian and Santa Elena
archaeological excavations, and through the Savannah River Site Archaeological
program. The underwater archaeological program has created two heritage

trails for visitors to either paddle or scuba dive to see remnants of South Carolina's maritime past. The organization also offers a Field Training Course to prepare divers to assist in the field on various projects (J. Spirek pers. comm.).

More locally, museums, historical societies, avocational archaeology groups and the like are conducting a very wide variety of programs designed to enhance public interest in archaeology. For instance, Pam Wheat, Director of Education, Houston Museum of Natural Science, says:

> The Houston Museum of Natural Science took six middle school students to a field school sponsored by the Texas Archeological Society in June 1999 near Del Rio. Each day the students added a page to the web site called 'Archeology X Pedition' at www.hmns.org which created an on-line journal complete with video clips illustrating the field work. They also conferred daily with a class in the Museum of Natural Science that was focused on archeology of the Pecos River. The middle school students were also featured in a 30 minute video that originated from KHOU-Houston PBS September 28, 1999, and was aired over 100 PBS stations nation-wide. Their commentary told the story of the archeological field school and of the ancient people of the Lower Pecos River valley. The video and web site will inform students and adults about the work done by archeologists in the field and empower other students to be involved.
>
> (P. Wheat pers. comm.)

Likewise, Kevin Bartoy writes the following statement about Colonial Williamsburg's extensive public educational and involvement program in archaeology:

> Colonial Williamsburg has demonstrated its commitment to public oriented research for almost 80 years now. This past summer we started a 'virtual dig' on the web. It deals with seventeenth-century Virginia and follows our excavations from this summer (and next summer).
>
> (K. Bartoy pers. comm.)

Eminent historical house museum scholar Barbara Heath has provided the following information about archaeology education at Jefferson's Poplar Forest:

> We have a group that has just begun to meet to discuss research and interpretive strategies on a regular basis in Virginia. It includes Gunston Hall (home of George Mason), Kenmore and Ferry Farm (Kenmore home of George Washington's sister, Ferry Farm is George

Washington's boyhood home), Poplar Forest (Thomas Jefferson), Monticello (Thomas Jefferson), Mount Vernon (George Washington), Stratford Hall (the Lee family). All of these sites have on-going archaeology programs that incorporate public programming focusing on archaeology, archaeological field schools, and exhibits.

(B. Heath pers. comm.)

Communities of special interest offer unique opportunities for public education. Rita Elliott of the LAMAR Institute at Watkinsville, Georgia tells us that:

> The LAMAR Institute has been conducting teacher workshops on archaeology since the mid 1980s. These one week workshops provide teachers with 3 Staff Development Unit credits. During the week teachers learn about all periods of Southeastern prehistory and history from professional archaeologists and other experts. They also learn about archaeological method and theory. Teachers discover why archaeology is a good multidisciplinary tool in the classroom and participate in hands-on (non-digging) activities that they can incorporate into their curriculums. They also attend fieldtrips to excavations. At the end of the workshop they produce a lesson plan incorporating archaeology into their specific subject. The LAMAR Institute has conducted children's archaeological workshops since 1992. Children learn, through a series of hands-on activities, about archaeology and why it is important. They also learn about site preservation and the damage that looting does. Children's workshops have ranged from one hour, to one day, to a three year session! They have included grades K-12 (in various sessions). Both children's and teachers' workshops have been held at various venues around the state, such as universities, museums, and botanical gardens, and even a few outside Georgia.

(R. Elliott pers. comm.)

The Society for Georgia Archaeology (SGA) just recently obtained non-profit status, although it has been doing public education for years. It sponsors Georgia Archaeology Week annually, with events, a poster, and an education guide. SGA published an education manual for teachers assisting them in using archaeology in their curriculums. It provides speakers for presentations and holds conferences and workshops. The non-profit Coosawattee Foundation conducts children's archaeological workshops in Georgia for students in grades 7–12. It offers public field classes, lectures, and seminars upon request. It has done programming outside the state of Georgia, as well (R. Elliott pers. comm.).

In South Carolina, the state Archaeological Society, founded 1968, hosts a number of public archaeology programs through hands-on events, conferences and publications. Wayne Neighbors of that organization calls it 'a cooperative effort of professional and avocational (amateur) archaeologists from the beginning'. The organization has an interesting history:

> South Carolina (USA) did not have any professional archaeologists until very late. The first (SC has had only two so far) 'State Archaeologist' was hired about 1967. . . . So, for some professional archaeologists as early as the 1930s, collaboration with avocation people became a very acceptable practice – outreach efforts, cooperation, motivation, and recognition for the avocational contributions. Yes, they even credited 'lay people' in their publications. And if they stayed in one place long enough, they found it greatly to their advantage to organize local archaeological societies and – if possible – be the sponsor until they were operating independently . . . at the University of North Carolina at Chapel Hill, Dr. J. Coe did the same thing. Indeed, Dr. Coe's first major publication many decades ago (related to a chronology of prehistoric culture in North Carolina) was based on several archaeological sites. All these archaeological sites were 'introduced' to him by amateur archaeologists. There is an ongoing project that has turned into a 'pre-Clovis' site in South Carolina. Professional archaeologists supervise. Avocational and lay folks do the digging under close supervision. And they pay for that opportunity each summer which removes the need to find funding year after year.
>
> (W. Neighbors pers. comm.)

One of the oldest and most active archaeological groups in the US is the Archaeological Society of Virginia. The Society, in cooperation with the Council of Virginia Archaeologists and the Virginia Department of Historic Resources has set up an Archaeological Technician Certification Program. This program is designed to provide training to interested avocational archaeologists to bring their skills up to the level expected by professional archaeologists who are hiring field techs for projects (M. F. Barber pers. comm.).

Louisiana has one of the most successful public educations in archaeology programs on the continent. Nancy Hawkins, the state educational archaeologist, has offered the following summary of her office's accomplishments over the past few years:

> The Louisiana archaeology outreach efforts began in 1975, but began expanding in 1981 when the state archaeologist hired an outreach coordinator. The program, within the State Historic Preservation Office, now distributes the following free materials: nine booklets about Louisiana archaeology, two exhibits for museums and libraries, two kinds of artifact activity kits for schools, three classroom activity

guides, a set of five information posters about Louisiana prehistory, a brochure about ancient mounds. Other activities and initiatives include: teachers workshops, a web site, and lending of archaeology books and videos to schools statewide Archaeology Week (we just had the 12th annual one). The two latest publications are the ancient mounds brochure and an interdisciplinary, hands-on activity guide about the Poverty Point site, with activities linked to state curriculum standards.

(N. Hawkins pers. comm.)

Finally, a great deal of public archaeology in North America is actually carried out by private consulting firms in the course of meeting their contractual obligations. Generally called 'CRM' (cultural resource management) on this continent, archaeological consulting includes a wide range of tasks which provides wonderful opportunities for enhancing public knowledge of the resource and the need for its conservation. Many archaeological consulting firms feel a strong commitment to public education, as the following commentary provided by some of the leaders in both Canada and the US demonstrates. For instance, Pat Garrow considers: 'all archaeology done by CRM firms [to be] essentially public archaeology because the public ultimately foots the bill in one way or another. We have an obligation to report our findings back to the public in forms they can understand and appreciate' (P. Garrow pers. comm.).

Likewise, Ron Williamson of Archaeological Services Inc. in Toronto, Canada describes a project undertaken in 1999:

> Archaeological Services Inc. was retained by Blythwood Group Inc. to conduct a Stage 4 mitigative excavation of the late 18th century, early 19th century historic Butler site (AhGs-18) in Niagara-On-The-Lake. Colonel Butler was a significant figure in the colonial history of Niagara. He was a town founder, Indian Agent, judge, and war hero. Initially, the excavation was conducted in conjunction with a public archaeology program. Approximately 375 students and 40 volunteers participated in the program which ran from May 31 to July 31, 1999 ... A second program with which we are involved is the Region of Hamilton-Wentworth's Archaeology Month. The Region, in co-operation with the Hamilton Regional Indian Centre, Archaeological Services Inc., The Ontario Archaeological Society and McMaster University-Department of Anthropology, have organized a series of public lectures, artifact identification days, as well as educational programs geared to middle and high school groups. The educational program includes an introduction to pre-contact history of the region through hands-on experience at the King's Forest Park site, an 800 year old Early Iroquoian village.

(R. Williamson pers. comm.)

Mary Maniery of PAR Environmental Services, Inc., Sacramento, California, decided in 1982 to do a project at a mining site called Altaville. The company decided to tie the project to Califorma's Sesquicentennial. Their role is to direct the project, and analyze and write up results, as Six Rivers has no historical archaeologist on their staff. She says:

> Our partnership agreement is based on us getting paid for half our time and all expenses and we volunteer an equal amount in staff hours, lab space. The project goes through weekends so we (PAR staff) volunteer on the weekends and I take vacation time for the field phase and then pay my staff. It's a blast because we all take our kids/families and camp out for 10 days. There are several other organizations that have partnered with Six Rivers for this project. The majority of the site is owned by a private mining venture, Cal Nickel. They allow excavation on their property and provide a staff geologist who does geology tours of the mines surrounding the town for those interested. The Del Norte Historical Society gives research hours and is doing some of the archival research. Americorps provided young strong bodies to buck brush, clear off features and do other grunt work. BLM provided some funds and personnel. Another local firm flew the site and provided free aerial photos of the entire mining district to help with defining old transportation routes and identifying mines.
>
> (M. Maniery pers. comm.)

Finally, Tom Wheaton, Vice-President of New South Associates in Stone Mountain, Georgia, and a leader in the field of CRM in North America offers the following commentary on the state of the field:

> In the United States, cultural resource management has matured greatly since its beginnings in the late 1960s and early 1970s. To meet the growing need for archaeologists and other professionals to conduct cultural resource projects, the private sector has grown considerably. Today, 80 to 90 percent of the archaeological research being conducted in the United States is by private firms. As these firms have matured and grown, they have become more and more involved in public education and outreach programs, and some firms are even specializing in public outreach. This growth in private firms has also seen an increase in support for local and regional archaeological associations, which in turn has caused an increase in the promotion and quality of local public archaeological programs and public outreach. As private, for-profit companies, these firms know the importance of obtaining public support for laws and regulations governing cultural resource management at the state and national levels.
>
> (T. Wheaton pers. comm.)

Conclusion

As we have seen, educational archaeology is flourishing in North America. It is generally unabashedly agenda-driven: public archaeologists work very hard to instill the stewardship message in as many members of the public as they can reach. Escalating site destruction, vandalism, looting and the ever-present and pernicious trade in antiquities demand a direct and aggressive professional response, and public archaeology is, to a large extent, it. Archaeologists from every branch of the discipline are becoming aware of the need to reach and teach the members of the general public. They do this in order both to engage their enthusiasm to help in site preservation, and to enlist their support in political, legislative and financial arenas where decisions that affect heritage conservation are made.

As archaeology education evolves, practitioners have become increasingly aware of the need to work with professionals in the fields of education, communications and marketing to ensure that appropriate messages reach their target audiences. The growing demand for experienced and skilled archaeology educators, and for curriculum-relevant and effective educational materials is being met through new university-based training programs and fresh-off-the-press literature on the subject. The popularity of archaeology with teachers, students, tourists and visitors to historic sites is undeniable, but the next few years will show whether or not it is all working – from the archaeologists' point of view, at least.

The proof is, as they say, in the pudding. Attitudinal change is the most difficult of all educational objectives to measure. How does one assess one's degree of success or failure? To a large extent, we who have been conducting public programs, writing textbooks on how to introduce archaeological subjects to various age groups, and developing wonderful instructional media, have been working on faith. We believe that involving ordinary people in the preservation of their own heritage will make them want to help us to preserve it. Archaeology is about time. And only time will tell if archaeology education will actually help make ordinary people into stewards of the past. But I believe that an educated public who understands why we ought to care if fragile heritage remains are preserved is the best hope we have to help 'save the past for the future'.

Acknowledgement

I am indebted to my old friend John Jameson of the US National Park Service both for his cogent commentary on this article, and for the contribution of information about archaeological education programs developed by the US government. His kind assistance – and incredibly rapid turn-around time – were both greatly appreciated. I would also like to thank the literally dozens of archaeologists who responded to my call for information about current public education programming. I received many thoughtful, enthusiastic and cogent e-mail communications from across the continent. I hope that I have in some measure done justice to the wonderful work all these people have been doing for so long.

I would also like to acknowledge the help of the many, many individuals, organizations and programs that are not specifically mentioned here. I will simply say, with the joy of a longtime advocate of public education who feels immensely privileged in her colleagues, that there are now so many of you that I can't fit everyone into a short article.

Note

1 The original email survey was undertaken in 1999, with follow-ups in subsequent years.
2 These included such eminent scholars as Douglas Leechman of the then National Museum of Canada, who had according to recent research at least 500 scholarly articles, a number of films, museum exhibits and a whole series of ethnological works to his credit (Dyke 1980, especially p. 128).

Bibliography

AnthroNotes. Washington DC: Smithsonian Institution (various editions).

Archaeology and Public Education Newsletter. Washington DC: Society for American Archaeology Public Education Committee (various editions, 1990–99).

Bazeley, S. 1999. Cataraqui Archaeological Foundation. URL: http://web.ctsolutions. com/carf/document/resource.html

Brown, M. III 1991. Introductory Remarks. In F.P. McManamon and K.C. Smith (eds) *Archaeology and Education: The Classroom and Beyond*. Archaeological Assistance Study, No. 2. Washington, DC: US Department of the Interior, National Park Service, Cultural Resources.

Butler, W. B. (ed.) 1992. *State Archaeological Education Programs*. National Park Service, Rocky Mountain Region, Interagency Archaeological Services.

Christensen, B. 1995. Mississippi Valley Archaeology Center's Archaeology in Education Program. In *Public Archaeology Review*. University of Indiana: Center for Archaeology in the Public Interest.

Christensen, B. 2000. Archaeology Education Programs: A long-term regional approach. In K.E. Smardz and S.J. Smith (eds) *The Archaeology Education Handbook: Sharing the Past With Kids*. Thousand Oaks, California: AltaMira Press.

Corley-Smith 1989. *White Bears and Other Curiosities: the First 100 Years of the Royal British Columbia Museum*. Special Publication, Victoria: Royal British Columbia Museum cited in Apland, B. (1993) The roles of the Provincial Government in British Columbia Archaeology. *BC Studies* 99 (Autumn): 7–24. URL: http:// galileo.enc.org/fedprogs/agencies/smith.html

Davis, E. M. 2000. Government education standards and K-12 archaeology programs. In K. E. Smardz and S. J. Smith (eds) *The Archaeology Education Handbook: Sharing the Past with Kids*. Thousand Oaks, California: AltaMira Press: 54–71.

Davis, H. 1990. *Training and Using Volunteers in Archaeology: A Case Study from Arkansas*. Archaeological Assistance Program Technical Brief No. 9. US Department of the Interior.

Devine, H. 1989a. School Curriculum and Archaeology. In *Proceedings, World Summit Conference on the Peopling of the Americas, Orono, Maine*

Devine, H. 1989b. Archaeology in Social Studies: An Integrated Approach. *The History and Social Science Teacher* 24(3): 140–7.

Dyke, I. 1980. 'Toward a history of archaeology in the National Museum of Canada: the contributions of Harlan I. Smith and Douglas Leechman, 1911–1950. In P.J. Smith and D. Mitchell (eds) *Bringing Back the Past: Historical Perspectives on Canadian Archaeology*. Mercury Series, Archaeological Survey of Canada Paper 158. Hull, Quebec: Canadian Museum of Civilization.

Ellick, C. 1991. Archaeology is more than a dig: educating children about the past saves sites for the future. In F.P. McManamon and K.C. Smith (eds) *Archaeology and Education: The Classroom and Beyond*. Archaeological Assistance Study, No. 2. Washington, DC: US. Department of the Interior, National Park Service, Cultural Resources.

Erickson, P. A. 1990. *Interim Report on Precollege Anthropology*. Committee on Research for the American Anthropological Association Force on Teaching Anthropology in Schools (Nov. 28, unpublished manuscript).

Erickson, P. and Davis, S. (eds) (1981–present) *Teaching Anthropology Newsletter*. Halifax: St. Mary's University Department of Anthropology.

Fagan, B. 1994. Perhaps We May Hear Voices. . . . In *Save the Past for the Future II: Report of the Working Conference, Breckenridge, Colorado, September 19–22, 1994*. Washington DC: Society for American Archaeology. 25–30.

Fagan, B. 1995. Timelines: Bad News From Toronto. *Archaeology Magazine* 48(1) (Jan/Feb): 26–33.

Fox, W. A. 1999. Aboriginal peoples, archaeology and Parks Canada. In Native Americans and Historic Preservation: 1990–1993, K. M. Banks and L. Sundstrom (eds) Special Issue of *Plains Anthropologist* 44(170), Memoir 31.

Haas, D. 1995. Education and Public Outreach in Federal Programs. In *CRM* 18(3): 43–48.

Hawkins, N. 1984. *Classroom Archaeology: An Archaeology Activity Guide for Teachers*. Baton Rouge: State of Louisiana Division of Archaeology, Office of Cultural Development, Department of Culture, Recreation and Tourism

Hidden Beneath the Waves, An Underwater Archaeology Educational Kit (1996/7) Underwater Archaeology Unit, North Carolina Division of Archives and History and the Cape Fear Museum.

Hoffman, T. L. and S. Lerner 1988. *Arizona Archaeology Week: Promoting the Past to the Public*. Technical Brief No. 2. Arizona State Historic Preservation Office, National Park Service.

Jameson, J.H. Jr. (ed.) 1997 *Presenting Archaeology to the Public: Digging For Truths*. Walnut Creek: AltaMira Press.

Johnson, E. and T.E.H. Jones 1999. The Saskatchewan Archaeological Society and the Role of the Amateur Societies. In P.J. Smith and D. Mitchell (eds) *Bringing Back the Past: Historical Perspectives on Canadian Archaeology*. Mercury Series, Archaeological Survey of Canada Paper 158. Hull, Quebec: Canadian Museum of Civilization.

Lipe, W. 1994. Introduction. In *Save the Past for the Future II: Report of the Working Conference, Breckenridge, Colorado, September 19–22, 1994. Washington DC: Society for American Archaeology.* 9–10.

McGimsey, C. R. III 1972. Public Archaeology. New York: Seminar Press.

McGimsey, C. R. III 1991. Forward: Protecting the Past: Cultural Resource Management – A Personal Perspective. In G. Smith and J. Ehrenhard (eds) *Protecting the Past.* Boca Raton, Florida: CRC Press.

McManamon, F. P. 2000. Preface: Public Archaeology: A Part of Archaeological Professionalism. In K.E. Smardz and S.J. Smith (eds) *The Archaeology Education Handbook: Sharing the Past With Kids.* Thousand Oaks, California: AltaMira Press.

McManamon F. P. and Smith, K. C. (eds) 1991. Introduction. In *Archaeology and Education: The Classroom and Beyond,* Archaeological Assistance Study, No. 2. Washington, DC: US. Department of the Interior, National Park Service, Cultural Resources.

McNutt, N. 1988. *Project Archaeology: Saving Traditions.* Longmount, Colorado: Sopris West, Inc.

Pokotylo, D. L. and Mason, A. R. 1991. Public attitudes towards archaeological resources and their management. In G. Smith and J. Ehrenhard (eds) *Protecting the Past.* Boca Raton, Florida: CRC Press.

Price, D. and Gebauer, G. 1990. *Adventures in Fugawiland!: A Computer Simulation in Archaeology.* Mountain View, California: Mayfield Publishing Company.

Reinburg, K. M. 1991. Save the past for the future: a partnership to protect our past. In G. Smith and J. Ehrenhard (eds) *Protecting the Past.* Boca Raton, Florida: CRC Press.

Save the Past for the Future II: Report of the Working Conference, Breckenridge, Colorado, September 19–22, 1994. Washington DC: Society for American Archaeology.

Schuyler, R.L. 1991. A 'Compleat' Curriculum: Historical Archaeology on the Undergraduate Level. In F.P. McManamon and K.C. Smith (eds) *Archaeology and Education: The Classroom and Beyond.* Washington, DC: Archaeological Assistance Study, No. 2. US. Department of the Interior, National Park Service, Cultural Resources.

Selig, R. O. 1991. Teacher Training Programs in Anthropology: The Multiplier Effect in the Classroom. In F.P. McManamon and K.C. Smith (eds) *Archaeology and Education: The Classroom and Beyond.* Archaeological Assistance Study, No. 2. Washington, DC: US Department of the Interior, National Park Service, Cultural Resources.

Selig, R. O. and M.R. London (eds) 1999. *Anthropology Explored: The Best of Smithsonian AnthroNotes.* Washington, DC: Smithsonian Institution Press.

Smardz, K. E. 1990. Archaeology and Education in Toronto. In P.G. Stone and R. Mackenzie (eds) *The Excluded Past: Archaeology in Education.* New York: Routledge.

Smards, K. E. 1991. Teaching people to touch the past: archaeology in the Toronto school system. In G. Smith and J. Ehrenhard (eds) *Protecting the Past.* Boca Raton, Florida: CRC Press.

Smardz, K. E. 1997. The Past Through Tomorrow: Interpreting Toronto's Heritage to a Multicultural Public. In J.H. Jameson Jr (ed.) *Presenting Archaeology to the Public: Digging For Truths.* Walnut Creek: AltaMira Press.

Smardz, K. E. and S.J. Smith (eds) 2000. *The Archaeology Education Handbook: Sharing the Past With Kids*. Thousand Oaks, California: AltaMira Press.

Smith, B. 1995. The Secret Archaeologist. *Archaeology and Public Education Newsletter* 5(3).

Smith, G. 1994. Education. In *Save the Past for the Future II: Report of the Working Conference, Breckenridge, Colorado, September 19–22, 1994*. Washington DC: Society for American Archaeology. 31–40.

Smith, G. and Ehrenhard, J. (eds) 1991. *Protecting the Past*. Boca Raton, Florida: CRC Press.

Smith, K.C. (ed.) 1990. *Pathways to the Past: An Educator's Guide to Resources in Archaeology*. Talahassee, Florida: Museum of Florida History, Department of State.

Smith, K.C. 1991a. At Last, A Meeting of the Minds. *Archaeology Magazine* 44(1): 3, 9.

Smith, K.C. 1991b. Archaeology in the Classroom. *Archaeology Magazine* 44(1): 80.

Smith, K.C. 1995. SAA Public Education Committee: Seeking Public Involvement on Many Fronts. *CRM: Archaeology and the Public* 18(3): 25–31.

Smith, P.J. and D. Mitchell (eds) 1980. *Bringing Back the Past: Historical Perspectives on Canadian Archaeology*. Mercury Series, Archaeological Survey of Canada Paper 158. Hull, Quebec: Canadian Museum of Civilization.

Society for American Archaeology Public Education Committee Formal Education Subcommittee Workbook Task Group (nd). *Teaching Archaeology: A Sampler for Grades 3 to 12*.

Stone, P. G. and R. Mackenzie (eds) 1990. *The Excluded Past: Archaeology in Education*. New York: Routledge.

Struever, S. 2000. Crow Canyon Archaeological Center: Why an independent, non-profit center makes sense. In K.E. Smardz and S.J. Smith (eds) *The Archaeology Education Handbook: Sharing the Past With Kids*. Thousand Oaks, California: AltaMira Press.

Talalay, L. E. 1991. Traveling Suitcases. *Archaeology Magazine* 44(1): 40–1.

Wells, P. S. 1991. 'Presenting the past: a conference series aimed at public education. In G. Smith and J. Ehrenhard (eds) *Protecting the Past*. Boca Raton, Florida: CRC Press.

Wheat, P. and B. Whorton 1990. *Clues from the Past: A Resource Book on Archaeology*. Dallas, Texas: Texas Archaeological Society and Hendrick-Long Publishing Co.

White, N. M. 2000. Teaching archaeologists to teach archaeology. In K.E. Smardz and S.J. Smith (eds) *The Archaeology Education Handbook: Sharing the Past With Kids*. Thousand Oaks, California: AltaMira Press.

4

INVOLVING THE PUBLIC IN MUSEUM ARCHAEOLOGY

Nick Merriman

Introduction

Museums are a significant and powerful vehicle for the public construction of the past and for public involvement in archaeology. For much of their history, archaeological museums have been relatively inward-looking and have tended to serve the needs of the academic discipline of archaeology over and above the needs of the wider public. In recent years, however, museums in general in the UK have begun to open themselves up to enjoyment and participation by a wider range of people and have begun to play a stronger role in contemporary society. Archaeological museums are taking part in this shift towards a focus on the visitor, with the keynotes being on access, active participation and even on tackling social exclusion.[1] In this paper, I shall explore some of the initiatives that are being undertaken in the UK, and argue that some of them represent a new way forward for a more publicly oriented concept of archaeology as a discipline which balances the former over-emphasis on the needs of the academic community and 'posterity'.

The power of museums

Museums can be described as mass media of the long term. They do not have the day-to-day audiences of television or film, but cumulatively, they are visited by large numbers of people over a long period of time. Thus, a gallery in a museum with 100,000 visits a year, will over the course of a generation (say, 25 years) be visited by around two and a half million people. In the UK, visiting museums and galleries as a whole is more popular as an activity than watching football matches or any other live sporting event (MORI /Resource 2001: 7). A recent survey by the Society of American Archaeology confirmed that a large proportion of the population is exposed to archaeology in museums. The survey, derived from a statistically representative sample of 1,016 American adults, found that 88 per cent of the US population had visited a museum exhibiting archaeological material at some time in their lives (Ramos and Duganne 2000: 21).[2]

85

Museums are powerful media of representation because they deal with the very material on which claims to identity and truth rest. Their concreteness, their possession of 'the evidence', their official status and their association with scholarship, give museums greater authority and claims to truth than many other media of representation. It is this which has made museums important symbols in the struggle to assert national or regional identity claims or to suppress the claims of others (Kaplan 1994). Thus, in many parts of the world, museums were often founded directly out of a desire to promote new identities in emergent states (Lewis 1992) and more generally to produce an ordered, self-regulating civil society which turned away from the temptations of the gin-house and learned to be satisfied with its place in the social order (Bennett 1995; Duncan 1995).

A key element in nineteenth century nation-building was the use of archae-ology to project backwards in time the idea of a shared ownership of identity within modern national boundaries (Trigger 1995; Skeates 2000: 90–5). Museums played their role in this by amassing material from the past that was found within their modern geographical boundaries and by using this to legitimate the existence of the modern state by situating it in the context of the deeper past (Broshi 1994). In the same way, in the twentieth century, the Nazi regime used the presence of ancient 'Germanic' finds to justify its claims to an expanded Greater Germany, and then used museum presentations of this material culture to justify its invasions and its treatment of certain peoples as inferior or sub-human (Arnold 1990; McCann 1990).

To the public in general, to competing interest groups, to politicians, to economists, to journalists and to academics, museums – including archae-ological museums or those with archaeological collections – continue to matter a great deal. They continue to be powerful cultural and civic symbols; they are used to spearhead economic regeneration and resurgent regional identities, as seen in the construction of the new Museum of Scotland (Ascherson 2000); and they continue to be fundamental targets in conflict, where they are looted and destroyed to erase identity claims, as has been seen recently in Kuwait, Bosnia, and Afghanistan (Layton *et al.* 2001).

And yet, despite these apparently large visitor figures, and despite the avowed importance of museums as attested by the amount of press coverage and controversy they generate, how effective are they at actually communi-cating about the past? I have argued elsewhere (Merriman 1991), that the intention of museum founders to disseminate a consensual view of identity amongst the populace has been subverted by the many different readings that museum visitors make of museums, and because many groups in society simply do not visit museums. As a result, the effect of museums for much of their history has been to bind together the educated and advantaged groups in society with a common culture, and to exclude others. The importance of archaeological museums, then, has to a large extent until recently derived from their symbolic role as the repositories of the raw material on which cultural identity is founded, rather than necessarily through the success of any wider educational functions which they may have performed.

Archaeological museums as servants of archaeology

Housing of archaeological evidence, and demonstration of a legitimating presence in the landscape that links past with present have then been the principal social roles demanded of the archaeological museum. This emphasis on 'authentic evidence' has meant that for much of their history archaeological museums have focused on the preservation and documentation of their collections, and on the academic needs of the discipline of archaeology.[3] Even relatively recently, for example, the concluding paper in a publication arising from a conference about museum archaeology in Europe restricted the role of museum archaeologists to undertaking fieldwork, and storing the results of survey and excavation (Biddle 1994).

In common with most other museums, for much of their history, archaeological museums have been 'top-down' institutions where the curators dispensed displays to a passive audience. The training of archaeological curators has been in archaeology, not in communication, and museum archaeologists have tended to look to their peers in other areas of the archaeological community for their validation and approval, rather than to the non-specialist public as a whole.

The difficulty of capturing the headline-grabbing excitement of discovery in the field, the apparent need to serve the rest of the archaeological discipline by coping with the storage of large amounts of material, and the consequent inward focus on matters of curation rather than on audiences, has led to a marginalisation of museum archaeology, whereby it is seen to be remote from the interests of most people today (Merriman 1991: 96–103). Indeed, a recent survey of the use of archaeological archives and collections in England (Merriman and Swain 1999) showed that despite the huge resources expended in generating them, they are barely being used even by archaeologists, let alone the public as a whole. A similar 'curation crisis' has been noted in the USA (Childs 1995) and Japan (Barnes and Okita 1999).

The consequences of this lack of focus on the needs of the public can be far-reaching. In Croydon, to the south of London, when local people were asked what sort of things they would like to see in a new community museum that was being planned, the majority said that they wanted nothing before the time which their grandparents could remember back to (MacDonald 1998). As a result, none of the local archaeological material from the prehistoric to late medieval periods found a place in the museum. When consulted, today's ethnically diverse community did not think it of interest or relevance.

The turn towards the public

However, it is the community museum movement which holds the key to understanding the changes that are being experienced by some archaeological museums today. From the 1960s, archaeological museums, like many others, began to experience considerable advances in the *technology* of presentation through the use of models, dioramas, 'reconstructions' and audio-visuals in new initiatives such as the Fishbourne Roman villa museum (opened 1968) and the Museum of London (opened 1976). These served to make museums more attractive to visitors, and a combination of greater leisure time and disposable income, effective marketing and presentation, coupled with a genuine desire to hold on to past certainties at a time of rapid change, led to a 'heritage boom' in the 1970s and 1980s. 'Experiences' such as the Jorvik Viking Centre (opened 1984) seemed to show a new way in which archaeology could be presented to popular acclaim. The success of 're-enactments' and first- and third-person interpretation in the United States (Anderson 1984) led to its adoption in open-air sites such as Ironbridge, and for occasional special events at archaeological sites and museums (Sansom 1996).

While their growth at this time demonstrated the popularity of museums and other heritage attractions, developments were strongly criticised by some academics for producing interpretations of the past which were comfortable and nostalgic and biased in favour of the dominant classes. Specifically for archaeology, Shanks and Tilley (1987: 87) argued that museums such as the Museum of London legitimate contemporary social relations by 'suppressing contradiction, fixing the past as a reflection of the appearance of the present'. The solution for such failings was, it was argued, for museums to become much more self-reflexive, more 'owned' by their communities, to work in partnership with different interest groups, and to represent different voices in their presentations (ibid.: 98–9).

In many ways, the community museum movement already showed the ways in which this might be accomplished. From the 1960s, the changing political climate which questioned traditional values and promoted civil rights, led to a gradual re-thinking of the museum and its role. The movement seems to have started with the Anacostia Neighbourhood Museum in Washington, DC, where the Smithsonian Institution established a branch in a Black neighbourhood in 1967 (Hudson 1981: 179–81). The ecomuseum movement began at around the same time under the influence of the thinking of Rivière and de Varine (Davis 1999). In these new kinds of museums, the keynote was on the participation and involvement of the local community in developing museums that met their own needs. In theory at least, the museum was to be run by, and orientated towards, the local people who lived in the area (ibid.: 75).

The access and inclusion agenda

More recently, partly inspired by the success of community museums, and building on the desire to ensure that public services are accountable to tax-payers and serve the needs of the entire community, a much more explicit social agenda has been given to museums in the UK by the government. Elected in 1997 on a manifesto which included improvements in education, tackling social exclusion and providing access for all to public services, the Labour government has required all of its ministries to identify means of contributing to this overall agenda. The department which covers both archaeology and museums, the Department for Culture, Media and Sport, has as a result placed a high priority, through a series of policy documents, on encouraging educational, accessible and socially inclusive programmes in the bodies it funds (DCMS 1998, 2000, 2001; Dodd and Sandell 1998). This agenda coincides with approaches already favoured by local government, and has influenced other funding agencies, such as the Heritage Lottery Fund, which also place a high priority on the promotion of access to cultural heritage, and the development of educational services. As a result, probably for the first time in the UK there is a situation in which publicly funded museums share an outward-looking agenda which places the public before collections management. This has itself been reflected in a changed definition of the museum by the UK's Museums Association, from one which focused primarily on processes and collections ('an institution which collects, documents, preserves, exhibits and interprets material evidence and associated information for the public benefit') to one which stresses outcomes and audiences: 'Museums enable people to explore collections for inspiration, learning and enjoyment. They are institutions that collect, safeguard and make accessible artefacts and specimens, which they hold in trust for society' (Museums Association 1998).

As a result, archaeological museums find themselves in a climate in which their funding bodies, and the public at large, are looking to them to develop programmes which engage contemporary audiences, and which are relevant not only to traditional visitors but which also reach out and connect with people who normally do not visit museums or have any particular interest in archaeology. Whilst the political impetus to use museums to implement government policy must be regarded extremely critically by those working in museums (cf. Moore 1997: 21–2), so far the move towards making museums more socially engaged has had the benefit of giving many of them a much-needed push to address their actual and potential audiences more closely.

As a result, widening 'access', defined simply as physical and intellectual, or further refined into physical and sensory, intellectual, cultural, attitudinal and financial (Lang 2000), has become the single most important driving force in museum development in the UK in recent years. I shall now turn to examine some of the ways in which this turn to the public has manifested itself in the work of museum archaeologists.

Digital access

One of the principal ways in which access to archaeological collections is being promoted is through the placing of collections information and images on the Internet, which allows them to be accessed in ways that break free of the constraints of the four walls of the museum.

For long seen as something dull but necessary for accountability purposes (Davies 1998), museum documentation has been transformed through digital technology into an element of museum access and communication (Keene 1998). Some museums, such as Hampshire Museum Service, have simply posted their collections information on the Web fairly undigested, but searchable by anyone with sufficient interest. The Petrie Museum of Egyptian Archaeology at University College London has developed a full on-line illustrated catalogue of all 78,000 objects in its collection, and plans to create a virtual museum linking all of the other Egyptian material excavated by Petrie scattered around the world, starting with a specific link-up with the Manchester Museum for the finds from the site of Lahun which are held in both museums (MacDonald 2000). At the Hunterian Museum in Glasgow, it is possible to see 'object movies' of prehistoric carved stone artefacts – by clicking on the object it can be made to rotate so that all sides and angles can be seen.

Many museums have moved beyond the object to use the Internet to create a virtual information resource. At the Museum of Antiquities of the University of Newcastle, it is possible to see a 'virtual exhibition' about Late Stone Age hunter-gatherers, enter the Hadrian's Wall education website, and explore the museum's re-created temple to Mithras three-dimensionally by moving around the room and clicking on elements of interest (Museum of Antiquities Website 2001).

Beyond the UK, the Alexandria Archaeology Museum in Virginia, USA, is one of the fullest archaeological explorations in a museum context of the possibilities of on-line access and information. As well as providing information on how to find the museum (including on-line maps), and its current pro-grammes, the website provides details of its current and past exhibitions, of the 'Archaeology Adventure Lessons' held in the museum and other activities such as the summer camp, public dig days and archaeological site tours. There are 'Kids Pages' which provide on-line or downloadable activities, and details of how to join the Friends' programme, become a volunteer or apply for an internship. There are also short on-line catalogues relating to publications and merchandising, with downloadable order forms, and, as an incentive to visit, 'eSavings coupons' which can be used by actual visitors to the museum to obtain discounts. In addition, there is 'behind the scenes' information on how collections are cared for and conserved, extracts from the collections policy, details on how the new storage facility was created, explanations about the laws on archaeological preservation and metal detecting, and downloadable forms for archaeologists, such as a 'Request for Preliminary Archaeological Assessment'. Finally, there is extensive information on local sites currently or previously excavated, themes from Alexandria's past, and a bibliography of publications relating to the archaeology of the town (Alexandria Archaeology Museum Website 2001).

Most Internet access involves remote visitors accessing a pre-prepared site. However, some museums are beginning to exploit the Web's potential for interactivity and broadcast. The National Museum of Wales' excavation of a Viking Age settlement at Llanbedrgoch became the focus of a project called 'Digging for Vikings. Archaeology as it Happens' in 2000. Perhaps borrowing from a format established by the television series 'Time Team', Web pages were set up giving the background to the excavation, details of the site team and their jobs, site reports, site plan, educational information, and daily updates. Enquirers were invited to send e-mails with their questions to the excavation team, which the team would reply to on a daily basis (National Museum of Wales Website 2001). Taking this a step further, a British Museum team excavating the Palaeolithic site at Elveden in Suffolk is experimenting with Webcam broadcasts (British Museum 2000), in a manner similar to that already undertaken in the National Museums and Galleries on Merseyside for scientific expeditions as part of the JASON project (Phillips 1998).

Digital media clearly provide a new dimension to the accessibility of museum archaeological resources. However, they are not the panacea that they are sometimes seen to be, because access to the Web is generally limited to those with the resources to afford it (Sarraf 1999: 233). The further provision of Internet access through the People's Network, which will hook all libraries to the Internet, and Culture Online, which is a new government agency devoted to providing digital content, may transform this situation, but at present there is a fairly close match between Internet users and those who tend to visit museums (ibid.). Non-visitors tend also to be non-users of the Internet, except perhaps in the case of young people, who are more likely to be Internet users but less likely to visit museums.

Paradoxically too, the use of digital media to provide 'access' to museum archaeological collections, can actually take people away from the real objects themselves by focusing their attention on digital reproductions of them. While digital information may alert users to the existence of certain collections and stimulate more enquiries to see the objects themselves, it is not clear whether digital media really provide any more 'access' to collections than photographs in books.

Behind the scenes

Another strand of the access agenda does however bring users into closer contact with the museum's collections themselves, for example, through the opening-up of storage and other 'back-of-house' facilities such as conservation, through the handling of collections in discovery centres and loan boxes, and through programmes of outreach beyond the museum building itself.

In the archaeological context, the opening-up of collections formerly held in store away from public gaze can mean the provision of pull-out storage drawers in the body of display cases, a re-invented Victorian tradition seen, for example, at the Verulamium Museum, St Albans, or it can mean the availability of the whole stored collection in a publicly accessible resource centre. The Museum of London's London Archaeological Archive and Research Centre, for example, makes the entire archive of some 3,000 excavations available to students, researchers, archaeological societies and interested members of the general public (Hall and Swain 2000: 87). Other museums which do not have the resources to develop facilities such as these will often have open days with guided tours behind the scenes, where visitors have the opportunity to see material in store and ask questions of the curators (CBA Website 2001).

The opening-up of the museum has also resulted in the exposure of previously hidden processes to public scrutiny. For archaeology, this seems to have begun with the Archaeological Resource Centre in York which, from its opening in 1990 (Jones 1995), not only allowed visitors to gain an insight into finds processing and analysis (see below), but also had offices with glass walls so that archaeologists could be seen at work.

Archaeological conservation has been brought out of the laboratory and into public view by the National Museum of Wales through its 'Celtic warrior' programme, which presents an in-gallery performance designed to show how materials survive or deteriorate. The 'warrior' (played by a member of museum staff), and his clothes and weapons are described to the audience who then help 'bury' him under a mound. The warrior is removed via a trapdoor and replaced by his grave as if it has just been excavated by archaeologists. Conservators then discuss with the audience how different aspects of the body, clothes and grave goods have changed in the course of burial. Using X-rays, photomicrographs and tools, they then show what excavation and conservation can discover about what may originally have been deposited. At the end, the Celtic warrior returns so that the visitors can again compare what was placed in the grave with the work of the conservators (National Museum of Wales Website 2001).

The most ambitious attempt to develop public access to conservation has been at the Conservation Centre in Liverpool, which is part of the National Museums and Galleries on Merseyside. The Centre provides accommodation for all of the museum service's conservation needs, including archaeology, and was designed from the outset to promote public access and understanding. It has a visitor centre, open seven days a week, which explains the processes of conservation in an interactive display, and at scheduled times visitors can sit in a small lecture theatre which has a live video-link to the laboratories. They can use this link to engage in an active question and answer session with conservators working in the labs. Tours of the labs themselves are also available at scheduled times (Forrester 1998).

It is notable that one of the characteristics of these initiatives to bring out formerly hidden museum functions into public view is that it seems to be only the technical processes themselves which are exposed. It is taken for granted that museums must undertake storage and conservation, for example, and debates about the ethics of collecting, disposal and conservation do not form part of the presentation. Visitors are, it seems, invited to admire the extent of the collections, and the expertise and scientific prowess of the museum staff, but not question the fundamentals of what they do or why they do it.

Hands-on the past

A major way in which visitors have been given further access to archaeological collections is by breaking a long-held taboo and being allowed to touch and handle some of them. To a large extent this has been influenced by the development of hands-on discovery centres, particularly those relating to scientific principles, of which the first was the Exploratorium in San Francisco in 1969 (Caulton 1998: 3). Owen (1999) has summarised recent approaches to hands-on learning in archaeological museums showing that the principles of discovery learning are well-suited to archaeological collections (but see her reservations, below).

For archaeology, the pioneering 'discovery centre' has been the ARC in York (Jones 1995) which concentrates primarily on providing hands-on experiences for booked school groups and family visitors. Visitors handle archaeological finds from sites, sort them into categories (pottery, bone, etc.), and are encouraged, through this, to understand something of the archaeological process. Staff are on hand to guide visitors through the process and answer questions.

The ARC is unusual in being a stand-alone facility entirely devoted to archaeology. Rather commoner is the generalised discovery gallery in which archaeology plays a part alongside other disciplines, such as the Discovery Centre at the National Museum of Scotland. Here, from amongst six activity areas, visitors can unpack a Roman soldier's kitbag, write on a wax tablet, handle artefacts from a Viking grave, or make a seal's tooth pendant. As well as being available for the general public, the Centre is aimed specifically to meet the demands of the curriculum for 5 to 14-year-olds. It has times reserved for school visits and is supplemented by teachers' packs and teachers' in-service courses. In similar vein, Hampshire Museum Service's hands-on centre, SEARCH, is aimed principally at primary school groups studying National Curriculum topics in science and history. One of the areas is 'Archaeology in Action' which has workstations equipped with microscopes and hand lenses for examining material. Following a slide show about evidence found during an excavation, children are encouraged to handle and sort real and replica Roman and Anglo-Saxon material, look for clues about their use, and build up ideas about the life of the inhabitants.

Figure 4.1 'The Dig': a temporary initiative carried out at the Museum of London.

The Museum of London has taken the notion of 'discovery' through participation in archaeological activities a stage further in its temporary exhibition, 'The Dig', which was held in 2001 (Figure 4.1). Here, visitors were able to participate in a mock excavation over twenty-four 'trenches', using trowels and brushes to uncover real and replica objects (Martin 2002).

Hampshire's 'SEARCH' is subtitled 'Hands on education centre for learning by discovery', and it is clear from all of the above initiatives that a consensus has developed that it is educationally beneficial for visitors to handle and closely examine authentic archaeological material. However, as Owen (1999) has observed, there is next to no work which actually demonstrates quite what the educational benefits of hands-on or discovery learning are for visitors. Despite this, they seem to be popular, and may well justify themselves from the enjoyment they provide through the experience of handling ancient objects alone, rather than through any enhanced learning which they may, or may not, stimulate. It is also uncertain how far such hands-on initiatives actually broaden the audience for archaeology rather than provide a richer experience for the existing profile of visitors, as currently visitor studies on this topic do not exist.

Loan boxes

One of the ways in which museums have been attempting to widen hands-on access to archaeological collections, and broaden the profile of their audience, is through the use of loan boxes, which are one of the oldest forms of museum outreach. Despite being quite well developed in the period before World War II (Markham 1938), many museum loan services were curtailed in the post-war period because of local authority funding cuts. However, with the rise of the access and education agenda, loan boxes have been reborn in many museum services as a vital component of educational outreach. The loan service run by Reading Museum, one of the few to survive intact for nearly a century, now consists of some 2,000 foam-padded boxes containing 20,000 objects, including a significant archaeological component comprising prehistoric, Roman, Anglo-Saxon, medieval, Ancient Greek and Ancient Egyptian material. The boxes are delivered to schools in the local area each term to support their curriculum needs and each year around 4,000 loans are made, which are used by 33,000 schoolchildren (Swift 1997).

Moreover, as part of the general move of museums to bring behind-the-scenes processes out into the open, Reading Museum has developed a 'box room' right by its entrance, which consists of a hands-on area where visitors can examine some of the loan boxes not currently out on loan and handle some of the objects, and an area where staff work in the open, preparing boxes for loan, receiving returned loans, and administering the scheme as a whole.

In a further development of the idea, the Museum of London has re-invented the loan box as a permanent transfer to local schools. Enquiries showed that the museum's schools' sessions on the Roman Gallery were not able to accommodate all of the school parties wishing to use it, and as many as 5,000 children a year may have been turned down (Hall and Swain 2000). In addition, it was found that the poorest schools were not able to afford to travel to visit the museum. As a result, the museum developed a scheme whereby boxes of Roman material were given to 200 schools in the London area. The boxes contain selected unstratified Roman material together with replica material such as a lamp and writing tablet, teachers' notes and a video. Each school now has a permanent mini-museum available to it, and the Museum has been able to use material which was archaeologically relatively unimportant because of its lack of context.

Outreach and inclusion

As the work with loan boxes implies, the socially engaged museum is now no longer to be conceived of as a building to which visitors are enticed, but as a service, which tailors its work to different target audiences. As a result, outreach work has become an important means of service delivery, both as an end in itself, and as a way in which the museum can publicise itself. Outreach in this context involves moving beyond the traditional provision of travelling exhibitions which are lent to other museum venues, to the provision of services to non-traditional venues and audiences. In some instances this can mean mounting archaeological displays in places such as the office buildings erected on the sites of excavations, or in pubs, airports or shopping centres, as has been done by the Museum of London, and in other cases it can mean taking mobile museums directly out to the community. Long-established in large countries with relatively few museums, such as India (Jain 1994), mobile museums have had a sporadic history in the UK, but like loan boxes, are becoming revived as outreach and public involvement become more important.

The National Museum of Scotland's 'Discovery on the Move', for example, is a travelling version of its discovery centre that can be booked by museums, libraries, schools, community halls and other public venues. It focuses on five topics, two of which include the use of archaeology. The first element, on 'How we use evidence to learn about the past', invites visitors to see what material from today would look like in 100 years' time, and piece together a three-dimensional jigsaw in the form of a broken pot. Another element displays objects and evidence specifically from the local area of each venue, and changes with each destination. A computer information point provides further information about objects and places in Scotland.

However, such forms of outreach do not necessarily mean that new audiences who would not normally consider visiting museums (particularly 'the socially excluded'), are reached. The issue of broadening audiences, particularly of reaching audiences who are socially marginalised, represents a major challenge to museum archaeologists. How can archaeological collections be made to resonate with people's lives today, especially those who feel excluded from museums?

One response to this has been to target specific groups. For example, the county museum services of Shropshire, Herefordshire and Worcestershire have come together to develop a 'Museum on the Move' which is specifically aimed at providing a community museum service to isolated rural communities, many of them suffering from considerable poverty. A purpose-built 7.5 tonne vehicle housing an exhibition is made available to visit schools, training centres, day centres for the elderly, sheltered housing schemes, village centres, hospitals, youth centres, and shopping centres. As with most of the outreach projects already noted, disciplinary boundaries are dissolved and archaeological material takes its place in thematic displays alongside material from other traditional disciplines. The first exhibition, 'Munch!: A short history of food through the ages', included archaeological material, and featured handleable real and replica objects, 'feely boxes' and 'smelly boxes', tapes, video, and an on-board interpreter who could answer questions.

Glasgow Museums Service, a pioneer of community involvement and outreach in the UK, has developed its 'Open Museum' service, which consists of a series of twenty exhibitions or displays which can be borrowed by community groups, and four handling kits for schools, playschemes and local events (Edwards 1996). One of the handling kits is called 'The Archaeology Game', which has been designed to be used by visually impaired children as well as sighted ones. It has accompanying Braille notes, as well as teachers' notes. All of the exhibitions and kits are available free of charge.

The exhibitions are distinguished by the fact that they have all been developed in partnership with local people, so the process of exhibition development is as important a part of the project as the final product. Some of the displays include an archaeological component, including one on 'Digging up Govan' which features Viking and other material from Govan Old Parish Church. They tend to be loaned not to other local museums but to church halls, libraries and community centres.

Archaeology and cultural diversity

Very few museum archaeological initiatives have targeted current ethnic minorities in their programmes, who, surveys show, tend to feel excluded from participation in museum culture (Trevelyan 1991, Khan 2000). This has also recently been emphasised in the UK government's review of the historic environment (English Heritage 2000). Informing it was a large-scale survey of attitudes of the public, and in particular members of ethnic minorities, to the history and heritage of the UK. The survey showed that Black people in particular felt alienated from mainstream white culture and its heritage, and did not feel that the historic environment is 'for them' (MORI 2000).

The issue of how archaeology and archaeological museums in the UK might include people from ethnic minorities in their audiences is a question that has generally not troubled archaeologists, and only a couple of examples are available of projects that might point the way forward. The 'Peopling of London' project at the Museum of London in 1993–94 combined archaeological and social historical evidence to demonstrate that London's cultural diversity was part of the essence of the city's history from its earliest times (Merriman 1997). The exhibition began with a survey of London in the post-war period, which established what most visitors perceived to be true: that immigration from the Commonwealth had been a significant part of London's story in this period. Visitors then went back to prehistoric times, to the last glacial maximum, when Britain was an uninhabited peninsula of northern Europe. The story then wound from the incursion of hunter-gatherers into lowland Britain following the retreat of the ice sheets, through the establishment of the Roman settlement of London, inhabited by people from all over the empire, the Anglo-Saxon and Norman settlements, the settlement of craft-workers and merchants from overseas in medieval times, England's expansion as a maritime and trading power in the Tudor period, the development of the slave trade and the first Black settlers in London, and through on into the eighteenth and nineteenth century settlements of Irish, Jewish, Chinese, Asian,

Italian, German and African-Caribbean people, back to the present. In doing so, the project involved members of ethnic minorities who previously felt unrepresented and unwelcome in the museum, and told a story that linked their lives with those of Londoners of hundreds or thousands of years ago. In addition to the exhibition itself, there was an extensive programme of events for schools and families, a teachers' pack, a book, a travelling exhibition, and an artist in residence. Nearly 100,000 people visited the exhibition during its six-month run, and survey and other evaluation techniques demonstrated that the exhibition successfully attracted a new audience to the Museum, with 20 per cent of people visiting the museum while the exhibition was on describing themselves as belonging to an ethnic minority, compared with 4 per cent before the exhibition (Merriman 1997).

The Cuming Museum in Southwark, London, is based on an antiquarian collection of Egyptian and British antiquities, which until just over a decade or so ago catered principally for a dwindling audience of mainly elderly people committed to archaeology and local antiquities. The museum's local area is today ethnically highly diverse. Rather than turning their backs on this local audience, in recent years the museum staff have attempted to make connections between the collections and the local people by transforming part of the galleries into a child-oriented hands-on local archaeology and history display with text written in an accessible, personal way and a hands-on excavation pit in the centre. Through the local council's education and outreach department, the museum reaches out to schools and community centres. Through handling sessions in the museum itself, connections are made between archaeological material and the visitor's experience, such as between Roman lamps and similar lamps used by Hindus at home today. Through targeting its very diverse local community, and in particular local schools, the museum now finds that some 60 per cent of its visitors are from ethnic minorities (J. Bird, pers. comm.). Here, perhaps, is an indication that by concentrating on the notion of 'place', archaeological collections can make connections with audiences who do not necessarily subscribe to the notions of a shared identity rooted in a deep common past that until recently archaeological displays promulgated.

The 'Art of Archaeology'

One particular method of developing new approaches to the use of archaeological (and other) collections has been through emphasising the creative and imaginative ways in which archaeological collections can be used. In most museum contexts, this has involved engaging the services of creative artists who have tended to use the collections as a source of inspiration and produce their own interventions in the museum space (Pearce 1999: 21–5). Whilst such interventions may play with ideas of the relationship between the historical display and the artistic installation, and may 'subvert the museum's dialectic by illuminating it with the beams of parody, irony and deliberate fiction' (ibid.: 24), it is not clear how far such questioning and subversion extend beyond the highly culturally literate core museum audience.[4] One exception to this is the work of Mark Dion, an American artist whose work challenges the boundaries between fact and fiction and between science and art, by collecting material in fieldwork 'expeditions' and assembling cabinets of curiosities from his discoveries, which are exhibited in art galleries rather than museums of history or science. His 'Tate Thames Dig' of 1999 was the fourth in a series of 'excavations' which collected debris from different parts of the world and arranged them on tables or in cabinets (Coles and Dion 1999). In this project, the process of collecting, cleaning and classifying material taken from the Thames foreshore by the sites of Tate Britain and Tate Modern were essential parts of the project, and were carried out in public in tents on the lawn of Tate Britain. Crucially, for this project, Dion chose as his 'field workers' representatives of the local community. Their role was to collect, clean, label and package the material from the river foreshore, answer questions from the public and attend the lectures given by 'experts' on aspects of the river and its history. This was effectively a kind of community archaeology project, in which over half of the community participants were from ethnic minorities, but took place within the context of an art gallery rather than an archaeological museum.

In order to explore new uses and new audiences for under-used archaeological collections, the Society of Museum Archaeologists, the UK's professional organisation for archaeologists working in museums, developed a project called 'The Art of Archaeology' which encouraged the creative use of archaeological collections. Ten museums took part between May 2000 and March 2001, helped by funding from the Heritage Lottery Access Fund. Some of these are worth describing in a little detail as they provide good examples of the ways in which museum archaeologists are currently trying to encourage wider use of archaeological collections.

Nottingham City Museums and Galleries developed a project called 'Archaeology Revealed'. One element involved young mothers from a particular area of the city in developing a ceramic art installation for the exhibition, and involved pupils at risk from exclusion in a local school in the production of the exhibition banner, using the Egyptian collection as inspiration.

In urban museums such initiatives are not unusual, although they have rarely been carried out using archaeological collections. It is much more unusual, though, for this kind of work to be undertaken in rural areas, despite their oft-neglected problems of poverty and poor services. Archaeological collections can potentially have a significant role to play in outreach projects in rural areas because they are found in almost every local history museum and because the general robustness of much of the material lends itself to active use.

Shropshire Archaeology Service, for example, used material from a Roman villa and a medieval friary to develop a series of events focused particularly on the Craven Arms district, which is a recognised area of rural poverty. Events included an art installation, song and poem workshops, and a workshop in which a stained-glass artist used medieval stained-glass fragments to discuss with participants how they could be used to reconstruct the past. Two of the workshops were also taken into local schools and all of them resulted in a series of exhibitions which toured local museums and libraries.

In another rural area, Herefordshire Museums' projects included one undertaken in partnership with the local Royal National College for the Blind, in which a five-week course on 'A History of Ceramic Technology' was held, based principally on the museums' collection of archaeological pottery. The course was held for students following a vocational qualification on recreational art and design, and the results of their work were displayed at one of the local museums.

North Lanarkshire Museum targeted two areas, Glenboig and Cardowan, as areas of deprivation and social exclusion, for a programme of creative writing focusing on the industrial heritage of the area through the museum's industrial archaeology and social history collections. Workshops involved a range of participants, from primary school pupils, youth group members and adults, and culminated in a public reading of their work, and a publication. In similar vein, Worcester City Museum developed creative writing workshops based on its archaeological collections, involving schools, a leisure club, and adult groups, including a group with disabilities.

Evaluation of the projects made it clear that the majority of projects were successful in bringing new uses and new audiences to archaeological collections. All of the museums involved felt that the projects represented new approaches for them, and would wish to undertake more of this work if resources would allow them to do so. It is clear that it is possible to encourage more extensive use of archaeological collections, and their use by a wider audience. However, it is also clear that such work requires a significant commitment in terms of time by museum staff, and it is not yet clear what the effects are or how long-term they may be (Owen 2002).

Observations

This overview has demonstrated that archaeological museums – or museums with archaeological collections – are now beginning to make significant strides in re-orienting themselves to the public following their former focus on the needs of their collections and of the discipline of archaeology. What is remarkable about many of the initiatives is that they represent a new way of thinking about archaeology in which the emphasis is not, as has traditionally been the case, on what the public can do for archaeology, but rather on what archaeology can do for the public (Smardz 1997: 103). This is not to say that archaeology can only justify itself if it can be proved to be 'relevant' to contemporary society, but it does mean that archaeology can no longer be solely justified by reference to notions of disinterested scholarship and objectivity:

it must also balance this with a commitment to deliver something back to present-day communities.

In terms of archaeological museums, in many ways the work in the UK leads the way, mainly because of the pressures exerted by non-archaeological impulses on the museums profession as a whole. However, the embracing by the whole archaeological profession of the notion of engaging with audiences, providing access and use of archaeological collections and knowledge, and provid-ing services for different parts of the community is an exciting prospect indeed for a more publicly oriented archaeology. There are nevertheless a good number of issues to be confronted (aside from the obvious ones such as funding) which arise from a review of current practice.

The return to the object

One of the most noticeable aspects of many of the access initiatives outlined above, such as visible storage, on-line databases, hands-on activities and the art projects, is that they seem to represent a return to the object. In contrast to some recent approaches to social history in museums (Fleming 1998; Jenkinson 1989), which have argued for a retreat away from the object in favour of historical context and interpretation, much recent museum archaeology has focused on the objects themselves, with minimal if any historical contextual-isation. The intrinsic properties of the objects are emphasised, be it their tactility, age or unusual nature. The visitor is invited to engage with the objects as objects, with their apparently intrinsic 'aura', rather than engaging with them as evidence forming an element in the construction of a historical understanding of past cultures. Where contextualisation is provided, it tends to be used to demonstrate processes of excavation, storage, conservation or research, but rarely will the possible historical meanings of the objects be explored beyond classification, date and technical function.

A focus on the objects themselves nevertheless highlights aspects of the visitor experience which engage well with current theories of museum educa-tion, which emphasise affective, non-linear, self-directed learning in which the visitor constructs knowledge him- or herself (Hein 1998). Plurality is welcomed, and proximity to 'truth' is not the standard against which visitor understanding is measured. Such approaches stress that what museums do best is to stimulate feelings such as wonder, awe, mystery and 'otherness' (cf. Tilden 1957). A focus on the individual 'aura' of each object stimulates an approach that is creative, poetic and anti-rational. It is also an approach that is accessible to all, in that knowledge of archaeology is not necessary, nor even encouraged. The visitor can admire the richness of the collections, may react to the aesthetic qualities of the object, and may develop a subjective emotional response to the material, without needing to know anything about the historical context and interpretation of the objects themselves. This is an aesthetic approach, which treats the collections essentially as if they are art objects.

The abandonment of interpretation implicit in such approaches may actually be a legitimate response to critiques of museum archaeological representation which have seen gallery narratives as irredeemably biased and partial. However, in concentrating on providing access, principally physical, to archaeological collections, museum curators are in danger of promoting the idea that the objects 'speak for themselves', or of concentrating on the exposition of archaeological and museum processes at the expense of historical interpretation. This point has been well made by Sharon MacDonald in relation to science interpretation, where she argues that although 'the active visitor' is seen as an ideal manifestation of democratic and accessible interpretation, the actual range of choices with which visitors are presented can in fact restrict possibilities for critical engagement rather than open them up:

> Thus, rather than just reading off 'democracy' or 'empowerment' from 'activity' or 'choice-making', it is important to try . . . to understand just how activities are conceptualised and performed by those involved, what kinds of questions are asked, and, equally crucially, what are not.
>
> (Sharon MacDonald 2002: 219)

This partiality of approach could mean that the post-modern fear of the past becoming a plaything, devoid of meaning other than as a thing to be consumed by visitors (e.g Walsh 1992: 113–5), could become fulfilled. Greater access may indeed be provided through such initiatives, but access to what? The challenge must now be for museum archaeologists not only to broaden the demographic profile of their audiences, but also to broaden their minds.

Use of 'informed imagination'

One of the ways in which intellectual access to archaeological collections might be broadened without sacrificing the role of museums to encourage knowledge of the past is to introduce historical contextualisation alongside the affective, hands-on and creative approaches outlined earlier. There already exist some models for this kind of approach, which I would term 'informed imagination'. By this I mean an approach to interpretation which is based on the knowledge of the archaeological and historical context of the material provided by the expertise of the curators, but which acknowledges diversity of views, the contingency of archaeological interpretations, and encourages imagination and enjoyment in the visitors' own constructions of the past.

Elements of such an approach could be seen in the former prehistoric gallery of the Museum of London, which used images of modern stereotypes of prehistory, an explicit agenda in its narrative, the ability to handle objects, links between past and present landscape, and a poetic approach to the writing of text, to communicate a sense of change over a period of half a million years

(Cotton and Wood 1996). The latter is also a strong feature of the main text panels in the early displays at the Museum of Scotland, as in this section on 'Bloodshed, weapons and heroes':

> . . . At first we fought with clubs and with bows and arrows. Later we fought with swords and spears. Our weapons got better, our warriors grew fiercer. The army of the Romans was uncountable. They moved with the purpose of ants. Their weapons were murderous, their war horses terrifying. But we fought them anyway.
>
> (Clarke 2000: 221)

This represents an entirely new kind of approach to archaeological interpretation in the museum. Instead of the dry and distanced writing of the scholar, we have an emotional, experiential narrative, which draws on poetry and fiction and by implication invites visitors to construct their own stories from the evidence and information they see in the galleries.

Galleries such as these tend to be informed by research on the preconceptions and attitudes of actual and potential visitors (Cotton and Wood 1996), which is one of the reasons that successful communication can occur. The recent temporary touring exhibition, 'Ancient Egypt: Digging for Dreams', mounted by the Petrie Museum of Egyptian Archaeology, Croydon Museum and Glasgow Museums, was similarly informed by such research, particularly amongst people who tended not to visit, such as members of ethnic minorities (Sally MacDonald 2002). The initial sections of the exhibition dealt with popular stereotypes about Ancient Egypt, as shown, for example, in films such as 'The Mummy'. The excavation and recovery of the collections by Flinders Petrie were discussed in terms of colonialism, and then the political usurpation of archaeology was explored, such as the Nazis' use of the mummy portraits discovered by Petrie to support racial arguments (ibid.: 4).

The main body of the exhibition was devoted to various issues relating to the relationship between Ancient Egypt and societies today (Figure 4.2). One of these concerns the treatment of human remains: in the exhibition, mummified remains were in a case covered by a shroud, which visitors could lift if they wished to view them. Visitors were invited to fill out postcards giving their views on the display of human remains. Other parts of the exhibition dealt with issues of race and colour, which were identified in visitor research as being of particular interest to Black people, and the way in which Ancient Egypt is drawn upon by New Age beliefs. A final section examined how Ancient Egypt is marketed and consumed. A short video showed the personal meaning of Ancient Egypt to different people, ranging from an academic Egyptologist to Black schoolchildren (Sally MacDonald 2002).

The last three approaches to the interpretation of the archaeological past in museums offer an exciting prospect for the future, in which experimentation and debate can occur about archaeological interpretations, in which visitors

Figure 4.2 'Ancient Egypt: Digging for Dreams': a temporary exhibition at University
College London.

and their understanding are placed at the forefront, and in which the best work
on opening up collections can be allied with innovative approaches to narrative and contextualisation. The public seem to respond well and without
surprise to what are often seen as radical departures by archaeologists and
museum professionals. It may be, then, that it is we who are holding ourselves
back, through fear of the disapproval of our peers. Perhaps it is time to listen
more to the views of our potential visitors, and take a few more risks in what
we do.

Acknowledgements

I am very grateful to Janet Owen, Chair of the Society of Museum Archaeologists, for allowing me to look at her report on the 'Art of Archaeology'
project in advance of publication, and to Jane Bird of the Cuming Museum
for telling me about the museum's work. I am also grateful to Sally MacDonald,
Stephen Quirke, Tim Schadla-Hall and Peter Ucko for reading and
commenting on an earlier draft of this paper.

Notes

1   Social exclusion has been defined by the Department for Culture, Media and Sport as: 'A shorthand term for what can happen when people or areas suffer from a combination of linked problems such as unemployment, poor skills, low incomes, poor housing, high crime environments, bad health, poverty and family breakdown' (DCMS 2000: 7).

2   However, this may be slightly misleading as the survey does not make clear whether visitors specifically went for the archaeology, or indeed whether they looked at the archaeology galleries at all in their visit.

3   There has nevertheless been a strong tradition of support for adult education and archaeological societies amongst museum curators since the expansion of museum provision in the nineteenth century in the form of lectures, evening classes and field excursions. The audiences for such initiatives, however, have tended to be those who were already strongly committed to archaeology.

4   Although there is some evidence that such approaches do serve to bring in a new audience of young people who relate to contemporary art and popular culture, as was witnessed in the 'Time Machine' project at the British Museum, in which contemporary artists installed artworks in the Egyptian Sculpture gallery (S. Quirke, pers. comm. 2001).

Bibliography

Alexandria Archaeology Museum Website. 2001. http://ci.alexandria.va.us/oha/archaeology. Accessed on 12 June 2001.

Anderson, J. 1984. *Time Machines. The World of Living History*. Nashville: American Association for State and Local History.

Arnold, B. 1990. The Past as Propaganda: Totalitarian Archaeology in Nazi Germany. *Antiquity* 64: 464–78.

Ascherson, N. 2000. The Museum of Scotland. *Public Archaeology* 1(1): 82–4.

Barnes, G. and Okita, M. 1999. Japanese Archaeology in the 1990s. *Journal of Archaeological Research* 7(4): 349–95.

Bennett, T. 1995. *The Birth of the Museum. History, Theory, Politics*. London: Routledge.

Biddle, M. 1994. Can we expect museums to cope? Curatorship and the archaeological explosion. In Gaimster, D. (ed.) *Museum Archaeology in Europe*. Proceedings of a conference held at the British Museum, 15–17 October 1992. Oxbow Monograph 39. Oxford: Oxbow Books: 167–71.

British Museum. 2000. *The British Museum Plan 2000/01 to 2004/05*. London: British Museum.

Broshi, M. 1994. Archaeological museums in Israel: reflections on problems of national identity. In Kaplan, F. (ed.). *Museums and the Making of 'Ourselves'. The Role of Objects in National Identity*. Leicester: Leicester University Press: 314–19.

Caulton, T. 1998. *Hands-on Exhibitions*. London: Routledge.

CBA Website. 2001. http://www.britarch.ac.uk/. Accessed 12 July 2001.

Childs, S.T. 1995. The Curation Crisis. *Federal Archaeology* Winter/Spring: 11–15.

Clarke, D. 2000. Creating the Museum of Scotland. A reply to Neal Ascherson. *Public Archaeology* 1(3): 220–21.

Coles, A. and Dion, M. (eds) 1999. *Mark Dion Archaeology*. London: Black Dog Publishing.

Cotton, J.F. and Wood, B. 1996. Retrieving prehistories at the Museum of London: a gallery case-study. In McManus, P. (ed.) *Archaeological Displays and the Public: Museology and Interpretation*. London: Institute of Archaeology, University College: 53–71.

Davies, M. 1998. Too much data. *Museums Journal* 98(8): 19.

Davis, P. 1999. *Ecomuseums: a Sense of Place*. Leicester: Leicester University Press.

DCMS (Department For Culture, Media and Sport). 1998: *A New Cultural Framework*. London: DCMS.

DCMS. 2000. *Centres for Social Change*. London: DCMS.

DCMS. 2001. *Libraries, Museums, Galleries and Archives for All. Co-operating Across the Sectors to Tackle Social Exclusion*. London: DCMS.

Dodd, J. and Sandell, R. 1998. *Building Bridges: Guidance for museums and galleries on audience development*. London: Museums and Galleries Commission.

Duncan, C. 1995. *Civilising Rituals. Inside Public Art Museums*. London: Routledge.

Edwards, N. 1996. The Open Museum. *Museum Practice* 1(3): 60–3.

English Heritage. 2000. *Power of Place. The Future of the Historic Environment*. London: English Heritage.

Fleming, D. 1998. Brave New World: the future for city history museums. In Kavanagh, G. and Frostick, E. (eds.) *Making City Histories in Museums*. London: Leicester University Press: 133–50.

Forrester, J. 1998. Opening up. *Museum Practice*, 3(1): 59–61.

Hall, J. and Swain, H. 2000. Roman boxes for London's schools: an outreach service by the Museum of London. In McManus, P. (ed.) *Archaeological Displays and the Public. Museology and Interpretation* (2nd edition). London: Archetype Publications: 87–95.

Hein, G. 1998. *Learning in the Museum*. London: Routledge.

Hudson, K. 1981. *Museums of Influence*. Cambridge: Cambridge University Press.

Jain, S. 1994. Mobile museums in India. In Pearce, S. (ed.) *Museums and the Appropriation of Culture*. New Research in Museum Studies 4. London: Athlone Press: 129–41.

Jenkinson, P. 1989. Material culture, people's history and populism: where do we go from here? In Pearce, S. (ed.) *Museum Studies in Material Culture*. Leicester: Leicester University Press: 139–52.

Jones, A. 1995. The Archaeological Resource Centre. In Hooper-Greenhill, E. (ed.) *Museum, Media, Message*. Leicester: Leicester University Press: 156–64.

Kaplan, F. (ed.) 1994. *Museums and the Making of 'Ourselves'*. Leicester: Leicester University Press.

Keene, S. 1998. *Digital Collections. Museums and the Information Age*. Oxford: Butterworth-Heinemann.

Khan, N. 2000. *Responding to Cultural Diversity: Guidance for Museums and Galleries*. London: Museums and Galleries Commission.

Lang, C. 2000. *Developing an Access Policy*. London: Museums and Galleries Commission.

Layton, R., Stone, P. and Thomas, J. (eds) 2001. *Destruction and Conservation of Cultural Property*. London: Routledge.

Lewis, G. 1992. Museums and their precursors: a brief world survey. In Thompson, J.M.A. (ed.) *The Manual of Curatorship: A Guide to Museum Practice*. London: Butterworth: 5–20.

McCann, W.J. 1990. 'Volk und Germanentum': the presentation of the past in Nazi

Germany. In Gathercole, P. and Lowenthal, D. (eds) *The Politics of the Past*. London: Routledge: 74–88.

MacDonald, Sally. 1998. Croydon: what history? In Kavanagh, G. and Frostick, E. (eds) *Making City Histories in Museums*. London: Leicester University Press: 58–79.

MacDonald, Sally. 2000. University museums and the public: the case of the Petrie Museum. In McManus, P. (ed.) *Archaeological Displays and the Public: Museology and Interpretation* (2nd edition). London: Archetype Publications: 67–86.

MacDonald, Sally. 2002. An experiment in access. *Museologia* 2: 101–8.

MacDonald, Sharon. 2002. *Behind the Scenes at the Science Museum*. Oxford: Berg.

Markham, S.F. 1938. *A Report into the Museums and Art Galleries of the British Isles, other than the National Museums*. Edinburgh: Carnegie United Kingdom Trustees.

Martin, D. 2002. Great excavations. *Museum Practice* 7(1): 21–3.

Merriman, N. 1991. *Beyond the Glass Case. The Past, the Heritage and the Public in Britain*. Leicester: Leicester University Press.

Merriman, N. 1997. The Peopling of London Project. In Hooper-Greenhill, E. (ed.) *Cultural Diversity. Developing Museum Audiences in Britain*. Leicester: Leicester University Press: 119–48.

Merriman, N. and Swain, H. 1999: Archaeological archives: serving the public interest? *European Journal of Archaeology* 2(2), 249–62.

Moore, K. 1997. *Museums and Popular Culture*. London: Leicester University Press.

MORI. 2000. *Attitudes Towards the Heritage. Research Study Conducted for English Heritage*. London: MORI.

MORI/Resource. 2001. *Visitors to Museums and Galleries in the UK*. London: MORI/Resource.

Museum of Antiquities Website. 2001. http://museums.ncl.ac.uk. Accessed 12 June 2001.

Museums Association. 1998. *Museum Definition*. London: Museums Association.

National Museum of Wales Website. 2001. http://www.nmgw.ac.uk/archaeology. Accessed on 12 June 2001.

Owen, J. 1999. Interaction or tokenism? The role of 'hands-on activities' in museum archaeology displays. In Merriman, N. (ed.) *Making Early Histories in Museums*. Leicester: Leicester University Press: 173–89.

Owen, J. 2002. *Society of Museum Archaeologists Art of Archaeology Initiative. Summary Report*. URL: www.socmusarch.org.uk/artofarch.pdf

Pearce, S. 1999. Presenting archaeology. In Merriman, N. (ed.) *Making Early Histories in Museums*. Leicester: Leicester University Press: 12–27.

Phillips, P. 1998. Developing digital resources. National museums and galleries on Merseyside. *Museum Practice* 9: 54–6.

Ramos, M. and Duganne, D. 2000. *Exploring Public Perceptions and Attitudes about Archaeology*. Washington, DC: Society for American Archaeology.

Sansom, E. 1996. Peopling the past. Current practice in archaeological site interpretation. In McManus, P. (ed.) *Archaeological Displays and the Public: Museology and Interpretation*. London: Institute of Archaeology, University College London: 118–37.

Sarraf, S. 1999. A survey of museums on the Web: who uses museum websites? *Curator* 42(3): 231–43.

Shanks, M. and Tilley, C. 1987. *Reconstructing Archaeology*. Cambridge: Cambridge University Press.

Skeates, R. 2000. *Debating the Archaeological Heritage*. London: Duckworth.

Smardz, K. 1997: The past through tomorrow: interpreting Toronto's heritage to a multicultural public. In Jameson, J. (ed.) *Presenting Archaeology to the Public. Digging for Truths*. London: AltaMira Press: 101–13.

Swift, F. 1997. Boxing clever. *Museum Practice* 2(2): 9.

Tilden, F. 1957. *Interpreting Our Heritage*. Chapel Hill: University of North Carolina Press.

Trevelyan, V. 1991. *Dingy Places with Different Kinds of Bits*. London: London Museums Consultative Committee.

Trigger, B.G. 1995. Romanticism, nationalism and archaeology. In Kohl, P. and Fawcett, C. (eds) *Nationalism, Politics and the Practice of Archaeology*. Cambridge: Cambridge University Press: 263–79.

Walsh, K. 1992. *The Representation of the Past*. London: Routledge.

5

UNCOVERING ANCIENT EGYPT

The Petrie Museum and its public

Sally MacDonald and Catherine Shaw

Introduction

Here are invalids in search of health; artists in search of subjects;
sportsmen keen upon crocodiles; statesmen out for a holiday; special
correspondents alert for gossip; collectors on the scent of papyri and
mummies; men of science with only scientific ends in view; and the
usual surplus of idlers who travel for the mere love of travel.

(Edwards 1877: 1–2)

Amelia Edwards was a popular writer and journalist with a passion for Egypt.
When she died in 1892 she left her collection of Egyptian antiquities, together
with some money, to University College London (UCL), to promote 'the
teaching of Egyptology with a view to the wide extension of the knowledge of
the history, antiquities, literature, philology and art of Ancient Egypt' (Will
of Amelia Edwards, dated 8/3/1891, copy in Petrie Museum archive). Edwards
clearly hoped that the new academic department she helped establish would
have an impact, long term, on the wider public understanding of this ancient
culture.

Her bequest funded the UK's first Chair in Egyptology. Flinders Petrie, her
protégé and first Edwards professor, added his collections to hers and through
his annual excavations and purchases built UCL's museum into one of the most
significant collections of early Egyptian material in the world. What came to
be called the Petrie Museum remained nevertheless a university rather than
a public museum: 'The collection is largely supplementary to the national
collection, and consists of objects for study rather than for popular show' (letter
from W.M.F. Petrie to Provost, UCL Managing Sub-Committee Minutes
5/11/1907 minute 10).

For Petrie and his immediate successors the collections were primarily
there to support the teaching of UCL's Egyptian archaeology students, although

the quality and range of the collections inevitably attracted specialist academic researchers from all over the world. It was not until the 1970s that museum staff took steps to broaden its audience and welcome interested amateur Egyptologists. External (non-UCL) visit numbers rose from around 200 per annum in 1970 to around 3,000 by 1997 and nearly 9,000 by 2000. As the museum became more heavily used by an 'outside' audience the inadequacies of its current accommodation grew more apparent and the need to find a safer, more spacious and more accessible home grew more acute. The search began for a suitable site, and at the same time the museum began a programme of research on its existing and potential audiences and what they might want from new displays on ancient Egypt in the new museum. This paper reports on that research, which examined for the first time, in relation to a museum of Egyptian archaeology, the attitudes of existing users alongside those of non-users such as the modern black and Egyptian communities in London, and the perspectives of amateur enthusiasts and children, alongside those of academics.

Audiences and questions

The process of defining existing and target audiences involved – as it would in any museum – understanding what was known about current visitors (here mainly from observation and old visitors books); looking in detail at the subject matter of the collection; and considering other potential interest groups and the media through which they currently access ancient Egypt. It was a long and rather woolly process involving much discussion and it is not over yet. Many museums – particularly in North America and more recently in the UK – now undertake formative research of the kind described here when planning new displays or programmes. This is part of a general trend away from single-perspective didactic exhibitions and towards more open, reflective presentations that take account of the perceptions, beliefs and biases that audiences – and, of course, curators – bring with them to any subject (Merriman 1999: 7). Although this kind of research appears inclusive and potentially allows many voices to be heard, it has to be remembered that it is almost always museum staff who set the agenda, decide the questions, choose the respondents, and, in the end, decide whether to use or ignore what they hear.

Amateur and 'alternative' Egypt

On the basis of observation, staff at the Petrie Museum broadly defined their existing adult audience as consisting of professional and amateur Egyptologists. The professionals are those who earn their living, or aspire to earn their living, from the subject; most hold relevant higher education qualifications. The amateurs are those for whom the subject is an interest rather than a job. Many members of the museum's thriving Friends organisation would fall into this latter category. In practice the difference between professionals and amateurs is not always clear-cut. Amateurs at the traditional end of the spectrum belong to many of the same societies as professionals, and read some of the same books. Many amateur Egyptologists develop specialised knowledge and some earn money and academic status by giving lectures or writing articles.

Move towards the alternative end of the amateur spectrum and a great divide appears to open up. Roth identifies this alternative sector as a broad grouping of New Age spiritualists, those who believe in reincarnation, or the mystical powers of pyramids and crystals. She points out that the media tend to emphasise disagreements between professional and alternative Egyptologists in favour of a good story (Roth 1998: 221). However, it is tempting to conclude that each side plays down the points of agreement between them. I have often heard academics refer to alternative Egyptologists as 'nutters' or 'pyramidiots', while alternative archaeologists seem to relish the banner of 'forbidden archaeology'. But as a group alternative Egyptologists are too numerous and too diverse to dismiss. The Questing Conference of 'forbidden archaeology', held in London in 1999 attracted over 800 people to hear papers on labyrinths, pyramids and the evidence for ancient astrology. Feder, who has catalogued and dissected many examples of what he calls archaeological pseudoscience, acknowledges and analyses their wide appeal and refuses to draw easy distinctions between what he calls 'scholars, charlatans and kooks' (Feder 1996: 252).

The academic/amateur distinction was not, of course, an issue in the early years of the museum, when the discipline was also in its infancy. Petrie encouraged amateurs, organising the Egyptology Library for lending as well as reference, to help those who could only study at home, and supporting specialised research. In his inaugural lecture in 1893 he remarked, 'Someone may not be able to touch more than a minute subject, in a few spare hours, now and then; but let him do that fully and completely and every student will thank him' (in Janssen 1992: 102). Montserrat has pointed out that Dr Margaret Murray, Petrie's assistant at UCL and a professional Egyptologist, was at the same time also a practising witch (Montserrat 2000: 21). Today the distinctions seem more clearly demarcated. In fact academic, popular and alternative Egyptologies seem polarised in a way that might appear very strange to someone coming from another discipline.

Academic Egypt

But while amateur Egyptology appears to be growing in all directions, academic Egyptology is a narrow field; in this country Egyptology is a 'minority' academic subject (as defined by the Higher Education and Funding Council for England). Some see a link between these developments. As Roth has pointed out: 'ironically, the academic field of Egyptology is increasingly being marginalised by the very popularity of its subject matter' (Roth 1998: 222). The experience of the Petrie Museum's curator, that within academic circles Egyptology is considered academically inferior to the study of other, less widely appealing, ancient cultures, supports this view (S. Quirke pers. comm.).

Roth argues that academic Egyptologists should welcome the public interest in their subject and engage with it. Instead she sees many of her colleagues retreating into more specialised studies which earn them peer recognition yet distance them not only from the lay public but also from colleagues in other academic disciplines (Roth 1998: 229). There are additional reasons for these interdisciplinary divisions. Thomas points to the traditional separation of classics departments from those concerned with the Near East and Egypt as being 'a relic of the secular separation in the late 18th century of classics from the study of the Bible' (Thomas 1998: 15). As a university museum, the Petrie is very much affected by these academic divisions. For most of its history, it was part of UCL's Egyptology Department. It was only in 1993 that the department was officially incorporated within the Institute of Archaeology (the Greek and Latin Department is still separate). Despite incorporation, the old disciplinary divisions are still in evidence. The museum houses extensive collections from Hellenistic and Roman Egypt, but remains little known and almost unused by Institute of Archaeology staff teaching courses other than Egyptian Archaeology (Merriman 2000: 1). It can easily be argued that discipline-bound thinking is a problem throughout academia. But within the academic study of archaeology ancient Egypt seems isolated in a way that, for instance, Bronze Age Greece does not.

The Petrie Museum is a university museum seeking to broaden its audience, both within and outside academia. Museum staff felt it was important to understand the common ground between academic and more general audiences. After all, Feder's surveys of college students found they were just as likely to believe in unorthodox archaeological statements as the general public (Feder 1996: 3–5). What periods and themes were of greatest interest? What meanings did ancient Egypt have for them? What was their attitude to modern Egypt, and more specifically, to archaeology in modern Egypt?

African Egypt

There are numerous recent examples of ethnographical and social history museums engaging with traditionally excluded audiences in an effort to redress the historic biases of their displays (Simpson 1996). Archaeological museums have been criticised for lagging behind, for failing, often, to see the relevance to their institutions and displays of such issues as cultural diversity (Merriman 1999:3). In a recent UK survey researchers found that three out of four people believed that 'the contribution of black people and Asians to our society is not thoroughly represented in heritage provision' (MORI 2000). The archaeology of Egypt presents interesting questions in this respect.

There is a long history of black scholarship on the subject of Ancient Egypt and its relationship to the rest of Africa (Hilliard 1994). Some of the more extreme aspects of what is often called Afrocentrism have been rightly criticised (for example by Howe 1998) as being themselves racist, and some academics argue that it is both misleading and dangerous to seek to establish, as many black scholars have done, what colour the Ancient Egyptians were (e.g. Brace *et al*. 1996: 162). To do so is, they argue, to apply modern concepts of race which did not exist in Ancient Egypt. Most of them would, however, acknowledge that, for almost two centuries, the study of Ancient Egypt in the Western world has been distorted by Eurocentric and racist bias (e.g. Young 1995: 118–41).

UCL has no black Egyptologists on the teaching staff. Of those students undertaking research or taught courses in Egyptian archaeology, less than one in ten is black. Friends of the Petrie Museum defining themselves as black are a tiny minority (less than 1 per cent). The proportion of black visitors to the museum is also, from observation, very low, though some have recently criticised the museum's displays and labelling as racist (T. Golding pers. comm.). This research sought to draw black audiences – both Egyptologists and members of the general public – into discussion about Ancient Egypt, its appeal, significance and representation in museums. It also took issues that have been important to black historians – Ancient Egypt's relationship with the rest of Africa, the skin colour of the Ancient Egyptians – and raised them in discussion with white audiences.

Egyptian Egypt

Modern Egyptians might be regarded as another group excluded by traditional Egyptology. The slow growth of indigenous Egyptology in the last century has been attributed in part to the prevalence of pan-Arab politics, favouring a study of Islamic rather than earlier periods (Trigger 1984: 359) and in part to the appropriation of Ancient Egypt by Western scholars and archaeologists (Reid 1985: 234). According to one source, less than 5 per cent of visitors to the Cairo Museum are Egyptians (Stone and Molyneaux 1994: 21). Professor Fekri Hassan, an Egyptian archaeologist and currently Petrie Professor of Egyptology at UCL, summarises the modern Egyptian relationship with the country's ancient past as follows:

> the Pharaonic past is a political card. It can arouse passionate responses among certain intellectuals, but it has not effectively become an integral or a predominant element of the materiality of Egyptian life. Perhaps the only vibrant continuity with Egypt's Pharaonic past is the Nile river. But it no longer floods and is imprisoned within its bounded channel. Lined with high rise Western hotels it belongs to the European and Arab tourists who can afford them.
>
> (Hassan 1998: 212)

Although UCL has an Egyptian Professor of Egyptology, the proportions of students and museum Friends who are Egyptians are again very low (one in twenty students, 1 per cent of Friends). This research sought the views of Egyptians, most of them Egyptologists, on general issues relating to the study and presentation of ancient Egypt. It also asked wider audiences about the issue of chronology, of when, in their view, ancient Egypt began and ended. It has been argued that the term Egyptology has imposed time limits on the subject, denigrating, for instance, a study of Coptic and Islamic Egypt (Reid 1985: 234). The narrowness of the academic field of study may also have restricted the interests of more general audiences. A study of visitors to the British Museum in 1998 indicated that most visitors made no connection between ancient and modern Egypt (Motawi 1998). In the research discussed here this issue was explored further with people who had visited Egypt, as well as those who had not, to establish whether a personal encounter with modern Egypt might be significant in re-shaping attitudes to past and present.

Specific areas of interest included tourism and archaeology. Wood has concluded that

> Europeans, even 'Egyptologists' must still have been motivated by a desire to possess 'treasure', if only for the prestige its ownership would entail . . . This cavalier attitude . . . that Europeans have the right to excavate, study and export Pharaonic remains however they see fit is rooted in an attitude that feels that, in the end, Egypt's past does not really belong to its present day inhabitants.
>
> (Wood 1998: 190)

Given that the museum is part of a department that employs and trains archaeologists, and whose staff and students excavate in Egypt, it seemed appropriate to ask questions about attitudes to archaeology, and to the ownership and treatment of what is excavated.

Children's Egypt

For some years now Ancient Egypt has been an option on the English National Curriculum history programme of study at Key Stage 2 (i.e. for children aged 7–11). It is not possible to establish how widely the subject was taught in English schools prior to that date, nor how many schools now choose the Ancient Egypt option from the seven options currently available to them as a World History Study (the alternatives are: Ancient Sumer, the Assyrian Empire, the Indus Valley, the Maya, Benin or the Aztecs). Anecdotal evidence from advisory teachers suggests however that it is a popular choice (D. Garman pers. comm.).

The National Curriculum requires the study of the key features of the chosen past society, which must include 'the everyday lives of men, women and children; the society in relation to other contemporary societies; chronology; the reasons for the rise and fall of the civilisation; significant places and individuals; distinctive contribution to history' (QCA 1999: 19). At Key Stage 2, children are also expected to acquire knowledge, understanding and skills applicable to any historical subject. Amongst other things they are required to be taught how to find out about the past from a range of sources (examples given in the guidance include documents, artefacts and visits to museums, galleries and sites). They should also be taught 'about the social, cultural, religious and ethnic diversity of the societies studied' and 'to recognise that the past is represented and interpreted in different ways, and to give reasons for this' (ibid.: 17).

The curriculum thus maps out what can be interpreted as a radical and stimulating agenda for the study of Ancient Egypt at primary level. However, although standard attainment targets (SATS) are set for history, they are not tested as they are for the core subjects of English, Maths and Science and there is no way of knowing, other than through inspectors' reports on individual schools, whether or not they are being attained. On the particular issue of cultural diversity, for instance, it has been said that 'Ancient Egypt is frequently chosen and taught as if this civilisation were actually white' (Claire 1996: 12). Certainly there are few currently available primary level support materials, in print or video format, that address questions of diversity or differences of interpretation in the study of Ancient Egypt.

There is evident demand from primary teachers for access to museum displays about Ancient Egypt. In the 12 months from November 1999 to November 2000, 1,032 school groups booked into the Egyptian Galleries in the British Museum, and according to the museum's Education Department the Egyptian galleries are more popular with schools than even the Greek displays, despite the fact that the study of Ancient Greece is compulsory, and that of Ancient Egypt an option (information from British Museum Education Department).

Since the Petrie Museum began offering sessions for primary schools in October 1998 these have been considerably over-subscribed. We wanted to understand through this research how we could best meet teachers' needs and which aspects of Ancient Egypt they wished to prioritise. We also wanted to understand what interested children, who access Ancient Egypt, as adults do, outside formal education; through toys and stories – Asterix, Lego, Scooby Doo – referring to the secret passages, codes and curses common in Western popular fiction. Their interests would be unlikely to accord exactly with the priorities of a curriculum written by adults.

About the research

There are two strands to the findings presented in this paper. The first has to do with examining the similarities and differences between academic and amateur Egyptologists in terms of their particular areas of interest. These findings are important in informing the museum's management about the interests and needs of its current users: those who visit in order to study. The second strand involves taking a broader and more exploratory look at perceptions, attitudes and beliefs relating to both ancient and modern Egypt. These findings provide a basis for developing the museum for a visitor population with a more general curiosity about Egypt. These two strands are fundamentally related to the overall aims of the research, which was to inform decision-making about access, display and service issues for the Petrie Museum. It did this by reviewing the particular areas of interest, research needs and priorities of existing study-users, and potential ones such as Key Stage 2 history teachers and their pupils, by exploring the nature of people's fascination with Ancient Egypt, and by examining attitudes to modern Egypt and its links with the past, including attitudes to archaeology.

In order to address these objectives effectively it was necessary not only to target a range of different respondents, but to employ a number of research methods.

Surveys of existing specialist user groups

The purpose of these surveys was to build an accurate description of what these 'core' groups of existing users wanted from the museum, and how much common ground there was between them in terms of themes and periods of particular interest.

In August 1999 a questionnaire was sent to all 650 Friends of the Petrie. A total of 252 completed questionnaires were received, representing a response rate of 38 per cent. A survey of students took place nine months later. Questionnaires were sent to all undergraduate and post-graduate Egyptology students at UCL (including those just taking a module as part of another degree) using the university's internal mail system. Thirty-nine responses were received, a response rate of 43 per cent, one-third of whom were studying for higher degrees.

Survey of known potential users – primary school history co-ordinators

As already described, Ancient Egypt is an optional area of study at Key Stage 2 (KS2) of the National Curriculum. This opens up the potential for thousands of school-age visitors to the Museum each year. What would the interests, and particular needs of this age group be, and to what extent would they overlap with those of older or more advanced students? Equivalent questions about themes and periods of interest to those asked of Friends and students were therefore included in the survey of KS2 history co-ordinators.

We decided to take primary schools within reasonable travelling distance from central London as our target population. As a high response rate was not anticipated, the questionnaire was mailed to a large number of schools, in order to ensure a return large enough to yield meaningful findings. A sampling fraction of 50 per cent was selected, and questionnaires were sent to the KS2 history co-ordinators of the 1,167 state and independent schools in Greater London thus randomly selected; 165 replies were received.

In-depth interviews

While the surveys were able to provide a quantitative description of the range and prevalence of particular themes and periods of interest within the existing user groups, they were unable to provide any insight as to why and how the individual respondents had developed their particular specialised areas of interest, nor their attitudes to various aspects of the subject. To this end, in-depth interviews were conducted with a sample of 24 individuals with a known interest in Egyptology. Interviewees were purposively selected to include both professionals (such as academics and museum workers) and amateurs, including those with alternative or fringe interests in Egyptology. Three of the inter-viewees were themselves Egyptian, another five were black, but not Egyptian, and the remainder were white.

Amongst other topics, the interviews explored the meaning and significance of Ancient Egypt for interviewees, their impressions of present-day Egypt, and their attitudes to excavation. These interviews, which lasted for up to 90 minutes, were tape-recorded and fully transcribed.

Focus groups

The fascination that Ancient Egypt holds for the general population was studied by means of a series of focus groups, commissioned from the Susie Fisher Group (Fisher 2000). The focus group setting allows respondents to explore and develop ideas and perceptions about a subject within a stimulating but non-threatening environment. Five groups were conducted: one of school-children aged 9–10 who had studied Ancient Egypt; people who had visited Egypt (one group of backpackers, and an older group of 'Nile cruisers' who had been on a cruise or organised tour); and two groups of people aged 25 to 45 who had never visited Egypt (one group of white and one group of non-white UK-born respondents). Each group contained six to eight respondents and lasted between 60 and 90 minutes.

Research findings

The findings presented below are drawn from the analyses of the questionnaires, interviews and focus groups. A large amount of varied data covering a wide range of themes was collected during the course of the research, but in a paper of this length it is possible only to summarise responses to some of the key questions.

Most popular themes

The questionnaires presented respondents with lists of pre-coded themes, of which they could tick as many as they wished. These lists were very similar on each questionnaire, although sub-themes were omitted from the teachers' version. Many general enthusiasts (particularly among Friends and undergraduates) took the opportunity to tick virtually every box, whereas academic specialists (including some Friends) indicated just one or two themes. There were nevertheless large areas of common interest to be found between students, Friends and primary school teachers (on behalf of their pupils). The results are presented in Table 5.1.

Table 5.1 Themes of interest to Petrie Museum user groups (%)

	Students (n = 39)	*Friends* (n = 252)	*Teachers* (n = 165)
Daily life	69	64	95
Society and social relations	56	55	44
Women / gender	36	35	
Agriculture, food and farming	21	37	73
Science and technology	36	50	46
Language / script (all or any)	59	64	85
Hieroglyphs	46	50	
Hieratic	23	15	
Demotic	18	11	
Trade, travel, transport	33	48	43
Architecture (all or any)	67	80	90
Temples	33	53	
Tombs	38	56	
Pyramids	33	51	
Palaces	28		
Arts and crafts	46	58	73
Pharaohs, politics and government	56	61	67
Religion, gods and goddesses	67	64	94
Death and burial – mummification	64	49	92
War and weapons	28	30	22
Archaeology and archaeologists	51	53	
Other	23		

Shaded boxes indicate themes or sub-themes which were absent from a particular questionnaire.

Five broad themes proved to be of universal interest, each indicated by over half of each of the user groups:

- daily life
- architecture (including pyramids)
- language and communication
- pharaohs, politics and government
- religion, gods and goddesses.

These five areas were particularly strongly indicated by primary-school teachers, the group which proved most homogenous in their interests, for reasons presumably related to the requirements of the National Curriculum. More than two-thirds of teachers expressed an interest in these themes and also in those of death / mummification, agriculture and arts / crafts. Perhaps of greater significance is the blanket *lack* of interest in certain aspects of Ancient Egyptian life. All groups of respondents showed a singular lack of enthusiasm for women, trade and war.

Most popular periods

The same user groups were also asked about which periods of Egyptian history were of most interest (Table 5.2).

It is perhaps of no surprise to find that Egypt under the Pharaohs is by far the most popular period among all three groups surveyed: 85 per cent of students, 94 per cent of Friends and an overwhelming 97 per cent of primary-school teachers expressed an interest in some or all of the period. Within this broad time-frame, interest for both Friends and students – we did not expect teachers to go into such detail – peaks at the Old Kingdom, Middle Kingdom and, in particular, the New Kingdom, after which interest tailed off markedly. Relatively little interest was expressed in the intermediate and late periods.

However, there is even less enthusiasm for more recent periods of Egyptian history, and expressed interest gradually declines. By the time the Islamic age is reached, we are down to a handful of individuals, some of whom indicated an interest in *every* period listed and therefore cannot be assumed to have any particular specialist interest in Islamic Egypt.

These findings are borne out by those of the focus group research; 'virtually nothing is known about modern Egypt or times since the pharaohs, and there is no desire to know' (Fisher 2000: chart 6). Among more general audiences there was no evidence of an understanding of chronology or sense of historical perspective: 'Ancient Egypt is a sealed bubble in which pharaohs, pyramids, slaves, tombs and Cleopatra float around in a rich soup' (Fisher 2000: chart 7).

Table 5.2 Periods of interest to Petrie Museum user groups (%)

	Students (*n* = 39)	*Friends* (*n* = 252)	*Teachers* (*n* = 165)
Predynastic Egypt	51	57	12
Egypt in the period of the unification	44	48	
Egypt under the Pharaohs (all or any)	85	94	97
Early Dynastic Egypt	33	49	
Old Kingdom	39	58	
First Intermediate Period	23	36	
Middle Kingdom	39	58	
Second Intermediate Period	31	41	
New Kingdom (all or any)	59	63	
Amarna Period	36	56	
Ramesside Period	28	52	
Third Intermediate Period	18	32	
Late Period	15	27	
Graeco-Roman Egypt (all or any)	33	43	10
Ptolemaic	26	26	
Roman	26	19	
Byzantine/Coptic (early Christian)	13	16	
Islamic Periods (all or any)	18	14	2
Medieval	10		
Ottoman	5		
Contemporary	8		

Shaded boxes indicate themes or sub-themes which were absent from a particular questionnaire

Most resonant ideas and images

The focus group research identified a number of 'mythic themes' associated with Ancient Egypt in the minds of general audiences: death; power; wealth; treasure; extinction; slavery; monumental building; command of the heavens; creativity and religion (Fisher 2000: chart 17). The most resonant images appeared to revolve around the size and splendour of the architecture (pyramids, tombs, sphinx); the exoticism of the landscape (sand, heat, camels); a collection of historical/mythical individuals (Cleopatra, Tuthankhamun, Indiana Jones) and a general sense of awe and mystery:

> I'd like to know how they built, like their pyramids and got everything perfect. The dimensions are so intelligent, it's scary.
>
> (non-white adult)

For non-white respondents ancient Egypt had a greater role, symbolising 'the theft of cultural capital' by white Europeans (Fisher 2000: chart 13).

The focus group findings suggest that, for general audiences:

> Ancient Egypt is a concept. It is not only a country. It is not purely history. It is not just a tissue of myths and artefacts. It is an amalgam of all of these; a magic terrain where myths may be real. The concept is created by school, media, archaeology, myths and museums, and is completely self-contained and satisfying.
>
> (Fisher 2000: chart 16)

The researchers found that white people seemed untroubled by the mix of fantasy and fact in their vision of ancient Egypt, whereas non-white respondents were more conscious of distortions (Fisher 2000: chart 33):

> I suppose I want to think that Cleopatra looked a bit like Elizabeth Taylor.
>
> (white adult)

> People think it's European history, Richard Burton and Elizabeth Taylor.
>
> (non-white adult)

In the in-depth interviews, it was not uncommon for a preoccupation with Ancient Egypt to develop from a more generalised interest in ancient history. However, for those interviewed, Egypt rapidly took over, exerting a stronger fascination which eclipsed previous interests. One interviewee refers to the study of Greeks and Romans as being a 'poor relation', these periods being 'too accessible, I suppose, and there didn't seem to be quite the mystery to them' (white, amateur). This is an interesting comment in relation to the survey finding that fewer people were interested in the later periods of Egyptian history. Another respondent describes how his interest wanes as more modern times are reached:

> We're then starting to come into the classical world, they were Macedonians from Greece, they themselves were Egyptian and they adopted the Egyptian culture and religion . . . but it's not the same . . . I have no interest in studying classical Greece or Rome or any other ancient civilisation.
>
> (white, professional)

What colour were the Ancient Egyptians?

The research concluded that the question of colour was an interesting and provocative one for all the adult respondents. White adults found questions about the skin colour of the Ancient Egyptians 'profoundly disturbing and largely unexpected'. There was evidence of a desire to maintain a white Egyptian identity (Fisher 2000: chart 35):

> Hollywood makes out they were white Europeans. Why didn't it dawn on me? I assumed they were all white and the dark ones were Nubian slaves.
>
> (Nile cruiser)

Non-white respondents felt passionate rather than threatened by the question. They were clear that Ancient Egypt had been appropriated as part of white history (Fisher 2000: chart 37):

> I went to the library, looking in the African section. It came under European history!
>
> (non-white adult)

> The black Africans were supposed to be ignorant, but we could build the pyramids.
>
> (non-white adult)

Feelings about modern Egypt and its relationship to Ancient Egypt

The focus group researchers found that most people, particularly white respondents, made no connection between ancient and modern Egypt, which was 'below nowhere on most people's agenda':

> Modern Egypt is simply the country you have to get to so that you can physically experience the myth of ancient Egypt. Many people aren't quite sure where it is, but . . . this doesn't matter because spiritually they feel ancient Egypt belongs to them too.
>
> (Fisher 2000: chart 26)

Those respondents who had visited Egypt seem to have come away with negative and racist views:

> The monuments are too breathtaking for words. It knocks you away and now they can't mend your toaster.
>
> (Nile cruiser)

The focus group researchers noted the strong contrast between Western European perceptions of the Ancient Egyptians ('aloof, spiritual, powerful, clever') and of the modern Egyptians ('grasping, pushy, poor, backward'), looking for their own roots among the first group. Non-white respondents were 'more open, insightful, sympathetic' (Fisher 2000: chart 29).

While the Egyptologists (amateur and professional) interviewed were more knowledgeable about Egypt's geographical location (as most of them had visited the country) they expressed similarly negative attitudes to modern Egypt and Egyptians. Many of their comments were indistinguishable from those of the focus group members. For example:

I wasn't too sure about modern Egypt, which I thought was very run down, poor and I didn't particularly like it very much. But ancient Egypt, yes, it lived up to everything I hoped it would.

(white, professional)

Another interviewee, who had never visited, remarked sardonically:

Well, apart from the heat, the flies, the food and the terrorism, it sounds wonderfully appealing . . .

(white, amateur)

Other interviewees spoke as if there was almost a duty – which was sadly neglected – for Egyptians to make their country more palatable for tourists. One interviewee described her surprise at the 'dirt' and the 'culture shock' she experienced on every visit:

No matter how much they try, and they do try much harder nowadays because they get so many Western visitors, it is still difficult . . . the argument that it's the climate . . . doesn't really pass muster, that's not really true, it's a cultural thing. They don't bother . . . I've never understood it.

(white, professional)

They pester you constantly . . .. they want to stick to all the Europeans, thinking they can get as much money from them as they can, but they don't understand the European mentality.

(white, amateur)

Among the interviewees a clear distinction was drawn between rural and urban Egypt. Most of the unpleasant images were derived from the cities or tourist areas whereas the countryside was viewed as very much unchanged from ancient times – 'like a Bible picture coming to life' (white, professional) – with agricultural practices most often being cited in this context.

Modern Egyptians were sometimes criticised by interviewees for showing insufficient interest in their own heritage, or for simply taking it for granted through familiarity. They 'don't give a toss about it' according to one amateur Egyptologist, although, on reflection, she does not judge them too harshly:

I was angry they didn't treat it any better but also, the poverty of the country in comparison to our wealth here, I could see they had other priorities.

(white, amateur)

It would, however, be unfair to present too one-sided a picture here, and it should be acknowledged that other – more sympathetic – views were also expressed in the interviews, particularly by those who had become more immersed in modern Egyptian life and had made Egyptian friends.

Feelings about archaeology

The focus group respondents, children and adults, were almost wholly positive in their view of archaeology, seeing it as a virtuous search for artefacts with a 'Boys' Own' appeal:

I would like to find a flight of stairs in the rock. They found the Anubis seal and there were four rooms blocked off.

(child aged 9–10)

They don't give up that chance they'll find something. It's a hobby and the achievement of finding something becomes an obsession. Your moment of glory.

(Nile cruiser)

The researchers felt that some young men saw it as a kind of game 'as though the Egyptians had buried their artefacts, daring future generations to find them' (Fisher 2000: chart 38). There appear to be strong parallels between people's descriptions of archaeologists and fictional representations such as Indiana Jones or the Tomb Raider video game. This theme was echoed in an interview with a professional archaeologist, who had been inspired by the glamorous heroine of a Hollywood movie:

So the image that I had was her in a safari suit with leather boots, chiffon scarf and a pith helmet, which is what I always wanted to be.

(white, professional)

Among the focus group members the only person expressing disquiet about archaeology was a child:

If I found a tomb, I would leave them. I wouldn't want to be dug up when I should be resting.

(child aged 9–10)

Some of the in-depth interviewees shared this concern, in particular those who approached Egyptology from a mystical or religious angle:

> Being a spiritual person by nature, I'm not sure about the merit of digging up people's tombs, when they obviously put so much effort into preserving their own dignity.
>
> (white, amateur)

The interviewees for the most part were more aware than focus group members of the debates around the subject of excavation, and expressed more equivocal views. Arguments in favour of continued digging included the thirst for more knowledge and increased archaeological skills, the benefit to the local Egyptian economy, and the race against time in a climate of deteriorating environmental conditions. On the other hand there was an awareness that there already exists an enormous quantity of uncatalogued and inadequately conserved finds, a feeling that enough was known already, and that nothing was being left for future generations to discover. Most interviewees were ambivalent in their views.

However, there was a clear consensus among interviewees that finds should remain in Egypt – 'they belong to the country that they're in' (white, amateur) – with just one dissenting voice:

> Ultimately it depends on the arrangement between the Egyptian authorities and the excavators . . . who finances the digs and so on. You can't afford to be sentimental about that.
>
> (non-white, professional)

It was assumed by white focus group members that archaeologists would be white Europeans or Americans (Fisher 2000: chart 40):

> We sort of had to do it, as they couldn't be trusted to look after it themselves.
>
> (white adult)

Sadly, this perception was borne out by the personal experience of a number of professional Egyptologists we interviewed. A young British Egyptologist is contemptuous of the attitudes of some of her colleagues:

> I do see a heck of a lot of 'We're the foreigners, we're here, we're going to dig your country, we're going to tell you all about it, and you're going to sit and listen'. . . . It's astounding, it's, 'We don't speak to them because they're Egyptian'. It's, 'We do our thing, they do their thing'.
>
> (white, professional)

Whereas this Egyptian describes the struggle to be accepted as a trainee on a dig in his own country:

> Still, after all these years, you can see it in foreign expeditions digging in Egypt, it's all foreign, they are happy to take foreign students to train them, they never take Egyptian students to train them. . . . I had to force myself onto anybody to take me for training, nobody was interested. They just don't take Egyptians.
>
> (Egyptian, professional)

Some non-white focus group respondents had a conviction that finds and findings should be shared:

> I think they should acknowledge and apologise and keep partnerships. A commonwealth, where everything is catalogued.
>
> (non-white adult)

The following interviewee went further, suggesting that knowledge should be shared not only across nations, but between different interest groups in Egyptology, blaming academics for not making their work more accessible to lay or specialist audiences.

> There's enough information around for God's sake, the academics are sitting on it, they're not sharing it . . . And I find that is very controlling and manipulative . . . and they make it into something boring and dry and unapproachable. So if there's any academics listening, get your arses into gear and you'll be more popular.
>
> (white, amateur)

Contemporary relevance of Ancient Egypt

All the interviewees were asked what they felt the legacy of the Ancient Egyptians had been. Most responses referred to social or spiritual concepts. Perhaps surprisingly, only a few mentioned the physical remains such as art and architecture. Two interviewees made a link to the people themselves, one describing the Egyptians as a 'root race' (white, amateur), while the other, an Egyptian, referred to the 'relics of our own ancestors', both material and spiritual. Some of the black interviewees highlighted the connections between ancient Egyptian society and language with aspects of modern and traditional African life. Others pointed to the connections between ancient and modern Egyptian cultures:

> There is a gradual harmonious transport of ideas from ancient Egypt to Coptic Egypt to Islamic Egypt, and you just need to scratch the surface to see ancient Egypt.
>
> (Egyptian, professional)

For many, Egyptian society was represented in an almost Utopian way, for example, 'perfect' (white, amateur), 'tolerant' (white, professional), 'non-racist' (non-white, professional). One interviewee suggested it should be revived as a model society:

> Very dedicated, obedient, liked working in groups, team work and things like that . . . If we go back to those disciplined days . . . it would be good for everybody.
>
> (Egyptian, professional)

Many of the amateur Egyptologists interviewed were interested in the spiritual aspects of the subject, and this is reflected in their comments about the legacy of the ancients, which emphasise the mythic archetypes, mysteries and mysticism associated with Egypt. For some, a deep religious truth endures:

> They knew something about the after-life . . . there's something really important there, they're trying to say . . . they've left messages if you like.
>
> (white, amateur)

As one interviewee pointed out, 'legacy can mean different things to different people' (Egyptian, professional), and as the examples above show, the meanings attributed by the interviewees were indeed very personal, underpinning and supporting their fundamental belief systems.

Children and education

One area that would clearly repay further work is that of children's interest in Ancient Egypt (Figure 5.1). The focus group report described children's vision of Ancient Egypt as 'bursting with life . . . a magnificent adventure play-ground' (Fisher 2000: chart 8):

> I want to see a tomb, go into a tomb, get the curse of the mummy.
>
> (child age 9–10)

> They had mummies in Egypt. I would have tea with them if they came to life.
>
> (child age 9–10)

The primary-school teachers' survey indicated that 75 per cent of respondents chose the Ancient Egypt option, rather than one of the others, at least partly because 'pupils find it interesting or inspiring'. Leaving aside the National Curriculum requirement 'to study an ancient civilisation', selected by 86 per cent of respondents, children's interest was by far the most significant factor in choosing the option.

Figure 5.1 Schoolchildren handling ancient artefacts in the Petrie Museum. Petrie Museum of Egyptian Archaeology, University College London, 2003.

Even before the National Curriculum, some schools had taught about Ancient Egypt, sparking the interest of around one-third (32 per cent) of respondents to the students' survey. School was the most commonly chosen source of early interest in Egypt for this group (now mainly in their twenties and thirties). The survey also suggests that formal education is more significant than other media or catalysts (such as films, magazines, exhibitions) in laying the foundations for later interest. Given that, because of the National Curriculum, a higher proportion of children are receiving formal education about Ancient Egypt, it seems possible therefore that the schoolchildren of today are more likely than their counterparts in previous generations to become Egyptology enthusiasts. This raises questions about how that interest might best be fostered in secondary and higher education and in informal settings such as museums.

Conclusions for museums

This research provides museums like the Petrie Museum with a basis for audience development and communication on a number of levels, many of which it has not been possible to examine here in detail. For now the most significant implications, and questions, to consider appear to be these.

- **Broadening audiences**. In theory it should be possible for museums like the Petrie to serve both a general and a specialist audience; they share an immense enthusiasm for the subject matter. The research confirmed the strength and diversity of interest in Ancient Egypt. If museums can harness this appeal together with the considerable academic resources at their disposal they have powerful tools with which to inform and inspire people.
- **Children**. There is a need to understand the role of formal education, and of museum visiting as part of this, in developing children's evidently high level of interest in this subject. In the meantime the level of enthusiasm for the subject among children implies that a high priority should be placed on this audience.
- **Difficult subjects**. Museums now have to decide how hard they should try to 'burst the bubble' in various areas. How far should they temper their broadly educational mission with an acceptance of the interests, or lack of interest, of their audiences? For example:
- **Chronology**. It would appear that general audiences have little idea of and little interest in understanding the chronology of Ancient Egypt. Educational audiences are required to be more interested, but curricula have their own demarcations. Some of the periods represented in the Petrie Museum's collections, for example, appear to have significantly less appeal than others, and the museum will have to work harder to 'sell' these. Alternatively, it may be decided that a chronological presentation is not always appropriate.
- **Unappealing themes**. Both general and specialist audiences may be less receptive to certain themes that museums may feel it is important to cover, such as trade. Again more work and effort may need to be put into presenting these themes in an appealing way, or working them into more attractive subject areas.
- **Modern Egypt and archaeology**. Although modern Egypt is rarely if ever the theme of museums of Egyptian archaeology, it may be important to include Egyptian people and perspectives in the displays in order for visitors to engage. However, it also needs to be borne in mind that attitudes to modern Egypt among some of the target audiences are very negative, and there is apparently little general interest in the ethics of archaeology.
- **Race and colour**. This is not a theme traditionally addressed within academic or popular Egyptology, except by black historians. Many academics fight shy of it as impossibly complex, dangerous and misleading territory. For white audiences the question will be disturbing. Nevertheless if museums are to address black audiences it is a fundamental issue to tackle.
- **Using science**. There is widespread support for an open approach to the subject, one which is academically honest but allows for alternative readings and leaves some questions unanswered. There is a history of argument

and debate around many aspects of the subject and this could be present in displays. There is a general desire to know more about the science of archaeology; science and the techniques of archaeology could be a bridge between the academic and popular audiences.

- **Using romance.** Effective communication with general audiences will require museums to address (and probably use the appeal of) the 'mythic themes' generally associated with Ancient Egypt as a framework for understanding the objects in the collections. In practice this may be difficult to achieve. Some of the popular myths – that slaves built the pyramids – may be too entrenched for museums to counter, and some of the romance more powerful than the evidence.

- **What makes Egypt special?** For many people, including some professionals, the study of Ancient Egypt has a contemporary relevance of a social or spiritual nature. It will be a challenge to create museum displays that allow for and support these personal readings while at the same time enabling people to reflect on and question them.

Inevitably the next stage, as far as the Petrie Museum itself is concerned, will involve a good deal of trial and error, testing and evaluating the most effective means of presenting important issues, unimaginable chronologies, unappealing or contentious subjects. However, exploring the effective communication of difficult subjects seems an entirely appropriate area for a university museum. Inspiring a broader audience to research this subject in more depth, to ask informed questions and to reach new interpretations is an aim of which Amelia Edwards, this museum's founder, would probably have approved.

Each must interpret for himself the Secret of the Sphinx.

(Edwards 1877: xvii)

Bibliography

Brace, C.L. with Tracer, D.P., Yaroch, L.A., Robb, J., Brandt, K. and Nelson, A.R. 1996. Clines and Clusters versus 'race': the case of a Death on the Nile. In Lefkowitz, M.K. and Rogers, G.M. (eds) *Black Athena Revisited*. Chapel Hill & London: University of North Carolina Press.

Claire, H. 1996. *Reclaiming our Pasts: Equality and Diversity in the Primary History Curriculum*. Stoke-on-Trent: Trentham Books.

Edwards, A. B. 1877. *A Thousand Miles up the Nile*. London: Routledge.

Feder, K. L. 1996. *Frauds, Myths and Mysteries: Science and Pseudoscience in Archaeology*. Mountain View: Mayfield.

Fisher, S. 2000. *Exploring Peoples' Relationships with Egypt: Qualitative Research for the Petrie Museum*. Susie Fisher Group (unpublished report).

Hassan, F. A. 1998. Memorabilia: archaeological materiality and national identity in Egypt. In Meskell, L. (ed.) *Archaeology under Fire: Nationalism, Politics and Heritage in the Eastern Mediterranean and the Middle East*. London: Routledge.

Hilliard, A. G. 1994. Bringing Maat, destroying Isfet: the African and African diasporan presence in the study of ancient KMT. In Van Sertima, I. (ed.) *Egypt, Child of Africa*. New Brunswick and London: Transaction Publishers.

Howe, S. 1998. *Afrocentrism: Imagined Pasts and Imagined Homes*. London: Verso.

Janssen, R. M. 1992. *The First Hundred Years: Egyptology at University College London 1892–1992*. London: University College London.

Merriman, N. (ed.) 1999. *Making Early Histories in Museums*. Leicester: Leicester University Press.

Merriman, N. 2000. *Institute of Archaeology Teaching Collections: Staff Survey* (unpublished).

Montserrat, D. 2000. *Ancient Egypt: Digging for Dreams*. Glasgow: Glasgow City Council.

MORI. 2000. *Attitudes Towards the Heritage: research study carried out for English Heritage*. London: English Heritage. Available on English Heritage Website: www.english-heritage.org.uk

Motawi, S. 1998. *Egypt in the British Museum*. MA Dissertation. Institute of Archaeology, University College London.

QCA (Qualifications and Curriculum Authority) 1999. *History: the National Curriculum for England*. London: HMSO.

Reid, D. 1985. Indigenous Egyptology: the decolonisation of a profession. *Journal of the American Oriental Society* 105: 233–46.

Roth, A. M. 1998. Ancient Egypt in America: claiming the riches. In Meskell, L. (ed.) *Archaeology under Fire: Nationalism, Politics and Heritage in the Eastern Mediterranean and the Middle East*. London: Routledge.

Simpson, M. 1996. *Making Representations: Museums in the Post-Colonial Era*. London: Routledge.

Stone, P. G. and Molyneaux, B. L. (eds) 1994. *The Presented Past: Heritage, Museums and Education*. London: Routledge.

Thomas, R. 1998. Learning from Black Athena. *British Museum Magazine* Autumn/Winter: 12–15.

Trigger, B. G. 1984. Alternative archaeologies: nationalist, colonialist, imperialist. *Man* 19: 355–70.

Wood, M. 1998. The use of the pharaonic past in modern Egyptian nationalism. *Journal of the American Research Centre in Egypt* 35: 179–96.

Young, R. J. C. 1995. *Colonial Desire: Hybridity in Theory, Culture and Race*. London: Routledge.

6

PRESENTING ARCHAEOLOGY TO THE PUBLIC

Constructing insights on-site

Tim Copeland

Presenting archaeology to the public is not a new idea. Wheeler stated that 'It is the duty of the archaeologist to reach and impress the public, and to mould his (sic) words in the common clay of its forthright understanding' (Wheeler 1954: 224). However this vision of public involvement in archaeology was a long time coming to fruition as evidenced by M. W. Thompson's (1981) account of the preservation and display of ruins in which the public audience is notably absent. He discriminated between primary interpretation 'in which someone has to confront the ruin and give an intelligible account of it' and secondary interpretation (presentation), 'the popular transmission of this account, or the more interesting parts of it, to other people'. However, he was quite clear about the archaeologist's role: 'The latter is in part an educational function and requires different skills from the former with which we are concerned' (Thompson 1981: 84). This is to be contrasted with the view twenty years later: 'This background in education and self-fulfilment, distinguishing between information and understanding, is pervasive today as the ideal to be striven for in the presentation of heritage attractions' (Prentice 1993: 171). During the intervening period archaeologists have taken on the educational role in response to the increase in visits to heritage sites. The reasons were outlined by the publication *Visitors Welcome*:

> Good on-site presentation of the archaeological dig is good for raising awareness, good public relations and good for generating income and support for continued work . . . your visitors should go away interested in and understanding the value of digging up the past, and appreciative of the role of the archaeologist . . . Heritage is now a considerable marketable commodity.
>
> (Binks *et al*. 1988: 2–3)

Archaeologists wanted to inform opinion-makers: 'it is paramount that archaeologists consider the manipulation of public opinion to further the cause

of preservation of the record for the use and education of future generations'
(Bower 1995: 34). However the underlying motivation for presentation was
to further archaeological ends rather than for general purposes of education and
enjoyment.

Clearly, there has been a shift from a positivist approach, where the public
were told what to see, to a more open rationale of helping the public understand
what archaeologists do, why they do it and why they should continue to explore
the material evidence for the past. There has also been a recognition that there
are many publics who have varying motivations for consuming archaeology
including education, entertainment and countryside recreation (Goulding
1999). The results of this change of position have been seen in many highly
successful ventures in the United Kingdom. Presentations at The Jorvik
Viking Centre (Addyman 1994) and Flag Fen (Pryor 1989) have heightened
interest in archaeology and ensured that wherever possible the public is part
of its audience. Television programmes such as 'Time Team' and latterly 'Meet
the Ancestors' have been successful partially due to the efforts to communicate
with the public using everyday language and following the archaeological
process from site discovery to interpretation of the evidence. Similar successes
such as the Young Archaeologist Club and the English Heritage Education
Service have demonstrated that there is a growing wish on behalf of a wide
range of public audiences to understand and take part in archaeology, perversely
at a time when there are fewer and fewer opportunities for involvement in
excavation.

There does seem to have been an imbalance in the equation of archaeology
and the public in favour of the archaeologist (Smardz 1997). However, the
growing literature in the field of public archaeology indicates this challenge
is being faced. 'It is dangerously easy to present an interpretation without
giving careful consideration to what our audiences want and need, and without giving careful consideration to the social agendas embedded within our
own interpretation' (Potter 1997: 37). This attempt to consider meeting the
public's needs rather than just those that coincide with those of the archaeologist has been dismissed by Clark: 'All this interpretation is a very worthy,
if gently patronising activity, that makes archaeologists feel better, and leaves
the few members of the public who visit archaeological sites marginally less
baffled' (Clark 1998: 229) but West (1990) suggests that all too often the past
is idealised and packaged, not to invite challenge but to act merely as a
backdrop for leisure events that attract the paying public. This paper is an
attempt to explore the nature of interpretation and presentation of archaeological sites to the public using a constructivist perspective which is
particularly amenable to exploring how public needs are identified and the
meanings they put on the presentations they experience.

A constructivist approach to interpretation and presentation

The implication of a constructivist approach (Ballantyne 1998; Copeland 1998) is that individuals are constantly constructing and reconstructing meaning as they react with the world, negotiating thought, feelings and actions. A constructivist would assert that events do not exist 'out there' but are created by the person doing the construing. Something exists, but we cannot perceive it completely objectively. Hence, there is no such thing as an independent reality which we can know, describe and communicate in an absolutely true sense. What we experience is a dynamic interaction of our senses, perceptions, memory of previous experience and cognitive processes which shape our understanding of events. Individuals actively create experience and meaning which contribute to a form of personal construction of the world.

Individuals experience evidence either directly or indirectly, and internalise information about the source by selecting aspects which are significant to them. The selection of these aspects is determined by the individual's prevailing values, attitudes and previous experiences. New information is then adapted and a new construction is made or the previous construction is modified. Learning is most effective when there is a 'cognitive dissonance', a contradiction between what is previously thought and the new information, that causes the learner to question and explore concepts and derive their implication.

Constructivism which emphasises personal constructs as the essential way in which we construe the world has been referred to as radical constructivism.

> radical constructivism . . . starts from the assumption that knowledge, no matter how it be defined, is in the heads of the persons, and that the thinking subject has no alternative but to construct what he or she knows on the basis of her/his own experience. What we make of experience constitutes the only world we consciously live in.
>
> (Von Glasersfeld 1995: 3)

Another important aspect of this process is that social interaction can aid this type of learning by offering occasions for questioning and exploration of concepts in order to form a shared construction. This shared learning context is known as social constructivism.

A constructivist perspective is particularly apposite in examining aspects of the past, particularly archaeology, as the nature of the evidence dealt with is such that it may be interpreted in various ways by the viewer.

> 'Then', although it has happened, and cannot change itself, far from being dead is dynamic, for essentially it is a construct of our minds. In a very real sense it is our past (wherever we may be born or live), for, to a degree, we fashion it as we will rather than just accepting it as it is, never mind what it was.
>
> (Fowler 1992: 5)

James has commented that 'there could be as many interpretations of history – in effect, as many pasts – as there are social interests; and, ultimately, that the relation between history and society is worked out in action, even among visitors mingling at a monument' (James 1986: 47). Stanley-Price (1994) has discussed the various values ascribed to site preservation.

In terms of the problems of interpretation and presentation, a constructivist perspective is valuable in that it considers the prior knowledge and values of the viewer from what Falk *et al.* (1985) would define as 'the visitor perspective', as opposed to the 'exhibit perspective' where the nature of the exhibit and its expert interpretation are the dominant framework. Hall and McArthur (1993: 13) have suggested that traditional presentation management is 'deficient because it generally takes inadequate account of the human element in heritage management and especially the significance of visitors'. A constructivist approach is also congruent with Tilden's oft-quoted dictum that interpretation must connect the topic or place 'to something within the personality or experience of the visitor' (Tilden 1977: 9). The importance of creating cognitive dissonance to aid learning is also well matched to Tilden's definition of interpretation as 'an activity which aims to reveal meanings and relationships as an art, and revelations based upon information whose aim is not instruction but provocation' (Tilden 1977: 8–9). Krippendorf used the term 'animation' to emphasise the importance of learning, self-help, stimulation of self-creativity and self-participation through exploration in presenting heritage to the public. He defines animation as:

> giving a person the courage to come out of his (sic) shell; laying free what is buried; providing information, ideas and stimuli; creating favourable preconditions and setting an example . . . (it) should help remove barriers, it should encourage the exploratory spirit and openness for new contacts, thus making it possible to escape from isolation.
>
> (Krippendorf 1987: 142)

Figure 6.1 illustrates the main processes of a constructivist approach in examining the processes of interpretation and presentation of archaeology. In the literature interpretation and presentation are often used synonymously, though the term 'interpretation can also be used with the meaning of acceptable presentation to the public' (Fowler 1977: 185) . In this paper interpretation and presentation are separated into two interrelated and dynamic phases. The interpretation of a site or artefact is seen as an 'expert construction' which results in a presentation while the second phase is the 'public construction' where that presentation is used to construct meaning by visitors. Figure 6.1 demonstrates that at the heart of the presentation process is the necessity to provide aids and dialogues of translating experience into more powerful systems for the understanding of archaeology.

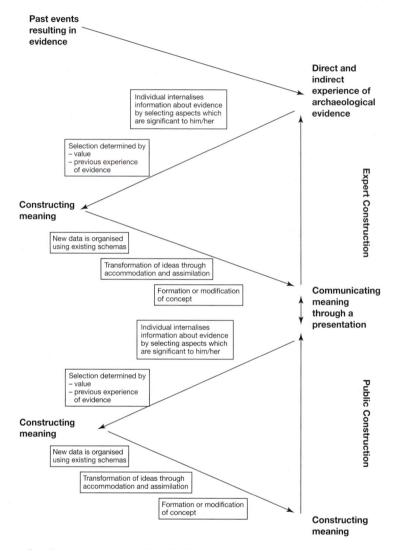

Figure 6.1 Constructions on archaeological sites.

The first phase begins when an archaeologist, or other expert, though not necessarily the excavator, has direct experience through handling objects or excavating the site, or indirect experience through the literature. A construction of the past is formed that will be unique to him or her and mediated through his/her own values and previous experience. Learning may take place in the process or previously held ideas and concepts may be reinforced. The formation or modification of concepts about the particular issue will be communicated to others through a presentation. The form of presentation should be congruent with the audience for whom it is intended. For other experts an archaeological discourse might be the most appropriate format, but for a range of other consumers it will be necessary to attempt to match the medium to the audience, and this includes the physical layout of the site as well as more formal educational media.

Touring a monument is a cultural negotiation between the terms laid out in presentation and the visitors' own pattern of interaction (James 1986: 51). Public visitors to archaeological sites or landscapes will often begin with the expert's presentation, but there may be other significant aspects to the visit such as companions or the setting. A similar process of construction will take place with the individual internalising aspects of the information, the selection of which is contingent on previous experience. This prior knowledge will also encompass formats of communication with which the individual is familiar and competent, the previous experience about a location or type of evidence. The values attached to the presentation will incorporate the reason for engaging with the evidence (casual tourist, amateur interest). If challenged by the presentation, fresh learning may take place and this meaning will be communicated usually verbally, but less frequently in writing or a visual format. This is an assessment point at which researchers can determine the meanings made on the site, and engage in a 'feed-back' loop of evaluation to the form of the presentation. Using this assessment of meaning, a reappraisal of the format of the presentation can be undertaken which will influence the expert values in relation to communicating with the public. The values of the interpreter need to be congruent with those of a variety of audiences and their previous experience of sites and presentational formats.

An improvement of presentations of archaeology to the public over the last two decades has been the result of increasing alertness to public constructions of the past, whereas previously this second phase was largely ignored by archaeologists and not evaluated. To ascertain the effectiveness of the presentation of archaeology to the public it would be more appropriate to identify successful presentations by discussing the evidence for public construction as detailed in research rather than to begin with the archaeologists' interpretation as this would compound old errors. Unfortunately there has been limited research into the use of archaeological sites (often referred to in the literature as 'heritage sites') by the public and much of what has been done is of a quantitative nature. This is particularly so in terms of research aimed at understanding public constructions on-site.

Representation formats

Representation formats are the most important aspect of presenting a site to the public, whether it is under excavation, permanently displayed or part of a 'heritage centre'. Table 6.1 summarises the main types of representation in use

Table 6.1 Representations used on archaeological sites

Enactive	Iconic	Symbolic
Experimental archaeology	Photographs	Plans
Touching	Drawings	Excavation reports
Re-enactments	Reconstructions	Audio tours
Walking around the site	3D views	Guided tours
	Models	Guidebooks
	TV programmes	Lectures
	Information panels	Information panels
	Maps	
	Multi-media presentations	
	The layout of the site	
	Directional signs	

on sites at the present time. It is based on Bruner's (1966) scheme categorising the representational media as enactive (through action), iconic (visual representation) or symbolic (in which words or numbers are the main device). Bruner also considered that increasing mastery of a concept, be it time, change, continuity, evidence, lifestyle or interpretation, needed to 'run the course of these three systems of representation until the human being is able to command all three' (Bruner 1966: 12). This implies a sequencing of formats of representation which will certainly overlap. It also implies that the most appropriate forms of communication for the inexperienced are the enactive and iconic formats, whereas those able to articulate concepts readily will be able to use symbolic forms also. Therefore, in order to foster constructions of the past from archaeological evidence the format of presentations will be crucial.

Prentice (1993) has pointed out that studies of the responses of visitors to the media used to present heritage attractions such as archaeological sites, as opposed to research in museums, are few in number. Herbert (1989) found that visitors to historic sites were strongly in favour of the provision of exhibitions of crafts, costumes and armour, but also favoured the partial reconstruction of ruined sites, re-roofing of rooms and 'events' portraying images of past happenings. Prentice (1993) undertook research into visitor preferences for presentational formats at archaeological sites on the Isle of Man. He concluded that in terms of tourist ratings, the media that were most successful in gaining and holding attention were models, including costumed figures; an introductory film or video; furnished rooms; directional signs; and live animals. There appears to be an emphasis on the enactive and iconic in these findings, which is supported by the public: 'When we stopped at Stonehenge we enjoyed going right up to the stones, touching them and even climbing on them. Surely this is the right use of such a place . . . Hands on Stonehenge!'(letter, 26 June 1999, *The Independent Weekend Review*: 2). Whilst some aspects of this behaviour are not to be encouraged, it is significant that an enactive format is seen as important to the visitor. Prentice (1993) also found that symbolic presentational media such as wall plates and panels, limited display of artefacts and guidebooks, were comparatively ineffective in encouraging tourist understanding.

Visitors' constructions

There are fewer studies of the constructions that visitors make on sites, and those that have been undertaken have been limited to the factual knowledge gained through interpretative media, ignoring what has been brought to the site by the visitor or what is taken away in personal experience. The main aim has been to identify whether the visitor has taken in what the archaeologist wishes them to. This is emphasised in Light's (1988) review of the problems of presentation as a means of on-site interpretation by visitors where he suggests that clear objectives are needed as to what a visitor is expected to achieve on a visit. This is emphatically an 'exhibit perspective' rather than a 'visitor perspective' (Falk et al. 1985). Prentice (1991:174) describes a study using multiple choice recognition tests to measure recall of higher education students at a Welsh monument and notes the lack of attention to interpretative media around the site. He comments that in terms of tourist visits such learning objectives cannot be to the fore. Prentice (1993) reports a similar multiple choice recognition test being used on Manx sites to test the benefits of visiting heritage attractions and suggests that tourist learning from information at such attractions cannot be assumed. Such positivistic identification of the meanings of archaeological sites for visitors ignores the prior learning and values of tourists and the meanings that they do make.

There is very little research into visitor experience at archaeological sites designed to explore the visitor perspective rather than that of the professional. However, Masberg and Silverman (1996) attempted to use a phenomenological approach with students in Indiana to assess what meanings heritage sites had for the participants and what they thought were the benefits of a visit. This research was not site-specific or undertaken at the time of the experience but retrospectively. However, the sites recalled were primarily archaeological sites: monuments, buildings and villages.

The research found that heritage sites were defined as having the past, or the past and culture, as the most important aspects. The salient aspects of the visit were:

- the activities engaged in, which were mainly enactive in nature such as walking around the site
- the presence of a companion
- the site personnel
- the information learned
- the built environment

- the natural setting of the site
- culture, defined as the ways of a people depicted or observed.

These factors illustrate not only the cognitive aspects of a site visit but also the importance of the social dimension in making meaning. Visitor outcomes were described as the knowledge gained, and personal experience such as the social benefits of significant interactions with companions and aesthetic experiences gained through the natural setting. Masberg and Silverman comment 'student visitors think of heritage sites as a mosaic of different aspects' (1996: 24), a combination of setting, landscape, people, personal experiences, and in the context of other places. This reinforces the importance of using prior learning, experiences and the values held by visitors in aiding the construction of learning.

In terms of the model illustrated in Figure 6.1, the research evidence illuminates some of the public's preferred presentation types and identifies some of the meanings made on archaeological sites. However, the process of constructing meaning is still a 'terra incognita' as far as research is concerned and there needs to be a further exploration of what people experience on sites, how they connect it to their prior experience and the values they attach to the materials they interact with.

The constructivist site

Moscardo (1996: 392) has discussed the circumstances that contribute to 'mindfulness' on heritage sites and which will result in more learning, higher satisfaction and greater understanding. These are detailed as:

- Visitors should be given variety in their experiences.
- Visitors should be given control over their experiences through opportunities to interact with or participate in the interpretation and good physical orientation systems.
- Interpretation needs to make connections to the personal experiences of visitors.
- Interpretation needs to challenge visitors, to question and to encourage them to question.

These aims are highly congruent with a constructivist approach, and Brooks and Brooks (1993) outline a number of constructivist settings for developing understanding which can here be adapted to an archaeological site context. Constructivist archaeologists undertake the following.

- *Encourage and accept visitor initiative.* While most members of the profession would endorse the idea that the public should be initiated into the way archaeologists think and work, the organisation and management structures on sites often militate against these goals. It is necessary to allow visitors to frame and articulate their own understandings, their own questions and to encourage searching for answers at different parts of the site.

- *Use primary sources alongside interactive and manipulative materials.* Allowing visitors to handle and see archaeological materials rather than just use interactive programmes and reading display boards encourages abstraction of ideas, rather than presenting a positivistic and 'expert' interpretation. Increasingly, it is the multimedia presentation that is used to engage the public without reference to primary sources. A variety of sources will also help to match visitor's individual learning profiles.
- *Use interpretation which asks visitors to classify, analyse and create.* Outlining the raw data and asking visitors to suggest a hypothesis helps them to make connections between contexts and create new understandings. Their own contributions are given value.
- *Use visitor responses to drive interpretation.* Careful evaluation of visitor prior knowledge and values when visiting sites allows the archaeologist to frame the presentation to suit the audience both in the long term of formal presentation programmes and in the short term of guided tours.
- *Inquire of visitors' own understanding of concepts before sharing their own interpretation.* When we give the public our own definitions and explanations of evidence, questioning by visitors of their own understanding is essentially eliminated. The 'expert view' dominates (Potter 1997: 43–4) and visitors are not motivated to 'waste their time' in developing theories if they are going to be 'wrong'.
- *Encourage visitors to engage in dialogue both with the expert and with each other.* Meaning-making is enhanced through social discourse as ideas are tried out with peers, and this is where change or reinforcement of concepts can occur most readily.
- *Encourage visitor inquiry by asking thoughtful, open-ended questions and encouraging visitors to ask questions of each other.* If archaeologists value their own opportunities to undertake enquiry and offer interpretations about the past they must also value it in others. Not only does archaeology rarely have the definitive response to a question, but questions to which there is only one 'correct' response do not encourage the public to think about what they see. The sharing of questions with peers also aids meaning-making.
- *Seek elaboration of visitors' initial responses to evidence.* Asking visitors to elaborate on their thinking enables an exploration of the public construction of sites and gives the opportunity for re-evaluation of an individual's initial concepts.
- *Engage visitors in experiences that might engender contradictions to their initial hypotheses and encourage discussion.* Understanding occurs when an individual revisits and reformulates a current perspective. Often visitors will come

to sites with tenaciously held views. By using questions that develop contradictions archaeologists can help develop thinking.

- *Allow time for posing questions and for students to construct relationships and create metaphors.* For a variety of reasons people are not prepared to respond to questions or other stimuli immediately. They need time to process information, and to do this before they are given an authoritative answer by the 'expert'. All of us create metaphors, to bolster our understanding of concepts. It is a way of understanding complex issues in a holistic way and to see what works. Archaeological sites and artefacts are extremely complex and we need to help the public to use their own experiences to forge similar scenarios in order to come to terms with this complex information.

Conclusion

Light (1987) suggested that interpretation and presentation are considered to be an art and Prentice (1993) considers that this is the reason why there has been little systematic assessment of either process. However, 'art' does usually not respond to the wishes of the viewer and tends to be the property of the maker and a form of self-expression. Clearly, in the case of presenting archaeology to the public there needs to be a two-way traffic of ideas and responsiveness on behalf of both archaeologist and the public and 'dialogue' might be a better term to describe the process. Archaeologists need to 'stop taking archaeology to the public for archaeology's sake and start doing it to meet the general public's educational, social, and cultural needs' (Smardz 1997: 103).

In this paper a constructivist approach has been used to highlight the processes that the public go through on an archaeological site and some of the ways in which archaeologists can help in aiding those constructions. Clearly not all sites are amenable to organisation in a manner to encourage constructivist approaches, but many of the most visited present a highly positivistic view of the past, almost a photograph of reality (Lewthwaite 1988: 86), rather than expressing the possibility of alternative views based on a wide number of interpretations and giving the opportunity for making personal constructions. The public may enjoy the spectacle but their learning and self-creativity are stunted by the presentation, and it is archaeology that is the loser in the long run.

A research agenda for heritage tourism must attend as a priority to evaluation if the users of heritage are to receive the benefits of an informed visit which they are seeking, however generalistic this requirement for information might seem to professional historians and archaeologists. The means of converting academic information into popular information should not fall to professional interpreters alone, for the translation of concepts into intelligible words and images also requires well grounded skills in identifying what is of relevance and setting these into a wider context.

(Prentice 1993: 231)

The nature of this current volume, and the increasing motivation on behalf of archaeologists to involve themselves with the public while taking cognisance of the public's needs, indicates that much progress has already been made in the profession's wish to present archaeology to a variety of audiences sympathetically and with integrity.

Bibliography

Addyman, P.V. 1994. Reconstruction as interpretation: the example of the Jorvik Viking Centre, York. In P. Gathercole and D. Lowenthal (eds) *The Politics of the Past*. London: Routledge.

Ballantyne, R. 1998. Interpreting 'visions'. Addressing environmental education goals through interpretation. In D. Uzzell and R. Ballantyne (eds) *Contemporary Issues in Heritage and Environmental Interpretation*. London: Stationery Office.

Binks, G., Dyke, J. and Dagnall, P. 1988. *Visitors Welcome. A manual on the presentation and interpretation of archaeological excavations*. London: HMSO.

Bower, M. 1995. Marketing Nostalgia: an exploration of heritage management and its relation to human consciousness. In M. Cooper, A. Firth, J. Carman and D. Wheatley (eds) *Managing Archaeology*. London: Routledge.

Brooks, J. G. and Brooks, M. 1993. *In Search of Understanding: The Case for Constructivist Classrooms*. Alexandria, Virginia: Association for Supervision and Curriculum Development.

Bruner, J. S. 1966. *Towards a Theory of Instruction*. Cambridge, Mass: Harvard University Press.

Clark, K. 1998. Review of 'Presenting Archaeology to the Public'. *Antiquity* 72: 275.

Copeland, T. 1998. Constructing history: all *our* yesterdays. In M. Littledyke. and L. Huxford (eds) *Teaching the Primary Curriculum for Constructive Learning*. London: David Fulton.

Falk, J. H., Koran, J. J., Dierking, L. D. and Dreblow, L. 1985. Predicting Visitor Behavior. *Curator* 19: 45–62.

Fowler, P. 1977. *Approaches to Archaeology*. London: A. and C. Black.

Fowler, P. 1992. *The Past in Contemporary Society: Then, Now*. London: Routledge.

Goulding, C. 1999. Interpretation and presentation. In A. Leask and I. Yeoman (eds) *Heritage Visitor Attractions: An Operations Management Perspective*. London: Cassell.

Hall, C. M, and McArthur, S. 1993. Heritage management: an introductory framework. In C. M. Hall and S. McArthur (eds) *Heritage Management in New Zealand and Australia*. Oxford: Oxford University Press.

Herbert, D. T. 1989. Does interpretation help? In D. Herbert, R.C. Prentice and C. J. Thomas (eds) *Heritage Sites: Strategies for Marketing and Development*. Aldershot: Avebury.

James, N. 1986. Leaving it to the experts. In M. Hughes and L. Rowley (eds) *The Management and Presentation of Field Monuments*. Oxford: Oxford University Department of External Studies.

Krippendorf, J. 1987. *The Holiday Makers: Understanding the Impact of Leisure and Travel*. London: Heinemann.

Lewthwaite, J. 1988. Living in interesting times: archaeology as society's mirror. In J. Bintliff (ed.) *Extracting Meaning from the Past*. Oxford: Oxbow Books.

Light, D. 1987. Interpretation at historic buildings. *Swansea Geographer* 24: 34–43.

Light, D. 1988. Problems encountered with evaluating the educational effectiveness of interpretation. *Swansea Geographer* 25: 79–87.

Masberg, B. A. and Silverman, L. H. 1996. Visitor experiences at heritage sites: a phenomenological approach. *Journal of Travel Research* 34: 20–25.

Moscardo, G. 1996. Mindful visitors: heritage and tourism. *Annals of Tourism Research* 23(2): 376–97.

Potter, B. P. Jr. 1997. The archaeological site as an Interpretive Environment. In J. H. Jameson (ed.) *Presenting Archaeology to the Public: Digging for Truths*. Walnut Creek, California: Altamira Press.

Prentice, R. C. 1991. Measuring the educational effectiveness of on-site interpretation designed for tourists. *Area* 23: 297–308 (London: Institute of British Geographers).

Prentice, R. C. 1993. *Tourism and Heritage Attractions*. London: Routledge.

Pryor, F. 1989 'Look what we've found' – a case study in public archaeology. *Antiquity* 63: 51–61.

Smardz, K. E. 1997. The past through tomorrow: interpreting Toronto's heritage to a multicultural public. In J. H. Jameson (ed.) *Presenting Archaeology to the Public: Digging for Truths*. Walnut Creek, California: Altamira Press.

Stanley-Price, N.P. 1994. Conservation and information in the display of prehistoric sites. In P. Gathercole and D. Lowenthal (eds) *The Politics of the Past*. London: Routledge.

Thompson, M. W. 1981. *Ruins: Their Preservation and Display*. London: Colonnade Books.

Tilden, F. 1977. *Interpreting Our Heritage* (3rd edition). Chapel Hill: University of North Carolina Press.

Von Glasersfeld, E. 1995. A constructivist approach to teaching. In L.P. Steffe and J. Gale (eds) *Constructivism in Education*. Hillsdale: Lawrence Erlbaum Associates.

West, A. 1990. Critical archaeology and black history. In F. Baker and J. Thomas (eds) *Writing the Past in the Present*. Lampeter: University College.

Wheeler, R.E.M. 1954. *Archaeology from the Earth*. London: Penguin Books.

7

ARCHAEOLOGY AND THE
BRITISH MEDIA

Neal Ascherson

Archaeologists, not only in the United Kingdom, profess themselves to be aggrieved at the exaggerations and misrepresentations which their profession attracts from the media. This is an old grievance, pre-dating the appearance of the early 'halfpenny press' and tabloid journalism at the end of the nineteenth century. But the fact is that for equally long there has existed a relationship between archaeology and journalism, a mutually profitable two-way relationship. The media seek news and stimulus from archaeology. In return, the profession has learned to manipulate and exploit media publicity with unexpected enthusiasm and success. It is probably true to say that archaeologists are more cunning and proactive in their handling of this relationship than news editors and reporters.

Media representations of archaeology

In the British press, at least, these are still founded to a surprising degree on nineteenth century images and stereotypes which were often caricatures even then. As numberless cartoons reveal, the archaeologist is conventionally imagined as a sub-species of explorer whose expeditions are conducted in distant and dangerous landscapes. He – it is usually an elderly he – wears a pith helmet and often commands armies of primitive local inhabitants who function as bearers, porters or diggers.

The persistence of this set of attributes is illustrated in the cyber-character of Lara Croft, heroine of the highly successful 'Tomb Raider ' computer games produced in the UK. Croft, in khaki hot-pants, glides through tomb-chambers seeking and often killing not only a variety of guardian-monsters but also villains of the illegal antiquities trade. She is only the most recent figure in a genre which reaches far back beyond Indiana Jones to late-Victorian thriller heroes like Rider Haggard's Allan Quartermain (in *King Solomon's Mines*, for instance).

The hegemonic press image of an excavation (or of 'the archaeological project', if you insist) remains the opening of Tutankhamun's tomb. This was the most lavish, sustaining and sustained feast ever offered to journalism by archaeology, as Lord Carnarvon and Howard Carter fed titbits to waiting reporters throughout the ten years (1922–32) of the operation. It is not entirely surprising that ancient clichés from that feast – themselves recycled from even more venerable Victorian clichés about archaeology – are still in circulation. The 'King Tut' story provided in abundance two elements which are still almost invariably sought by British journalists from every reported archaeological enterprise. These are 'Buried Treasure/Gold/Wealth', and 'Access to the Supernatural'.

'Buried treasure': the value question

Almost all media reports on archaeological finds or discoveries are required to include some information about value. The idea that something may be old, interesting and worthless is not acceptable. Archaeologists on a site will accordingly be asked the How Much Is It Worth question. An answer will be expected not only for a gold torque or coin find (items which can be said to have some sort of market price attributable to them) but for polished stone axes, beakers or fragments of painted wall plaster. If the excavator replies that in all honesty he or she has no idea of how much a corroded bronze rapier is worth, then it will probably be reported as 'priceless'.

Access to the supernatural

Exploration, that arch-Victorian pursuit, was represented as a challenge to some hostile environment of jungle, desert and 'savage tribes'. Archaeology, associated with exploration, was assumed to face not only those perils but also the 'mysterious forces' which might be guarding buried treasure. Lara Croft confronts scaly monsters in her crypts which are no more than the dragons which used to protect crocks of gold in their caves. The 'Curse of the Pharaohs' myth, so beloved by the old Fleet Street, seems to survive indestructibly (the e-mail bulletins of the Institute of Archaeology, in London, regularly carry appeals from newspaper or TV editors and researchers for 'experts' prepared to discuss the Curse of King Tut and the 'mysterious' fate of those who disturbed his rest).

There are two interesting points to be made here. The first is about the pedigree of such myths. They derive directly from a vast mass of spooky fiction produced in the last two centuries, ranging in quality from pulp chillers up to M.R. James's *Ghost Stories of an Antiquary* (James 1994), in which peculiarly horrible guardians of treasure abound. But that fiction, in turn, drew on a pre-existing corpus of legend and folk-tale, dealing with hidden treasures and the monsters or spirits appointed to watch over them (Westwood 1986). In Britain, at least, such tales were already current in the post-Roman centuries and may be much older. The mounds which open to the correct spell and display a chamber full of gold, protected by physical monsters, curses or time-shift enchantments, the Arthurian dragons standing sentinel over something buried or concealed in a cave . . . almost all these narratives in their countless variants contain a cautionary tale against intruders and tomb-robbers. This transition from oral tradition to twentieth century Fleet Street commonplace is also illustrated by the equally indestructible Loch Ness Monster stories. Nessie arrived in the tabloid press via the genre of 'monster unknown to science' fiction as practised by Conan Doyle and Jules Verne. But it derives ultimately from the marriage of Jules Verne to long-established Gaelic myths about the existence of 'water-horses' in fresh-water lochs (Adomnan 1995; Mackenzie 1972).

The second point is about the moral implication of such myths. Quite clearly, they convey a view of archaeology as transgression. One could syn-thesise, or ventriloquise, that view in terms like these: the act of excavation – or exhumation, or appropriation – was a breach of ancient, unwritten law, a gross and ominous crime even when it was licensed by some contemporary social authority. It was assumed that, in the far-off epoch when the deposit was made, society's leaders would have imposed a penalty for impious robbery and desecration. Now that penalty would be exacted by the dead ancestors or their monstrous agents, through the power of magic. While the twenty-first century mass media do not believe in dragons, it is apparent that they are still, on occasion, inclined to see the archaeologist as desecrator and violator. England produced a typical example of this instinct in 1999, following the discovery of so-called 'Sea-Henge' (a circle of timber uprights around a single massive, up-ended tree which came to light on the Norfolk coast). When it became clear to the public that English Heritage intended to remove the timbers for conservation and display elsewhere, New Age protesters who attempted to block the removal on grounds of magical integrity and chthonic piety received much sympathy and wide coverage from press and television. *The Guardian* reported on 16 June that 'an alliance of druids, eco-warriors and the head of a plant company won the first round yesterday in a seaside battle over Britain's only "sea-henge"'. The Press Association agency report the same day, syndicated to hundreds of press and broadcasting media throughout the country, tilted its report even more distinctly against English Heritage. It did so by emphasising the case of the objectors both in the space given to them and through the 'these-are-serious-people' language allotted to them: 'locals are battling to prevent English Heritage from moving the structure . . .', or 'Villagers in Holme Next The Sea have asked [the minister] to impose some form of listed building status on the structure . . .'. The chairman of the parish council was quoted at some length when he claimed that most locals wanted the monument to be 'left in the care of the sea'. In contrast, the English Heritage case for removing the timbers received only a single sentence.

Archaeology as nationalist/patriotic undertaking

The media are also apt to represent archaeology as the search for evidence of superiority – national or local. This superiority may be demonstrated in at least two ways: by evidence of priority, in settlement, development or the achievement of 'civilisation'; or by evidence of a higher cultural/technical level at a time/times in the past.

This is a competitive context. Superiority is required in order to support local, ethnic or national grievances or claims, to reverse the presumptions of an overbearing neighbour-nation or an arrogant national metropolis. As such, the search for superiority powerfully encourages the hankering for superlatives which is so strong an element in journalese: ' the earliest known . . .', 'the biggest in Europe . . .', 'the most valuable hoard . . .' and so on. Archaeologists will constantly be invited to proclaim a site or artefact to be 'unique'. If they cannot bring themselves to agree, then they will often be implored to state on record that the object is at least 'very unique'.

A second, more intriguing consequence of the 'superiority' discourse is the implicit assumption of continuity. For material evidence of the past to support that discourse, there must be some arguable connection between those who in remote times left that evidence and those today who are using it to promote their own claims. The media frequently suggest a direct biological link, as if contemporary inhabitants of a territory were the linear descendants of Neolithic or perhaps even earlier families in the area: 'these people were our forefathers'. Another approach is to suggest a retrospective continuity between all inhabitants of a specific territory regardless of their origins. In other words, all groups who ever lived in the lower Thames basin, even bands of hunter-gatherers, may be referred to as 'Londoners'.

Box 7.1, from a local newspaper, uses the well-known Mesolithic site at Star Carr, in Yorkshire, to claim that 'Yorkshire was the cradle of civilisation'. Two observations are worth making. The first is that, while the journalist's tongue here is to some extent in his cheek, the 'cradle of civilisation' slogan is spun to appeal to contemporary Yorkshire's deep-rooted resentment of the south of England, whose inhabitants are proverbially seen as effete, over-privileged and technically incompetent.

The second observation relates to the mutuality of the relationship between archaeologists and journalists. A close look at that newspaper cutting will suggest that the 'cradle of civilisation' line might not in fact have originated with a journalist. Instead, it may have been deliberately, if unattributably, floated by an archaeologist or somebody else associated with the excavation on the occasion of an organised media visit to the Star Carr site. The line, picked up and used by almost every journalist on that visit, certainly ensured wide, enthusiastic and friendly coverage in the papers they represented.

Box 7.2 refers to the 'Cramond Lioness'. Found in 1997, in the mud of the River Almond at Cramond near Edinburgh, the sandstone effigy of a lioness

Box 7.1 Yorkshire as the cradle of civilisation. Courtesy of *Yorkshire Evening News.*

'Cradle of civilisation' is found near Flixton

ARCHAEOLOGISTS have discovered that a site near Scarborough was home to a bunch of stone age sophisticates.

Evidence uncovered by a research team from Cambridge University and the Vale of Pickering Trust suggests that an advanced community of hunters thrived at Star Carr, between Seamer and Flixton, 10,000 years ago.

Their grasp of carpentry and animal husbandry was more advanced than their contemporaries in Europe and has drawn comparisons with Jericho and the Middle East – traditionally thought of as the cradle of civilisation.

Archaeologists have spent 13 years excavating the site at Star Carr and the new discoveries are the culmination of that work.

The excavation team found that the community living at Star Carr was so advanced that it knew how to make planks from trees and use them, and how to entice animals into the area so that they could be caught for food.

Planks which were used for a prehistoric wood track and lakeside jetty were made by splitting timber from trees using tools made from from the tips of deer antlers.

Researchers discovered that reed beds had been repeatedly set alight each spring for 300 years to encourage the growth of new shoots and to attract animals to the lake edge where they could be hunted.

Prof Paul Mellars, professor of prehistory and human evolution, at Cambridge University, said: "What we have found is extremely important. It is unique and shows that this community was more advanced than anything else in Europe at that time.

"Star Carr is a very well-known site and was first investigated in the 1950s.

"There is in fact a big display in the museum at Scarborough showing the early work that was done, but this is something new."

There is little at Star Carr today to suggest that a sophisticated Stone Age culture once thrived there.

A rubbish dump backs on to the site, with the soil fit only for growing potatoes.

(Stuart Arnold, *Evening News*, 11 May 1998)

devouring a warrior is thought to have formed part of an unknown funerary monument associated with the Roman fort at Cramond. It has been dated to the second or early third century AD.

The report comes from the Scottish edition of the London-based *Daily Mail* tabloid. The climate of the time was one of fervent national self-assertion in Scotland, and it may be thought that a popular newspaper fighting a bitter circulation war against Scottish-based rivals was anxious not to be outbid in the nationalism stakes.

There is no evidence whatever that the Lioness was 'meant to scare Scots'. Neither is there the slightest evidence that she was deliberately thrown into the river by 'the Scots in a defiant show of patriotic joy' when the Romans departed – not least because the Scots did not arrive in the land ultimately known as Scotland until some three or four centuries later. As for relations between the Roman military authorities and the local population – the large and technically proficient confederation known as the Votadini – they appear to have been quite cordial. Far from chafing under the yoke of the foreign occupier, the Votadini were more likely to have been well rewarded for supporting the Empire and its troops, and were probably distressed to see them go.

The media invented a totally spurious nationalist myth around the Lioness. But sensational discoveries can create problems for the curators of national tradition. Nothing remotely like the Lioness had been found in Scotland before, and she had to be integrated into the conventional account of the Scottish past – which in turn had to be modified to accommodate her.

'Lost civilisations'

The media appetite for news of vanished cultures more advanced than our own is old, but now expanding with unprecedented greed and urgency. The examples are endless. So are the names of those – including some with archaeological or other scientific qualifications – who are prepared to feed it. Any parascientific tale about Atlantis or about vanished white or sometimes black colonisations of the Americas appears capable of finding a market in the British media, above all in television.

In looking for an explanation, one clue is the enduring attraction to pseudo-science and journalism of ultra-diffusionist theory. There appears to be a compulsion to believe that all material culture, all languages and all belief-systems must have emanated from one central point. The difficulty of actually finding that central point is met by the proposal that it is 'sunken' – hidden on the ocean bed or obliterated by flood, meteorite, eruption or earthquake.

Why, though, should ultra-diffusionism exert such allure? One plausible explanation is that this is a way of clinging unconsciously to the ideology of Empire. The imperial self-image – British, Russian, German, French – was of a superior civilisation destined to send its elites across the world to spread their

Box 7.2 Newspaper coverage of the discovery of the Cramond Lioness. Courtesy of the *Daily Mail*.

Roar for a lion after 1,600 years in mud

WHEN the Romans erected a tomb to commemorate the burial place of one of their most powerful warriors, they probably did not give much thought to how much commotion it would cause 1,600 years later.

But yesterday an excited crowd of 200 watched in biting cold for more than two hours as archaeologists mounted a military-style operation to bring a rare piece of history gently into the 20th century.

A one-ton statue, which marked the tomb, was found in the murky waters of Cramond Harbour on the banks of the River Forth, near Edinburgh, last week.

The terrifying image of a lioness devouring a man was intended to scare and intimidate the people who lived under Roman rule. But when the Romans departed, the Scots in a defiant show of patriotic joy, threw the sandstone monument into the River Almond, according to experts.

It lay undiscovered until last week when ferryman Robert Graham noticed the carved head protruding from the water. He called in council archaeological experts who were astounded.

The stone lioness is the only one of its kind to be found in Scotland and only the fourth to be discovered in Britain.

Yesterday, as the salvage operation got under way, one village local said: 'The last time there was this many people in Cramond was probably when the villagers threw it in after the Romans left.'

A team of five archaeologists, headed by Mark Collard, have been working at the site since last week. Yesterday, after two hours and a roar of approval from spectators on the harbour walls, the lioness was lifted from the muddy pit where she has lain since the third century and placed in a truck.

Mr Collard said: 'People have often asked me what is the most interesting thing I have found; now I have an answer for them.'

Ferryman Mr Graham, 36, who lives opposite the site, said: 'It will be a wrench to see it moved. I don't feel any pride for finding it, I was just very lucky.'

Experts say the statue dates from the second or early third century and is a fine piece of Roman provincial art with a great deal of detail still visible.

Mr Collard said: 'It depicts a big cat holding down the shoulders of a male figure with its front paws, with the man's head in its jaws. 'It is miraculous that the construction of concrete foundations for the ferry steps in the 1930s did not damage the statue, as they are less than six inches from the head of the lioness.

'The subject matter has been interpreted as showing the destructive power of death, represented by the lioness, or guarding the dead person in their tomb.'

Remains of a Roman fort overlook the site and the latest find may be the starting point for a larger examination into the use of the River Almond by the Romans. The statue and a plinth were transported to a conservation centre to be restored.

Mr Graham will be entitled to an award under the Scottish law of Treasure Trove, which is administered by the Crown Office. An independent panel of experts will decide where the sculpture should be exhibited.

(Andrew Walker, *Daily Mail*, 21 January 1997)

technical, cultural and even spiritual attainments to lesser breeds. To remain convincing, this image required that the attainments of the lesser breeds should be impressively inferior. Much as the white Rhodesians felt compelled to believe that black Africans lacked the intelligence and skills required to have constructed Great Zimbabwe, which they ascribed variously to lost white tribes, 'Phoenicians' or Arabs (Mallows 1985), so media treatment of archaeological themes has often exaggerated the technical sophistication of prehistoric monuments in order to leave them explicable only by the thesis of visitors from lost civilisations. To synthesise once more, a typical article might ask: 'Who were these mysterious high priests of a vanished culture who taught Stone Age folk to build megalithic calendars predicting star positions to within a single degree of accuracy?'

And it takes only a glance at the UFO and intergalactic entertainment industry to recognise a similar ideological structure: a second, closely related image of imperial ultra-diffusion. Colonial Secretaries, from about the middle nineteenth century on, drew a distinction between 'empty' territories (i.e. cleared of their indigenous population by genocide or deportation) where the white race might settle, and those indelibly black and fever-ridden coasts from which wealth might be extracted but where permanent European settlement was considered impossible.

Once those places had 'risen' from the status of colonial trading-ports with hinterlands to full tropical colonies complete with Governor, there arose the idea that the colonial presence itself should be only temporary. At some time in the future, those black colonies would be ripe for self-government or even independence. Then the white visitors of the *mission civilisatrice* would fade away and efface themselves, their task completed. In the same way, almost all science-fiction narratives end with the departure of the superior aliens to their own galaxy. They educate and/or destroy, and then, leaving their hosts to absorb the incredible technology they leave behind them, they vanish.

The archaeologist as mad professor

Something has already been said about the 'explorer' associations in many media representations of archaeology. Another, related expectation – also drawn from nineteenth century stereotypes – is the archaeologist as academic street-fighter. Victorian memories of the great scientific controversies, slugged out in public debate between bearded giants of the intellect, encourage editors to hope for duels between personalities. It is assumed that any announced discovery, in archaeology or any other scientific discipline, is one professor's victory but the shattering defeat and discrediting of another.

It was difficult to set up media cockfights between British archaeologists during the first half of the twentieth century, as a period of cautious positivism succeeded the vast generalisations of the late Victorian period. But it has been easier in the last 30 years or so, as genuine full-scale intellectual controversy revived. At the same time, journalists find it much harder to personalise profound theoretical disagreements into annihilating vendettas between rival protagonists. Feuds may still be common between archaeologists, but they generally have roots in personal antipathies or bureaucratic competition for careers and funding. Spectacular collisions between archaeologists now seldom arise, as they so often did a hundred years ago, from a head-on clash of interpretations. This means that really important debates within the profession are hard for journalists to identify, unless archaeologists take the trouble to bring them to media attention in a succinct and intriguing form.

Other media stereotypes

In *Antiquity and Man* (1981), a volume of essays published in honour of Glyn Daniel, Warwick Bray contributed a chapter on 'Archaeological Humour' in which he identified three satirical representations dear to the media, and especially to cartoonists.

The first is the 'archaeologist as explorer' image. Bray wrote: 'He comes in various forms, from the cartoonist's stand-by (an endearing, incompetent figure in pith helmet and baggy shorts, with ill-concealed inclinations towards lechery) to the tough and somewhat sinister characters of popular fiction'. The second image is the 'archaeologist as collector': sometimes with a ruthless acquisitive obsession, sometimes enthusiastic but gullible. The third is the archaeologist as 'antiquarian scholar', which Bray elaborated as follows:

> he or she is slightly dotty, single-minded, elderly and rather dull, incompetently amorous, possessive about data, jealous of reputation and concerned with matters of no relevance to the world of real life – in short, a natural candidate for that much quoted, but alas! apocryphal Directory of Archaeologists Broken Down By Age and Sex.
>
> (Bray 1981: 227)

Bray goes on to remark that, while the world changes, these images do not. There was an immutable 'Archaeologyland' in which cavemen, dinosaurs, missing links and lost tribes continued to cohabit. Acutely, Bray identified the startling anachronism, even archaism, of this imagery:

> The Explorer, the Collector and The Antiquary have been with us, virtually unchanged, for well over a century. The archaeological milieu they inhabit is that of the bygone imperial era so engagingly described by Sir Leonard Woolley in his reminiscences (1961), a time when great museums behaved like institutional private collectors and even the 'official' archaeologists dug as much for loot as for information. And there, at about 1939, the clock stopped. For the majority of people

> ... the technical and intellectual developments of the last 40 years
> have never taken place.
>
> (Bray 1981: 228)

But Bray's witty account of Archaeologyland needs to be qualified. He is right about the archaisms, and right to see the 1930s as the moment when 'the clock stopped' for the media. It is not fair, however, to assume that 'the majority of people' are locked into these representations. The popular media are an exceedingly bad guide to the state of public knowledge about a branch of science, and the media claim to mirror and even to create public opinion is misleading. Newspapers, especially, may stick for decades, even generations, with obsolete formulae about what their readers like or know. Meanwhile, the real quantity and quality of knowledge among the general public changes rapidly.

Nowhere is this more true than with the popular grasp of archaeology. News and features editors may continue to cater for readers who like jokes about cavemen, dinosaurs and boffins in baggy shorts. Archaeologists often enjoy them too. But the readership section which seriously perceives archaeology in those images is now elderly and diminishing. Most readers, especially the young, will have come into contact with working archaeologists at some time in their lives. They see the profession as about local finds of pottery and stone tools, rather than of gold and silver in remote lands. Many of them have enjoyed books or television programmes about early hominids or 'Celtic Civilisation'. There is an expanding awareness that there are arguments about where *Homo sapiens* developed or how agriculture began, and there is a big non-specialist audience which finds these debates interesting (witness the audience averaging 2.5 million for BBC-2's recent five-part television documentary on the Neanderthal problem). The tide of interest in modern archaeology and its concerns is still rising.

Why, then, are British news editors so often stuck with stereotypes which were obsolescent even by 1939? To answer that fully would require a digression into media studies. But it is important to remember that it was not just for archaeology that the tabloid clock stopped some 60 years ago. The whole ethos of those newspapers is a relic: the weirdly dated slang, the lickspittle yet resentful servility to 'rank', the grotesque double standards about sexuality, all derive from the Fleet Street formula of the 1930s.

In fairness, the media have also made positive contributions to archaeology. There have always been editors and journalists, some of them formidably learned, who specialised in historical and archaeological stories. While no British newspaper today would employ a full-time Archaeology Correspondent, most serious papers have a 'Heritage Correspondent ' who relies on a network of freelance journalists trying to market specialised stories about the past and its exploitation – and archaeology is a profitable freelance specialism in this sector. However, the pressure to hype or distort stories about archaeology continues. This is in part because most archaeology stories in newspapers are consigned, by tradition, to news pages rather than feature pages. Archaeology is still reckoned to be about discovering things – 'finds ' – and a discovery is a news story, not a more reflective feature offering space to discuss background and implication. This means that the freelance is trying to sell the story to a newsdesk in competition with 'Judge Charged With Drunk Driving' or 'Council Tenants Storm Housing Committee'.

Hyping archaeology stories for sale to a busy news desk is a rare skill. One technique, perfected by *The Independent's* legendary David Keys but widely imitated, is the 'Even in Those Days . . .' gambit. To invent an example, a story might begin: 'The Romans Had An Answer to High Street Gridlock. Archaeologists in the Roman city of Verysillium have unearthed alterations to the street plan, designating streets one-way in busy shopping areas . . .'. This could introduce a perfectly respectable report on new evidence that Verysillium's market quarter was replanned after a fire in the second century. At the tabloid end of things, 'Did Skinheads Build Stonehenge?' could be the way into a news story about a Wiltshire hoard including a bronze blade which might have formed part of a hair-shears. And so on.

In contrast, television – carrying little baggage from that distant period of the 1930s – has found it easy to move into the gap and provide lively archaeological programmes which deal with the profession's real concerns and excitements. But this success was not only a matter of historical timing. In Britain, where television broadcasting began in earnest in the 1950s, a group of well-established archaeologists took the initiative and dominated the planning and presenting of the first generation of archaeology programmes. Glyn Daniel and Sir Mortimer Wheeler launched 'Animal, Vegetable, Mineral?' for the BBC as early as 1952 – a high-spirited and long-lived series in which the presenters were challenged to identify objects placed before them and to hold forth on their associations. AVM was followed by 'Buried Treasure' and then, in 1966, by 'Chronicle'.

But the archaeologists, inevitably, were gradually dethroned by professional TV presenters. British television today has plenty of regular programmes devoted to archaeology, Heritage or 'the past' in general. Their quality of research and – potentially – of information can be high, in terms of what is being discussed. Too frequently, though, much of that quality is thrown away by the dominant style of presentation: often an approximation to the hectic, garish gabble of breakfast entertainment TV. A good many of today's pro-gramme researchers have degrees or experience in archaeology. But their work is filtered through the producer's and presenter's constant anxiety to avoid 'being boring'. In consequence, the outcome can be trivial, and sometimes misleading. 'Time Team', a hugely successful archaeology programme launched by Britain's Channel 4 in 1991, shows symptoms of this sort of pressure, above all through the constraint of having to complete the fieldwork shown within three days. On the other hand, this is one of the first television treatments to concentrate on the aims and methods of excavation, rather than on 'finds'. This is a highly significant change, given that it rests on research by programme planners which suggests that modern TV audiences are as fascinated by the process of investigation as by the objects which may – or may not – come out of the earth (Cleere 2000).

How archaeology uses the media

Archaeology, in Britain as in some other countries, is well down the road to privatisation as the third millennium opens. In this situation, the profession must constantly and proactively use press, radio and television, or perish. As state support and funding shrivels, the media have proved able to offer several different services to archaeology.

One, an old-established practice, is the sponsorship by newspapers or other media of expeditions and excavations. This is a speculative bargain: we finance your operations in return for exclusive rights to publish the stories and pictures which the dig provides. In the 1920s, Mortimer Wheeler sold exclusive coverage of his excavation of the Roman legionary amphitheatre at Caerleon to the *Daily Mail*, and a few years later made a similar deal with Pathé Newsreels to finance his work at Verulamium. In the 1960s, *The Observer* had at least a participating sponsorship role in Yigal Yadin's spectacular excavations at Masada, and put money into the dig at Cadbury Castle. *The Sunday Times* underwrote and reported on the sensational discoveries at the Roman sites of Vindolanda and Fishbourne. BBC television invested in the digging of an investigatory tunnel under Silbury Hill, in the Avebury complex, but – to the sponsor's vexation – practically nothing 'visual' was found to justify the expenditure.

It would be fair to generalise that in almost all these bargains, archaeology – or at least archaeologists, their careers and to some extent their students – came off best. The media took a chance with their money, but were much less likely to feel afterwards that they were the exploiters rather than the exploited.

A second service which the media can provide is to promote and sustain a generally saleable image for the profession – archaeology as an approvable cause which is lumped into the whole patriotic heritage industry. This positive sort of coverage can reach the really big individual or institutional donors, suggesting to them that support for an archaeological trust is good business in many different ways, of which tax avoidance is only one.

Equally important, the media and television in particular are not only recruiting new generations to the profession, but successfully persuading the public to identify with archaeology as an occupation. Archaeology ceases to appear awe-inspiring and alien – an activity typically ordered and carried out by higher authority – when you can see schoolchildren who might be your own enjoying themselves at casual jobs on a site, or when you can encounter on screen a group of foul-mouthed, mud-caked practitioners who are patently not mad professors from another planet but plebeian individuals recognisable to you or me.

And, in conclusion, it must be repeated that the profession itself has shown a talent for journalism, individual self-promotion and the manipulation of publicity which nobody could have predicted a couple of generations ago. In Britain, at least, this is the factor which more than any other has ensured that the media–archaeology relationship has been a two-way one. The first academics to become famous TV personalities in Britain were archaeologists. Long before history professors or Nobel laureates of physics established themselves on screen, millions of women lusted after Sir Mortimer Wheeler as he flashed his great moustache at something which might have been a toy, a gaming piece or a ritual object.

The proactive media skills of the profession mean that editors seldom have to go out and seek archaeological stories these days. Everyone knows of cases where the director of an excavation tries to keep his site as private as a vampire funeral, but these are the exceptions. It is more normal to find the digger on the fax or e-mail, putting his or her own spin and hype into a press release, expertly laying out wares for the media market. The excavator will usually contact the local press and broadcasting outfits in order to arrange a site visit; the archaeological team will be trained to know how much a non-scientific reporter in a hurry can be expected to take in, or how a rubble wall-core or a line of postholes can be made to look alluring to the cameras.

Most archaeologists, moreover, are now aware that their work ought if possible to be set in the context of the living community around them. Most try to learn the skills of, for example, convening and running village-hall meetings at which the digger and the priest, the farmers and the commuters all talk about what ought to happen to 'our bones' in the end. And this sort of process, which in one sense is the democratisation of archaeology and in another its *aggiornamento* – the overthrowing of the mental barriers which kept archaeology 'in the past' – is also the grassroots level of a new relationship with the media.

Archaeologists, in short, are no longer waiting resignedly to be asked all the wrong questions. Through their growing media skills, they are able not only to set the agenda for the debate about what they are up to, but to pose many of the questions themselves. And these include the most interesting question of all: 'What does what I am doing mean to you? '

Bibliography

Adomnan. 1995. *Life of Columba*, translated by R. Sharpe. London: Penguin.

Bray, W. 1981. Archaeological humour: the private joke and the public image. In J.D. Evans, B. Cunliffe and C. Renfrew (eds) *Antiquity and Man: Essays in Honour of Glyn Daniel*. London: Thames & Hudson.

Cleere, H. 2000. Behind the scenes at Time Team. *Public Archaeology* 1(1): 90–2.

James, M.R. 1994. *Ghost Stories of an Antiquary*. London: Penguin.
Mackenzie, O. 1972. *A Hundred Years in the Highlands*. London: Bles.
Mallows, W. 1985. *The Mystery of the Great Zimbabwe*. London: Hale.
Westwood, J. 1986. Albion: *A Guide to Legendary Britain*. London Guild.
Woolley, L. 1961. *As I Seem to Remember*. London: Allen & Unwin.

8

TOWARDS A MORE DEMOCRATIC ARCHAEOLOGY?

The Internet and public archaeological practice

Carol McDavid

Introduction

It is now commonplace to point out that the Internet is the fastest-growing communication medium that humankind has yet invented. Indeed, some of my taken-for-granteds are that all of this book's readers will know what the Internet is,[1] and that they use it more or less regularly – for e-mail, to participate in online discussion groups, to view web sites, or to transmit other sorts of information electronically.[2] I also suspect that even if the readers of this book have not actually used the Internet to present their work to the public, most have considered it. A quick search of Internet web sites (using the 'search engines' Yahoo©, Google©, and Altavista®) reveals that at the time of writing (2001) there are between 1,060,001 and 1,870,000 Internet web sites that either deal with or are about archaeology.[3]

Even taking into account the extremely slippery nature of those numbers (and the certainty that some of those web sites focus on, say, Foucauldian archaeologies instead of the sort being examined in this book) it is apparent that archaeologists and their publics are embracing this new technology in huge, and growing, numbers. There are archaeological web sites that are primarily gateways to other archaeological web sites,[4] those that focus on universities, organizations, exhibitions, and journals,[5] and those in which archaeologists discuss and present their data.[6] Some sites are devoted to archaeology and children,[7] and several include interactive elements such as discussion forums, questionnaires and feedback forms. Quite a few of these web sites were not created by archaeologists, but, rather, by other people using archaeological information for their own purposes[8] (some of which are disconcerting to archaeologists; Meskell 1997). In any event, there are far too many archaeological web sites for any archaeologist interested in communicating with the public to ignore.

It is also safe to assume that most archaeologists today do believe that this sort of communication is important and worthwhile. What is, perhaps, not as commonplace is the idea that it should take place in democratic, open ways, so that people with diverse points of view can question our archaeological interpretations, and so that we can respond to these questions seriously. As more and more archaeologists embrace the view that 'multiple voices' should participate in conversations about the past (e.g. Hodder 1999; McDavid and Babson 1997; Meskell 1998; Schmidt and Patterson 1995), the Internet would appear to hold much promise as a forum for this sort of 'democratic' interactive and multivocal discourse (Bolter 1991; Landow 1992; Rheingold 1993).

Whether it actually does so is, of course, another matter. In this paper, I will examine the question of the 'democratization' of cyberspace by tacking back and forth between two levels of analysis. The first level of scrutiny is directed at the particular, in that it draws on the systematic study of one archaeological web project, the Levi Jordan Plantation Web Site (McDavid 2002a, 2002b, 2003). Therefore, I will first situate this particular project in practical/ technological, disciplinary, and sociopolitical terms. Broadening my gaze, I will then provide an overview of the recent 'state of the Net', especially as this relates to the particular audiences I wish to reach with the Jordan site. The objective of doing this is three-fold: to provide a sense of who it is that we reach when we use Internet web sites to talk about archaeology; to argue that we must be sensitive to this sort of data as we participate in this new communicative environment; and to provide resources for others who want to review data pertinent to their own projects.

I will then re-narrow my focus to discuss two concepts central to any web site: interactivity. First, I will comment on interactivity generally, and then will discuss some of the specific strategies used by Jordan project collaborators (both archaeologists and local citizens) to build in interactivity *outside the technology*. Next, I will critically examine two interactive components of the Jordan web site that are made possible *within the technology*: an online discussion forum (including a brief comparison to forums at other archaeological web sites) and the personal e-mails and feedback forms received from members of the public throughout the period of this case study.

My discussion of the Jordan data, and data from other sites, may seem at times to be somewhat particularistic and anecdotal. I make no apologies for this, as it is important to remember that my observations are, like all good archaeology, rooted in the realities of *practice*. These examples must be seen as firmly situated within the historical particularities of individual experience – my own and others. Drawing on these experiences, I will conclude this paper with some more general observations about whether the Internet can be a part of a more 'democratic' archaeology.

One point of view: the Levi Jordan Plantation Internet Project

For the past several years I have been involved with a project in which archaeologists and local citizens are collaborating to create an Internet web site to discuss the politically and emotionally charged archaeology of the Levi Jordan Plantation (located in the rural community of Brazoria, Texas, USA; McDavid 1998b). We are attempting to see whether 'the Net' can provide a way for the descendants of both African-American and European-American residents of this plantation to conduct critical dialogues with archaeologists, with each other, with people elsewhere – and with 'the past' (McDavid 1998a, 1999, 2002a, 2002b, 2003).[9] If we want to use the Internet to create meaningful, open 'conversations' (Rorty 1995: 122) with our publics, we have to understand the limits of the technology, and how to reach beyond it – therefore, part of my interest is practical and technological.

However, my work is also firmly situated within specific disciplinary and political frameworks, in that it represents one segment of a growing movement within American historical archaeology to share control of archaeological research with the people who are most affected by it – the living descendants of the individual people who left the material and historical remains that are the object of study (LaRoche 1997; McCarthy 1996; McDavid 1997a; Roberts and McCarthy 1995). It is part of an even more general move to embrace the inherently political nature of historical archaeological practice (Leone et al. 1987; Handsman and Richmond 1995; Potter 1994) particularly as this pertains to archaeologies which study and publicly interpret the lives of previously enslaved and disenfranchised peoples (Agbie-Davies 1999; Bograd and Singleton 1997; Brown 1997; Leone et al. 1995; McDavid and Babson 1997).

These political frameworks extend to engagements with local, community, 'everyday' politics, in that the archaeological research itself sometimes reveals fresh (and sometimes contested; McDavid 1997a, 1999, 2000) information about political and social relationships between people who owned, or were owned by, each other (Brown and Cooper 1990; Brown 1994; Barnes 1998, 1999). Individuals in Brazoria, Texas, are still negotiating issues of power and control – issues that spring from their ancestors' relationships during the slave and tenant period (Barnes 1998; McDavid 1997a; Powers 1994; Wright 1994). Contemporary aspects of these relationships do not necessarily play out in predictable ways, as I have discussed elsewhere (McDavid 2000, 2002a, 2002b, 2003), but they do play an active role in the ways that this Internet project has developed. In this context, archaeologists cannot evade being part of the local political scene, and cannot evade the necessity of dealing reflexively, critically and responsibly (Leone et al. 1987; McDavid 1997b; Potter 1994) with the power we hold as members of the academic establishment. We must also be aware of the flow between these local contexts and national/global ones.

As Lynn Meskell put it:

> The past is not a static, archaic residue, rather it is an inherited artefact which has an active influence in the present through the interplay of popular and officially inscribed meanings . . . An aware, responsible and engaged global archaeology might be a relevant, positive force which recognises and celebrates difference, diversity and real multivocality . . . In the process, knowledge and culture can be reworked, and with them, power and politics . . . Engagement is the first step.
>
> (Meskell 1998: 4–5)

Engagement, in the case described here, refers to both engagement with one local community (with its own needs and agendas) as well as engagements with 'publics' that extend beyond local audiences to audiences across the globe. The Internet provides both the impetus for, and a location for, these engagements. The next question is, therefore, whom do we reach when we use the Internet to discuss our work?

Who is on the Net? Why should we care?

Statistics about Internet usage are extremely difficult to pin down, not only because they change so quickly, but also because there are no standard protocols for measurement. Indeed, both factors make it very difficult to write *about* the Internet *outside* the Internet, in 'permanent' media such as books and journals; by the time this volume is published, it is certain that the figures here will be out of date. The web sources cited here should, however, continue to be available, and readers should be able to access them for current data relating to other projects as needed. Much of the data discussed here will focus on the United States, but will highlight information about minority and rural use of the Net (as described above, the audience for the Jordan web site includes, or ideally should include, African-Americans and rural citizens. It is therefore necessary to be concerned with the ways that they do – or do not – use the Internet).

Data updated in November 2002 (NUA 2002) suggest there are about 605 million users of the Internet, worldwide. About 190 million of those users are in Europe, and some 182 million in the US and Canada. The remaining users are divided between Africa, Asia/Pacific, the Middle East and Latin America, with most of those located in Asia/Pacific (almost 105 million; NUA 2000). By the year 2003, some sources predict that there will be 545 million user acounts worldwide (Datamonitor 1999). Others predict that two-thirds of US homes will have Internet access (Yankee Group 1999) and that one-third of European homes will be on the Net (Datamonitor 1998) by that date. It is apparent that the Internet is still primarily used by people in the so-called

'Western industrialized nations', and will be for some time (although trends suggest that this is slowly changing, particularly in terms of online access in Asia; see Conlin 1999; NUA 2002).

Although Internet use (in the United States at any rate) is moving quickly towards 'critical mass' (Novak and Hoffman 1998), it is not true that this rapid growth is balanced equally amongst various ethnic and geographic groups. African-Americans, Hispanics, and Native American groups tend to access the Internet at lower rates than European Americans (Novak and Hoffman 1998; GVU 1998; NCIA 2000). Rural access is lower than urban access, and the American South (where the Jordan project is located) trails in Internet access across the board (NCIA 2000; Novak and Hoffman 1998). At the lowest income levels, people in urban areas are more than twice as likely to have Internet access than people earning the same income in rural areas (NCIA 2000).

There is some good news, however. Although this 'digital divide' still exists, online access is increasing in all demographic groups and geographic locations, in terms of raw numbers (NCIA 2000; Novak and Hoffman 1998, Pew Internet Project 2000). In addition, the divide between whites and blacks[10] at the higher income levels has narrowed considerably in recent years (NCIA 2000, Pew Internet Project 2000). One study indicates that, in the US, Hispanics and African-Americans are more likely than European-Americans to say that they will subscribe to an Internet service 'this year' (that is, 2001) (NUA 2001). Another indicates that the number of home Internet users in the US increased by 33 percent in 2000, and that African-Americans led that online growth (Yahoo 2001).

Because of these positive trends, some African-American leaders are not as concerned about this 'digital divide' as the other researchers cited here. Some have suggested (Lemos 1998) that, because African-Americans are using the Net in greater numbers than before, and because (amongst high-income groups) Internet usage is about the same between African-Americans and European-Americans, the 'digital divide' will continue to narrow as the Internet becomes of more interest to the general public (and as computer prices and Internet access continue to drop in cost). One point of agreement between most analysts, however, is that in the meantime both government and private efforts should be aimed at increasing access points in public community access centers (such as schools and libraries), because most studies indicate that these centers are well used by groups who lack access at home or work.

Other observers have suggested that a lack of relevant content could be another reason that blacks (even those with Internet access) do not use the Internet as actively as do whites, and some maintain that more African-Americans and Hispanics will come online as the Net becomes more relevant to their daily lives (USA Today 1999). It is true that content issues are slowly being addressed: there are, for example, a growing number of web sites that focus on African-American content listed in 'gateway' or 'portal' sites.[11] Similar 'portal' sites exist for members of other ethnic and social groups.

Archaeologists who are interested in Net communication need to be aware of this type of data, in that it can serve both to encourage continued work in this area and to temper naïve enthusiasm about it. We obviously need to maintain a degree of healthy cynicism – it is premature to see the Internet alone as a way to 'democratize' archaeological discourse, when large percentages of the groups we want to reach are still economically and technologically disenfranchised. Even so, the raw numbers are impressive – the Internet does allow us to reach larger audiences than we could by relying solely on museums, site tours, and other more traditional forms of public outreach. Therefore, when our archaeological interpretations are potentially of interest to multicultural audiences (as the Jordan interpretations are), we need to market our web sites aggressively and directly towards these audiences. We did this early on, by contacting the webmasters of appropriate African-American interest sites; during this process we discovered that we were, in many cases, the only archaeological web site that had ever approached them in this way. The result is that we are now listed on many of these 'portal' web sites, and a growing percentage of our visitors come to us from them.

Finally, to the degree that we can, we need to find ways for people without Internet access to participate in the development of, and use of, our web sites. This paper will address some strategies we have employed in Brazoria, Texas, to do this; before this, however, I should make clear what some of our 'taken-for-granteds' are, with regard to the words I am using here.

Clarifying terms

So far I have used the terms 'democracy', 'democratic' and 'interactivity' rather uncritically, and before continuing I should explain what they mean for the Jordan web site project – and, by extension, what they can mean for other archaeology projects on the Internet. 'Democracy' can of course be used to discuss specific problems associated with differential access to Internet technology, as described above. It can also refer to social equality (a classless, egalitarian, and uncensored social environment) or can describe a system or organization which is self-ruled and independent (such as a democratic state or group). To evaluate whether 'democracy' is being enacted by the Jordan project, it is therefore necessary to examine the planning organization which directs it, the Levi Jordan Plantation Historical Society, to see how deeply the idea of democracy (in the first sense) is embodied in the structure of the organization (democracy in the second sense). What was done – in terms of organization, content, and process – to create an egalitarian and uncensored social environment? Were people free to challenge the archaeological and historical information presented on the web site? Did people attempt to communicate with the people who created the site, and, when they did so, what things did they want to communicate about? Did they challenge or argue with information presented on the site? Did people who might have had alternate points of view appear to have visited the site at all? Was traditional academic authority and power dispersed or mitigated?

In terms of the democratic structure of the organization, the Levi Jordan Plantation Historical Society was explicitly organized to *be* democratic, in the sense of being egalitarian and decentralized. For example, there is only one archaeologist on the Society's eight-person Board of Directors. Though he began his research working only with the plantation's owner (a Jordan descendant), his power-position shifted when the Board of Directors was created and officially 'hired' him. Now he continues to serve as the Archaeological Director, but he does so at the pleasure of this Board, whose members represent the interests of various descendant groups (my 'official' role is as a volunteer consultant). It is true that recommendations that he (and I) make carry a great deal of weight, and that Board members do defer to us on many issues. The structure of the organization, however, was explicitly designed to give the Board the legal right to continue working with us – or not.

Likewise, organizational power between various descendant groups is also shared. Even though descendents of Levi Jordan still own the property, it has been leased to the Society for 99 years; this lease is tied to a legally instituted tax-exempt organization and thus cannot be terminated easily. The Society's democratic structure is reflected in the structure of the web site as well, in that archaeological 'truths' are not positioned in dominant position with respect to other ways of knowing the past; those organizational and content elements will be described more fully later in this paper.

I also need to situate the term 'interactivity' in terms of our 'democratic' agendas. In 'Netspeak', activities referred to as 'interactive' reflect three increasing levels of sophistication: navigational interactivity, functional interactivity, and adaptive interactivity (Guay 1995). *Navigational* interactivity is a fundamental feature of any web site, and refers to the basic tasks of using links, menus, search engines, and the like. It is integral to the Net experience, but it is passive; users are limited to making simple choices about links to click, animations and video clips to see, sound bites to hear and so on. *Functional* interactivity takes this a bit farther and allows users to send e-mails, fill out online forms, order products and win games (or in the case of some archaeological sites, identify artefacts; Abram 1999). Generally the results of these interactions do not become a part of the web site's content. *Adaptive* interactivity is more sophisticated still, and allows users some measure of creative control; that is, they are able to change the site in ways that are visible to other visitors. Discussion forums operate at the most accessible level of adaptive interactivity, in that messages to forums are posted to the site for others to read. At higher levels, users are allowed to change other elements of a site's content. At this writing the World Wide Web offers few opportunities for users to experience this highest level of interactivity, although it is an important feature of hypertext authoring systems used in classrooms (Joyce 1999; Slatin 1994), in hypertexts discussed by early hypertext theorists

(Joyce 1995; Landow 1992) and in more recent hypertexts by writers (including archaeologists) who have experimented with collaborative web authoring, some examples of which have been or will be published on the World Wide Web (Joyce 2000 *et al.*; Tringham 2000).

In this paper, and this project, I am most concerned with the ways that navigational and functional interactivity can be deployed to create a democratic social environment, outside the technology, and a democratic communicative environment, within the technology. The next section of this paper will describe the former.

Interactivity and democracy *outside* the technology: structuring principles and strategies for the Levi Jordan web site

Early on, those of us involved in the Jordan web site made a conscious decision to avoid many of the more technologically demanding features described in the above discussion of interactivity because they usually require long down-load times (unless the user has a fast, high-bandwidth connection, which was extremely uncommon when this project began) and because they demand the latest, fastest software and hardware – in short, because of access. For that reason, we did not include Java© applets, Quicktime© videos, audio files, large graphics, and the like. We do have graphics, of course, but they are small. We do have a clear navigational system, key to the first level of interactivity, but it is not tied to 'frames' or blinking icons, drop-down menus and the like. Our priority was, and is, to enable people to see and enjoy the site with a minimum of frustration – even people with dial-up connections, slow computers, and slow modems.[12] We directed most of our time and effort, during the planning phase of this project, at developing *content* interactively and multivocally, rather than just relying on the technology to create an interactive environment.

I call this sort of thing 'interactivity from the ground up' (or, to borrow a phrase, interactivity 'from the trowel's edge'; Hodder 1997, 1999). This way of thinking of interactivity is akin to that used by Net critic Stephen Doheny-Farina, who pointed out that we should be

> suspicious of any net enterprise that defines interactivity as simply clicking a mouse from display to display . . . If the net is going to transform communications for the better, it will engage us less in viewing displays and more in substantive interactivity . . .
> (Doheny-Farina 1996: 183)

Consequently, we have attempted to define the 'substantive' interactivity referred to by Doheny-Farina as the *ongoing process of communication* between members of descendant communities, archaeologists and others to *collaboratively create web site content*. This interactively developed content then becomes part of the interactive online environment, when we do employ some of the interactive mechanisms made possible by the technology, as will be discussed later.

Themes and principles

A number of guiding principles proved to be particularly useful to me and my collaborators as we developed this content. First, we came to conceive of this web site as a *conversation* (Rorty 1989) about archaeology. In adopting this explicitly 'conversational' trope, we consciously rejected the more dominant ways of 'doing' public archaeology – 'presentation' and 'education' – because both of the latter have an unavoidably authoritative, hierarchical flavour. The ideologies underlying the terms 'presentation' and 'education' speak more of 'indoctrination' than a mutually empowered, democratic communicative process (Mouer 2000). By rejecting them, we came to see our archaeological voices as only one part of a contingent, historically situated conversation – a conversation which allows space for alternate truth claims, and different ways of looking at history. Interestingly, in doing this, we found that our archaeological findings began to have more credibility in the community, not less – contrary to the expectations of those who bemoan so-called 'relativist' approaches in public presentations of archaeology (e.g. Moore 1994; South 1997). Local people began to provide more family stories, more documents, more pictures, and so on than they did before this shift in orientation. Some began to feel that they, as project participants, had more of a vested interest in the web site and, more generally, in the Jordan archaeological project. This had a direct and positive effect on the content included in the web site; it now includes major sections on genealogy, oral history, diary-writing, and community, in addition to sections provided by academics on archaeology and 'formal' history.

In addition to developing this 'conversational' theme, we are also employing what has been termed a 'self-reflexive postprocessual methodology' in 'real site' (as opposed to 'web site') contexts (Hodder 1997, 1999). That is, we attempted to incorporate elements of reflexivity, multivocality, interactivity and contextuality in various phases of the web site's design, content, and delivery, in order to create opportunities for openness, democracy, relevance, and the expression of shifting and multiple voices in understanding the past. I should emphasize that the Jordan web site does not purport to be reflexive, multivocal and so on, but, rather, to employ all four elements in varying degrees on different parts of the site. There is material on the site that is decidedly non-reflexive and univocal (academic papers, for example), although the attempt was to use this material in a reflexive, transparent way. In this paper I am focusing on strategies used to incorporate interactivity to create a democratic environment, both on the screen and behind the scenes – strategies dealing with reflexivity, multivocality and contextuality are addressed in some detail elsewhere (McDavid 1999).

Strategies

As discussed earlier, the Jordan excavations took place in Brazoria, Texas, a small rural Texas town. Many of the people I work with in Brazoria are descendants of the people whose material lives we study. They include the elders – the gatekeepers – and their voices are an important part of both past and present in these communities. However, many of them have little or no interest in purchasing or using computers. We needed to find ways for these important voices to appear on the web site – a web site that some of them will never see (though frequently their children and grandchildren can, and do).

Therefore, we met with some of these key individuals and conducted oral history interviews. These interviews were transcribed and portions of the transcripts were included on the web site, and linked to other parts of the web site that came up during these off-line conversations. Usually another family member and I conducted the interviews together, and frequently I found family members asked most of the questions. These jointly led interviews, without question, led to inter-family discussions about history, genealogy, etc. that would not have occurred if the interviews had not taken place. Transcripts of the interviews were given to the family members involved and subsequent meetings were held to clarify information, approve the interview segments used for the web site, obtain pictures, and the like.

Second, we adopted a policy of asking permission to put certain kinds of information on the web site – even when we did not have to, legally. Much of the material we wanted to use was from public records; we needed to include it, but we decided not to do so without explicit permission from at least some of the family's descendants. Doing this had two positive results. First, it assured descendants that we respected their privacy and their families' privacy, and reinforced our position as collaborators, not authorities with some right to use their families' histories for our own purposes. Second, it opened avenues for additional information – this new information has not only enhanced our understanding of the past, but it has also helped contemporary people to see their ancestors in ways they had not before.

For example, it was during one of these 'asking permission' interviews with an African-American descendant that we learned something new, and important, about an individual named McWillie Martin. Martin owned the plantation when the quarters area was suddenly abandoned in the late 1880s (Brown and Cooper 1990, 1994) and had been very involved in white supremacist activities in the late nineteenth century (Barnes 1998, 1999). Both archaeological and historical research have indicated that Martin's activities had a great deal to do with the reasons that the tenants left the plantation suddenly, leaving so many things behind to be excavated today.

We learned that Martin apparently regretted the actions of his youth – to the point that, according to the person who volunteered the information, he 'repented' these actions before his death. We learned of this from a descendant of the family of George Holmes, a person who had been enslaved on the plantation, as we met to discuss the possibility of putting some of the Holmes family's genealogical records on the web site. This explicitly expressed regret was unknown to any of the Martin descendants we have spoken with – many of whom continue to struggle with the harsh reality of their ancestor's actions. This new information was, of course, included on the web site, and serves to put earlier historical information about Martin's life in a more long-range historical context. More importantly, it serves to reinforce the ways that people's lives, identities, and knowledge about each other overlapped (and continue to overlap) in sometimes unexpected ways.

These two strategies I have just discussed have helped us to ways to develop interactive content 'from the ground up', including people who do not own computers, but we are also attempting to find ways for people without computers to actually see and use the web site itself. First, we held a series of online Internet workshops for students and members of the public in the computer labs of local schools and libraries. I was present to help people who had not used computers before, and to gather information about how people interacted with the web site, with me, and with each other while the workshop was going on. During these workshops I encouraged them to use the on-line interactive elements, such as the discussion forums, feedback forms, and questionnaire.[13] In addition, we also arranged for several computers to be donated to the local community library. These now provide another public access point, and in return, the library promotes the web site and mentions it in signage located near the public access computers.

A final note on interactivity, as it relates to multivocality: we have also developed a participants' section of the web site, which includes short biographies of descendants, academics, students, and other participants, as well as links to information they wish to put on the site under their own names. Whenever possible, the biographies are written by the individual participants, and sometimes they have used their own pages to publicize information about various community causes. This not only allows more local voices to be represented on the web site, but it also highlights our interactive, collaborative approach. On these participant pages, archaeological and local agendas merge in mutually empowering, reciprocal ways and the web site project becomes more firmly situated within the social context of the local community, even though it is accessible to people all over the world. It is this larger context, and the use of the technology itself to create an interactive environment, which is the focus of the next section of this paper.

Interactivity *within* the technology: discussion groups and e-mails/feedback forms

First, I will discuss online discussion forums as one form of functional interactivity, drawing on observational data from the Jordan forum as well as a few others. I will not consider 'Usenet' newsgroups, 'Listserv' or 'Mailbase' discussion groups, or 'chat rooms',[14] but will concentrate instead on discussion forums located on specific archaeologically oriented web sites.[15] Second, I will then discuss data from e-mails and feedback forms that Jordan web site received during the period of my case study (January–December 1999). Each section will conclude with a brief discussion about the specific sort of interactivity addressed in that section; this will be followed by concluding remarks about what this all means in terms of the 'democratization' of archaeological discourse on the Net.

Discussion forums

Forums associated with specific archaeological sites are, overall, relatively inactive, at least in terms of creating meaningful and ongoing conversational opportunities between archaeologists and the public. I will make some specific observations about two: the Levi Jordan Plantation forum (http://www.web archaeology.com), which I manage, and the forum located on the Çatalhöyük web site (http://catal.arch.cam.ac.uk/catal/catal.html), under the direction of Anja Wolle and Ian Hodder. Information about the former is based on personal experience; comments about the latter are based on my observations as well as conversations with both of the individuals directing the site. Both the Jordan and Çatalhöyük web sites were established, in large part, for the explicit purpose of opening and democratizing conversation between archaeologists and the public, and as such, their results are especially pertinent here.

Despite having a total visitorship of over 31,000 visitors during 1999,[16] the Jordan forum generated only 13 discussion topics (six of which were created by me) and 43 messages (18 of which were also from me, either to attempt to initiate discussion or to respond to a query). Most of the discussions were about archaeology, other than occasional postings about the alleged presence of ghosts at the Jordan Plantation site and a few other non-archaeological topics. I was the only project participant who posted regularly to the site; to my knowledge, no other project participant ever visited the forum. They did, however, continue to use technology to interact with me in other ways (such as e-mail); those interactions will be discussed shortly.

I experimented with a number of strategies to increase forum participation. In addition to posting messages myself, I also conducted Internet workshops in a number of local schools, and set up special discussion topics for students in individual classes to use – the idea was that students and teachers could use the forum to discuss what they were seeing on the web site with each other. This turned out to be a rather bad idea; students did *not* wish to use the forum to talk about the site, about history, or, indeed, anything related to the site. Rather, they used the forum to play – to talk about upcoming football games, to post anonymous 'naughty' comments, and the like. I deleted these topics from the forum after the workshops were over. I also included numerous links to the forum throughout the primary web site, and distinguished them visually from the rest of the text in a number of ways. The texts themselves also discussed the forum; specifically, there were frequent descriptions of our desire to receive challenges and questions about the information presented on the site. I also occasionally posted messages originally received as e-mails or feedback forms to the forum in the hope of generating more group discussion.

The Çatalhöyük site had a somewhat higher number of visitors (A. Wolle pers. comm. 1999) than did the Jordan Plantation web site during 1999, and the forum was also slightly more active. From the period of 25 February to the middle of September 1999, there were an average of about 40 postings a month – taking into account periods in which the forum was offline (A. Wolle pers. comm. 1999). Topic threads about matriarchy/patriarchy, human origins and 'the goddess' were lively but, for the most part, consisted of acrimonious debate between two to four individuals who tended to dominate the forum. According to the site's managers, some people seemed to use the Çatalhöyük discussion page as a point of departure to air their own beliefs about any number of topics, few of which had to do with the Çatalhöyük archaeology. Although a few Çatalhöyük team members occasionally posted messages to the site, most of the message posters did not appear to be archaeologists or other archaeological specialists. When Çatalhöyük team members did enter the discussions, participants seem to both notice and appreciate this – sometimes even brief input from a team member would refocus message threads that were moving into vociferous and tedious argument.

In an effort to improve the quality of the online discussions, in late October of 2000 the Çatalhöyük web site was reorganized to include two different discussion forums: an unmoderated one similar to the original forum, and a new moderated forum. The moderated forum had only 17 messages posted from October of 2000 to April 2001; these did not include occasional inappropriate messages deleted by Wolle or messages forwarded to individuals for direct reply. She has indicated (A. Wolle pers. comm. 2001) that participation by other team members was, as it was for the earlier version of the forum, uneven. Postings on the unmoderated forum are still dominated by a few non-archaeologist visitors, some of whom seem to want to use the forum to make personal attacks on other posters and to grandstand about issues that have little to do with Çatalhöyük archaeology (though some do have to do with so-called 'pseudo-archaeology'). The unmoderated forum is slightly busier than the moderated one – 35 messages were posted during the same time period. Software used for this forum tallies the number of times that each message has been viewed; the 35 messages on the site were viewed by site visitors 820 times during the pertinent period – therefore obviously the forum had a much larger audience than its low level of participation would initially suggest. The more acrimonious, provocative postings were, not surprisingly, the ones that generated the most 'views'.

The most active, productive Internet discussion forums about archaeology tend to be those that are affiliated with 'gateway' sites, not those connected to individual web sites like the Jordan site and Çatalhöyük. Two are worth special note: the About.com web site, located at http://archaeology.about.com/, and the forum centered around the British television Channel 4 Time Team Live web site, located at http://www.channel4.com/history/timeteam/.

The About.com discussion is moderated by Kris Hirst, an archaeologist who also manages the About.com Archaeology hierarchical directory. This directory functions as a 'search engine' of sorts – it contains articles, a newsletter, online chat, employment information, a rather large and well-organized list of links to other archaeological sites, and, at the time of writing, has about 70,000 visitors a week (K. Hirst pers. comm. 2001). The discussion forum is still fairly active, and in the past has included message threads about Moche tombs, Donald Johanson and 'Lucy', Giza's monuments, the Great Wall of China, questions about how to become an archaeologist, debates about pseudo-archaeologies – and more. Hirst takes an active role in these conversations, as do a number of regular contributors, several of whom appear to be professional archaeologists. Some postings originate as e-mails that have been posted to Hirst personally; she re-posts them to the forum in order to generate more discussion (a strategy also employed by Wolle for Çatalhöyük). Many discussion threads begin in response to one of the articles posted by Hirst on the site – the web site acts as a sort of 'magazine' about archaeology, and visitors are encouraged to join the e-mail list related to the site, which in turn enables them to receive regular newsletters and other items of interest. The e-mail newsletters include announcements of new articles by Hirst, news items about archaeology, a 'quote of the week', and a list of new topics posted to the discussion forum. Therefore, people who subscribe to the e-mail newsletter are reminded to go to the web site to see the new materials.

The discussion forum on the Time Team site is even more active, and is associated with Channel 4's Time Team, a popular series of television broadcasts that feature short-term archaeological excavations in various parts of the United Kingdom. An archaeological team is taped as it conducts a three-day excavation, and a television programme is aired after the excavation on Channel 4. Presenters for the program include known television personalities as well as archaeologists and other specialists. For a typical Time Team excavation, the tapes for one excavation are consolidated into one television broadcast, shown later. In addition to these taped broadcasts, however, the series also features occasional 'live' excavations, in which a given excavation takes place over a three-day weekend. During these 'live' events members of the public are encouraged to visit excavations in progress, to watch several live Time Team TV episodes aired over the weekend, and to visit the Time Team web site and discussion forum to discuss their experience. The fanfare associated with these live presentations is extensive.

Not surprisingly, this publicity generates a great deal of response on the Time Team discussion forum. During one three-day event monitored in late 1999, over 1,700 messages were posted. Some of these threads were relatively serious and very active ('Any questions on medieval medicine?' and 'Any questions for Time Team?'), while some were meant mostly as good fun ('Name that leech!'). Quite a few of the threads (both official – posted by the programme – and public) did discuss the excavations underway – there were, for example, questions and comments about specific finds as well as debates (e.g. 'exhumation or grave disturbance?'). Most of the 'non-official' postings revolved around a huge variety of topics that had little or nothing to do with the archaeology itself. These included several threads about the personal attributes of presenters and archaeologists (hairdos, presentation style, marital status, etc.); threads with compliments or gripes about the web site; greetings between web site regulars (who call themselves 'Time Team Forum Friends'); as well as a number of other topics (e.g. 'First Americans', 'Welcome back Mary in Madrid', 'Welsh Lingo', and 'Did Britain have to enter WWII?').

Comments: discussion forums

First, it appears that the content of an individual web site matters very little in whether or not people actively participate in that site's discussion forum – that is, whether a web site is interesting and provocative will not necessarily predict whether the web site's discussion forum provokes interesting and provocative conversation. My bias is obvious, in my assumption that the Jordan content is both interesting and provocative; likewise, the Çatalhöyük site is also compelling and well presented. The point is that web site content alone does not appear to be the driving factor in whether a forum takes off.

Second, archaeologists who bother to create their own forums should also bother to participate in them; even when – or even especially when – the public is apparently more interested in 'pseudo-archaeologies' of the sort that have dominated the unmoderated Çatalhöyük forum. Being willing to be 'open' and 'democratic' has little positive effect, other than to create a forum for a few loud voices, if we are not willing to make our own truth claims loudly and forcefully *within that particular conversational context*. Real 'democratization' may only occur when archaeologists are willing to (as Hodder has done with his e-mail communication with 'Goddess' groups[17]) engage seriously in conversations with people with whom we disagree.

Third, it is apparent that people do not visit discussion forums to talk about 'the past', *in and of itself*. They may find the past interesting, and they may well enjoy talking about it – but they are motivated to participate in online discussion forums because these forums connect to something that is ongoing in their 'real' lives. With About.com, the connection is simple – regular e-mail reminders, reinforced by the occasional use of the site as a search tool. In the case of Time Team, the connection is to everyday social activity– such as television watching and excavation watching. It follows that if we are going to incorporate these sorts of forums in our web sites, we also need to create more active, ongoing connections between our forums and the 'real lives' of our publics. We will need to find local, even parochial, analogues to create the kinds of connections that the larger forums can employ.

Fourth, most importantly, it would appear that forums which rely solely on 'themselves' to generate repeat visits and discussion have much less, and much less varied, visitor participation than forums which use collateral media publicity. The newsletters that the About.com site sends, the fact that it is widely publicized on a myriad of other archaeological portal sites, and its corollary function as an archaeological search engine mean that it receives a large number of visits. Thus, the postings on its forum are varied and relatively numerous. This is true to an even larger degree with the Time Team site.

The implications of this in terms of a more 'democratic' archaeological practice are significant. If an archaeological forum has to be connected with a large commercial television network, or even just a large Internet resource, to attract response, does this mean that more local and individual efforts have any chance of being a part of the larger goal of 'democratizing' archaeology? The above findings suggest not. If we do want to use this particular form of interactivity to talk about our individual archaeological efforts, our efforts might be better aimed at being loud and forceful discussants in precisely those forums that are *already* powerful and well funded. The structure of the two larger forums described allows this; all we have to do is to sign on and speak up.

Feedback forms and e-mails

Most web sites offer opportunities to contact the 'webmaster' or some other individual – this form of functional interactivity is a very common one. However, I know of no other web sites that have attempted to systematically examine whether these mechanisms are successful in opening and democratizing conversations about archaeology. Therefore, tracking this form of interactivity became an important component of my case study of the Jordan web site.

In order to encourage people to contact us, a link to my personal e-mail address appeared on the bottom of every page. In addition, each page featured a prominent link to a feedback form page, and links to other participants' e-mail addresses were included on pages for which they had contributed content. Finally, much of the text actively solicited visitor response; requests for challenge, comment, and questions were a major part of the content on each page. The feedback forms were designed to be flagged by the sender as either intended for me or for delivery to one of the other project participants. In all cases, I was the person who received the form first. After responding to all messages, I then referred messages to other project participants as necessary, asking them to copy me if they replied to the message.

To my knowledge, no participant other than me ever received a personal e-mail from any of the links on the site, although I received 378 e-mail messages and feedback forms during the study period. Most people previously unknown to me preferred to use feedback forms rather than personal e-mails for their first contact with the site; however, people who identified themselves (or that I was able to identify) as archaeologists frequently sent personal e-mails. I suspect that this is because I was seen as a member of their peer-group; therefore they may have been more comfortable communicating directly with me, rather than using the more anonymous (in appearance, at any rate) form.

Most of the 'conversations' that resulted from these efforts were very short (two or three messages in a stream), with the exception of a few individuals with whom I continued to communicate for extended periods. Other archaeologist-participants in the Jordan project replied to very few of the messages I forwarded to them. One team member in particular has indicated (Brown 2000) that he found the task of dealing with questions about his archaeological interpre-tations from 'people with little to no training in archaeology' a frustrating and 'humbling' experience; it was certainly a time-consuming one. I made a point of answering every e-mail and form, and of continuing to reply to people as long as they sent messages to me. Responding to initial messages, and keeping these 'conversations' going, took a fair amount of time on my part – sometimes up to 10–12 hours a week.

Many of the messages received were quite long and included a number of topics, and frequently different themes emerged during the course of message streams with individual respondents. A disappointing number of messages dealt specifically with African-American archaeology or history; only 2 percent of the total. Eight percent of the messages received were primarily concerned with the archaeology on the site, and 11 percent were sent to complement the content, organization and format of the site. Seventy-five respondents were high school students in the local area; 16 percent of these asked specifically about the ghost stories that are a large part of local lore about the still-standing plantation house.

As would be expected given the site's content, a number of e-mails and forms came from archaeologists (8 percent of the total messages). Sixty-one percent of the total messages came from sources previously unknown to me; these individuals did not have a vested or personal interest in the site, as would be the case with community participants, colleagues and friends, many of whom also sent in forms and e-mails. Therefore it would appear that there were messages from people who *might* have been willing to challenge the archae-ological and historical information on the site. During the entire study period, however, only two people questioned, or even elaborated on, any of the archae-ological or historical information presented. Indeed, most people who did communicate about the archaeology were the same ones who were full of complements and praise for the site.

All of the correspondents who identified themselves as 'Family members' (that is, as descendents of the plantation's original residents), and were previously unknown to me or the other project participants, contacted the web site in order to discuss genealogy. Interestingly, they seemed quite willing to correct information presented in the genealogy pages of the web site. None of them appeared to be interested in the archaeological, or even historical, information at all.

Comments: feedback forms and e-mails

First, both e-mail and feedback forms were important in generating response; feedback forms were used more often by members of the 'unknown' public, while e-mails tended to be used by people with some connection (personal or disciplinary) to me.

Second, people did not appear to want to communicate directly with project participants other than myself; the power I held as the leader of the project was not dispersed by my efforts to share that power with others.

Third, it appears that our efforts to democratize the *content* of the site – that is, to provide an important place for other 'ways of knowing' – did have the positive effect of drawing more people into the site than would otherwise have been the case. Site descendents, not surprisingly, had a particular and positive response to genealogical information, and were even willing to correct it on occasion.

Fourth, as with discussion groups, it is apparent that feedback forms and e-mails are only as effective as their recipients– the archaeologists, in this case – are willing to make them. I seriously doubt whether most archaeologists, without a research project about the Internet as a prime motivator, could be expected to invest the time and energy to communicate, one-on-one, with members of the public at the level required to make this form of communication meaningful in a disciplinary sense. Certainly, my archaeologist-collaborators were less willing than I was to engage at this level, despite their willingness to provide content for the web site and their stated support of this aspect of the project. It is likely that, as the project director of the web site, I allowed my own enthusiasm about 'democratic' conversation to mask a lower level of commitment to this on the parts of some other participants.

Finally, most important, despite our entreaties for challenge and debate, openly written texts, and frequent interactive opportunities within the technology, the site's correspondents did not seem to be willing to question or challenge the archaeological or historical information presented on the site. They were willing to praise the content and, occasionally, ask for additional information, but very few were interested in engaging in sustained, meaningful discourse about archaeology or history with either me or with other project participants. This has important implications in terms of our desire to de-center the archaeologist/academic as the authoritative figure in conversations about the past – despite our best efforts, power stayed with the powerful. It could be that this 'democratization' agenda was 'ours', not 'theirs'; that is, people may simply prefer to interact with archaeological and historical information somewhat passively. It could also be that our requests for criticism and feedback were not seen as credible – at least seven people commented that they were surprised that we had responded to them at all, or that we responded so quickly. While this is hardly a significant number, it is revealing that anyone said this sort of thing at all.

Even so, the importance of the few long message streams should not be discounted. Perhaps it is not important whether these conversations were always about archaeology; it may be more important that an *archaeological* web site provided a bridge between academia and the public for at least a few individuals. In these cases, the original purpose of initiating the exchange was transcended in favour of simple communication between human beings. Considering this, it appears that people were as open as they wished to be with us, and that we were *perceived* to be open, accessible, and willing to accept challenges about our work. This is significant, although it is, perhaps, not enough.

Conclusion

My goal here was to lay out some issues about the 'democratization' of archaeology on the Internet; to provide a snapshot about the 'state of the Net' generally, with respect to democratic access; to examine (with a case study and other examples) some ways in which some archaeologists are using it to reach their publics; and to examine whether a more 'democratic' archaeology is being enacted by these efforts. In concentrating on this, I have not dealt with several troublesome issues that are outside the scope of this paper; they do, however, demand mention here, and further analysis and discussion in other settings.

For example, I have not addressed the problems in blending academic agendas with purely commercial ones (a question the Time Team and About.com professional archaeologists have, no doubt, considered). Nor have I examined the increasing globalization of multinational corporate media (Hodder 1999) and the impact this will have on Internet access, especially in terms of economically and politically disenfranchised groups worldwide.

I have also not discussed in any detail one particular issue with regard to the 'democratization' of archaeology that is frequently troubling to archaeologists – and that is that the democratic *structure* of the Internet tends to give equal weight to both 'uninformed' voices and 'informed' ones. Sometimes these 'uninformed' voices are relatively benign, and sometimes they are not. Many web sites promote, for example, white supremacist views, and use archaeological information to do so. How does the typical Internet user identify what might be termed 'legitimate' archaeological knowledge? (see McDavid (1998c, 2000) for discussions of this topic in terms of pragmatist philosophy; see also Meskell (1997) and Hodder (1999)). It may be that the fact that the Internet already allows space for alternate archaeologies – pseudo-archaeologies

– to be presented is, itself, proof that to some degree it has already 'democratized' archaeology. Archaeologists may or may not wish to participate in this sort of 'democracy'; I would argue that we had better, if we want 'legitimate' archaeology to have a voice in the more general milieu of 'archaeology on the Net'.

The proposition for this paper, however, was simply that we need to be knowledgeable and critical about what the Internet can, and cannot, do if we believe that opening archaeology to other voices and groups is a good thing to do (Hodder *et al.* 1995; Shanks and Tilley 1987; Shanks 1992). As Ian Hodder has pointed out recently:

> Archaeology has tended to see an absolute divide between 'deep' specialist information . . . and 'shallow' popular books, films and exhibits. Modern information systems allow the two to be provided together . . . Public access to 'depth' can be provided, and alternative perspectives empowered.
>
> (Hodder 1999: 165)

It is true that the Internet has provided a certain degree of public access to archaeological knowledge, and has also given archaeologists more opportunities for meaningful conversations with diverse publics than we had before the 'rise of the network society' (Castells 1996). However, it is likely that access to this knowledge and these conversations will, for the foreseeable future, be limited to people who also have access to a wide range of other economic and technological resources. Therefore, the degree to which the Internet is actually a pathway to 'democratization' of archaeological discourse is an open question – even though, admittedly, our audiences on the Internet are huge, and growing.

In the case of the Jordan Plantation project, we attempted to mitigate this by involving 'non-networked' people in the content and delivery of the web site. This effort had a number of positive results,[18] especially in terms of our credibility within the local community; indeed, the *process* of working with descendants to create the Jordan web site was extremely worthwhile. It was in this very process – the ways that the Jordan organization itself was created and instituted, and the ways that the diverse multiple voices were involved in creating the web site – that typically disenfranchised and marginalized groups *were* empowered. Some of the strategies described here could likely have been deployed in *any* 'public archaeology' project – such as museum displays, real-site tours, and the like. This is not a bad thing; it is even a very powerful and good thing. As one site descendant put it recently, referring to both the process and the web site itself, 'Even if we never do anything else, it will have been worth it'. Developing a collaborative democratic process in which local people could help to create a product about their own history is part of what good public archaeology is all about.

Unfortunately, however, the unimpressive activity on the discussion forum, coupled with the tendency of e-mail and feedback respondents not to challenge our archaeological and historical interpretations, leads me to believe that the question of whether the Internet *itself* can help to 'democratize' archaeological discourse must be viewed sceptically. Archaeologists may be able to learn to use the Internet in ways that are democratizing and equalizing, but they will need to depend less on the technology itself and more on strategies to encourage interactivity 'from the ground up', some examples of which are described in this paper. We are not, yet, at a place where the technology can do that job for us. In this historical moment, we might be better served by having a non-technological approach to a technology that many, including myself, find seductive and even occasionally liberating. Our responsibility in the short term is to learn to use the Internet to communicate about our work, but to use it cautiously. We must be critical of claims made by the Internet's utopiasts, who tend to see the technology itself as liberating and equalizing (Bolter 1991; Landow 1992; Rheingold 1993) and equally wary of those writers who take a more apocalyptic view (Kester 1994; Kroker and Weinstein 1994; Postman 1992). The Internet can communicate and empower, and it can also exclude and disenfranchize. In the end it will depend on how we – and our publics – choose to use it.

Notes

1 Because of these taken-for-granteds, I will assume that the readers of this paper will know what certain words mean, at least in terms of commonly accepted use, e.g. 'e-mail', 'web sites', 'Internet', 'search engines', 'World Wide Web' and 'Web', 'web browsers', 'bandwidth', 'download', etc. The 'Net', in this paper, refers primarily to the 'Internet' (in particular, Word Wide Web sites located on the Internet). For readers who require formal definitions of these and related terms see Rheingold (1993) and Clemente (1998).

2 This paper will not address other forms of Internet communication, such as the thousands of online 'Usenet' discussion groups (sci.archaeology, alt.archaeology, etc.) and special interest e-mail (listserv) discussion groups such as histarch, arch-theory, rad-arch, etc. Other studies have examined how discourse takes place on those forums; see for example Shade (1996) and Tepper (1997). It is also important to note that the term 'the Net' frequently refers to networked communication more generally – that is, fax machines, television, telephones, satellite and cellular communications, etc. (Doheny-Farina 1996: xiii).

3 Yahoo©, Altavista® and other 'so-called' search engines sometimes find drastically different numbers of web sites. This is because some 'search engines' (like Yahoo©) are not really 'search engines' but, rather, hierarchical directories. In order to be listed on these directories, writers (sometimes known as 'webmasters') of individual web sites must register their sites, along with a request to list them in certain specific, predetermined categories – such as 'archaeology'. On the other hand, Altavista® and similar 'real' search engines employ searching software called 'spiders', 'robots', 'web crawlers', etc. This software scans every page in each web

site, looking for the search terms requested. Therefore, they are likely to find many more web sites than searches done with 'hierarchical directory'-type 'search engines'.

4 For example, ArchNet (http://archnet.asu.edu/)
   About.com (http://archaeology.about.com/)
   Archaeology on the Net (http://www.serve.com/archaeology/main.html)
   A Guide to Underwater Resources Archaeology on the Net
   (http://www.pophaus. com/underwater/)
   Biblical Archaeology Resources
   (http://www.lpl.arizona.edu/~kmeyers/archaeol/bib_arch.html)
   Voice of the Shuttle Archaeology Page
   (http://vos.ucsb.edu/shuttle/arcahaeol.html)
   Anthropology Web Ring Site, (http://www.unc.edu/~lgmull

5 For example, Society for Historical Archaeology (http://www.sha.org/)
   Society for American Archaeology (http://www.saa.org/)
   Peabody Museum of Archaeology and Ethnology
   (http://www.peabody.harvard.edu/)
   Current Archaeology (http://www.cix.co.uk/~archaeology/)
   National Parks Service (http://www.cr.nps.gov/)
   Ashmolean Museum of Art and Archaeology, Oxford
   (http://www.ashmol.ox.ac.uk/)

6 For example, Crow Canyon Archaeological Center (http://crowcanyon.org/)
   Archaeology of Teotihuacan Mexico (http://archaeology.la.asu.edu/teo/)
   Dan Mouer's Digweb
   (http://saturn.vcu.edu/~dmouer/digweb/digweb_home.html)
   Çatalhöyük (http://catal.arch.cam.ac.uk/catal/catal.html)
   Levi Jordan Plantation Web Site (http://www.webarchaeology.com)

7 For example, Archaeology's Dig (http://www.digonsite.com/
   The Aztecs (Snaith Primary School)
   (http://home.freeuk.net/elloughton13/aztecs.htm)
   Mysteries of Çatalhöyük (http://www.smm.org/catal/home.html)

8 For example, The Name of Bast (http://www.per-bast.org/)
   Rabbit in the Moon (information on Maya art) (http://www.halfmoon.org/)
   Sacred Journeys (about the goddess and Çatalhöyük)
   (http://www.wordweb.org/sacredjo/index.html).

9 The Internet project derives from research about the slave and tenant quarters at the Jordan Plantation, which is under the direction of Kenneth L. Brown at the University of Houston, Texas (Brown and Cooper 1990; Brown 1994). Brown and his students provided all of the archaeological data on the Jordan web site. The quarters were occupied by slaves from 1848 to 1865 and by tenant farmers (many of whom were the same people) from 1865 to about 1888. Archaeologically, the Jordan site is unique in the American South – in its deposition, its preservation, and in the ways in which it is being interpreted. It appears that in about 1888 the plantation's tenants moved out and took very few of their possessions with them. The quarters were then locked, abandoned, and, gradually, the decaying remains were flooded and silted over – the area was then essentially undisturbed until excavations began some 18 years ago.

10 I use the terms 'African-American' and 'black', and 'European-American'

and 'white', interchangeably, as do the people (both black and white) in my study area.

11 A few of these include:
African America Online
  (http://home.zdnet.com/yil/content/roundups/african_america.html)
Universal Black Pages (http://www.ubp.com/)
Net Noir (http://www.netnoir.com/)
African-American History (http://historicaltextarchive.com/)
African-American Web Ring (http://www.soulsearch.net/aawr/)

12 Recent data supports our early decisions in this area. According to a prominent Internet commentator, Jakob Nielsen:

> For the next five years, the Web will be dominated by users with so slow connections that any reasonable Web page will take much longer to download that the response time limits indicated by human factors research. Thus the dominant design criterion must be download speed in all Web projects until about the Year 2003. **Minimalist design rules**.
>
> (Nielsen 1998c; emphasis in original)

In addition, some research suggests that as web users are becoming more conservative, there is greater reluctance to accept innovations in web page design – again, from Nielsen:

> Web users are conservative; they don't want inconsistent site designs or fancy pages filled with graphic gimmicks and animations. And they frequently don't have the latest client software available. As a result, Web designers have to be conservative in what they show to users: **page design must be conservative and minimalist**.
>
> (Nielsen 1998b; emphasis in original)

13 This paper will not discuss the results of this questionnaire, but it should be pointed out that it, too, was a form of functional interactivity.

14 'Usenet' is a worldwide system of discussion groups, in which individual users pass around comments on hundreds of thousands of machines. It is completely decentralized, with more than 25,000 discussion areas, called newsgroups (Clemente 1998: 170). Some newsgroups are moderated (that is, filtered for topic-appropriate content), but most are not. Readers do not need to subscribe – just to log on, read previously posted comments which are organized by 'topic threads', and post replies if desired. These groups tend to be very open, and to attract many non-specialists (such as people interested in 'fringe' archaeologies; Hodder 1992). 'Listservs' and 'Mailbase' groups, on the other hand, are subscription-only special-interest mailing lists. The words 'Listserv' and 'Mailbase' refer to the software used to manage most of these lists; other software packages are also available. They tend to be somewhat more focused on particular interest areas (historical archaeology, British archaeology, archaeological theory, etc.), and, while many are moderated, many are not. Individual members tend to self-regulate the discussion, and to protest (vociferously) if people post comments which are perceived by the rest of the members to be inappropriate. They tend to attract more serious professional or

avocational archaeologists, although anyone can usually join. Most of the gateway web sites list both sorts of discussion groups. Finally, 'chat rooms' are online, real-time discussions, usually pre-scheduled, although the busier chat rooms are 'open' all the time. Few of these exist on archaeological web sites; see the scheduled chat rooms at http://archaeology.about.com/ for one example.

15 Although it is likely that the forums mentioned here will be active for some time, they may not exist indefinitely; there is a somewhat ephemeral quality to much of the content available on the Internet. Both published data (Nielsen 1998a) and personal experience suggest that at least 10–12 percent of links on web sites are 'broken' at any given time, and some survey data indicate at least 60 percent of web users cite broken links as a major problem when using the web (GVU 1997). Broken links mean that the link destinations have either been taken off the web or have moved.

16 This number refers to user sessions, not to 'hits', which measure the download of any file; each user session contains, therefore, a great number of 'hits'. Even so, this is a small number compared to that received by many web sites. For the first year of operation for an independent site, focused on one archaeological site in rural South Texas, we were not displeased with this number of visitors.

17 See the web page which archives this correspondence, at http://catal.arch.cam. ac.uk/catal/goddess.html.

18 It should be noted that the larger case study (of which the 'democracy' question is only one component) also analyses other qualities of archaeological web sites – such as their ability to be 'relevant' to multiple groups. To a large degree these results are more positive than the results presented here concerning 'democracy'.

Bibliography

Abram, E. S. 1999. *Archaeological Analysis: Pieces of the Past.* Royal Ontario Museum. URL: http://www.rom.on.ca/digs/munsell/, accessed on 12 April 2001.

Agbie-Davies, A. 1999. The legacy of 'race' in African-American archaeology: A silk purse from a wolf's ear? Paper presented at World Archaeological Conference 4, Cape Town, South Africa.

Barnes, M. K. 1998. Everything they owned. Paper presented at Annual Meetings of the Society for Historical Archaeology, Atlanta, Georgia.

Barnes, M. K. 1999. *Church and Community: An Archaeological Investigation on the Levi Jordan Plantation. Master's Thesis, Department of Anthropology, University of Houston.*

Bograd, M. D. and Singleton, T. A. 1997. *The Interpretation of Slavery: Mount Vernon, Monticello and Colonial Williamsburg. In Jameson, J. H. Jr (ed.)* Presenting Archaeology to the Public: Digging for Truths. Walnut Creek, London, New Delhi: Altamira Press.

Bolter, J. D. 1991. *Writing Space: The Computer, Hypertext, and the History of Writing.* Hillsdale, NJ: Lawrence Erlbaun Associates.

Brown, K. L. 1994. 'Material culture and community structure: the slave and tenant community at Levi Jordan's Plantation 1848–1892. In Hudson, L. E. (ed.) *Working Toward Freedom: Slave Society and Domestic Economy in the American South.* Rochester, NY: University of Rochester Press.

Brown, K. L. 1997. Some thoughts on archaeology and public responsibility. *Newsletter of the African-American Archaeology Network* Fall: 18.

Brown, K. L. 2000. From archaeological interpretation to public interpretation: collaboration within the discipline for a better public archaeology (Phase One). Paper presented at: 65th Annual Meeting of the Society for American Archaeology, Philadelphia, Pennsylvania.

Brown, K. L. and Cooper, D. C. 1990. Structural continuity in an African-American slave and tenant community. *Historical Archaeology* 24(4): 7–19.

Castells, M. 1996. *The Rise of the Network Society*. Oxford: Blackwell.

Clemente, P. 1998. *The State of the Net: The New Frontier*. New York: McGraw-Hill.

Conlin, R. 1999. Internet fast becoming a global draw. *E_commerce Times*. URL: http://www.ecommercetimes.com/news/articles/990610-7.shtml , accessed on 31 August 1999.

Datamonitor. 1998. One in three European homes online by 2003, December 10 1998. NUA Internet Surveys. URL: http://www.nua.ie/surveys/index.cgi?f= VS&art_id=905354575&rel=true, accessed on 15 April 2001.

Datamonitor. 1999. 545 million user accounts globally by 2003. August 11 1999. NUA Internet Surveys. URL: http://www.nua.ie/surveys/index.cgi?f=VS&art_id =905355185&rel=true, accessed on 15 April 2001.

Doheny-Farina, S. 1996. *The Wired Neighborhood*. New Haven, London: Yale University Press.

Foucault, M. 1972. *The Archaeology of Knowledge*. London: Tavistock.

Guay, T. 1995. WEB Publishing Paradigms. Simon Fraser University. URL: http://hoshi.cic.sfu.ca/~guay/Paradigm/Paradigm.html, updated April 1995, accessed on 12 April 2001.

GVU. 1997. Problems Using the Web, GVU's 8th WWW User Survey. Graphic, Visualization, and Usability Center; Georgia Tech Research Corporation. URL: http://www.gvu.gatech.edu/user_surveys/survey-1997–10/graphs/use/Problems_ Using_the_Web.html, accessed on 13 September 1999.

GVU. 1998. GVU 10th WWW User Survey. May 4 1999. Graphic, Visualization, and Usability Center; Georgia Tech Research Corporation, http://www.gvu.gatech. edu/user_surveys/survey-1998–10/index.html, accessed on 31 August 1999.

Handsman, R. G. and Richmond, T. L. 1995. The Mahican and Schaghticoke Peoples and Us. In Schmidt, P. R. and Patterson, T. C. (eds) *Making Alternative Histories: The Practice of Archaeology and History in Non-Western Settings*. Santa Fe, New Mexico: School of American Research Press.

Hodder, I. 1992. *Theory and Practice in Archaeology*. London, New York: Routledge.

Hodder, I. 1997. Towards a reflexive excavation methodology. Antiquity 71(273): 691–700.

Hodder, I. 1999. *The Archaeological Process: An Introduction*. Oxford: Blackwell.

Hodder, I., Shanks, M., Alexandri, A., Buchli, V., Carman, J., Last, J. and Lucas, G. (eds) 1995. *Interpreting Archaeology: Finding Meaning in the Past*. London and New York: Routledge.

Joyce, M. 1995. Of Two Minds: Hypertext Pedagogy and Poetics. University of Michigan Press, URL: http://www.press.umich.edu/webhome/09578-intro.html (segments only), accessed on 12 April 2001.

Joyce, R. 1999. Multivocality and authority: implications from a hypertext writing project. Paper presented at: Annual Meetings of the Society for American Archaeology, Chicago, Illinois.

Joyce, R., Guyer, C. and Joyce, M. 2000. Sister Stories. New York University Press, URL: http://www.nyupress.org/sisterstories, updated in 2000, accessed on 12 April 2001.

Kester, G. 1994. Access Denied: Information Policy and the Limits of Liberalism. University of Rochester, URL: http://www.rochester.edu/College/FS/Publications/ KesterAccess.html, accessed on 9 September 1999.

Kroker, A. and Weinstein, M. A. 1994. *The Theory of the Virtual Class: Not a virtual culture, but a culture that is wired shut.* New York: St. Martin's Press.

Landow, G. P. 1992. *Hypertext: The Convergence of Contemporary Critical Theory and Technology.* Baltimore and London: The Johns Hopkins University Press.

LaRoche, C. 1997. Seizing intellectual power: the dialogue at the New York African burial ground. In McDavid, C. and Babson, D. (eds) *In the Realm of Politics: Prospects for Public Participation in African-American Archaeology. Historical Archaeology* Vol. 31(3). California, Pennsylvania: The Society for Historical Archaeology.

Lemos, R. 1998. NetNoir head criticizes coverage of online race study. April 17 1998. ZDNet, URL: http://zdnet.com.com/2100-11-509080.html, accessed on 12 April 2001.

Leone, M. P., Potter, P. B. Jr and Shackel, P. A. 1987. Toward a Critical Archaeology. *Current Anthropology* 28(3): 283–302.

Leone, M. P., Mullins, P. R., Creveling, M. C., Hurst, L., Jackson-Nash, B., Jones, L. D., Kaiser, H. J., Logan, G. C. and Warner, M. S. 1995. Can an African-American historical archaeology be an alternative voice? In Hodder, I., Shanks, M., Alexandri, A., Buchli, V., Carman, J., Last, J. and Lucas, G. (eds) *Interpreting Archaeology: Finding Meaning in the Past.* London and New York: Routledge.

McCarthy, J. P. 1996. Who owns these bones?: descendant community rights and partnerships in the excavation and analysis of historic cemetery sites in New York and Philadelphia. *Public Archaeology Review* 4(2): 3–12.

McDavid, C. 1997a. Descendants, Decisions, and Power: The Public Interpretation of the Archaeology of the Levi Jordan Plantation. In McDavid, C. and Babson, D. (eds) *In the Realm of Politics: Prospects for Public Participation in African-American Archaeology, Historical Archaeology* Vol. 31(3)> California, Pennsylvania: Society for Historical Archaeology: 114–31.

McDavid, C. 1997b. Editor's Introduction. In McDavid, C. and Babson, D. (eds) *In the Realm of Politics: Prospects for Public Participation in African-American Archaeology. Historical Archaeology* Vol. 31(3). California, Pennsylvania: Society for Historical Archaeology.

McDavid, C. 1998a. The Levi Jordan Plantation Historical Society: The History of a Collaborative Project. Levi Jordan Plantation Historical Society, URL: http:// www.webarchaeology.com/html/about.htm, updated on 27 February 1999, accessed on 15 September 1999.

McDavid, C. 1998b. The Levi Jordan Plantation Web Site. Levi Jordan Plantation Historical Society, URL: http://www.webarchaeology.com, updated on 27 February 1999.

McDavid, C. 1998c. Archaeology and "The Web": writing multi-linear texts in a multi-centered community. Paper presented at Annual Meetings of the Society for Historical and Underwater Archaeology, Atlanta, Georgia.

McDavid, C. 1999. From real space to cyberspace: contemporary conversations about the archaeology of slavery and tenancy. *Internet Archaeology* 6, Special Theme:

Hingley, R. 2000. Medieval or later rural settlement in Scotland – the value of the resource. In J.A. Atkinson, I. Banks and G. MacGregor (eds) *Townships to Farmsteads. Rural Settlement Studies in Scotland, England and Wales*. BAR British Series 293. Oxford: BAR: 11–19.

Hutton, W. 1995. *The State We're In*. London: Jonathan Cape.

Jones, A. 1995. Integrating school visits, tourists and the community at the Archaeological Resource Centre, York, UK. In E. Hooper-Greenhill (ed.) *Museum, Media, Message*. Leicester: Leicester University Press: 156–64.

Liddle, P. 1989. Community archaeology in Leicestershire museums. In E. Southworth (ed.) *Public Service or Private Indulgence?* The Museum Archaeologist 13. Liverpool: Society of Museum of Archaeologists: 44–6.

Lowenthal, D. 1998. *The Heritage Crusade and the Spoils of History*. London: Viking.

MacInnes, L. and Wickham-Jones, C.R. (eds) 1992. *All Natural Things: Archaeology and the Green Debate*. Oxbow Monograph 21. Oxford: Oxbow Books.

Mackay, D. 1993. Scottish rural Highland settlement: preserving a people's past. In R. Hingley (ed.) *Medieval or Later Rural Settlement in Scotland. Management and Preservation*. Historic Scotland Ancient Monuments Division Occasional Paper Number 1. Edinburgh: Historic Scotland: 43–51.

Merriman, N. 1991. *Beyond the Glass Case. The Past, the Heritage and the Public in Britain*. Leicester: Leicester University Press.

Merriman, N. 2000. The crisis of representation in museums. In F. P. MacManamon and A. Hatton (eds) *Cultural Resource Management in Contemporary Society. Perspectives on Managing and Presenting the Past*. London: Routledge: 300–309

MORI. 2000. Research conducted for English Heritage. URL: www.english-heritage.org.uk.

Morris, R. 2000. On the Heritage Strategy Review. *Conservation Bulletin* 37: 2–5.

Murray, T. 1989. The history, philosophy and sociology of archaeology: the case of the Ancient Monuments Protection Act 1882. In V. Pinsky and A. Wylie (eds) *Critical Traditions in Contemporary Archaeology*. Cambridge: Cambridge University Press: 55–62.

Ponting, C. 1986. *Whitehall: Tragedy and Farce*. London: Sphere Books.

Potter, P.B. and Chabot, N.-J. 1997. Locating truths on archaeological sites. In J. Jameson (ed.) *Presenting Archaeology to the Public. Digging for Truths*. London: Altamira Press: 45–53.

Robertson, M. 2000. *Conservation Practice and Policy in England, 1882–1945*. Master of Studies dissertation, Department of Continuing Education, University of Oxford.

Samuel, R. 1994. *Theatres of Memory*. London: Verso.

Saunders, A.D. 1983. A century of ancient monuments legislation. *The Antiquaries Journal* 63: 11–33.

Simpson, M.G. 1996. *Making Representations: Museums in the Post-Colonial Era*. London: Routledge.

Start, D. 1999. Community archaeology: bringing it back to local communities. In G. Chitty and D. Baker (eds) *Managing Historic Sites and Buildings: Reconciling Presentation and Preservation*. London: Routledge: 49–59.

Walsh, K. 1992. *The Representation of the Past. Museums and Heritage in the Post-Modern World*. London: Routledge.

10

PUBLIC ARCHAEOLOGY IN BRAZIL

Pedro Paulo A. Funari

Introduction: Brazilian society and the Brazilian public

The concept of Brazilian society is as elusive as any generalisation and most foreigners are likely to have a fairly blurred image of Brazil. Probably the most ubiquitous image of the country is of the Carnival and the streets of Rio de Janeiro, mixed with sounds of the *bossa nova* hit 'Girl from Ipanema' (*Garota de Ipanema*) by Tom Jobim, whose rendering by Frank Sinatra, among others, spread Brazil's image around the world. Rio de Janeiro is still considered by many people the world over to be the capital of Brazil (or even Argentina). The fact is that, even though Brazil is relatively unknown as a country, some of its culture is widely known abroad, from such personalities as Pelé and Airton Senna, and from its rhythms. But, what about Brazilian society? Is there a society in Brazil? It depends on one's definition of society, of course, for 'a system of common life' (Williams 1983: 294) is a difficult definition to apply to the Brazilian case, given the lack of subjective links between the different social strata. Perhaps a shocking news piece is enough to alert us about this lack of social commitment: 'A beggar has been burned alive in Porto Alegre. The incident happened downtown, close to the main bus station and witnesses say that there were several aggressors, some of them adolescents' (Gerchmann 1998).

This kind of crime is so common that it goes generally unreported, although there has been a lot of publicity about arsonists since an indigenous Brazilian was killed the same way, on 19 April 1997, in the capital, Brasília, just when school children were celebrating 'Indigenous Brazilian day'. The arsonists were caught by the police, and these middle class youngsters were indicted sometime later, not for murder, but for 'unconsciously risking a life'. In the wake of the murder, several cases were reported in the press, as several poor people were put to death by 'unconscious', but usually not persecuted, citizens. In some quarters, it has since been 'fashionable' to set fire to poor people. Who are these poor Brazilians, do they represent a tiny minority of expendable human beings?

Brazil is now the tenth largest economy, with a gross domestic product (GDP) reaching some eight hundred billion United States dollars and a per capita GDP around US$ 4700 (*Latin American Monitor* 1997: 5) but, after some sources, it is the most iniquitous country on earth, as the poorest 40 per cent earn only 7 per cent of the national income, whilst the richest 10 per cent earn 51.3 per cent, a worse imbalance than in any other American, African or Asian country (*Folha de São Paulo* 1996a). Just the richest 1 per cent earn 13.9 per cent, whilst the poorest 10 per cent earn 1.1 per cent (*Folha de São Paulo* 1996b), and in the last forty years or so the imbalance has been increasing, rather than decreasing (Dantas 1995), to the despair of economists, such as Zini (1997) and writers, such as Rui Mourão (1997), among others. Children still work, instead of going to school (Filho 1997; Ribeiro 1997; Sérgio and Rocha 1997) and illiteracy is rife.

The vast majority thus live on less than US$ 60 a month (Fuentes 1996) and are, as a consequence, out of the consumer market, as emphasised some time ago by Edward J. Amadeo (1991), now minister for labour affairs. While this goes a long way to explain the poor status of ordinary Brazilians, two other features must also be mentioned: the patriarchal roots of Brazilian social relations and the recent history of authoritarian rule. A hierarchical society, the Brazilian system operates secularly through such institutions as the elite family and its side effects: patronage and the resulting fear of the good, powerful masters (DaMatta 1991: 399). Slaves, poor people, and all non-proprietors are thus not citizens, but subjects and dependants (Mota 1977: 173) and patronage (Carvalho 1998) is still pervasive today (e.g. *O Estado de São Paulo* 1998). This authoritarian tradition was strengthened by military rule between 1964 and 1985, when 'lots of people suffered, have been exiled, tortured and killed', in the words of a historian who lived the experience (Iglésias 1985: 216). After the restoration of civilian rule there has been no enquiry into the abuses of the authorities in this period, even though human rights activists stress that 'the state of law and democracy demand that truth be revealed, if governments do not respect the law and the rights of citizens' (Pinheiro 1995; cf. Rebelo 1990). There has been no 'Truth and Reconciliation Commission' in Brazil, as was the case in South Africa (Cose 1998; Mabry 1998), and even other countries in the southern cone, like Argentina, were able to at least partially investigate the abuses of military dictators and their supporters. The result has been that the discourse of power, articulated by intellectuals who are themselves power-holders, systematically denies 'the Other' (Velasco e Cruz 1997: 21–2) and dismisses the need to integrate Brazilian society beyond the huge social cleavages that pertain.

In this social context, what does it mean to 'do archaeology for the public', as Parker Pearson (1998) put it? The wider audience for archaeology in the United States and Europe includes a broad spectrum of social strata, and the pages of the *National Geographic Magazine* bear witness to the popular appeal of archaeology for a wide readership. Even though the constituency for archaeology is not much wider than the middle class (Merriman 1991; McGuire and Walker 1999), in the United States and Europe the middle classes are themselves not restricted to being an upper crust. The public for archaeology in Brazil, on the other hand, is limited to probably less than two hundred archaeologists (Barreto 1998: 774) and to school children, newspaper readers and sometimes a mass of television viewers, as more than 80 per cent of homes have television sets (*Folha de São Paulo* 1996c), and the middle classes are proportionally not as large as in Europe or the United States. The aim of this paper is thus to discuss the relationship between archaeologists and their different audiences and to assess the outlook for changes in the future.

Brazilian archaeology and Brazilian audiences

The public is usually perceived as an aggregate, non-organised community of people and hence it is used as a collective noun. In this sense it is too general to be used to deal with a variety of different social audiences. The narrowest audience of Brazilian archaeologists are other local archaeologists, and most practitioners are not worried by the fact that they limit themselves to this very special public. Usually, archaeologists do not publish their reports, as there is no explicit and abiding rule demanding research and publication of the results, as is the case in many other countries. In this case, the audience for several field seasons is restricted to the volunteers who assisted with the excavations. When there are unpublished reports or dissertations, the readership is restricted usually to a few people who have access to the original and/or to copies in libraries.

Increasingly though, archaeologists have been publishing their papers in local journals, enabling the readership to become wider: up to several hundred fellow archaeologists. Most archaeologists write in Portuguese and have no intention of addressing a non-Brazilian scholarly audience; few journals publish papers in foreign languages and/or are multi-lingual. Considering that there are fewer than two hundred archaeologists in the country, and that they deal with a variety of different subjects, if a paper is read by more than ten people it is an exception. Papers which address a much wider international archaeological audience are still rare but since the restoration of civilian rule in 1985 there has been a growing production of studies addressing the world archaeological community, as is the case in the recent 'Special section: issues in Brazilian archaeology', published by *Antiquity* (Barreto 1998; Gaspar 1998; Gonzalez 1998; Heckneberger 1998; Kipnis 1998; Neves 1998; Noelli 1998; Wüst 1998). Still, references to wider interpretive problems which could interest archaeologists who are non-specialists in Brazilian subjects are very rare, even though in the case of historical archaeology Brazilian subjects and standpoints are now being discussed by archaeologists in general, not only by the narrow group of foreign experts on Brazil, as recent books demonstrate (Orser 1996; Funari *et al.* 1999). This was already the case with papers produced by Brazilians on classical archaeology (e.g. Sarian 1989) and books (e.g. Funari 1996a) published in Europe (cf. Funari 1997a), which have had a much wider archaeological readership, as shown by consultation ratings on virtual sites.

The world archaeological public is, however, more interested in ideas than merely recovering and describing evidence because archaeology must be relevant to society at large and to the human and social sciences in particular (Tilley 1998: 691–2). There is thus another important audience, the other social sciences, whose concerns must be matched by archaeology, for there is a growing acknowledgement that archaeology is always socially engaged (Hodder 1991: 22), directly linked to ideologies and political uses (Slapsak 1993: 192), and that the way we interpret the past cannot be divorced from the way we perceive the present (Nassaney 1989: 89). So much so that even the study of the prehistoric past is a political act (Hodder 1990: 278) and archaeology, as a mode of production of the past (Shanks 1995: 34), assembles the past (Shanks and McGuire 1996: 82) and is a discipline inevitably linked to the public in general. In this respect, archaeologists in Europe and the United States are increasingly aware of the need to interact with historians, anthropologists, heritage managers, and educators. Their Brazilian counterparts should pay more attention to these audiences (Funari 1997b), inside and outside the country, as is beginning to be the case now (cf. Funari 1998), for the way to reach the wider public is to interact with fellow social scientists. A greater diversity of views and approaches, fostering pluralistic dialogue (Bintliff 1995: 34), enables archaeologists to be aware of the fact that there are other audiences, not strictly professional and archaeological (Funari 1996b).

Archaeologists have been confronting complex dilemmas when rulers and ruled (Ucko 1990: xx), or people excluded from power, compete for their services. Archaeology is the only social science that can provide access to all social groups, not only elites, but also peasants, indigenous people, nomads, slaves, craftsmen and merchants (Saitta 1995: 385), and for this reason ordinary people have the potential to recognise themselves in what we as archaeologists offer them. In recent decades, anthropologists, historians and other social scientists have been keen to study the excluded and to address a variety of audiences. Indigenous people have been active interlocutors and scientists have been campaigning for the rights of Indians, particularly for the demarcation of indigenous peoples' lands. Blacks are in a similar situation, and now some school textbooks mention Indigenous people, Blacks, ordinary poor people, immigrants and other excluded strata, both in the present and the past. Environmental concerns have also been addressed by different sciences, as is the case with urbanism and vernacular architecture from a perspective of poor people. Archaeology has also addressed some of these concerns, and this was so almost from its inception in the nineteenth century, even if this was the concern of a minority.

At the beginning of the twentieth century, when a state museum director and practising archaeologist, Von Ihering, defended the traditional approach to Indigenous people, proposing the genocide of ethnic groups, practising archaeologists from the National Museum in Rio de Janeiro, then the capital of the country, reacted and defended the Indians (cf. Funari 1999, with references). In the same vein, in the first decades of the twentieth century, some books on the archaeology and prehistory of Brazil were published. Their readers were not particularly numerous, nor their approach necessarily sympathetic to the Indians, but they did at least demonstrate the existence of an interest in indigenous material culture, and the desire of some practising archaeologists to understand 'the Other'. In a context when dominant groups used their power to push their own heritage to the fore (Byrne 1991: 275), the mere fact of looking for prehistoric artefacts was a way of challenging the dominating concerns and fashions.

However, those historical artefacts that were protected as heritage were overwhelmingly from the elite, resulting in ordinary people's alienation and lack of interest in the preservation of historical material culture. Looting of church art, for instance, has always been a problem, in Brazil as elsewhere (cf. Calabresi 1998), as ordinary people are not concerned by elite heritage and the elites themselves are usually lured by the market value of these artefacts (cf. the British case in Tubb and Brodie 2001). Even today, the eulogy of past upper class material splendour, in the form of ceramics or other elite items, is common currency (eg. Lima 1995), and museums promote exhibitions of these archaeological artefacts, with little concern for a critical approach, now common in both archaeology and museum studies worldwide.

Black material culture was as a consequence absent for a long time from archaeological discourse or displays, as were any humble artefacts, what Mediterranean archaeologists call the *instrumentum domesticum*, ordinary pottery, post holes, remains of suffering, not of the joy of wealthy aristocrats and their fine pottery. On 30 October 1998, at the historic colonial town of Ouro Preto, in Minas Gerais State, an Oratory Museum was opened with 'artefacts expressing the religious variety of our people. Rich and poor had a place of honour, in their homes, to shelter a domestic shrine', in the words of the Archbishop Luciano Mendes de Almeida of Mariana, a human rights activist who has taken part in the fight against oppression in the last few decades (Almeida 1998).

The main public concern of Brazilian archaeologists has always been in establishing that our heritage is a world heritage, that humble remains are as important as learned European ones, and that the excluded are also a part of the public. It is symptomatic that archaeologists engaged in human rights, in a very broad sense of the expression, have been those who have addressed a wider audience and fought for the right of future generations to be able to learn about their roots (Hudson 1994: 55). Paulo Duarte, an intellectual who fought the dictatorship in the 1930s and early 1940s, returned to Brazil after World War II and struggled to publicise the importance of shell middens, as a common heritage of all Brazilians, considering the remains of Indians worthy of preservation and study (cf. Funari 1995). Thanks to his efforts, legislation was passed in the Congress to protect archaeological heritage in the early 1960s, just before the military clampdown whose consequences are still felt, some fifteen years after the restoration of civilian rule in 1985. While official Brazilian archaeology was reinvented by the training of a new generation of Brazilian practitioners, under the guide of Betty Meggers and Clifford Evans, concern about the wider public gradually faded. However, even in those dark years (1964–85), several archaeologists continued to be concerned with the public and with heritage, some of them in line with the French-inspired humanism of Paulo Duarte, as was the case with the study of rock art by André Prous and Niede Guidon, among others, or the continued study of shell middens. African and/or African-Brazilian heritage was also a concern of Mariano Carneiro da Cunha.

Only after the restoration of civilian rule, though, did Brazilian archaeologists address wider audiences more directly. The first manuals on archaeology were published (Funari 1988; Prous 1991), historical archaeology began to pay attention to excluded people, such as Indians in Missions (Kern 1989) or Blacks in runaway settlements (Funari 1996c), and for the first time Brazilian prehistory was introduced for millions of school children as a search for Indigenous peoples' culture (Guarinello 1994). The increasing resonance of the ideals of the World Archaeological Congress in Brazil, as attested by a recent international conference (Funari 1998), shows a growing social awareness within the archaeological community. Overall, and in the context of a Brazilian society so marked by cleavages, there has been an active engagement of several archaeologists with broader social strata and issues, from land rights for Indian and Black people, to a less unbalanced picture of excluded people in museum exhibitions (Tamanini 1994). Processes and products (Merriman 1996: 382) of archaeological activities are directly linked to the public and Brazilian archaeologists are now resuscitating an enduring humanist approach, felt since the inception of the discipline in the country, whose concerns for the people are central to the archaeological practice. Indians, Blacks, ordinary people are being reintroduced in archaeological discourse, and public archaeology is beginning to be felt as an essential aspect of the discipline in Brazil, as it already is the world over.

Acknowledgements

I owe thanks to the following colleagues: Eduardo Goes Neves, Randall McGuire, Dean J. Saitta, Haiganuch Sarian, Michael Shanks, Sebastião C. Velasco e Cruz, Peter Ucko, Irmhild Wüst . I must also mention the support of FAPESP and the Institute of Archaeology (University College London). The ideas presented here are my own, for which I am therefore solely responsible.

Bibliography

Almeida, L.M. 1998. Museu do Oratório. *Folha de São Paulo* 24 October, 1: 2.

Amadeo, E.J. 1991. O núcleo protegido da economia brasileira. *Folha de São Paulo* 22 October, 3: 2.

Barreto, C. 1998. Brazilian archaeology from a Brazilian perspective. *Antiquity* 72: 573–81.

Bintliff, J. 1995. 'Whither archaeology?' revisited. In Kuna, M. and Venclová, N. (eds) *Whither Archaeology? Papers in honour of E. Neustupny*. Prague: Institute of Archaeology.

Byrne, D. 1991. Western hegemony in archaeological heritage management. *History and Anthropology* 5: 269–76.

Calabresi, M. 1998. Priest versus pilferers. *Time* 23 February: 19.

Carvalho, J.M. 1998. *Pontos e Bordados*. Universidade Federal de Minas, Belo Horizonte Gerais.

Cose, E. 1998. The limitations of the truth. *Newsweek* 26 October: 25.

DaMatta, R. 1991. Religion and modernity: three studies of Brazilian religiosity. *Journal of Social History* 25: 389–406.

Dantas, V. 1995. Concentração de renda aumentou desde 90. *O Estado de São Paulo* 13 August, Economia: 1.

Filho, T. 1997. Trabalho que empobrece. *Estado de Minas* 18 May: 42.

Folha de São Paulo. 1996a. Os números da desigualdade. *Folha de São Paulo* 9 July, 1: 5.

Folha de São Paulo. 1996b. Evolução do rendimento mensal do brasileiro. *Folha de São Paulo* 6 September, 1: 8.

Folha de São Paulo. 1996c. Percentual de residências com alguns serviços e bens. *Folha de São Paulo* 6 September, 1: 9.

Fuentes, C. 1996. From the boom days to the boomerang. *Newsweek* 6 May: 50–1.

Funari, P.P.A. 1988. *Arqueologia*. São Paulo: A[ac]tica.

Funari, P.P.A. 1995. Mixed features of archaeological theory in Brazil. In Ucko, P.J. (ed.) *Theory in Archaeology. A World Perspective*. London: Routledge.

Funari, P.P.A. 1996a. *Dressel 20 Inscriptions from Britain and the Consumption of Spanish Olive Oil*. Oxford: Tempus Reparatum.

Funari, P.P.A. 1996b. Pluralism and divisions in European archaeology. *Journal of European Archaeology* 4: 384–5.

Funari, P.P.A. 1996c. A Arqueologia de Palmares – sua contribuição para o conhecimento da História da cultura afro-brasileira. In *Liberdade por um Fio*. São Paulo: Companhia das Letras: 26–52.

Funari, P.P.A. 1997a. European Archaeology and two Brazilian offspring: classical archaeology and art history. *Journal of European Archaeology* 5: 137–48.

Funari, P.P.A. 1997b. Archaeology, history and historical archaeology in South America. *International Journal of Historical Archaeology* 1: 189–206.

Funari, P.P.A. 1998. *Teoria Arqueológica na América do Sul*. Campinas: Instituto de Filosofia e Ciências Humanas.

Funari, P.P.A. 1999. Brazilian archaeology: an overview. In Politis, G. (ed.) *Archaeology in Latin America*. London: Routledge.

Funari, P.P.A., Hall, M. and Jones, S. (eds). 1999. *Historical Archaeology: Back from the Edge*. London: Routledge.

Gaspar, M.D. 1998. Considerations of the *sambaquis* of the Brazilian coast. *Antiquity* 72: 592–616.

Gerchmann, L. 1998. Mendigo tem 13 per cent do corpo queimado em Porto Alegre. *Follha de São Paulo* 6 August, 3: 10.

Gonzalez, E.M.R. 1998. Regional pottery-making groups in southern Brazil. *Antiquity* 72: 616–25.

Guarinello, N.L. 1994. *Os Primeiros Habitantes do Brasil*. São Paulo: Atual.

Heckenberger, M.J. 1998. Manioc agriculture and sedentism in Amazonia: the Upper Xingu example. *Antiquity* 72: 633–48.

Hodder, I. 1990. *The Domestication of Europe*. Oxford: Basil Blackwell.

Hodder, I. 1991. Archaeological theory in contemporary European societies: the emergence of competing traditions. In Hodder, I. (ed.) *Archaeological Theory in Europe*. London: Routledge.

Hudson, K. 1994. The great European museum: the museum one cannot and does not need to enter. *Institute of Archaeology Bulletin* 31: 53–60.

Iglésias, F. 1985. Momentos democráticos na trajetória brasileira. In Jaguaribe, H. (ed.) *Brasil, sociedade democrática*. Rio de Janeiro: José Olympio: 125–221.

Kern, A.A. 1989. Escavações arqueológicas na Missão Jesuítico-Guarani de São Lourenço. *Estudos Ibero-Americanos PUCRS* 15: 111–33.

Kipnis, R. 1998. Early hunter-gatherers in the Americas: perspectives from Central Brazil. *Antiquity* 72: 581–92.

Latin American Monitor. 1997. Brazil: macroeconomic data and forecasts. *Latin American Monitor* 14(5): 5.

Lima, T.A. 1998. Pratos e mais pratos: louças domésticas, divisões culturais e limites sociais no Rio de Janeiro, século XIX. *Anais do Museu Paulista, N.Ser.* 3: 129–91.

Mabry, M. 1998. Look back in horror. *Newsweek* 26 October: 22–4.

McGuire, R.H. and Walker, M. 1999. Class confrontations in archaeology. *Historical Archaeology* 33.

Merriman, N. 1991. *Beyond the Glass Case: The past, the Heritage and Public in Britain*. Leicester: Leicester University Press.

Merriman, N. 1996. Understanding heritage. *Journal of Material Culture* 1(3): 377–86.

Mota, C.G. 1977. História contemporânea da cultura. Os anos 50: linhas de produção cultural. *Revista de História* 111: 155–81.

Mourão, R. 1997. As idéias que se traduzem em palavras. *Estado de Minas* 26 January: 8.

Nassaney, M. 1989. An epistemological enquiry into some archaeological and historical interpretations of seventeenth century Native American–European relations. In Shennan, S.J. (ed.) *Archaeological Approaches to Cultural Identity*. London: Unwin Hyman.

Neves, E.G. 1998. Twenty years of Amazonian archaeology in Brazil (1977–1997). *Antiquity* 72: 625–33.

Noelli, F.S. 1998. The Tupi: explaining origin and expansions in terms of archaeology and historical linguistics. *Antiquity* 72: 648–63.

O Estado de São Paulo. 1998. Paternalismo ainda domina relações políticas na cidade. *O Estado de São Paulo* 11 October, C: 4.

Orser, C.E. 1996. *A Historical Archaeology of the Modern World*. New York: Plenum.

Parker Pearson, M. 1998. The beginning of wisdom. *Antiquity* 72: 680–6.

Pinheiro, P.S. 1995. Não forcemos contas de chegada. *Folha de São Paulo* 6 August, 1: 3.

Prous, A. 1991. *Arqueologia Brasileira.* Brasília: Universidade de Brasília.

Rebelo, A. 1990. Dívida com a História. *Folha de São Paulo* 8 October, C: 3.

Ribeiro, L. 1997. A única alternativa de um pai. *Estado de Minas* 18 May: 42.

Saitta, D.J. 1995. Marxism and archaeology. In Cullenberg, S. and Biewoner, C. (eds) *Marxism in the Postmodern Age, Confronting the New World Order.* New York and London: Guildford.

Sarian, H. 1989. L'heritage mycenien: la civilisation. In Treuil, R. (ed.) *Les Civilisations Egéenes du Néolithique et de l'Âge du Bronze.* Paris: Presses Universitaires de France.

Sérgio, E. and Rocha, R. 1997. Lavoura esvazia escolas. *Estado de Minas,* 18 May: 42.

Shanks, M. 1995. Archaeological experiences and a critical romanticism. *Helsinki Papers in Archaeology* 7: 17–36.

Shanks, M. and McGuire, R. 1996. The craft of Archaeology. *American Antiquity* 61: 75–88.

Slapsak, B. 1993. Archaeology and the contemporary myths of the past. *Journal of European Archaeology* 2: 191–5.

Tamanini, E. 1994. *Museu Arqueológico de Sambaqui: um olhar necessário.* Unpublished Master's degree dissertation. Campinas: Faculdade de Educação.

Tilley, C. 1998. Archaeology: the loss of isolation. *Antiquity* 72: 691–3.

Tubb, K. W. and Brodie, N. 2001. From museum to mantelpiece: the antiquities trade in the United Kingdom. In Layton, R., Stone, P.G. and Thomas, J. (eds) *Destruction and Conservation of Cultural Property.* London: Routledge.

Ucko, P.J. 1990. Foreword. In Gathercole, P. and Lowenthal, D. (eds) *The Politics of the Past.* London: Unwin Hyman.

Velasco e Cruz, S.C. 1997. *Restructuring World Economy. Arguments about 'market-oriented reforms' in developing countries.* Campinas: Instituto de Filosofia e Ciências Humanas da UNICAMP.

Williams, R. 1983. *Keywords. A Vocabulary of Culture and Society.* London: Fontana.

Wüst, I. 1998. Continuities and discontinuities: archaeology and ethnoarchaeology in the heart of the Eastern Bororo territory, Mato Grosso, Brazil. *Antiquity* 72: 663–76.

Zini, A.A. 1997. Desigualdade de renda no Brasil. *Folha de São Paulo* 2 March, 2: 5.

11

ARCHAEOLOGY FOR WHOSE INTEREST – ARCHAEOLOGISTS OR THE LOCALS?

Bertram Mapunda and Paul Lane

Introduction

Archaeological research in East Africa started over eighty years ago with two major spatial foci, one centred on the interior along the Eastern Rift Valley, and the other along the coast from Somalia south as far as Mozambique. Initially, research in the interior was mostly concerned with hominid evolution and the Early Stone Age, and Later Stone Age rock art, resulting in the discovery of numerous internationally famous archaeological localities and sites, that include Olduvai, Laetoli, Koobi Fora, and Lake Turkana and the rich collection of rock art sites in the Kondoa region of Tanzania. Pioneering researchers included Hans Reck, Ludwig Kohl-Larsen, Louis Leakey, Mary Leakey and E.J. Wayland (a geologist by profession). The work on the coast, on the other hand, focused on a much more recent period of the region's history – the architectural monuments of the Swahili towns such as those at Kilwa Kisiwani, Kaole, Manda, Gedi, Lamu, Pate and many others. Much of this early research was conducted by the likes of James Kirkman, Neville Chittick, and Peter Garlake.

Since these early efforts to develop the discipline, archaeological research in the region has continued to expand both spatially and thematically (for a more detailed overview, see Robertshaw (1990) and Posnansky (1982)). Today almost every district in Eastern Africa has been visited by an archaeologist, and almost all classes of monument and all periods from the Early Stone Age through the Iron Age to the late nineteenth century have been the subject of investigation. The broad archaeological sequences for the different geographical and cultural zones are known, and widely exhibited in numerous national, regional, and site museums. Parties of school children are frequently to be seen being led through these displays, and in some cases can attend 'Archaeology Days' organised by one of the museums. In the past two decades, the opportunities to take courses leading to BA and MA degrees in archaeology have become increasingly available at the various universities in the region, and as a consequence there is a growing number of qualified East African archaeologists and palaeoanthropologists. Despite quite severe budgetary constraints, the antiquities services in most East African countries are still able to sustain a basic programme of archaeological resource management, and in some instances have a relatively high public profile. At least one National Museum service, the National Museums of Kenya, has recently launched its own web site.

Given the extent of this work, and the considerable sums of public, donor and research foundation money that have been invested in developing archaeological research in the region, it is legitimate to ask: 'How much of this reflects the needs of the general public, the *wananchi*, in East Africa?' Equally, one is entitled to ask: 'In what ways have archaeological research projects benefited local populations in the region?' The answer to both of these questions is 'very little!' Do members of the public know that there has been so much archaeological work going on in, so to speak, their backyards, for almost a century? Again, we are inclined to answer 'very few do!' If this is indeed the case, then why? Why, despite the efforts of museums, antiquities departments, universities and visiting researchers, do so few of East Africa's population have any knowledge about archaeology – to such an extent that far from being 'public', archaeology in the region could be better described as a very private and intellectually elitist affair?[1]

In this paper we try to account for the low impact that archaeological research has had on the majority of East Africans. We also suggest methods that may be more suitable for bringing archaeology closer to the rural and urban populace than those which archaeological bodies across the region currently rely on.

Archaeology and the public: the current situation

Engagement by archaeologists with members of the general public in both rural and urban areas in East Africa takes two broad forms. On the one hand, the various national antiquities and national museums services, as in other parts of the world, have either statutory or *de facto* powers and responsibilities to curate, manage and research the archaeological resources in their respective countries. The extent to which these different bodies actually fulfil their duties, however, is extremely variable. In some respects, this can be attributed to the different levels of economic prosperity and relative strengths of the national economies across the region. However, it is also the case that certain national museums and/or antiquities services have had a far more proactive approach to promoting archaeological awareness among the general populace, than others. The Zambian Heritage Commission, for example, has a long record of establishing regional and site museums, and of producing information sheets and other low-cost publications aimed at sensitising the public to the importance of archaeological remains and the need for their protection. In Kenya, where there is no formal antiquities service, the National Museums of Kenya, partly because of greater and more sustained funding, have made even more strenuous efforts to communicate the importance of archaeology through a variety of media and events. Yet, despite such efforts, site destruction through ignorance, neglect, complete disregard and even malicious intent remains an ongoing and major problem across the region (for a discussion of recent examples from Kenya, Somalia and Tanzania, see Brandt and Mohamed (1996), Karoma (1996), Kusimba (1996), Mturi (1996) and Wilson and Omar (1996)).[2] A further common problem faced by those bodies with statutory responsibility for the archaeological heritage, is that they are often negatively perceived by the rural and urban populace as yet another arm of central government interference and state control. That is, of what Foucault has termed 'govern-mentality'.

Public awareness and support for archaeology in the region are also not greatly helped by the level and quality of site interpretation media. On-site interpretation panels, signing, visitor orientation centres, self-guided leaflets, knowledgeable guides and even site custodians are absent from all but a tiny handful of publicly accessible archaeological sites and monuments in the region. Even where some of these media are employed, the style of writing and presentation are geared more towards foreign visitors and the educated elite, than for a mass audience. Perhaps because of this, there is only a very rudimentary culture of visiting museums and archaeological sites among the East African public. Equally, although there has been some recent improvement across the region in formal education about archaeology, especially at university level but also in secondary and primary schools, many text-books are woefully out of date and Eurocentric in their interpretations (Wandibba 1990).[3] Viewed in this light, the decision by the Village Museum in Dar es Salaam to allow the use of their premises for traditional performances such as initiation ceremonies and wedding dances, and for organising events to promote indigenous cuisine and traditional dances, seems to us to be a step in the right direction.

The other broad category of opportunities for contact with members of the public is within the context of field research projects, by both local and visiting researchers. Typically, researchers involve local people only as generators of information or as labourers. Rarely do archaeologists deliberately inform villagers about the objectives and significance of their research before they start working or about the research results at the end of their projects. Consequently, any critical evaluation of archaeological awareness among rural communities would most likely show that very few people know what archaeology is about or what archaeologists do. This would seem to imply that not only have archaeologists failed to inform, train and/or educate local people but also have not even made themselves and their projects especially visible to those who live in their research areas. This is true even with regard to ethnoarchaeological field projects, where the interaction between a researcher and the local people is a methodological necessity.

In many cases, the failure to recognize the importance of engaging villagers in the research process has alienated the local people from their own cultural heritage instead of retrieving, studying and preserving it for them. To a large extent, archaeologists have only succeeded in talking about the academic significance of artifacts, architectural monuments and faunal remains amongst themselves, as opposed to showing the significance of these materials to local people. Yet, it is the latter who are the caretakers, and in many cases the direct heirs, of the cultural heritage the archaeologists seek to retrieve from other peoples' homes. The general failure of the archaeological profession to get members of the public to recognise the rationale of protecting heritage resources from destruction, looting and illicit trafficking is a direct consequence of this. Lack of communication may well explain, for example, why local people, the Maasai, were ready to vandalise the roofing materials covering the DK^4 site at Olduvai Gorge; why residents at Kilwa Kisiwani continue to mine this World Heritage site for building materials; why villagers continue to use parts of the earthworks at Bigo and Ntusi for cultivating crops; and why numerous similar cases can be drawn from many other sites in East Africa.

Such continued neglect of East Africa's archaeological resources is perhaps understandable where sites are remote and poorly researched. Surely, though, at such well-known and intensively researched localities as Olduvai, Kilwa, and Bigo, which have all been visited periodically by teams of researchers for at least several decades, there can be no such excuses. And much of the blame for the continued lack of public regard for such sites must lie with the archaeological research community and our preferred *modus operandi*.

To try to change this sorry state of affairs, we argue here that researchers should be obliged to inform, train and seek to educate local people, so that they become aware of both the scientific significance of archaeological materials and the historical and cultural ties which link them to these remains. Drawing out the cultural and/or historical links, in turn, may well help to create a sense of ownership and hence an obligation among the local people to conserve and protect the archaeological materials. At the same time, there is a need to make archaeology a useful discipline for local people, just as it is for archaeologists themselves (Mapunda 1991; see also Lane 1990), and to fulfil our ethical obligations to return something to the communities that have hosted archaeological researchers for so long.

Suggested methods

There are several ways that archaeologists can impart archaeological knowledge to local communities. The conventional methods have been those involving mass media such as television, radio and newspapers. These popular methods have been used with varying levels of success. On Pemba, for example, Adria LaViolette found that coverage of her excavations at Pujini by Zanzibar Television stimulated considerable interest amongst the inhabitants of both Pemba and Zanzibar and encouraged many local people to visit the site (LaViolette 1991). Equally, several researchers working in Uganda, including Andrew Reid, Rachel Maclean and Pete Robertshaw, have found coverage of their research projects in the national press encouraged widespread local interest in archaeology and cultural remains (pers. comm.). On the other hand, many journalists are almost as uninformed about the archaeology of the region as the readers archaeologists would wish them to target, and as a consequence reports carried by newspapers and other mass media often contain many inaccuracies. Also, with the exception of radio, the mass media may not be the most effective mechanism to use, especially when trying to target rural communities. Television, for example, which is possibly the best medium for educational purposes, is poorly distributed in rural areas because the majority of the rural population cannot afford TV sets, and often have no access to electricity. Newspapers, in many cases, may not have reliable circulation in rural areas, and given the variable levels of literacy, readership figures can be quite low in some areas, especially among rural communities. Moreover, some countries do not have a recognised *lingua franca*, thus, the languages used in such media are foreign to many people.

Given these constraints, we suggest methods executable by researchers and ones that can be applied to all people, commoners and the affluent and educated elites. These include: (1) recruiting local people as field researchers; (2) conducting field site tours; (3) organising exhibitions of research results; (4) field public lectures; and (5) low-cost publications.

We know that some of these strategies are commonly used. For example, a good number of foreign researchers employ local people as interpreters in interviews or as labourers on site surveys and excavations. Typically, however, this type of local participation is not deliberately aimed at teaching local participants but rather exploiting their skills and labour. Similarly, with site visits and exhibitions, local visitors are usually treated as if they were tourists coming to admire excavation trenches and the 'dirt' collected therein, instead of as students who come to learn from and exchange views with researchers (Figure 11.1). Villagers should be allowed and encouraged to observe what is going on, to see what kind of materials are recovered and, most importantly, to be told about the cultural and scientific significance of the materials recovered and asked to provide their own intellectual input.

To do this, we propose the following model that one of us has been developing while conducting research in southern Tanzania over several years (Mapunda 1992), and which we also plan to implement as part of a new joint project in the Kondoa region of central Tanzania.

1. **Research goals.** Prior to the commencement of survey or excavation, a researcher needs to visit the villages covered by the respective research universe,

Figure 11.1 Public lecture to primary school pupils during the Ruvu River Basin survey, eastern Tanzania 1998. Photo by Bertram Mapunda.

Figure 13.1 Sydney Cove (right of the Opera House). The site of the first Government House, demolished in 1848, is immediately behind the tall black office tower to the right of the Botanical Gardens, formerly the Governor's Domain. Fairfax Photo Library.

of the Eora's dispossession as inevitable once the decision had been taken in London to dispatch the fleet. The inevitability comes from our understanding of the realities of power and our consciousness of the geo-imperial design. The fence around the governor's garden is thus merely an instant in a mapping project which would see a grid of boundaries spreading out across the landscape from this first fence (Byrne 2003). It also comes from our understanding that this mapping project, which had begun with the coastal charts drawn during Captain Cook's voyage of discovery in 1770, had a certain momentum: the First Fleet, when it sailed up the harbour on 20 January 1788, carried these charts but it also carried the intention to extend the mapping inland.[2]

The force and momentum of European territorial expansion was beyond the power of the Eora and the other tribes to prevent. This does not, however, mean they put aside their own prior and radically counter conception of local space or their own conception of belonging. In the following pages I contend that Aboriginal people have privately, as it were, refused to concede the dispossession that publicly seems so incontrovertible. I suggest that evidence of this is seen in the variety of ways that Aboriginal people not only give precedence to local space but orchestrate the movement of people and objects in the direction of the local. And I further suggest that this particular way of resisting colonisation has done a lot to make the archaeology of Aboriginal Australia a very public archaeology.

241

introduce him or herself to the village officials and traditional leaders so as to. inform them about the research goals and what he or she perceives as being the significance of the research. During this time the researcher should welcome and encourage local people to visit the research in progress, and also encourage members of the local population to contribute their own suggestions as to how the research may be of benefit to their communities. Efforts should also be made to ascertain how the local population perceive their past, and how archaeological research may contribute to global understanding of this.

2. **Labour recruitment**. Employment of local people as field assistants should go beyond simply meeting the labour needs of the project, so as to include members of the local populace as ambassadors to their respective communities. In case the research universe covers more than one village, the researcher should make sure that at least one person is employed from each village. In situations where employing a representative from each village would cost more than can be covered by the available budget, employment should be on a turn by turn basis as opposed to permanent persons for the entire research duration. As a matter of principle, the best 'ambassador' is one who is picked by the people represented. So the researcher should let the local people pick their own candidate provided he or she meets the basic qualifications needed for such a role. These may include physical fitness, hard work, acquaintance with the people and the research area and trustworthiness. If recruitment is on a turn by turn basis, the 'village ambassador' should join the research team when the work is conducted in his or her village or area. Apart from the usual research activities, the village ambassador could assist the principal researcher by satisfying the curiosity of local residents, and allaying the suspicions that the public usually have about archaeologists and archaeological fieldwork. In our experience, it is almost impossible to eradicate such suspicions through a non-local crew member.

Exercises of this type have also been carried out by other archaeologists working elsewhere in Africa. In the late 1970s and early 1980s, for instance, a team of archaeologists from Eduardo Mondlane University while excavating the site of Manyikeni in Mozambique employed a team of over 450 local people, each of whom was given on-site training and encouraged to learn more about the archaeology and history of their area. The strategy appears to have been greeted with considerable enthusiasm by the local populace, and even the government, and led, among other things, to the construction of on-site displays (Sinclair 1990).[5] An even more radical approach, which would certainly have long-term benefits, would be to provide more intensive on-site training for a few selected members of the local community in archaeological field techniques. This approach has been used to good effect by Andy Smith and Richard Lee among Ju/'hoansi in northern Bushmanland, Namibia, as part of a strategy aimed at empowering the communities in their research area so that they can engage in the production and representation of their past (Smith and Lee 1997).

3. **Exhibition**. Towards the end of the research period, the principal researcher needs to organise exhibitions of selected finds and preliminary results for public viewing (as happened at Manyikeni). The number of exhibitions would depend on the size of the research area. In extensive areas, where more than one exhibit may be necessary, concurrent exhibits could be conducted provided that there are a sufficient number of competent assistants to draw on. Where the researcher lacks able assistants, one way of mounting the exhibitions could be on a rotational basis. Alternatively, it may be worthwhile getting competent members of the adult education departments at local universities to assist.

The exhibition need not last more than a day, or at most two. Also, so as to achieve maximum public exposure, it ought to be arranged to coincide with a day of rest, such as Sunday or a public holiday. The event needs to be advertised well in advance to encourage participation. Public viewing should be preceded by a lecture. This should touch on the following: the research objectives, the reasons for picking the respective research area, the methods employed, the materials retrieved and their relevance to local culture, knowledge and beliefs (emphasising the connection with the local people), and the contribution of the results to world culture and science.

4. **Project assessment**. Researchers should cultivate a habit of conducting project assessments in the field so that the input of the local people is honoured and incorporated. The evaluation should be done at the end of fieldwork. Participants should include a cadre of local intellectuals such as village elders, officials and spokespersons, government workers (teachers, agricultural officers, medical officers etc.) religious leaders, and those villagers who have contributed in any important way to the project, e.g. as key informants or guides. From the local people the researcher should tease out views on the educational impact the project has had for their communities. At the same time, the researcher should seek their opinions and suggestions as to how the project could have been improved. The incorporation of local people in this exercise does not only enrich the researcher with suggestions for planning similar projects in the future, but also cultivates a sense of pride and confidence amongst them. In the longer term, this should enable them to carry out their own decisions in the future regarding the protection and preservation of heritage resources. Our experiences have shown that local people are highly motivated once they have been involved in this type of intellectual discourse.

5. **Popular publication of results**. There is a great dearth of popular, low-cost literature on archaeology and the results of archaeological research in the region. With the greater availability of desk-top publishing systems, and the concomitant fall in publication costs, such a situation is no longer acceptable. Although we recognise the value of using the World Wide Web as a means of disseminating research results and project information, access to such technology is limited to a few, comparatively wealthy members of the middle classes, most of whom are likely to be well educated professionals. This pattern of access is likely to continue for some years to come.

Accordingly, researchers should endeavour to produce, at relatively low cost, some tangible reminder of their research and the main results for public distribution, especially in their research area but also beyond. The types of publication can be quite modest, such as a double-sided sheet of A3 paper, folded for ease of handling, and should be easy and inexpensive to reproduce.[6] In the longer term, small booklets, written in the local language, with line illustrations and, if funds permit, photographs should be produced and made available locally and nationally.

Conclusion

We have stated earlier that there are many techniques one can use to increase public awareness of archaeology. These include increased coverage of discoveries, field projects and interpretations by the mass media, the use of mobile cinema and museums, public lectures and enhanced interpretive media in museums and on sites open to the public. All are useful methods, and can be used to good effect. However, we argue that public awareness in African contexts has to be hastened by the direct involvement of researchers while in the field. There are several reasons for this. First, we have both attempted to accomplish this while conducting our own research, and the results have been encouraging. This is particularly true of the more systematic work carried out by Bertram Mapunda over the last decade.

The first occasion these methods were tested was in 1990, when he began research for his Master's thesis in his home village of Lithui in southern Tanzania. As a direct consequence of his choice of field area, a need to share the information collected with local people arose as a result of pressure from two sides – the villagers who felt that they had some right to ask 'their boy' to explain what he was doing and what he uncovered, and, the obligation the 'boy' felt to inform his fellow villagers and relatives what he was planning to do.

On this occasion, the research universe was roughly 20 km^2 and encompassed seven separate villages. At the outset, visits were made to each village, at which the research team was introduced and the research goals were explained to the relevant village officials. The next step was to recruit labourers. The ideal strategy, as discussed above, would have been to employ a minimum of seven individuals and at least one person from each village. However, because of budgetary constraints, only four locals could be employed. The dilemma as to who should be picked was resolved by employing both full-time and part-time workers. Three villagers from two of the seven villages were hired full-time, with the remaining labourer being employed on a rotational basis depending on the locality in which fieldwork was being undertaken on a particular day. Each village was asked to select their representative to work with the research team whenever they were in their area. In addition to assisting in the field, on their return to their village, these individuals were also expected to satisfy the

Figure 11.2 Village elders examining archaeological materials found during the Ruvu River Basin survey, eastern Tanzania 1998. Photo by Bertram Mapunda.

curiosity of their neighbours and allay any suspicions they might harbour about the presence of researchers.

The last two Sundays of the seven-week field project were used to mount open exhibitions for two groups of villages based on their proximity to one another. The exercise began with a lecture on the meaning and relevance of archaeology, and how the research was related to understanding the cultural history of the area (Figure 11.1). This was followed by a guided viewing of a sample of materials collected during the project (Figure 11.2). Finally, the villagers were allowed to ask questions about the project and the research results. At the very end of the fieldwork, time was also set aside for a project assessment in which at least two senior officials from each village, important informants, and local intellectuals (e.g. primary school teachers, medical officers, agricultural extension workers and so forth) participated. The objective of this gathering was to tease out views and suggestions from the local populace on the various techniques employed during the research, for the purpose of sharing with them the archaeological information obtained during the project.

The results from both types of gathering were constructive in terms of both research methods and the promotion of public awareness of archaeology. The majority of the local population was highly impressed by the approach used to inform them of the research goals, and appreciative of their involvement in the project from its inception. They also admitted to having learned more about their history, and understood it better than they had before the project began. As an indication of their increased awareness of heritage resources, the villagers promised to pile stones around important sites so as to alert others to their presence in an effort to avoid damage to the sites in the future, and to preserve them for their offspring. They also requested the principal researcher to encourage future researchers in the area to consult with the local population and to involve them in their projects in a similar fashion.

Based on the good results from that first experience, the same methods have been used and refined on future field projects undertaken by Bertram Mapunda, and are now a research norm for him. Similar encouraging results have since been achieved using these methods in other parts of Tanzania, including the areas of eastern Lake Tanganyika and southwestern Tanzania (1992–93), the upper Ruvu River basin, eastern Tanzania (1998), and around Geita, western Tanzania (1999).

We appeal, therefore, to field researchers in East Africa, and Africa in general, to share the archaeological knowledge from their research with the people who live in their research areas. This is because the local people need and have the right to know about their cultural heritage. Also, this knowledge may provide some incentive to local people to conserve the archaeological materials that they may encounter in their neighbourhood. The use of researchers as educators requires neither additional labour nor money, only decision-making and planning, and adopting the type of strategies we have outlined may well go a

long way to strengthening the effectiveness of the other 'public archaeology' measures currently used by museums and other bodies in the region.

Notes

1 See Nzewunwa (1990) for a similar argument with regard to the situation in Nigeria.
2 A very similar range of concerns was expressed at two international gatherings held in Nairobi: The Archaeological Heritage of Eastern Africa: Conservation, Presentation and Research Priorities Workshop (February 1997) jointly organised by the British Institute in Eastern Africa and the National Museums of Kenya, (Sutton 1997); and the International Workshop on Urban and Monuments Conservation (May 1997) organised by the National Museums of Kenya.
3 For a discussion of these problems as they affect the teaching of history in schools, see Zeleza (1990).
4 DK = Douglas Korongo; i.e. Douglas Leakey's (the discoverer) gully.
5 Note, however, that these displays have not been maintained and both access to the site and the condition of the site have now deteriorated (Macamo 1996). Although this may be attributable to the difficulties Mozambique has faced given the recent civil war, it makes the point that there is a need to ensure the long-term sustainability of interpretation facilities at any site, and thought must be given to this when planning such ventures.
6 For example, the leaflet produced in 1995 by Ras Kono, as part of his Certificate in Museums Studies course at the University of Botswana, on the recent excavations by Nick Pearson at Modipe Hill, Kgatleng District, to accompany an exhibition about the site at Phuthadikobo Museum, Mochudi.

Bibliography

Brandt, S.A. and Mohamed, O.Y. 1996. Starting from scratch: The past, present and future management of Somalia's cultural heritage. In P.R. Schmidt and R.J. McIntosh (eds) *Plundering Africa's Past*. London: James Currey: 250–9.

Karoma, N.J. 1996. The deterioration and destruction of archaeological and historical sites in Tanzania. In P.R. Schmidt and R.J. McIntosh (eds) *Plundering Africa's Past*. London: James Currey: 191–200.

Kusimba, C.M. 1996. Kenya's destruction of the Swahili cultural heritage. In P.R. Schmidt and R.J. McIntosh (eds) *Plundering Africa's Past*. London: James Currey: 201–24.

Lane, P.J. 1990. Archaeology and development in Africa: present dilemmas and future prospects. Paper presented at the 2nd Pan-African Association of Anthropologists Conference, University of Nairobi, Kenya, September 1990.

LaViolette, A. 1991. Alternative approaches to East African archaeology and historiography: The archaeology of a Swahili fortification. Paper presented at the 34th Annual Meeting of the African Studies Association, St. Louis, USA, November 1991.

Macamo, S.L. 1996. The problems of conservation of archaeological sites in Mozambique. In G. Pwiti and R. Soper (eds) *Aspects of African Archaeology*. Harare: University of Zimbabwe Publications: 813–16.

Mapunda, B.B. 1991. The role of archaeology in development: The case of Tanzania. *Transafrican Journal of History* 20: 19–34.

Mapunda, B.B. 1992. Sharing archaeological knowledge with the local people: the case of the Ruhuhu River basin. Paper presented at the 11th Biennial Conference of the Society of Africanist Archaeologists, Los Angeles, USA, March 1992.

Mturi, A.A. 1996. Whose cultural heritage? Conflicts and contradictions in the conservation of historic structures, towns and rock art in Tanzania. In P.R. Schmidt and R.J. McIntosh (eds) *Plundering Africa's Past*. London: James Currey: 170–90.

Nzewunwa, N. 1990. Archaeology in Nigerian Education. In P. Stone and R. MacKenzie (eds) *The Excluded Past: Archaeology in Education*. London: Unwin Hyman: 33–42.

Posnansky, M. 1982. African Archaeology comes of age. *World Archaeology* 13: 345–58.

Robertshaw, P. 1990. The development of archaeology in East Africa. In P. Robertshaw (ed.) *A History of African Archaeology*. London: James Currey: 78–94.

Sinclair, P.J.J. 1990. The earth is our history book: archaeology in Mozambique. In P. Stone and R. MacKenzie (eds) *The Excluded Past: Archaeology in Education*. London: Unwin Hyman: 152–9.

Smith, A.B. and Lee, R.B. 1997. Cho/ana: Archaeological and ethnohistorical evidence for recent hunter-gatherer/agropastoralist contact in Northern Bushmanland, Namibia. *South African Archaeological Bulletin* 52: 52–8.

Sutton, J.E.G. 1997. The archaeological heritage of Eastern Africa: Conservation, presentation and research priorities. Report submitted to sponsors and participants, on file at BIEA, Nairobi.

Wandibba, S. 1990. Archaeology and education in Kenya. In P. Stone and R. MacKenzie (eds) *The Excluded Past: Archaeology in Education*. London: Unwin Hyman: 43–9.

Wilson, T.H. and Omar, A.L. 1996. Preservation of cultural heritage on the East African coast. In P.R. Schmidt and R.J. McIntosh (eds) *Plundering Africa's Past*. London: James Currey: 225–49.

Zeleza, T. 1990. The production of historical knowledge for schools. *Transafrican Journal of History* 19: 1–23.

12

PUBLIC ARCHAEOLOGY AND INDIGENOUS COMMUNITIES

Mike Parker Pearson and Ramilisonina

This paper examines different strategies of public involvement in two communities at opposite ends of the world which we have both visited for purposes of archaeological research. One of these is the semi-arid region of Androy in southern Madagascar and the other is the island of South Uist in the Scottish Western Isles, also known as the Outer Hebrides. Problems of what constitutes 'indigenous' and whether there is a standardized 'indigenous public archaeology' are examined. The concept of 'indigenous' is fraught with problems – of purity and exclusivity – which can be overcome by focusing on the more inclusive concept of 'local'. Within an increasingly globalized society, everyone is a local somewhere.

What is 'indigenous'?

Both of us were lucky enough to attend the World Archaeological Congress in Cape Town in January 1999, thanks to a windfall of building society shares. One morning we were intrigued to see that conference-goers were invited to 'an indigenous archaeologists' breakfast'. Neither of us went and we wondered whether anyone from the 'first world' – with or without a white skin – would dare to go. Could our session chair, Tim Schadla-Hall, have gone? He is, after all, a member of a community with a distinct identity within Britain, known for its peculiar customs, dialect and folkways. As a Yorkshireman doing fieldwork in Yorkshire, he could surely consider himself to be an indigenous archaeologist. Yet might even his considerable charm and engaging self-confidence have been insufficient to mask a certain awkwardness were he to have sat at that breakfast table?

The dictionary definitions of 'indigenous' – as native to a country or aboriginal – are wholly insufficient to do justice to the political nuances of the word. When 'indigenous' is used by archaeologists, can they be presumed to be talking about the same thing, given that there are at least four possible meanings to the term?

1. *A person native-born to the region or place where they work.* This definition, close to that of the lexicographer, includes people such as Tim together with many amateurs or avocational archaeologists, some of whom might consider that their roots in a country or region endow them with a justification to excavate and interpret that place's past which is not available to any incoming team of professional archaeologists.

2. *A member of a small-scale community with long-term and ancestral ties to its land.* But in the globalized and uprooted cultures of today can those who have become displaced for their work, education or livelihood still consider themselves 'indigenous' once they are no longer resident in their place of origin? Perhaps only those who have not suffered such upheavals – those who have never left – can lay claim to the term.

3. *Everyone apart from Europeans or people of European descent.* In other words, those inhabitants of colonized or post-colonial nations whose ancestors were there before the arrival of the colonists. In this definition, 'indigenous' is commensurate with 'first-nation' status within the developing world – the ethnically distinct people who were there first, before the arrival of the colonizers. Although the term is commonly used thus by archaeologists, such a definition avoids the thorny question of pre-colonial migrations and settlement, presupposing a past both immobile and unchanging before colonization and 'the beginning of history'.

4. *Anyone whose community has been colonized or subjected to outside political control or suppression, regardless of skin colour, language or global location.* By including Europeans, this broader definition raises another temporal problem. How recent does the colonization have to be? The conquest of England by French invaders in 1066 is just too long ago – the oppositional identities of Norman/Saxon have long vanished, subsumed into an English (or British) identity and not still 'suffering' from the effects – whereas the French colonization of Madagascar between 1895 and 1960 is so recent that the difference between Malagasy and French is unmistakeable.

Many archaeologists would probably feel comfortable with this last definition yet still be prepared to accept that the other three are also used in specific circumstances. 'Indigenous' is as slippery a term as 'ethnicity' and it contains within it the unspoken presupposition of an identity of opposition and contrast. Our example from the Western Isles of Scotland illustrates the complications.

The Western Isles – an indigenous community?

'No offence pal but I hate the f**king English' is one of those immortal phrases which summarizes certain Scottish attitudes to the descendants of their conquerors of old. During fieldwork in the Western Isles, university students from England react with hurt puzzlement when their hosts cheer for the opposing side whenever the English football team is playing an international match. For

many of the students have never been to Scotland before and, politically naive, are startled to discover that being Scottish is an oppositional national identity – the Scots are vehemently not English.

Identities in the Western Isles are even more complex since the people of the islands have an utterly distinct and unassailably self-confident regional identity which other Scots often find annoying. Scottish Gaelic may be spoken by only 2 per cent of the Scottish population but it is an almost universally spoken first language in the Western Isles. Even lowland Scots culture is thus excluded by language and by traditions. The tiny population of the islands is also subdivided by religious identity – Protestants live in the north and Catholics in the south – which on a day-to-day basis is probably invisible to many outsiders. People also express a local identity, belonging to a particular township (parish or dispersed settlement).

Hebrideans – the people of the Western Isles – can be considered 'an indigenous community' for several reasons. They have been perceived as not just different, but primitive. Until the 1930s archaeologists considered the people of this ethnically distinct community to be 'living Ancient Britons', inhabiting drystone longhouses and occupying the lower rungs of the Victorian evolutionary ladder. They are a colonized people with a recent history of exploitation and forced emigration as bitter as that of many of the world's colonized nations.[1] They are a small community with strong ties to their land, and an identity in opposition to that of the rest of the nation. Like other peripheral communities living under the control of a far-away dominant elite and political system, their existence is economically precarious, dependent on global changes outside their control such as EC subsidies, the defence industry and limited tourism.

Yet this community fails to meet one of the apparent criteria for being considered 'indigenous', the question of ancestry and long-term ties to the land. Strangely enough, a large number of the people who live in the Western Isles today cannot be described as indigenous in this sense since the ancestors of many families arrived only in the nineteenth century, after the forced migrations of most of the native population to North America. Many descendants of the true indigenes actually live in Nova Scotia, in Canada. To add to the confusion of definitions, the Medieval and Norse period evidence suggests that this deported population may well have had few genetic links to the people who lived on the islands before the area was colonized by the Vikings.

So does this mean that the term 'indigenous' is useless and misleading or that only certain groups who fulfil all the criteria may be considered 'indigenous'? It is from the perspective of self-definition that 'indigenous' has meaning: it serves to distinguish insiders from outsiders. As used by archaeologists, the term always possesses a political dimension, in that 'indigenous' exists only in relation to 'colonized'. People who are indigenous can only be defined as such through their relationship to outsiders or to colonists who have obtained rights over their current and former lands. And yet within the two communities in which we

have worked, the Western Isles and Madagascar, this definition is still inadequate since the relationship between the community, the archaeologists and the archaeology contains further subtleties.

Public archaeology in the Western Isles

From a Malagasy perspective, South Uist is exceptionally cold, with weather so unrelentingly stormy that it seems to presage hurricanes which would destroy our caravan accommodation in an instant. And yet it is an ideal world from many other perspectives. People can remain close to the land, keeping animals and cultivating, whilst at the same time they enjoy running water, electricity, television, telephones and impressive access to education, protected by the copious government and European subsidies which make modern economic life possible and prevent these islands from being instantly depopulated should the jobs and money disappear.

The islands are a tightly knit community free from car theft, robbery and burglary, where misdemeanors are largely drink-related. After some sticky moments ten years ago, the archaeologists – formerly referred to in the bar as 'the gynaecologists' – have become a recognized part of annual life. In the early years of the project there was relatively little communication and dissemination of results, generating a degree of mutual suspicion. Since then archaeology has made a big impact in terms of information, economic benefit, community life and prospective development.

People on South Uist are no more or no less interested in archaeology than anyone else in Britain. Some individuals are passionate about it and others cannot see the point at all. It is mainly the men and not the women who take an active interest, coming along to join in the digging, helping with the environmental sample processing, or providing other help in kind. Children are also encouraged through visits with parents or school parties. Archaeology gives them opportunity to learn about their own place's history because otherwise they learn nothing about it in the national curriculum.

The archaeological presence has risen to an annual complement of 120 people from five universities over two summer months. This makes a profound impact on a population of only 2000 people. The archaeologists not only provide a resource for tourists – albeit modest in the form of archaeological sites under excavation – but they are also themselves part of the tourist trade. Large block bookings of accommodation and heavy use of local shops, garages and bars provide a substantial cash injection to the local economy. The project's staff and students also join in with the life of the community in ways that other tourists do not. They participate fully in the public parts of community life, attending events such as the *ceilidh* dances and building friendships that strengthen over the years. The private life of the inhabitants, dependent on family ties and the Catholic faith, remains fairly closed, since few students are churchgoers and no-one has as yet pursued a romantic liaison as far as marriage and local residence.

In this sense the archaeologists remain outsiders, transient visitors. Indeed, they are ideal tourists because they are predictable, relatively high spenders and are known to the community. South Uist has a relatively embryonic tourist trade, especially when compared to Skye, its neighbour in the Inner Hebrides. No one locally seems to want Uist to become a tourist mecca to the extent that Skye has become. Yet tourism is seen as the growth industry to replace a defunct seaweed industry, the uncertain prospects of the military rocket range and base, the declining building trade and the increasingly lean returns from farming and fishing. Tourism currently revolves around specialized holidays. The upper classes come here to fish and shoot. The middle classes come for birdwatching and cycling holidays. Few come – as yet – for the heritage aspects of Gaelic culture and archaeology but the recent £0.5 million extension of the museum and a growing number of heritage-related activities and sites to be seen are laying the foundations for this new direction.

If visitors come to South Uist to explore their Hebridean roots, are they part of the 'indigenous community'? Such tourists are certainly not local, but in terms of self-identity they may well perceive themselves as having a very strong link to the land of their ancestors. The Western Isles have a long history of movement away from the islands, both for emigration and in search of work, before and after the clearances. The population of South Uist has never been static. Today many native-born islanders leave either temporarily or permanently and new residents arrive. People who settle in small communities without pre-existing family ties – 'incomers' – always have to negotiate their social position. In a society with an identity as strong as that of South Uist, being an incomer can be a difficult social role. Some non-native residents are deeply interested in the island's history and archaeology and as archaeologists we often have contact with this part of the population – those members of the community who are certainly 'local' but who are not 'indigenous'.

This difference between the 'local' and the 'indigenous' in practice goes far beyond defining the status of individual community members. Even on an island as small as South Uist – only some 30 km long north to south, with all settlement confined to a strip barely 5 km wide east to west – our contacts with the inhabitants are at two levels. Island-wide contact is made with the indigenous community as a whole (including the incomer members) at a fairly formal, semi-official level. Through leaflets, magazine items, site tours, local radio and television news items, open days, museum exhibitions and public lectures people have the opportunity to find out that South Uist has some of the rarest and best preserved archaeological remains in Britain.

Yet our most successful presentations of archaeology are at a local level, in the geographically tiny area in the south of the island in the townships where we live and work. Personal relations are crucial: people know who we are and what we are doing and their driving interest in the archaeology is that it is on their doorsteps. With the discovery in 1998 of a 1500-year-old skeleton in a tomb on the beach – referred to as 'Kilpheder Kate' – there has been an

explosion of interest in archaeology in the immediate area, leading to packed houses at archaeological talks and presentations arranged not for the island-wide community, nor for the tourists, but for the residents of the township. Local community involvement is the key and has been extremely successful on South Uist because of our own efforts at creating personal relationships combined with the overarching sense of identity of the indigenous community.

The indigenous community in southern Madagascar

From an English perspective, the region of Androy is a dry, hot and desolate desert lacking in all the creature comforts that make life bearable. In the words of a Tandroy saying, it is 'drier than a dog's crotch in the dry season'. There is no electricity or running water and the tiny wooden houses possess no furniture other than straw mats. There is scarcely any standing water in the nine-month-long dry season and the dry riverbeds are pockmarked by holes dug into the sand to seek out the hidden water below. There are fleas, lice, cockroaches, poisonous spiders, scorpions and (non-poisonous) snakes.

Most Tandroy are still pastoralists. People here in the arid south sometimes struggle to ensure that their families stay alive, as they watch their cattle herds dwindle and their crops wither. Drought and famine are ever-present dangers in this fragile and hostile environment. Medical and hospital provision is exceedingly limited and there has been barely any provision for education since the government lost its ability to pay village teachers' salaries some ten years ago. There are Tandroy politicians in central government but promises of government aid and subsidies have largely come to nothing. Many have emigrated to find work in the plantations and cities in other parts of Madagascar, working as wage labourers, nightwatchmen and mechanics.

Tandroy attitudes to outsiders are largely antagonistic. The politically and economically dominant people of Madagascar's central highlands, more Indonesian in appearance than most southerners, have been referred to for centuries as 'dog-pigs'. The delicacy and politeness of the highlanders is alien to the Tandroy who pride themselves on speaking their mind, and being blunt and forthright in their dealings. Anyone who is not Tandroy is a *vazaha*, a stranger or foreigner, regardless of whether they are Malagasy or not. Like the relationship of Scottish to English culture, Tandroy culture is a distinct regional variant with its difficult dialect, its own economic practices (cattle pastoralism and manioc cultivation as opposed to the prevalent rice cultivation of the rest of the island) and its disdain for the soft life lived by other Malagasy, in opposition to which the distinctive lifestyle of the Tandroy has been forged.[2]

The Tandroy know and talk about their fairly recent arrival in Androy. Genealogies list clan ancestors and oral histories tell how these ancestors came from the east and migrated across the south; archaeological survey places these migrations in the sixteenth to nineteenth centuries. It could be claimed that existing Tandroy notions about the past, manifested in genealogies, oral

traditions and the presence of the ancestors, make archaeology an intrusive and unnecessary form of knowing the past. Much the same was once conveyed to the archaeologists working on South Uist until people realized that there was an unknown and fascinating history being retrieved and reconstructed.

Our own approach is not that archaeology should serve to undermine traditional authoritative discourses but that it is a complementary and integral aspect of knowing the past. The past is important to people and archaeology is a way of broadening horizons and stimulating curiosity. There are certainly conflicts and contradictions between orally transmitted and archaeologically derived interpretations of particular archaeological sites but these are not to be shied away from. The Tandroy know that they have not always lived on the land they now occupy and seem to have no philosophical problem with accepting archaeological evidence of their own migrations or with the knowledge that there were other people living in the region before they arrived.

Public archaeology in southern Madagascar

Madagascar is the sixth poorest nation in the world. In this economic climate archaeology will seem to some to be an unnecessary luxury and yet the state supports a Musée d'Art et d'Archéologie, a Centre d'Art et d'Archéologie at the Université d'Antananarivo and a few archaeology and history posts in the provincial universities. Even during the years of Malagasy cultural reconstruction, when foreign influences and products were largely discouraged or unavailable, the Musée built up its international links and welcomed foreign archaeologists, ensuring that its research efforts went that much further through contact with French, American, and British academic institutions. Museum staff have worked intermittently in the south, and specifically in Androy, since 1961, carrying out field surveys of settlement sites and tombs, and excavations of major type sites dating from 1000–500 years ago.[3]

After 1984 there was a hiatus in Musée research in Androy until our own project commenced in 1991. However, Georges Heurtebize (a French resident of Androy, a geologist by training and an ethnographer by vocation) has carried out a certain amount of field survey and, together with the anthropologist Sarah Fee, has constructed an impressive museum of Tandroy life in the nature reserve and tourist attraction of Berenty in eastern Androy.[4] He also encouraged and trained our Tandroy colleague Retsihisatse as an archaeologist and anthropologist.

Our work in Androy is not possible without Retsihisatse.[5] There is a powerful social norm of hospitality throughout the south but people are very suspicious of outsiders. Retsihisatse's participation in the project enables us to break through this barrier. We have come across many stories of misunderstandings and confrontations between Tandroy and outsiders, both Malagasy and European, which have occasionally resulted in murder. There have long been tales of how 'foreigners', especially white ones, will steal hearts, livers and

230

tongues. In 1993 a new rumour began that white people were head-hunting to extract brains in the search for an AIDS cure. The rumour started in association with two Frenchmen in a red car ostensibly on a fact-finding mission into primary education – of which there is none. Within this climate of suspicion it was only a matter of weeks before the description of the suspects matched our team and Landrover – the head-hunters were now pretending that they were looking for old pottery . . .

The head-hunting rumour is still circulating today and has made fieldwork extremely slow and difficult. Few people know anything at all about archaeology, let alone what our research team is doing. In one sense this is a good thing because it means that we must spend even more time than we would ordinarily in talking to everybody about what we are looking for, and why. As one little girl asked when out fieldwalking with the team, 'Are these the good foreigners or the head-hunting foreigners?' In Androy we are considerably restricted in terms of the media available for communication and dissemination of our fieldwork intentions or results. In a society which has a low rate of literacy and where paper is valued primarily for rolling cigarettes, the printed word is of little use in public presentation. Our only means of communication is face-to-face. There are no 'village halls' so meetings take place in the open air within the framework of *kabary*, the Malagasy style of public speaking and debate.

Yet practice rather than talk is the best way of involvement and in the last eight years many more Tandroy than Hebrideans have done some archaeology. Many people, especially the children, come fieldwalking (Figures 12.1–12.3). The novelty and interest tend to fade after the first day or so and yet there are some individuals who have a strong interest and a good knowledge of the archaeological remains in their locality. Several people, young and old, have shown the level of interest out of which may develop a life-long enthusiasm

Figure 12.1 Children joining fieldwork on the site of the nineteenth-century royal village at Ambaro in 1993. Photo by Jean-Luc Schwenninger.

231

Figure 12.2 Excavations at Ambaro in 1995, the site of a nineteenth-century royal village, are inspected by Tsihandatse, whose ancestors, the royal dynasty of the Tambaro Andrianmañare, formerly lived here. Photo by Karen Godden.

Figure 12.3 Children of the village of Montefeno took part in excavations in 2000 on this seventeenth-century royal village site. They were particularly talented at identifying species and parts of animal bones. Photo by Mike Parker Pearson.

but there is no infrastructure of community funding or support which could ensure that Retsihisatse has protégés and a local 'amateur' network for the future.

Tandroy manners are such that people are not slow in coming forward and the archaeologists are a known and reliable source of presents, medicines and free rides to market. Our bizarre behaviour is also a source of sometimes hilarious entertainment for both children and adults. Our financial input to the local economy is substantial through gift-giving, food purchasing, market shopping, accommodation payments, fees to guides and provision of animal sacrifices. Yet there are aspects of people's lives which we cannot begin to improve. Access to drinking water, professional medical and hospital facilities, a better transport infrastructure, bigger cattle herds, and even more enormous stone tombs are the things that people most want.

Our mission is primarily archaeological and can only provide a very intangible benefit. We think that our work is appreciated for two reasons. People enjoy telling us what they know about their history in terms of the places, traditions, genealogies and stories about the past. Perhaps our most significant role is in validation of Tandroy heritage. It is not only just as important as anyone else's but specialists have come from the national museum and from far away overseas to find out about it. Secondly, people are often interested in our discoveries but to a lesser extent and often only if they themselves have a pre-existing interest and aptitude. This is particularly the case with some of the men who have worked as paid guides and local helpers.

But, just as in South Uist, it is difficult to distinguish whether the communities with whom we have had contact are best described as 'indigenous' or as 'local'. Working with Retsihisatse, an indigenous archaeologist by most definitions, we are able to explain our motives and the importance of the ancient settlements on Tandroy territory as well as calm any suspicions about what we are up to. Archaeologists working with 'indigenous' communities are there at the behest of their hosts or by their agreement. This means participating on the community's terms, respecting their beliefs and traditions. Even though both of us were raised as Christians we are happy to participate in non-Christian rituals, such as sacrificing to the ancestors to gain their blessing before embarking on an excavation.

Despite a climate of fear in which our appearance has occasionally caused children to run away screaming, we have nevertheless managed to build good relations with many of the local presidencies and villages in Androy. But Androy is a big region of 5000 square kilometres with a population of about a quarter of a million. Our worst problems, such as being held hostage, have happened when we were furthest from Retsihisatse's home village, in areas where no-one had ever heard of him or his family. Retsihisatse may be indigenous but, crucially, he isn't always *local*.

In both Androy and South Uist, people are intrigued by archaeological finds on their own land but expanding that local interest to encompass their entire

region and ethnic group needs methods beyond personal contact, and becomes a goal which is difficult to attain in South Uist and currently still distant in Androy. In addition, much as we have obligations to the local communities with whom we work, we also owe duties to a myriad of different public audiences that archaeology serves. In national terms, for example, we have a responsibility to disseminate knowledge to the people of Madagascar. Although in 1989 there was an exhibition on Androy in the capital Antananarivo, prejudices against the people of the south, seen as fearsome, uncivilized and dangerous, are still strong throughout the rest of the country.[6] In international terms we have an audience to reach amongst both scholars and the wider public. This is not simply because the long-term archaeology and history of Androy is fascinating for its contributions to understanding issues like megafaunal extinction and monumental tomb-building but because it is also a location where European and Malagasy history became inextricably entwined during the pre-colonial period of the sixteenth to nineteenth centuries.

How can this be expressed at a local level in Androy? Primarily through Georges Heurtebize's efforts, there is a growing sense of a history to be objectified and preserved. Oral traditions are being recorded, new archaeological sites are being discovered and there are the beginnings of a museum collection for the benefit of the local community in one of the oldest houses in Androy at Benonoke. Although the museum at Berenty is for the benefit of tourists, its very existence is a first crucial step which indicates to the Tandroy and the wider world that Tandroy culture and history are valued by people outside the indigenous community.

Just as tourism to the Western Isles has increased over the last ten years, so the numbers of American and European tourists to Madagascar have grown in tandem with newspaper articles describing it as a stylish adventure playground inhabited solely by cuddly lemurs. As our project's results are published to a wider European and American public so more people will want to visit Androy. Currently Androy is well off the beaten track of tourism. Public buses and tour buses pass through without stopping. Some non-Tandroy and Europeans live in the few small towns but otherwise the only white people to be seen, other than some of the archaeologists, are occasional aid workers and UNICEF water engineers, the Catholic priests and Protestant missionaries, some conservation personnel and the rare tourist who manages to explore beyond the roadside towns. The lemur reserve at Berenty is, however, specifically directed at overseas tourists. Many come to this insulated shady paradise unaware that they have the only running water, electricity, French food and cold beer for miles around. In Georges Heurtebize's' museum there they can learn about Tandroy life without the discomforts of having to live it or, conversely, without inflicting themselves on the Tandroy.

In spite of their wariness of strangers, some Tandroy are keen that more visitors should pass through. There may not be a tourist infrastructure as such but there are marketing opportunities for women to sell the beautiful woven

mats and locally made textiles that are distinctive to the region. This is a contradictory state of affairs in which tourists will be feared and welcomed at the same time. Many in the tourism industry consider that Tandroy culture would suffer from the exposure and that overseas tourism in Madagascar should be restricted as far as possible to the 'honey pots' at places like Berenty. For better or for worse, our work will – to an admittedly minute degree – increase the influx of travellers who wish to encounter Tandroy life and culture for themselves at first hand.

Indigenous archaeologists, local archaeologists

If we fail to apply any political loading to the term 'indigenous', both authors of this article may be described as indigenous archaeologists. Each usually works in the island (or islands) to which they belong by birth and citizenship, one in Britain on British prehistory, the other in Madagascar on Malagasy prehistory. With the added political dimension, only one author may be described as 'indigenous' in that his island was colonized in recent history. And yet is this term acceptable to cover an entire nation?

There are enormous problems to be tackled in the history of colonialism, the condition of the post-colonial nations and the public perception of non-European history but we must address these questions with a more sophisticated approach than one which resorts to categorizing our colleagues. The lumping together of all non-European archaeologists creates an oppositional identity – an 'us and them' defined by skin colour – which has an inherent danger of attaching certain qualities to (and disguising differences in experiences and attitudes within) that 'indigenous' identity.

The political dimension of the term 'indigenous archaeologist' indicates a relationship of opposition. There are two such oppositions at work here. One is economic – the inequalities between nation states. The other is intellectual – the unequal value still ascribed to the histories of European as opposed to indigenous (non-European) peoples. But these relationships which patently hinge on gross inequalities should not be conflated with the relationships between members of the archaeological community. Archaeology in Madagascar certainly has minimal funds and a fragile infrastructure when compared to archaeology in Britain but in terms of its professional practitioners, it is of qualitatively the same calibre – the only inequality in the relationship between Malagasy archaeologists and British archaeologists today is in their access to money and resources. We wish to emphasize, not deny, the economic, political and academic struggle faced by the post-colonial nations and would suggest that it should be supported by open debate and action by the archaeological community, not ghettoized by inviting under-funded archaeologists to have breakfast together.

At the local level, in the two regions described neither of us is an indigenous archaeologist in any meaning of the term. We rarely work in the particular

areas within each island – Bezanozano and Wessex – which we consider ourselves to be from, in terms of ancestry and birth. Both of us are outsiders when we work in the Western Isles and in southern Madagascar because the communities with which we work perceive us as such. In some ways, these are situations to be cherished since they provide interactions, economic as well as cultural, which would not come about if we restricted ourselves to our own patches.

There is no indigenous archaeologist on South Uist but there is a local history society which has supported and advised the archaeologists over the last decade. Other support comes from a locally based museums officer and from the regional council archaeologist based on the Isle of Lewis far to the north. Native-born islanders and incomers all play their part in community involvement. Although we would argue that many of the inhabitants of South Uist make up an 'indigenous community', it is the *local* community which is most involved in archaeology. Even in such a technologically sophisticated environment, personal contact has proved the best way of communicating our interpretations of the archaeology of the Western Isles to the people on whose land we found it.

In Madagascar, our colleague Retsihisatse is a member of the Tandranatelo lineage of the Afomarolahy clan of the Tandroy people – an indigenous archaeologist *par excellence*. Although he makes his living predominantly from his animals and crops, his income is augmented by our project. He enjoys his role as part of an international team, associate of the Musée d'Art et d'Archéologie, and 'fixer' for all visiting specialists researching fauna, flora, local arts, and ethnography as well as archaeology. He mediates between local residents and outsider archaeologists, protecting the interests of both because he has a stake in both. At a different level, the quasi-indigenous identity of Georges Heurtebize in Tandroy society has echoes of the identity acquired by the socially adept incomer on South Uist. Such an individual's inside/outside status can make important contributions to public archaeology and should never be denigrated.

Conclusion

Some people might think that archaeology amongst indigenous communities should be done only by indigenous archaeologists and only for the benefit of the indigenous audience and no one else. Such feelings are entirely understandable in an academic world which is recoiling from – and still in the grip of – colonialist and nationalist agendas in archaeology by which cultural treasures have been removed to a distant capital or country, and histories written with little or no local input and no concern for local self-determination. Yet this antithetical stance is as untenable as the colonialist/nationalist ethos which it seeks to replace. Archaeology can be a way of removing us from the concerns of the here and now and breaking down the political and cultural barriers that

divide people. It is a way of bringing together people with a common interest in the study of the past. The success of the Cape Town conference was precisely that people working in their small area could listen to others working in their adjacent – or even distant – small areas and grasp the bigger picture and the shared theme. They were not alone in their local problems and dilemmas.

Without the continuous interaction between indigenous and outsider archaeologists we will never learn to see the world from different perspectives. One of the greatest gifts that archaeologists can bring to each other and to the communities with which they work is that of their experiences and ideas (money and equipment also help, it has to be said!). Over the years in which we have worked together, each of us has profoundly changed the other's way of seeing our own culture. Retsihisatse has also opened our eyes to aspects of his culture that would otherwise have been closed to both of us.

Our experiences in the Western Isles and southern Madagascar have made us think more carefully about what it is to be indigenous and about the pitfalls that surround its definition and championing. Equally, working with these two communities has made us appreciate the need to work closely with their representatives. The attitudes, needs, interests and facilities of these two indigenous communities in Madagascar and Scotland have been wholly different but we would argue that in both cases *local* communities are the level at which archaeologists must operate in the field since personal contact is an irreplaceable means of communication.

In neither South Uist nor Androy do we claim to be working there for the indigenous community's exclusive and sole benefit: archaeology is driven by research which has to be multi-layered just as its audiences are multiple and globally dispersed. The world is too small to allow retreat into self-referential and closely circumscribed 'parish pump' archaeologies which feed local chauvinisms about indigenous purity and exclusion of the wider world, erecting instead barriers of intolerance and misunderstanding. Yet in the practice of field archaeology, that parish pump may be all important. Local communities call many of the shots, and rightly so, but archaeologists must be conscious of the inherent dangers in any 'indigenous' archaeology. Archaeology may sometimes lend itself to the redressing of great injustices but it will not always support beliefs held very dear by a dominated or disenfranchized community. In neither South Uist nor Androy, for example, can our research ever be used to confirm the present population as autochthonous. These indigenous communities live today on land once inhabited by others, people who were not their ancestors. These traces of past societies are nevertheless 'their' history which they can learn about with pride and interest, recognizing that there are others in this world who also have the right to know, either because they are the descendants of the thousands of enslaved Malagasy or impoverished Hebridean peasants shipped to North America, or because the projects were financed with public money, or just because archaeology fascinates them.

Acknowledgements

This paper was first delivered at the 1999 WAC session entitled 'Public Archaeology' and we wish to thank its chair, Tim Schadla-Hall, and all those who provided feedback on the paper. We wish to thank Karen Godden for editing this text. Funding for the projects in question has been provided in recent years by the National Geographic Society and Historic Scotland.

Notes

1 Our colleague Jim Symonds has been studying the archaeology of resistance during that unhappy time (Symonds 1999a, b, c).
2 The thorny question of Tandroy ethnicity has been addressed elsewhere (Parker Pearson *et al.* 1999b).
3 Notable contributions have been made by Pierre Vèrin and Chantal Radimilahy (Battistini *et al.* 1963; Radimilahy 1988; Radimilahy and Wright 1986).
4 Georges Heurtebize has many publications on Tandroy ethnography and archaeology, of which the principal ones are Heurtebize (1986a, b, 1997).
5 For some of this work see Parker Pearson *et al.* (1994, 1999a).
6 The museum exhibition was accompanied by a publication (Musée d'Art et d'Archéologie 1989).

Bibliography

Battistini, R., Vérin, P. and Rason, R. 1963. Le site archéologique de Talaky: cadre géographique et géologique; premiers travaux de fouilles; notes ethnographiques sur le village actuel proche du site. *Annales Malgaches* 1: 111–53.

Heurtebize, G. 1986a. *Histoire des Afomarolahy (extrême-sud de Madagascar)*. Paris: CNRS.

Heurtebize, G. 1986b. *Quelques aspects de la vie dans l'Androy*. Antananarivo: Musée d'Art et d'Archéologie.

Heurtebize, G. 1997. *Mariage et Deuil dans l'Extrême-Sud de Madagascar*. Paris: Harmattan.

Musée d'Art et d'Archéologie 1989. *L'Androy*. Antananarivo: Musée d'Art et d'Archéologie.

Parker Pearson, M., Godden, K., Ramilisonina, Retsihisatse and Schwenninger, J.-L. 1994. Finding Fenoarivo: fieldwork in central Androy. *Nyame Akuma* 41: 41–5.

Parker Pearson, M., Godden, K., Ramilisonina, Retsihisatse, Schwenninger, J.-L. and Smith, H. 1999a. Lost kingdoms: oral histories, travellers' tales and archaeology in southern Madagascar. In P. Funari, M. Hall and S. Jones (eds) *Back from the Edge: Archaeology in History*. London: Routledge.

Parker Pearson, M., Ramilisonina and Retsihisatse 1999b. Ancestors, forests and ancient settlements: Tandroy readings of the archaeological past. In P.Ucko and R. Layton (eds) *Landscape Archaeology*. London: Routledge.

Radimilahy, C. 1988. *L'Ancienne Métallurgie du Fer à Madagascar*. Oxford: BAR Supplementary Series 422.

Radimilahy, C. and Wright, H.T. 1986. Notes sur les industries de pierre taillée dans le sud de Madagascar. *Taloha* 10: 1–8.

Symonds, J. 1999a. Songs remembered in exile: integrating an unsung archive of highland life. In A. Gazinch-Schwartz and C. Holtdorf (eds) *Folklore in Archaeology*. London: Routledge.

Symonds, J. 1999b. Toiling in the vale of tears: everyday life and resistance in South Uist, the Outer Hebrides, 1760–1860. *International Journal of Historical Archaeology* 3: 101–22.

Symonds, J. 1999c. Surveying the remains of a highland myth: investigations at the birthplace of Flora MacDonald, South Uist. In M. Vance (ed.) *Myth, Migration and the Making of Memory: Scotia and Nova Scotia 1700–1990*. Halifax: Fernwood.

13

ARCHAEOLOGY IN REVERSE

The flow of Aboriginal people and
their remains through the space of
New South Wales

Denis Byrne

A death at Port Jackson

Baloderree died in December 1791 after a very short illness and was buried in the governor's garden at Sydney Cove. He was a young member of the Eora people whose country took in the shores and immediate hinterland of Sydney harbour where the British fleet had arrived in January 1788 to establish a penal colony. According to David Collins (1798: 601–5), Baloderree had been brought to the hospital which the British had set up, but when, during the night, his fever worsened, 'his friends, thinking he would be better with them, put him into a canoe, intending to take him to the north shore'. But he died on the way across the harbour.

Collins (1798: 602) tells us that it was agreed between Bennelong, a senior man of the Eora, and Governor Phillip that Baloderree should be buried in the governor's garden which extended from the shore of the cove to Government House on the slope above.[1] Collins goes on to describe in some detail the funeral: the placing of the body in a bark canoe, the procession to the grave, the sorrow of Baloderree's father. He describes the British drummers who at Bennelong's request played at the graveside, and the native funeral rites performed. All of this took place just a few hundred metres from where the Sydney Opera House now stands (Figures 13.1 and 13.2).

But I wish to dwell for a moment on the agreement to bury Baloderree in the governor's garden and, specifically, to wonder whether this represented a magnanimous invitation by Phillip to situate the grave in the imperial space of his garden, this space being a direct projection of British imperial power, or whether it represented a failure or refusal on Bennelong's part to concede that the fence around the governor's garden denoted that the enclosed space had ceased to be part of his people's own domain. To wonder, in other words, whether behind this 'agreement' there is not a profound disagreement, which turned on the issue of sovereignty. It is difficult for those of us 'in the West' not to think

Figure 13.2 'Balloderree' Artist unknown (Port Jackson Painter). Watling Collection drawing No. 58, The Natural History Museum, London.

A variety of dispersions

Over the last two decades or so, indigenous minorities in Australia, the US and elsewhere have used what power and persuasion they have to facilitate a return to their custody of human and cultural remains. The original process of collection has been reversed. Bones and artefacts now flow from collections in

242

the former imperial centres back to the former colonies; they also flow from collections in the cities of the former colonies back to local indigenous communities. In some cases, these communities choose to house them in keeping places or local cultural centres; in other cases they ferry them back to their ultimate destination, the multitude of points in the landscape from which they were originally collected.

I am foregrounding here the spatial dimension of collection (the movement of objects through space). Some archaeologists, however, see this as secondary in importance to the act of science. The fact that the remains ended up in centralized vaults, laboratories and display cases, they would see as incidental to the quest for knowledge about what happened in the past. Indeed many archaeologists have felt that if those pressing for repatriation would focus more on the knowledge and revelations that archaeology has been able to produce from these remains – knowledge which has the potential to enhance respect for indigenous culture and history – they would be less concerned about the precise spatial disposition of the remains (for an overview of the reburial debate see Hubert 1989). 'Dispersion', in fact, turns out to be a malleable term. I use it here to describe the way Aboriginal skeletal remains and artefacts were removed from local sites to collections in far away places. Mulvaney (1958) and Griffith (1996) both describe how collections of the bones and artefacts of the Aboriginal people were formed in the nineteenth century and the first half of the twentieth century in Australia, collections that were held privately or curated by universities and museums. I am aware, though, that many archaeologists may regard the return of material in these collections back to the original source sites and localities as itself constituting a dispersion. This, of course, testifies to the way collections acquire their own meaning and integrity over time, as discrete entities, as well as to the sense in which collections are creative enterprises, creative acts (e.g. Torgovnick 1994).

My present object, though, is to understand the privileged position of 'the local' in contemporary Aboriginal society and politics in Australia, specifically in New South Wales, and to this end dispersion and return will here be understood as connoting, respectively, movements away from and back to local space. In order to shed light on the issue of repatriation I turn now to a consideration of the significance of local cemeteries in Aboriginal New South Wales, drawing upon research I have been undertaking at the NSW National Parks and Wildlife Service since 1997 aimed at understanding the history and conservation needs of Aboriginal post-contact period cemeteries and the attachment which Aboriginal people have to these places.

It may help here to briefly sketch in the history of these cemeteries. Almost from the moment of British arrival in New South Wales in 1788, white settlement radiated out from Sydney until by about 1880 even the most distant and inhospitable areas of the colony had some degree of white presence. At first Aboriginal people continued to be buried in traditional locations and in traditional modes, most commonly in mounded graves with associated carved trees. But as the mosaic of settler farms and pastoral 'runs' crept across the landscape these locations became inaccessible and people began to bury their dead in or near the homestead graveyards of settler families, in church and municipal graveyards in the white towns and villages, or in unofficial burial grounds on land not yet taken up by settlers.

Beginning in the 1880s, the most dramatic result of the new government policy of segregation was the concentration of Aboriginal people on small reservations, the twenty-two largest of which were designated 'stations' and presided over by white managers appointed by the government's Aborigines' Protection Board.[3] Most Aboriginal stations and many of the smaller reserve communities had their own cemeteries but only rarely were these officially gazetted through the bureaucracy (Byrne 1998a; Kabaila 1995, 1996, 1998; Ward *et al.* 1989). The result of this was that when the reserve lands were later revoked and sold to white farmers, as the majority of them were by the 1960s, the cemeteries did not appear on the title deeds of the land. Many of the cemeteries ended up in the middle of white farmers' paddocks with the graves being trampled by grazing stock (Byrne 1998a: 22).

The change in government Aboriginal policy in the 1940s from segregation to assimilation put pressure on Aboriginal people to move from the reserves to nearby country towns. This occurred at a time when many other Aboriginal people were leaving the reserves for the cities because mechanisation of agriculture and other changes in the rural economy had left them unemployed and still others, taking advantage of the lifting of state controls on Aboriginal movement and residence, were moving to town to take advantage of educational opportunities or just to be part of the new urban modernity (Gale 1972; Morris 1989). Altogether this amounted to a major dispersion of Aboriginal people away from local, concentrated settlements. And when we weigh the effects of this dispersion, this taking to the road (and, in a real sense, recontentualising the road), this new power to flow through space (see Massey 1993: 61), we note that apart from anything else it ultimately enabled Aboriginal people to discover in the museums and universities of the cities the bones of their local countrymen and countrywomen. It also enabled the mixed pleasure of discovering their local place names written on labels attached to nineteenth century spears, boomerangs, baskets and stone tools.

If mapped, the dispersion of 'local' Aboriginal communities, radiating out from the old reserve settlements like so many exploding stars, would inscribe the landscape with a myriad pathways. The term 'beat' has been coined by Beckett (1988: 119) to describe the networks of movement between dispersed kin in western New South Wales and he has provided an account of how these 'beats' have expanded through space (1988: 132). In the southwest of Western Australia Birdsall (1988) has used the words 'lines' and 'runs' to describe the dispersion of Nyungar extended families through particular sets of towns, the latter term evoking the continual visiting that takes place between kin along the roads of that region.

A spectrum of returns

The work of Beckett and Birdsall, along with that of others, cautions us against supposing that the trajectories of dispersal represent lines of movement that have always taken people away, detaching them from local sites; we are made aware that these trajectories are the same pathways along which contact is maintained. They are lines of communication that have, in a sense, allowed the local to expand. Each local landscape with its particular memory sites (such as the old mission, the old cemetery) now has a constituency of 'locals' spread over several hundred kilometres. A refining or expansion of our understanding of the 'local' would seem to be called for (Massey 1993: 64–5, 67; 1994).

These networks are more than conceptual: they are real in space and they are alive with movement. For instance, on virtually any day of the year somewhere in New South Wales Aboriginal people will be converging at a graveside in a local cemetery and in so doing will be retracing their steps along the lines of their earlier dispersal. Great efforts are made to return the bodies of the dead for burial in what people regard as their own country (whether that country is traditional or adoptive). These 'returns' are often made over long distances and at considerable financial sacrifice (e.g. Morris 1989: 178) and they involve taking people home from the city to a cemetery in a country town or from a country town back to a cemetery on an old reserve (there being perhaps a dozen reserve cemeteries in NSW which have continued in use). Aboriginal funerals are rites of convergence where kin and friends from different parts of the web of dispersion gather at the graveyard, the graveyard being an important geographic anchor for this web. The homeward flow of the dead and the living, reversing the direction of dispersal, mirrors the return journey we see occurring with reburial and repatriation (Figure 13.3).

The homeward flow of the dead – both the bodies of the recently deceased coming home for burial and the skeletal remains of the long dead coming home for reburial – is also importantly a ritualised occurrence. The fact that these returns do occur is testimony to the drawing power, or 'pull' of the local; but the movement backwards through space, both the long haul down the road back from the city and the final slow ceremonial approach to the cemetery, with all the connotations of steps being retraced, departures being undone, life trajectories being rewound, families being reunited in death, this movement powerfully *creates* the idea of home and builds an aura around it. The coherence of Aboriginal extended families and the significantly lower life expectancy of Aborigines compared to the general population means that these ritual returns are one of the most familiar motifs of Aboriginal social life in NSW.[4]

An instance of dispersion not mentioned earlier was the removal by the white authorities of thousands of Aboriginal children from their families in the period from the early 1880s to the late 1960s (Report of the National Inquiry into the Separation . . . 1997). The children were taken, along roads and railroads, to institutional 'homes', principally the Cootamundra Girls Home and the

Figure 13.3 Funeral of 'Queen Narelle' at the Wallaga Lake Aboriginal Reserve, *c.* 1895, south coast of New South Wales. National Library of Australia.

Kichela Boys Home, before being adopted into white families or sent to work as domestics or apprentices for white employers across NSW. The authorities took care to cover the tracks of these removals but later in life many members of the Stolen Generations,[5] painstakingly and with the aid of organisations like Linkup (Edwards and Read 1989), did find their way back. They found their way home by drawing on people's memories, and by backtracking through the records. And then by travelling, physically, along the road home, in journeys which have often proven to be nerve-racking, heart-rending, epochal moments in people's lives. As Joy Williams said of her trip back to Erambie, 'You never forget [the trip home]. Never forget it' (1989: 133). My contention, then, is that reburial and repatriation are not ruptures of normality but are companions to a whole formation of other homeward movements.

Reburial and the ethos of return

The return of the recently deceased for burial in local cemeteries parallels the return of bones and artefacts in the repatriation context to the extent that both appear to reflect an unease or anxiety at the distancing of people and objects from local space. Others have argued that, generically, this anxiety is part of the condition of global modernity and post-modernity (e.g. Chambers 1994);

I suggest that it is an anxiety which is intensified in particular ways by the condition of being an indigenous minority. I turn now to the issue of reburial.

During the last two centuries the remains of several hundred Aboriginal people from New South Wales went into public and private collections. The private collecting of Aboriginal skeletal remains by amateur and professional scientists, beginning at the time of white settlement and involving chance finds as well as grave openings, was superseded from the early 1900s by large scale collecting in which hundreds of graves were systematically dug up. This phase was in turn superseded by the excavation of burial grounds by professional archaeologists in the 1960s and '70s (Donlon 1994: 73–4).

There is a parallel with natural history in much of the early collecting, in the way the graves and their contents were often treated as if they were naturally occurring phenomena. One collected skeletons much the way one collected butterflies or rocks. Little or no regard was shown for the feelings of living Aboriginal people who were the descendants or even the immediate kin of the disinterred.

This surely has its context in the fact that at the time the collecting was taking place Aboriginal people had been emptied from the landscape where the old burial grounds were to be found. Emptied not just through attrition by massacre or epidemic but by the survivors having been moved from their old hunting grounds and camps to fringe camps, reserves, and institutions where, in a sense, they became invisible.[6] There are two aspects to this invisibility. Firstly, their visibility was low because these new places were on the outskirts of white habitation and thus on the periphery of white vision. Secondly, the specific visibility of these people as *Aboriginal* was low because so many of them had a white parent, grandparent, or great-grandparent; when whites did observe them it was through the lens of a racism in which the darkness of skin was the measure of 'real' Aboriginality. And also, of course, because genetic hybridity had its cultural counterpart: they were not seen as authentically Aboriginal because their ways and their material culture were not 'traditional' enough.

Local space and national space

The non-urban landscape in NSW – the bush or the countryside – quickly became a space associated with the ancestors of living Aboriginal people (the 'old blacks') and with white pioneer bushmen and pastoralists, but not with living Aboriginal people themselves. Revealed in the writing and art produced by the first Europeans is an understanding of 'the ground of the colony as a virgin tract' and hence an understanding of European settlement as 'a kind of pure beginning' (Thomas 1999: 36). The Aborigines presence in this landscape had been replaced by a population of Aboriginal 'sites' (rock paintings, carved trees, coastal shell middens) which tended to be thought of by whites as belonging to a period well removed in time (Allen 1988; Byrne 1998b). For white

Australians, the 'real' Aboriginals were always away on the frontier or away in the past. The challenge for Aboriginal people has thus been to re-establish their visibility in the colonised landscape and one of the ways of doing this has been to mobilise an idea of landedness in the form of an archaeological footprint.

This has seen local Aboriginal communities all over NSW emphasise their connectedness to the thousands of Aboriginal archaeological sites present in the landscape. It has seen them become unofficial guardians of these sites. To this extent, then, I would say that the 'return' which reburial represents is part of a larger 'return' – a return of Aboriginal visibility in the colonised landscape.

It is probably true of all settler colonies that the white colonists have seen themselves, retrospectively, not as invaders but as inheritors of the true spirit of the land (Byrne 1998b). By the 1880s in Australia white settlers were reinventing themselves as the 'new natives' and the traces of former Aboriginal occupation, along with the indigenous flora and fauna, became vectors for contacting or connecting with this 'spirit of the land'. Eventually, by the 1960s, these traces would be appropriated as part of the national heritage. As Benedict Anderson (1991) has argued, the very idea of the nation state is tied up with the act of collection: the museum, the census, and the heritage inventory all contribute substance to this often elusive geopolitical entity. I suggest that for indigenous minorities to retain identity within the 'invented community' of the settler nation they have had to mount various localising, decentring, 'counter-collection' strategies, and it is in the realm of such activity that I situate what I am calling here a 'reverse archaeology'. My contention in this paper is that Aboriginal people in New South Wales – and perhaps indigenous minorities in general – are more interested in getting things back into the ground than in getting them out of it.

I suggest that Aboriginal people may see the presence of their cultural remains in museums and other repositories as not only, in their own terms, improper or offensive, but as strategically undermining their moral claim to land. We should bear in mind that, historically, the concept of ethnic or racial identity coalesced in the European mind around the idea of the nation. Under the terms of this notion you cannot have identity without land. In places like NSW where indigenous people have been very largely dispossessed of land this mindset has led them to emphasise the physical traces of their former tenure as landholders. It has led them to emphasise, in our terms, the archaeological evidence of their former presence. This might account for a tendency for at least some Aboriginal people to treat archaeological sites as if they were 'title deeds'[7] and it might also account for the way they tend to regard collections – which to us represent convergences – as dispersals. From their point of view the act of collection evaporates the evidence of their entitlement to land since this evidence loses efficacy the moment it ceases to be *in situ*. I do not think it would be going too far to say that in appropriating the discourse of heritage, Aboriginal people in places like NSW have reworked it into a discourse of land.

'Real' Aboriginals and 'real' conservation

Indigenous concern about the material past is, then, an 'archaeology in reverse' to the extent that it is driven by a desire to heal a rupture – a rupture that archaeology, as practised by whites, had a part in creating. Before going on to consider what happens to repatriated remains when they get home – the end point of the journey alluded to earlier – I must attend to one critical dimension of the act of separation which has gone largely unmentioned here. This involves the issue of authenticity. I have argued elsewhere that the physical traces of past Aboriginal presence in the landscape came to be seen by settler society as a more authentic manifestation of Aboriginality than the acculturated persons of the Aborigines themselves (Byrne 1998b: 87–8, 99–100). The sort of white people who showed an interest in the Aboriginal rock engravings around Sydney harbour, or in the ground-edged stone hatchet heads ploughed up by farmers in their wheat fields, associated these remains with that 'timeless' culture of the 'real' Aboriginals living in the north of the continent. Any claim for continuity between such remains and the living Aboriginal people of NSW was likely to be met 'with shock and disbelief' (Sullivan 1985: 144).

One of the critical challenges Aboriginal people have faced in places like New South Wales over the last thirty or so years has been to stake their claim to cultural continuity, a key component of which is their ownership of and curatorial responsibility for the traces of their past. As with the rest of us in the modern world, though, the daily life of Aboriginal people in NSW requires them to be sensitive readers and manipulators of a wide spectrum of institutions, protocols and discourses which have the power to act on them. When, for example, these people are negotiating or remonstrating with a white developer, land owner or town councillor over the protection of a shell midden, rock art site or burial ground they must have one eye on the likelihood that this white person will believe that because they drive a car, use a cellular phone and do not have dark enough skin, they are not 'real' Aboriginals.

If, as I maintain, white Australia employed the discourse of heritage in order to appropriate the Aboriginal past as part of a national patrimony then Aboriginal people have employed this same discourse in order to get it back (Byrne 1998b: 94–101). In the same way they have had little choice but to become as conversant in the discourse of heritage as they are, say, in the discourses of land law, human rights, welfare bureaucracy, and parliamentary democracy. Inevitably it has meant a degree of complicity with the essentialist view of culture which privileges the 'traditional' over the contemporary, the 'timeless' over the innovative. So to some extent Aboriginal people have to play up to white expectations and be able to produce performative versions of 'traditional' culture when this is what white people want to see. This, however, is what Gayatri Spivak (1987: 202) would term a 'strategic essentialism'. The right of Aboriginal people to engage in this kind of essentialism is strongly argued by Andrew Lattas (1990, 1993). As far as I am aware, the only Australian archaeologist to take up the issue has been Tim Murray (1993, 1996) who has noted that 'both archaeologists and Aboriginal people trade in the currency of essentialism' (Murray 1996: 76), each for different reasons, and while he has warned of the dangers this may pose to free scholarship he also sees how there can be valid reasons for Aboriginal people to 'emphasize continuity' (Murray 1996: 81; 1993).

Aboriginal people's use of the familiar language of heritage should not lead us to imagine they do not have alternative interpretations of concepts like conservation. Indeed it seems that many indigenous people regard reburial as an act of conservation and in this they join, as it were, that alignment of other non-Western peoples who do not subscribe to the West's 'conservation ethic'. This would include the pious Thai Buddhists whose 'restoration' of ancient stupas typically entails completely encasing them within glittering new stupas sometimes twice the size of the original (Byrne 1995: 274–5).

From my own vantage point in a heritage agency there are a number of indications that the practice of heritage by Aboriginal people in New South Wales is increasingly at variance with – even at odds with – archaeological practice. I would include here not just the reburial and repatriation movements but the establishment of local site registers which may not be made available to archaeologists or the state heritage agency, the carrying out of heritage impact assessments by people without formal archaeological credentials (Aboriginality being seen as a sufficient or superior credential) and a preparedness in some cases to sanction the destruction of 'archaeological' sites by developers in return for jobs or the funding of community facilities.

Owning the place

The spatial or geographic dimension is obviously critical in considering reburial and repatriation. What is involved here is a return to local space which retraces and reverses the journey made by artefacts and human remains on the way to the laboratory, the show case or the museum vault. I want to focus briefly on what it is that makes it so important to indigenous minorities that cultural remains do not stray from their resting places in the ground.

To begin with there is the matter of spiritual integrity. Since the 1970s in Australia large numbers of sacred ritual objects have been returned from museums and other collections to keeping places and sacred sites. These returns have been made on the grounds that they are necessary in order to restore the spiritual health of the land and by extension that of the people of that land. It is probably true to say though that in Australia the balance of concern among Aboriginal people in the north of the continent has been with the integrity of sacred sites – mostly natural landscape features such as rock outcrops or river beds whose sacred significance is invisible to white people. It may also said, though, that the sacred site has been 'over-emphasised' by the white legal system and that Aboriginal people in the north have had to accommodate their attachment to country, as experienced by them, to white constructions of sacredness and a white conflation of sacredness and authenticity (Jacobs 1988; 1993: 102). In the south, the act of dispossession made it impossible for Aboriginal people to maintain the precise spiritual/ritual linkage with sacred sites, though there are significant exceptions to this (Creamer 1988). Here Aboriginal concern has been mostly to do with the protection of non-sacred 'archaeological' sites. The proposition here is that, for Aboriginal people in the south who were totally dispossessed of their land, the continued presence in the colonised landscape of pre-contact archaeological sites has value as a critical reminder to Australians at large that until a mere 215 years ago Aboriginal people were in occupation of the entire landscape.

To pursue this line of thinking, the *visibility* of these archaeological sites to white people has become a crucial part of their significance to Aboriginal people. To this extent the remains are fetishised by Aboriginal people in a way they undoubtedly would not have been in pre-contact times. The vital difference is that in pre-contact times Aboriginal people did not have to contend with the doctrine of *terra nullius* (land unoccupied), 'the foundational fantasy of the Australian colonies' (Jacobs 1996: 105).

None of this should be taken to mean that Aboriginal people are not genuine in their desire to protect cultural remains in the landscape. For my own part I have more than once been in the company of Aboriginal people in New South Wales who have been moved to tears at the sight of shell middens or stone artefact scatters that bulldozers have gone through. What I am saying here is simply that it is wrong to seek the meaning and motivation of this desire purely within Aboriginal culture and not in the relationship Aboriginal people have with the larger, settler culture. To do so would imply a reified understanding of their culture as something which can be quarantined, even for the purposes of discussion, from its entanglement with settler culture.

One of the methods that colonisers have employed to disempower their indigenous subjects has been to valorise some of the very attributes of the latter's subjectivity that they are simultaneously suppressing. A good example would be the suppression of indigenous languages by punishing children for speaking them in school or forbidding their use on reserves, this occurring at the same time that these people were being denigrated as not being 'real' Aborigines partly on the grounds that they could not speak their own language. Similarly, after a century and a half of de-localising Aboriginal people by moving them away from their camps and their country to distant reserves we, the colonisers, now privilege the attachment local people have to local sites and, through the Native Title process, effectively penalise those who cannot demonstrate continuous attachment to place. One can only agree with Nicholas Thomas when he suggests that it has often been the illogicality, the internal contradictions, the very doubleness of 'colonialism's culture' that has made it so difficult for the colonised to fight (Thomas 1994: 60, 142).

It is appropriate to conclude by returning to Baloderree and to Sydney Cove. The exact location of Baloderree's grave, should any trace of it have survived in this heavily developed part of downtown Sydney, remains unknown. One can stand on the deck of the Neutral Bay ferry and approximately retrace the route of the bark canoe which carried the dying Baloderree on the short trip across the harbour. Governor Phillip's 1789 presence is somewhat more tangible: you can stand on the granite-paved forecourt of the Museum of Sydney and peer down through a plate glass window at a section of the foundations of the first Government House (demolished in 1845). A number of members of the Eora tribe, including Colebe, Bennelong, Bungaree and Baloderree, were encouraged by Phillip to frequent and even reside at Government House and it was been noted that they seemed remarkably comfortable and at home there. Watkin Tench, for instance, describes Bennelong, returning after an absence, 'running from room to room with his companions'(1961: 189) – 'as if they owned the place,' you might say. If we are surprised by this it is because we would expect the Eora with their 'simple' material culture to be awkward, even intimidated, by the relative complexity and splendour of the governor's house. But are we not projecting onto the Eora our own tendency to valorise built over unbuilt space? Remember, it was only three years since the British landed at Sydney Cove. Might not the burial of Baloderree in the governor's garden and the Aborigines' habit of running through his house both suggest the Eora regarded the presence of the house and garden as incidental to their ownership of the 'place' upon which these were constructed? If this is the case it would imply that same reversal of priorities that this paper takes as its key theme.

Notes

1 A small number of other Aboriginal 'friends' of Governor Phillip were also buried in or near the garden of Government House, the first being Arabanoo in 1789 (Tench 1961: 150). See McBryde (1989) for an account of the exploratory and ambivalent relationship between the first British governors and the Aborigines of the Sydney area.

2 Paul Carter (1988: 204) shows how the rapidly developing European technology of mapping made it possible to divide and allocate space in advance: 'Located against the imaginary grid, the blankness of unexplored country was translatable into a blueprint for colonization'.

3 'At the height of Aboriginal holding of reserve lands in 1911, there were 115 reserves totalling 26,000 acres. Of these, 75 were created on Aboriginal initiative' (Goodall 1996: 96).

4 Current life expectancy for Aboriginal people in Australia is 57 years for males and 66 years for females while the figures for the general Australian population are 75 years for males and 81 years for females (McLennan 1998: 144, 154).

5 The term 'stolen generations' first gained currency with the publication of Peter Read's booklet, *The Stolen Generations* in 1982.

6 In *Edge of Empire* (1996) Jane Jacobs makes the point that under the segregation policy you were invisible because you were on the reserve, under assimilation you were invisible because you were 'bred out' and absorbed, and under integration

you became invisible in undistinguished bungalows pepper-potted through suburbia.
7 Personal communication from D. Collett, Australian Heritage Commission, Canberra.

Bibliography

Allen, H. 1988. History matters – a commentary on divergent interpretations of Australian history. *Australian Aboriginal Studies* 2: 79–89.

Anderson, B. 1991. *Imagined Communities* (first published 1983). London: Verso.

Beckett, J. 1988. Kinship, mobility and community in rural New South Wales. In I. Keen (ed.) *Being Black*. Canberra: Aboriginal Studies Press: 117–36.

Birdsall, C. 1988. All in one family. In I. Keen (ed.) *Being Black*. Canberra: Aboriginal Studies Press.

Byrne, D. 1995. Buddhist *Stupa* and Thai social practice. *World Archaeology* 27(2): 266–81.

Byrne, D. 1998a. *In Sad But Loving Memory: Aboriginal Burials and Cemeteries of the Last 200 Years in New South Wales*. Sydney: NSW National Parks and Wildlife Service.

Byrne, D. 1998b. Deep nation: Australia's acquisition of an indigenous past. *Aboriginal History* 20 (1996): 82–107.

Byrne, D. 2003. Nervous landscapes: space and race in Australia. *Journal of Social Archaeology* 3(2): 169–93.

Carter, P. 1988. *The Road to Botany Bay*. New York: Alfred A. Knopf.

Chambers, I. 1994. *Migrancy, Culture, Identity*. London: Routledge,.

Collins, D. 1798. *An Account of the English Colony in New South Wales*. London: T. Cadell & W. Davies.

Creamer, H. 1988. Aboriginality in New South Wales: beyond the image of cultureless outcasts. In J. Beckett (ed.) *Past and Present*. Canberra: Aboriginal Studies Press.

Donlon, D. 1994. Aboriginal skeletal collections and research in physical anthropology: an historical perspective. *Australian Archaeology* 39: 73–82.

Edwards, C. and Read, P. (eds). 1989. *The Lost Children*. Sydney: Doubleday.

Gale, F. 1972. *Urban Aborigines*. Canberra: Australian National University Press.

Goodall, H. 1996. *Invasion to Embassy: Land in Aboriginal Politics in New South Wales, 1770–1972*. Sydney: Allen and Unwin.

Griffith, T. 1986. *Hunters and Collectors*. Cambridge: Cambridge University Press.

Hubert, J. 1989. A proper place for the dead: a critical review of the "Reburial" issue. In R. Layton (ed.) *Conflict in the Archaeology of Living Traditions*. London: Unwin Hyman.

Jacobs, J. 1988. The construction of identity. In Beckett, J. (ed.) *Past and Present*. Canberra: Aboriginal Studies Press: 31–43.

Jacobs, J. 1993. 'Shake 'im this country': the mapping of the Aboriginal sacred in Australia – the case of Coronation Hill.' In Jackson, P. and Penrose, J. (eds) *Constructing Race and Place*. London: University College London Press: 100–18.

Jacobs, J. 1996. *Edge of Empire*. London: Routledge.

Kabaila, P. 1995. *Wiradjuri Places: The Murrumbidgee River Basin*. Canberra: Black Mountain Projects.

Kabaila, P. 1996. *Wiradjuri Places: The Lachlan River Basin.* Canberra: Black Mountain Projects.

Kabaila, P. 1998. *Wiradjuri Places: The Macquarie River Basin.* Canberra: Black Mountain Projects.

Lattas, A. 1990. Aborigines and contemporary Australian nationalism: primordiality and the cultural politics of otherness. *Social Analysis* 27: 50–69.

Lattas, A.1993. Essentialism, memory and resistance: Aboriginality and the politics of resistance. *Oceania* 63: 240–67.

McBryde, I. 1989. *Guests of the Governor: Aboriginal Residents of First Government House.* Sydney: Friends of First Government House.

McLennan, W. 1998. *1998 Year Book Australia.* Canberra: Australian Bureau of Statistics.

Massey, D. 1993. Power-geometry and a progressive sense of place. In J. Bird, B. Curtis, T. Putnam, G. Robertson and L. Tickner (eds) *Mapping Futures: Local Cultures, Global Change.* London: Routledge.

Massey, D. 1994. A place in the world. In A. Bammer (ed.) *Displacements.* Bloomington: Indiana University Press.

Morris, B. 1989. *Domesticating Resistance: the Dhan-Gadi Aborigines and the Australian State.* Oxford: Berg.

Mulvaney, J. 1958. The Australian Aborigines 1606–1929: opinion and fieldwork. *Historical Studies – Australia and New Zealand* 8: 131–51, 297–314.

Murray, T. 1993. Communication and the importance of disciplinary communities: who owns the past? In N. Yoffee and A. Sherratt (eds) *Archaeological Theory: Who Sets the Agenda?* Cambridge: Cambridge University Press.

Murray, T. 1996. Creating a Post-Mabo Archaeology of Australia. In B. Attwood (ed.) *In the Age of Mabo: History, Aborigines and Australia.* Sydney: Allen & Unwin.

Read, P. 1982. *The Stolen Generations: The Removal of Aboriginal Children in N.S.W. 1883 to 1969.* Sydney: N.S.W. Ministry of Aboriginal Affairs.

Report of the National Inquiry into the Separation of Aboriginal and Torres Strait Islander Children from their Families. 1997. *Bringing Them Home.* Canberra: Commonwealth of Australia.

Spivak, G. 1987. Subaltern studies. In Spivak, G. (ed.) *In Other Worlds: Essays in Cultural Politics.* London: Routledge.

Sullivan, S. 1985. The custodianship of Aboriginal sites in Southeastern Australia. In I. McBryde (ed.) *Who Owns the Past?* Melbourne: Oxford University Press.

Tench, W. 1961. *A Narrative of the Expedition to Botany Bay (1789) and A Complete Account of the Settlement at Port Jackson (1793).* Reprinted as *Sydney's First Four Years*, edited by L.F. Fitzhardinge. Sydney: Angus & Robertson.

Thomas, N. 1994. *Colonialism's Culture.* Melbourne: Melbourne University Press.

Thomas, N. 1999. *Possessions: Indigenous Art / Colonial Culture.* London: Thames & Hudson.

Torgovnick, M. (ed.) 1994. *Eloquent Obsessions.* Durham: Duke University Press.

Ward, G., Egloff, B. and Godwin, L. 1989. Archaeology of an Aboriginal historic site: recent research at the Collarenebri Aboriginal Cemetery. *Australian Aboriginal Studies* 2: 62–7.

Williams, J. 1989. Joy Williams. In C. Edwards and P. Read (eds) *The Lost Children.* Sydney: Doubleday.

14

THE COMFORTS OF UNREASON

The importance and relevance of alternative archaeology

Tim Schadla-Hall

Introduction

Despite apparent increases in the coverage of archaeological topics in newspapers, and in viewing figures for archaeological television programmes, the vast majority of the public has no interest or direct contact with what members of the archaeological profession consider to be their subject. The development of archaeology as an academic subject across the world in the last two hundred years has left most of humanity untouched and unworried. Nevertheless, many archaeologists have continued to express concern, particularly from the mid-twentieth century, about the continued use of myth and wild and (in their eyes) unsustainable assertions about the past. This approach to archaeology is one for which I prefer to use the term 'alternative archaeology', rather than fringe or fantastic (see for example Williams 1991) or lunatic (e.g. Jordan 1981: 212) or cult or pseudo-scientific archaeology (e.g. Harrold and Eve 1987a) because all of these describe a series of alternatives to what might neutrally be described as mainstream archaeology.

Despite the relative lack of concern in academic and professional circles about the way in which the public perceives archaeology in the broadest sense, there are good reasons for continuing to monitor (and sometimes counter) some of the wilder shores of alternative archaeology, which, judging by sales of books and viewing figures for television programmes, in fact has a larger public audience than mainstream archaeology. As I shall be showing, some of the propositions of alternative archaeology deserve to be countered because of their implicit or even explicit support for racist, ultranationalist or other fundamentalist beliefs. In addition, alternative archaeology deserves the attention of archaeologists because it presents a challenge to the fundamentals of archaeological interpretation. Because the boundaries between conventionally accepted academic wisdom and wilder speculation continually shift over time, a study of alternative archaeology helps us to understand, and justify to others, what constitutes reasonable and rational conclusions based on rigorous and scholarly use of theory and a full range of archaeological evidence, and what constitutes unreasonable and irrational conclusions. This is made all the more difficult because within this has to be accommodated the usual spectrum of archaeological opinion, and, more recently, a recognition of the plurality of valid archaeological interpretations and the inability of archaeologists to discover a single true explanation of the past. A study of alternative archaeology, then, teaches us to be good archaeologists.

Defining alternative archaeology

This paper takes as its theme the continuing and currently expanding number of books and television programmes that appear on both sides of the Atlantic and that use archaeology to make often ludicrous claims about the past through the construction of modern mythologies. It is therefore also about the ways in which the developed world, with its mainly European genesis, has exported its manufactured search for its own myths mainly to North America – not least because it was colonised by Europeans – and developed a series of bogus bases for exploring its past. Some of these myths have their origin in the distant past, although most are a product of the eighteenth, nineteenth and even twentieth centuries. They often seem to develop as a means to explain colonial discoveries or rationalise the apparent pre-eminence of European culture, and often, and increasingly, display a veneer of academic respectability and methodology.

The problem with definition is that there are no easily defined parameters, as the boundary between what is acceptable mainstream archaeological opinion and what is 'alternative' speculation, shifts through time. A century ago many archaeologists believed that Aboriginals really did represent living versions of prehistoric peoples, and could directly give an insight into the lives of people in the European Palaeolithic. Archaeologists do not believe this today. Likewise in the 1950s many European archaeologists believed that Myceneans visited Stonehenge. Today, this opinion would only be held by non-archaeologist diffusionists. However the (then authoritative) publications that made these claims remain in print and in libraries. While archaeologists tend to know that interpretations are refined through time and ideas that can be disproved with new information are discounted, this is not at all clear to those reading out-of-date books in public libraries or the works of alternative archaeologists like Hancock (2002) and von Däniken (1969, 1997). The latter, in particular, apparently have no need to view published information critically and instead use the whole of published archaeology uncritically to suit their own particular requirements. It might be best therefore to define alternative archaeology as anything that disagrees with the generally accepted facts that archaeologists use to explain and reconstruct the past.

It is not my intention here to review exhaustively the principal manifestations of alternative archaeology, as this would require book-length treatment, and there already exist some useful summaries (e.g. Harrold and Eve 1987a; Roth 1998; Williams 1991). After noting some of the principal themes, I shall instead move on to examine how arguments promoting alternative archaeology are put forward, and the reasons for their popularity and growth. I shall conclude by discussing how archaeologists have responded to the challenge proffered by alternative archaeology.

Some themes in alternative archaeology

Although alternative archaeology has developed into a complex web of different perspectives, a number of underlying themes are discernible, most of which emerged at an early stage. I have attempted below to list briefly a few of these in order to show how they constantly recur as people search for more attractive explanations of the past than those provided by archaeologists.

Origins and hyperdiffusionism

This strand in alternative archaeological thinking postulates a single point of origin for all civilisation, spread out for example by Egyptian navigators (Perry 1923; Smith 1923; Heyerdahl 1950, 1958, 1970), by Phoenicians (Fell 1976) or through wanderings of the Lost Tribes of Israel (Parfitt 2002). It is strongly linked to notions of imperialism in the West (e.g. Ascherson, Chapter 7, this volume). The single point of origin for all civilisations is also sometimes seen in now drowned civilisations, principally Atlantis in the West (Ashe 1992; Berlitz 1969; Flem-Ath and Wilson 2000; Michell 1983) and Mu in the Pacific (Churchward 1926).

Ancient knowledge and power

Here, ancient peoples are seen as endowed with greater knowledge and power than contemporary civilisations. Ley lines in particular are seen as ancient force fields harnessed by past peoples (Nye 1987; Sullivan 2000), who are also seen sometimes as possessing other lost technologies (Knight and Lomas 1999; Tomas 1971).

Under this thinking, ancient monuments such as pyramids and megaliths are places where particular force fields are concentrated and are seen as centres of wider zodiacal or other power (Cope 1998; Tompkins 1978). This kind of approach to the ancient past can also link to wider contemporary 'New Age' beliefs in an earth spirit such as Gaia (Lovelock 1987; Michell 1975) and to paganism in general (Hardman and Harvey 1995).

Astro-archaeology

In this, one of the main strands of alternative archaeology, it is argued that visitors from outer space came to earth in ancient times and ruled for a while, and/or genetically engineered modern humans into existence (von Däniken 1969, 1972, 1974, 1997). These beliefs can also link to beliefs in other paranormal phenomena such as UFOs and abduction by aliens (Gray 1987).

The 'truth' of religion and mythology

Archaeological sites are often seen as being associated with the practitioners of ancient religions such as Druids, or with fertility cults (Meaden 1999), Mother Goddesses and the like (Johnson 1988; Sjoo and Mor 1991), and archaeological material from such sites is interpreted in a circular argument to 'prove' the existence of these religions.

In a similar way, archaeology can be harnessed to 'prove' the truth of mythologies, such as that of King Arthur (Higham 2002), or to support creationist beliefs about the literal truth of the Bible in general, such as the flood and Noah's Ark (LaHaye and Morris 1976).

As we can see from the above, one of the difficulties of examining alternative archaeology is the interlinked nature of so many of the beliefs which impinge on archaeological evidence, and how they also link to a wider network of non-archaeological concerns such as modern-day paganism, Gaia, and other New Age phenomena. As Merriman (1991) has shown in a survey of 'sanctioned' and 'non-sanctioned' approaches to the past, there can actually be quite a wide overlap in the range of beliefs held by individual people, with those who are interested in 'mainstream' archaeology also sometimes believing in 'alternative' interpretations.

It is tempting to suggest therefore that a more fruitful approach towards definition would be to examine the techniques used to present and write alternative archaeology rather than attempting to divide it up in order to create categories.

The presentational methods of alternative archaeology

The 'X-Files' approach and 'it is obvious' statements

A frequent feature in presenting alternative archaeology is to ensure that the writer or presenter has the chance to identify with the consumer by making comments which imply that 'I am only a normal human being, but it seems clear that the archaeologist has missed the following points', or by holding up archaeologists as the enemy – the elite who do not understand. This starts very early in the genre with the development of the factoid approach. James defines this as 'an unproven fact or assumption that is repeated so often that it becomes accepted as factual truth' (James 1999: 145). Another variant is converting a possibility or assumption into fact over a series of pages. Finally there is the approach that suggests that 'they' (archaeologists) are keeping something back from 'us' (the public/reader/viewer). This can be described as the 'X-Files' approach. It involves convincing the viewer/reader that s/he has not been told everything by the expert and that only this particular author will do so. This can also be characterised as an anti-elitist approach. An example of most of these approaches is encapsulated in Hancock's discussion about the origins of the human occupation of Malta and the significance of the unique Maltese neolithic temples:

> So I don't mind too much when the surviving megalithic temples were built. The counter-hypothesis that I offer for their origins is that they are the end-result of a very long process of development in Malta that began in the Palaeolithic and that has been veiled from us by rising sea levels, cataclysmic land subsidence, academic mendacity and a self-protecting old boys' club closing ranks.
>
> (Hancock 2002: 438–9)

Artistic associations

There is a long history of using apparently similar images or aspects of similar images to develop connections between cultures and countries. The technique dates back to the nineteenth century at least and frequently involves the use of sketches or interpreted images as line drawings. As an example, there is the oft-repeated argument that the carvings of macaws that form part of the lexicon of Mayan art are not macaws but elephants, and therefore 'prove' colonisation from the Old World. Smith and Perry both used these comparisons in the 1920s, and 80 years later Hancock used the same evidence and arguments to suggest an earlier society in *Fingerprints of the Gods* (1995). It seems to matter little that however often such dubious associations are demonstrated at minimum to be questionable, they still recur.

Linguistic associations

In alternative archaeology, simplistic linguistic associations are often made between different places in order to justify theories of ancient links between them. Wauchope uses the example of the work of J. C. Wise who used this technique in *Americas: The Background of Columbus*:

> Wise's technique seems to have been to pick up one syllable from a word or place name and then see where else he could find it in an atlas. Thus he finds it significant that the following places all contain the same letters bra: 'La-bra-dor, the sacred peak of Bra-zo in New Mexico,

the Br-zos in Texas, Bra-za in Argentina next to Bra-zi-la, Bra-za in Austria, and Brahma-poo-t-ra in India'.

(Wauchope 1962: 111–13, quoting Wise 1945)

Wauchope points to the use of similar linguistic acrobatics by Heyerdahl (1950) in *Kon-Tiki*, where readers of his work 'are convinced irrevocably that Thor Heyerdahl and his companions . . . demonstrated beyond all doubt that a Peruvian god named Kon-Tiki was the same as a white chief god named Tiki mentioned by an old man on an island in the south seas!' (Wauchope 1962: 112–13).

Geological phenomena

Geological occurrences, particularly those involving straight lines, are frequently interpreted in alternative archaeological texts as man-made, and as evidence of ancient (often drowned) civilisations. Jordan describes the 'so-called Bimini Road' of the Island of Bimini in the Bahamas, which he effectively demonstrates to be a geological formation. A geologist and an archaeologist who examined it promptly declared it natural in origin and belonging to a well-known feature of the Bahama shorelines: Pleistocene beach rock (Jordan, 2001: 100–3). Nevertheless, this has not stopped the formation being cited as a drowned road relating to an earlier civilisation. Indeed Hancock revives the Bimini road in his most recent book (2002) by adopting the 'X-Files' approach to his discussion of rock formations off the coast of India, Japan and Malta, which he claims are ancient cities drowned by the flood at the end of the last Ice Age.

Pseudo-science and selective quotation

Pseudo-scientific works of alternative archaeology often exploit the interest created by astro-archaeology to create a whole range of unlikely connections, using apparent methods of scientific measurement and analysis. It has a veneer of scientific respectability that is often added to by extensive reference to other published works that are themselves dubious, and the careful selection of 'facts' that are lifted out of context from mainstream archaeological publications. In many ways the approach is to assume the clothing of academic work, and to mimic academic respectability to such a degree that the product appears to be the same as mainstream academic work.

One of the most all-embracing publications of this nature in recent years was *Uriel's Machine: the Prehistoric Technology that Survived the Flood* (Knight and Lomas 1999). This publication manages to link freemasonry with archaeological research and demonstrate that there was a worldwide flood around 10,000 years ago. In doing so, the authors manage to quote established academics in such a way as to make it seem that they support their arguments, as where they write about how they wondered if the global flood could be more than a legend. This spurred us to look into what is known of prehistory, and we were pleased to find that some of the greatest scholars in this area have already found out what we discovered – that existing ideas are wrong. Professor Colin Renfrew, Disney Professor of Archaeology at Cambridge University expressed it perfectly when he said: 'The study of prehistory is in a state of crisis'.

(Knight and Lomas 1999: xiv)

Later they again quote Renfrew's view that:

Several commentators have spoken recently of a revolution in pre-history, of the same fundamental nature as a revolution in scientific thinking. It has been suggested, indeed, that the changes now at work in prehistory heralded a shift to a new paradigm, an entire new framework of thought, made necessary by the collapse of the 'first paradigm'.

(Renfrew 1978; quoted in Knight and Lomas 1999: 1–2)

They then use this to justify their contention that there are good reasons for their reassessment of the past, in which they claim to have demonstrated that:

Yes, the world was all but destroyed by a flood caused by a cometary impact less than 10,000 years ago . . .

Yes, the oral traditions of Freemasonry do record real events and there was an advanced group of people in the British Isles who appear to have had a major influence in the Middle East and even in China.

Yes, there is a new paradigm of prehistory to construct. We have just started to shed a little light on a new way to explain how we arrived at the world we live in today.

(Knight and Lomas 1999: 338–9)

However, Renfrew (1978) was writing about the radiocarbon revolution and its impact on the (then) accepted dating of European prehistory, and would no doubt be surprised to see his work quoted by two freemasons who were aiming to demonstrate the existence of 'Grooved Ware People' who were probably 'the Watchers who might well have survived the [comet] impacts of 7460 BC, and later, observing the 3150 BC comet' might have decided to warn as many people as possible (Knight and Lomas 1999: 151).

261

The growth of alternative archaeology

In the UK over the last 30 years, and particularly the last ten years, there has been an increasing interest in archaeology on the part of the public, despite there being no related increase in membership of a majority of archaeological societies and organisations with the possible exception of the Time Team Club (Schadla-Hall 1999: 151). Archaeology has continued to be widely covered in newspapers and even more so on the television, particularly with the increased number of channels brought by satellite and cable television. In addition, the advent of the World Wide Web has led to an unprecedented growth in archaeological and related information because of the web's capacity to cover a wide range of minority interests. However, despite earlier claims that the field of pseudo-science and alternative archaeology was in decline from its peak in the 1960s and 1970s (Feder 1987: 44–5), the best-selling publications dealing with the ancient past, and the most viewed television programmes, have tended to be in the areas of alternative rather than 'mainstream' archaeology.

For example, one of the most notable recent entrants into the field is Graham Hancock (Hancock 1995, 2002; Hancock and Faia 1998). Hancock is, apart from being an exponent of the hyperdiffusionist myth, an excellent exponent of the 'X-Files' approach to looking at the past. He always manages to imply that the keepers of the past – the archaeologists – are keeping the real facts from the rest of us, and to aid him in this approach he frequently emphasises his non-archaeological credentials. He has recently set out to demonstrate that there is a secret underwater ancient empire that archaeologists have all missed, and backed this up with a formidable mini series that had over four million viewers in the UK. This has been accompanied by a recently published book (Hancock 2002). This followed an earlier and very successful mini-series, which was also followed up with a similarly best-selling book, *Heaven's Mirror* (Hancock and Faia 1998).

The influence of these authors can be significant. In 1998 I asked a selection of undergraduates – admittedly not a scientifically derived sample – about their early introduction to archaeology. Three of them told me that they had read a book by Erich von Däniken, *Chariot of the Gods* (von Däniken 1969) and one had been given Julian Cope's book (Cope 1998) by her parents as a present, because they had read about it in a review in the broadsheet press, and assumed that it was therefore an important book. It is a sobering thought that even at the Institute of Archaeology at a discussion on the work and techniques of Hancock's most recent series of programmes, a number of the student audience were less than dismissive of his claims. This may well have something to do with a desire to support the underdog, and to engage in debate. But as Gray demonstrated, there were significant percentages of American students who were prepared to believe in the claims of von Däniken and also in UFOs, even after three years of university education (Gray 1987: 30–3). In addition, as we shall see, Harrold and Eve were able to demonstrate that significant numbers of students did hold creationist beliefs (Harrold and Eve 1987a: 86–7). Their other main category was that of

> pseudo scientific beliefs about the past [which they defined as] *cult archaeology*, which includes a whole variety of fanciful claims. Examples include von Däniken's 'ancient astronauts,' as well as the belief that a great civilisation once existed on the continent of Atlantis before it sank beneath the waves in a giant cataclysm, or claims that Romans, Phoenicians or many other Old World visitors left rock inscriptions all over North America.
>
> (Harrold and Eve 1987a: x)

The overlap between alternative and mainstream archaeology in the minds of younger people is not new. I am one of those who were vastly cheered by reading that other archaeologists (e.g. Williams 1991: 1) have read the work of Churchward and still survived to become archaeologists, thus proving that alternative archaeology does not necessarily do permanent damage. I can look back on the fact that at the age of 13 I was giving lectures on the Lost Continent of Mu (Churchward 1926), because the original publication had just been reprinted, and was available in my local library. As Williams notes in an earlier work (Williams 1987: 130), one of the reasons for exploring alternative archaeology with students is to teach them how to assess data and the plausibility of different arguments.

One of the reasons for the growth of alternative archaeology may well be that archaeologists, especially academic archaeologists, are so wrapped up in the development of their own subject that they really are leaving the public behind and that the void that they are creating is being filled by alternative archaeology. Certainly archaeologists ignore what is happening at their peril.

The idea of promoting an interest in the past for the public does not figure widely until relatively recently in archaeological research or discourse, although there have been warnings aplenty about the problem:

> The public feels much more comfortable with mythologies. This is partly because it is a function of mythologies to be retold. Unless we come up with better ones, public mythologies – about Druids, dancers or gold under the hill, or ley-lines – will continue to be reiterated. Yet our own frameworks could replace them provided we have the nerve and imaginative flair to embed them in the public consciousness, or maybe I mean public unconsciousness. In effect, we must provide new myths, which have the potential to be more viable than the fantasies, which currently rule. Myths? If you recoil, you make my point, which is that we have overlooked some of the public's needs. Fantasies flourish because to many people the past is an open field in which the imagination can wander. It is because they do not know exactly what

stone circles were for that they find them fascinating. Many of the public are suspicious of us. Is that because they fear that given half a chance we will destroy their dreams? Dream is a word you won't find in MAP2. Yet for many, the past is one of the few remaining refuges from scientific rationalism and materialism.

(Morris 1993: 12)

The point I wish to make here is that there is no clear and obvious separation between 'mainstream' and 'alternative' archaeology, and that individuals' subscription to different views may depend on their own attitudes towards rational scholarship and critical enquiry, or towards the importance of romantic imagination and fantasy. In addition, we need to explore whether subscription to 'alternative' ideas is a damaging foolishness on behalf of members of the public, or whether it is an entirely legitimate means of exploring the past. In order to do this, I want now to examine some of the responses of archaeologists to alternative archaeology over the last half century.

Various forms of alternative archaeology have been with us for centuries, but sustained responses to it did not begin until the 1950s, and until recently have entirely consisted of rebuttals.

Attempts to rebut alternative archaeology

That the continued growth and development of alternative archaeology at the same time as theoretical objectivity and fact should, apparently, have been dominating the subject, was a matter of concern for many archaeologists. In the last century both the first and second editors of *Antiquity* frequently used their editorial space to lambast alternative archaeology. The late Glyn Daniel used his editorship, which was 'learned, and accessible and funny when laying into sacred cows such as bogus Druids' (Howard 1992: 7), to repeatedly poke fun at a wide range of offerings. As early as the 1950s there was concern about the Midsummer celebrations at Stonehenge, and especially after the summer solstice of 1961, when there were reports of considerable damage as crowds gathered to watch the Druidic ceremony:

We do not expect the Minister and his advisers to evaluate what of religion and what of fantasy, what of truth and what of rubbish, exists in the claims of these bodies. They are all foolish people confusing fact with fiction.

(Daniel 1992: 25)

He continued his attacks on Druids for some considerable time:

Stonehenge was closed to the public from 7pm on the 20th of June 1964 but was open to the dotty Druids Lair! . . . What a ridiculous, ludicrous, silly affair! There should be a total ban on all solstice ceremonies from now on. These strange neo-druidic organisations have no claim in history and archaeology to Stonehenge. . . . it is to us most mysterious why these latter-day druids were ever allowed their junketings at Stonehenge, and why permission is annually continued. There must be some very special reason. Could it be that the staff of the Ministry of Public Buildings and Works is riddled with secret druids? Shall we hear, if we visit the Ministry, a curious melodious twang echoing down the corridors, and, suddenly turning a corner, find a harpist with furled umbrella at the ready?

(Daniel 1992: 34)

Daniel was ceaseless in his exposure of alternative archaeology in all its forms, and it was he who inspired the title of this chapter by his frequent references to the 'comforts of unreason' (e.g. Daniel 1992: 41, 65, 75). I suspect that this term – although never attributed – relates to the work of Crawshay-Williams (1947). Crawshay-Williams discussed the propensity that people display for believing the 'big lie' and the apparent desire to believe that which is clearly unprovable, and unsustainable. The crucial point that he discussed is the problem that humans often seem unable to accept that there is no external mechanism or agency that moulds what they have done or has happened to them, and they therefore invent them to explain an otherwise unpredictable world (Crawshay-Williams 1947: esp. 142–60).

The tradition of countering alternative archaeology within the archaeological community has been much more serious and sustained in the USA. As Wauchope (1962) has pointed out, American archaeologists became concerned quite early on by the hyperdiffusionist ideas given academic respectability by the anatomist Elliot Smith (1923) and the anthropologist Perry (1923). As far as the Americas were concerned, one of the crucial strands of their argument was that mummification was developed solely in ancient Egypt, and was spread out from a single point by Egyptian seafarers. Mummified remains in South America therefore 'proved' that the Americas had been colonised by Ancient Egyptians, who also brought the practice of pyramid-building with them. Their views were countered by the work of Dixon (1928), who demonstrated, for example, that the process of mummification was not the sole province of the ancient Egyptians, and similarly that there was no evidence of any Egyptian artefacts anywhere in South America that could be associated with any of the monuments. In doing so, Dixon seems to have been the first archaeologist to deliberately challenge, in an accessible way, the claims of alternative archaeology. It is worth reflecting that despite this early and masterful piece of work, hyperdiffusionist myths still abound on television (e.g. 'Mystery of the Mummies', a documentary series screened on Channel 4 in the UK in 1999–2000 that hinted at a single ancient origin for mummification (Schadla-Hall and Morris 2003)).

One of the enduring features of the progenitors of alternative archaeology is that many turn to archaeology from other professions and academic pursuits. I refer to a number of these in this paper, for example Perry, Smith and Meaden. Others, such as Harold S. Gladwin (Wauchope 1962: 71–2), were amateurs in the fields of archaeology and anthropology, who developed their own theories and published them. Gladwin was one of the first to develop the approach of attacking professionals and suggesting that academics were closed in their thinking, and appealed to the public on the basis of what can only be described as false logic.

> All the lights in the House of the High Priests of American Anthropology are out, all the doors and windows are shut and securely fastened (they do not sleep with their windows open for fear that a new idea might fly in); we have rung the bell of Reason, we have banged on the door with Logic, we have thrown the gravel of Evidence against their windows; but the only sign of life in the house is an occasional snore of Dogma.
>
> (Gladwin, quoted in Wauchope 1962: 71)

Wauchope wrote *Lost Tribes and Sunken Continents* (1962) because he wanted to challenge what he recognised was the continuing growth of alternative interpretations. He aimed, in a balanced way, to demolish through careful examination both the people and the ideas that held sway within the non-archaeological community in the USA and Europe as late as the 1950s.

Harrold and Eve (1987a) produced a serious analysis of the dangers of creationism and cult archaeology. The main thrust of their work and that of their fellow contributors was to examine the enduring and possibly growing belief in creationism after a century and a half of scientific evidence that has increasingly demonstrated the nature of human evolution. Creationism involves:

> an account of human origins taken more or less literally from the opening of the Book of Genesis in the bible. According to creationists, the earth is only a few thousand years old and humans, along with all other living things, were directly created pretty much as they are today. Creationists vehemently deny the scientific concept of the evolution of humankind and other life forms via descent from ancestral species. They explain fossils as the remains of creatures wiped out by the Great Flood in the time of Noah.
>
> (Harrold and Eve 1987b: ix)

Apart from showing the limited impact that teaching has had against the trend of alternative archaeology, they demonstrated that more than half of the American college students in their sample believed that God created Adam and Eve and that more than a third believed that men and dinosaurs co-existed.

They felt that 'such findings do not simply represent an inadequate science education but rather reflect a failure for many people to experience even a modest encounter with good scientific instruction during public education' (Eve and Harrold 1987: 136).

The tradition of countering alternative archaeology has been continued by books such as that of Williams (1991) on 'fantastic archaeology', and Jordan (2001) on 'the Atlantis syndrome'. The approach remains the same throughout, which is essentially that of showing archaeology as an objective scientific discipline, and of demonstrating the falsity of alternative claims. But is this the most effective approach to the issue of alternative archaeology, or is it more a case of the discipline attempting to stake out clearly its own academic territory and exclude the non-initiated?

Attempts to accommodate alternative archaeology

A number of organisations and individuals concerned with the public representation of archaeology have now begun to feel that coming to some sort of accommodation with alternative archaeology is a more fruitful way forward than rebuttal. This is partly no doubt because at least half a century of rebuttal does not seem to have had a significant effect on the volume of alternative material. It is worth noting, for example, that despite Glyn Daniel's long-running and hilarious campaign, the number of Druids has increased ten-fold at least since the 1950s (R. Maughling pers. comm.).

A new factor, however, has become archaeologists' general recognition, following two decades of theoretical debate, that interpretations of the past are historically contingent, and are multivalent and contested at any particular time. Contemporary archaeology does not have the same faith in a scientific and relatively objective view of the past that characterised the rebuttals of the 1950s to 1980s, and once a plurality of archaeological opinion is allowed in the academy, the division between mainstream and alternative becomes less clear. This is particularly brought into focus when we consider the question of indigenous archaeology. Archaeologists now, rightly, respect the myths and beliefs of indigenous peoples in relation to archaeological sites and landscapes, even if they do not accord with mainstream archaeological interpretations. In many cases (e.g. Pokytolo and Brass 1997) indigenous myths are presented on-site along with the academic archaeological conclusions.

Respect for the non-mainstream views of others is also being extended to other groups besides indigenous peoples. At Stonehenge, there is a continuing acceptance not only of Druids but also, following a ban, the re-admission of 'New Agers' and associated groups at the solstice in 2001. The work of Bender (1998) has shown a possible way in which multiple interpretations of Stonehenge can be advanced. Followers of the Mother Goddess cult are given space to air their views in interpretations of the site of Çatalhöyük (Hodder 1998).

Is accommodation, and respect for the views of others, therefore the most productive way forward? The answer, I think, is that it depends on what kind of views are being expressed. One of the problems that has affected the analysis of alternative archaeology has been the tendency to treat all its manifestations with the same weight. We now need to differentiate between different kinds of views, treating some as legitimate individual myth-making, but some as dangerous and denigrating to others.

For example, Aryans, Atlanteans and Cro-Magnons figure in much of the literature surveyed by Wauchope (1962: 116–24), and the conclusions of alternative archaeological literature can be taken up to support extreme views of racial superiority or cultural primacy.

Racist stereotyping also litters alternative archaeology to the current day, as Hancock demonstrated in *Heaven's Mirror* (Hancock and Faia 1998), which was also a Channel 4 mini-series, when he suggested that some of the Olmec heads from La Venta and other sites were 'pronouncedly African' and drew comparisons with Ancient Egyptian sculpture (ibid: 38–40). He also argued that other sculptures from the same sites depicted Caucasians. Both imply that civilisation could only be diffused from the Old World and not developed independently by the local populations.

In relation to creationist beliefs, Alice Kehoe (1987: 11) makes the point that:

> Scientific Creationists claim to be able to scientifically support statements in the King James English Bible, which they believe to have been dictated by God. This would be merely curious if it were not part of the credo of a political movement that advocates measures many opponents consider unconstitutional and policies tending to harden international hostilities. The movement hinders the emancipation of women from traditional constraints and fosters a pessimistic view of human nature that some followers interpret to justify harsh treatment of children and the indigent.

Whilst most archaeologists would probably wish to respect the views and interpretations of indigenous peoples, and some now wish to reflect a diversity of alternative perspectives in their public interpretations, most would no doubt also want to challenge alternative perspectives that would support the oppression or lack of respect for others. Where the line is to be drawn between the two attitudes is not always clear, which is the reason why public archaeology will always be about conflicts over identity and ultimately therefore a question of ethics for professional archaeologists.

Conclusions

Alternative archaeology has been around from the beginning of humanity's interest in the past, when fantastic stories and myths were used to give meaning to ancient remains. The development of archaeology as a discipline has been in part one of trying to distinguish rational enquiry from unreasonable speculation. However, as objectivity is now less certain as a goal, there is a spectrum of opinion from 'lunatic' to 'sanctioned', and with what constitutes legitimate discourse shifting through time, archaeologists have to realise that the black-and-white distinction between 'them' and 'us' is not as clear as may previously have been imagined. Archaeologists must engage with 'alternative' opinion, sometimes to mutual benefit. Archaeologists must also distinguish qualitatively between different kinds of alternative archaeology, rather than treating it as if it were all the same. Some alternative views should be strongly challenged on the grounds of their implicit or even explicit ideology or blatant commercial distortion; other alternative views should be acknowledged and celebrated as elements in the diverse ways in which people experience the past.

Bibliography

Ashe, G. 1992. *Atlantis. Lost Lands, Ancient Wisdom.* London: Thames and Hudson.

Bender, B. 1998. *Stonehenge. Making Space.* Oxford: Berg.

Berlitz, C. 1969. *The Mystery of Atlantis.* New York: Norton Publications.

Churchward, J. 1926. *The Lost Continent of Mu; The Motherland of Man.* New York: W.E. Rudge.

Cope, J. 1998. *The Modern Antiquarian – A Pre-Millennial OdysseyThrough Megalithic Britain.* London: Thorsons.

Crawshay-Williams, R. 1947. *The Comforts of Unreason. A Study behind the Motives behind Irrational Thought.* London: Kegan Paul, Trench, Trubner and Co.

Daniel, G. 1992. *Writing for Antiquity. An Anthology of Editorials from Antiquity.* London: Thames and Hudson.

Dixon, R.B. 1928. *The Building of Cultures.* New York: Charles Scribner's Sons.

Eve, R. A. and Harrold, F. B. 1987. Pseudoscientific beliefs: the end of the beginning or the beginning of the end? In F.B. Harrold and R. A. Eve (eds) *Cult Archaeology and Creationism.* Iowa City: Iowa University Press: 134–52.

Feder, K.L. 1987. Cult archaeology and creationism: a coordinated research project. In F.B. Harrold and R. A. Eve (eds) *Cult Archaeology and Creationism.* Iowa City: Iowa University Press: 34–48.

Fell, B. 1976. *America B.C.: European Settlers in the New World.* New York: Pocket Books.

Flem-Ath, R. and Wilson, C. 2000. *The Atlantis Blueprint.* London: Little, Brown and Company.

Gray, T. 1987. Educational experience and belief in paranormal phenomena. In F.B. Harrold and R. A. Eve (eds) *Cult Archaeology and Creationism.* Iowa City: Iowa University Press: 21–33.

Hancock, G. 1995. *Fingerprints of the Gods. A Quest for the Beginning and the End.* London: Heinemann.

Hancock G. 2002. *Underworld. Flooded Kingdoms of the Ice Age.* London: Michael Joseph.

Hancock, G. and Faia, S. 1998. *Heaven's Mirror: Quest for the Lost Civilization.* London: Michael Joseph.

Hardman, C. and Harvey, G. (eds) 1995. *Paganism Today* Wellingborough: Thorsons.

Harrold, F.B. and Eve R.A. (eds) 1987a. *Cult Archaeology and creationism. Understanding Pseudoscientific Beliefs about the Past.* Iowa City: University of Iowa Press.

Harrold, F.B. and Eve R.A. 1987b. Introduction. In F.B. Harrold, and R.A. Eve (eds) *Cult Archaeology and Creationism. Understanding Pseudoscientific Beliefs about the Past.* Iowa City: University of Iowa Press.

Heyerdahl, T. 1950. *Kon-Tiki.* Chicago: Rand McNally.

Heyerdahl , T. 1958. *Aku Aku. The Secret of Easter Island.* London: George Allen and Unwin.

Heyerdahl, T. 1970. *The Ra Expeditions.* London: George Allen and Unwin.

Higham, N. J. 2002. *King Arthur: Myth-making and History.* London: Routledge.

Hodder, I. 1998. The past as passion and play: as a site of conflict in the construction of multiple pasts. In L. Meskell (ed.) *Archaeology Under Fire. Nationalism, Politics and Heritage in the Eastern Mediterranean and Middle East.* London: Routledge: 124–39.

Howard, P. 1992. Introduction. In G. Daniel *Writing for Antiquity.* London: Thames and Hudson: 7–9.

James, S. 1999. *The Atlantic Celts. Ancient people or modern invention?* London: British Museum.

Johnson, B. 1988. *Lady of the Beasts: The Goddess and Her Sacred Animals.* London: Harper-Row.

Jordan, P. 1981. Archaeology and television. In J.D. Evans, B. Cunliffe and C. Renfrew (eds) *Antiquity and Man. Essays in Honour of Glyn Daniel.* London: Thames and Hudson: 207–13.

Jordan, P. 2001. *The Atlantis Syndrome.* Stroud: Sutton Publishing.

Kehoe, A. B. 1987. Scientific Creationism: world view not science. In F.B. Harrold and R. A. Eve (eds) *Cult Archaeology and Creationism.* Iowa City: Iowa University Press: 11–20.

Knight, C. and Lomas, R. 1999. *Uriel's Machine: the Prehistoric Technology that Survived the Flood.* London: Century Books.

LaHaye, T. and Morris, J. 1976. *The Ark on Ararat.* San Diego: Creation-Life Publishers.

Lovelock, J. 1987. *Gaia: A New Look at Life on Earth.* Oxford: Oxford University Press.

Meaden, T. 1999. *The Secrets of the Avebury Stones. Britain's Greatest Megalithic Temple.* London: Souvenir Press.

Merriman, N. 1991. *Beyond The Glass Case. The Past, the Heritage and the Public in Britain.* Leicester: Leicester University Press.

Michell, J. 1975. *The Earth Spirit: its Ways, Shrines, and Mysteries.* London: Thames and Hudson.

Michell, J. 1983. *The New View over Atlantis.* London: Thames and Hudson.

Morris, R. 1993. A Public Past? In H. Swain (ed.) *Rescuing the Historic Environment.* Hertford: Rescue: The British Archaeological Trust: 9–16.

Nye, E. 1987. *Ley Lines Worldwide: Explained with History, Map and Examples*. London: DLM Publications.

Parfitt, T. 2002. *The Lost Tribes of Israel*. London: Weidenfeld & Nicholson.

Perry, W.J. 1923. *Children of the Sun: a Study in the Early History of Civilisation*. London: Methuen.

Pokytolo, D. and Brass, G. 1997. Interpreting cultural resources: Hatzic Site. In J. Jameson (ed.) *Presenting Archaeology to the Public. Digging for Truths*. London: AltaMira Press: 156–65.

Renfrew, A.C. 1978. *Before Civilisation. The Radiocarbon Revolution and Prehistoric Europe*. London: Penguin Books.

Roth, A. M. 1998. Ancient Egypt in America: claiming the riches. In L. Meskell (ed.) *Archaeology Under Fire. Nationalism, Politics and Heritage in the Eastern Mediterranean and Middle East*. London: Routledge: 217–29.

Schadla-Hall, R.T. 1999. Editorial: public archaeology. *European Journal of Archaeology* 2(2): 147–58.

Schadla-Hall, R.T. and Morris, G. 2003. Ancient Egypt on the small screen – from fact to fiction in the UK. In S. Macdonald and M. Rice (eds) *Consuming Ancient Egypt*. London: UCL Press: 195–215.

Sjoo, M. and Mor, B. 1991. *The Great Cosmic Mother: Rediscovering the Religion of the Earth*. London: Harper Collins.

Smith G. E. 1923. *The Ancient Egyptians and the Origins of Civilisations*. London: Harper and Brothers.

Sullivan, D. 2000. *Ley Lines: A Comprehensive Guide to Alignments*. London: Piatkus Books.

Tomas, A. 1971. *We Are Not The First. Riddles of Ancient Science*. London: Souvenir Press.

Tompkins, P. 1978. *Secrets of the Great Pyramid*. New York: Harper Colophon Books.

Von Däniken, E. 1969. *Chariots of the Gods. Unsolved Mysteries of the Past*. London: Souvenir Press.

Von Däniken, E. 1972. *Gods from Outer Space*. New York: Bantam Books

Von Däniken, E. 1974. *Gold of the Gods*. New York: Bantam Books.

Von Däniken, E. 1997. *The Return of the Gods. Evidence of extra terrestrial visitations*. Shaftesbury: Element Books.

Wauchope, R. 1962. *Lost Tribes and Sunken Continents. Myths and Methods in the Study of American Indians*. Chicago: Chicago University Press.

Williams, S. 1987. Fantastic archaeology: what should we do about it? In F.B. Harrold and R. A. Eve (eds) *Cult Archaeology and Creationism*. Iowa City: Iowa: 124–33.

Williams, S. 1991. *Fantastic Archaeology. The Wild Side of North American Prehistory*. Philadelphia: University of Pennsylvania Press.

Wise, J.C. 1945. *Americas: The Background of Columbus*. Charlottesville: Monticello Publishers.

15

THE TREASURE ACT AND THE PORTABLE ANTIQUITIES SCHEME

A case study in developing public archaeology

Roger Bland

This paper discusses two initiatives undertaken by the UK government, the Treasure Act 1996 and the accompanying initiative to promote the voluntary recording of all other archaeological finds. Even after the passage of the Treasure Act the legal protection afforded portable antiquities in England and Wales is at the same time more limited in scope and more permissive and also more liberal in its treatment of finders than in virtually any other country in Europe. This paper examines the advantages and disadvantages of this approach.

Because there have never been any restrictions on the use of metal detectors in Britain, except on scheduled ancient monuments, detector users are now responsible for finding several hundred thousand archaeological objects each year. For this reason, it was not thought practicable to introduce legislation requiring all archaeological objects to be reported, such as exists in many European countries. The Treasure Act was merely designed to remove the worst anomalies of the medieval law of Treasure Trove which it replaced and the Act has led to a ninefold increase in cases during its first four years.

Of greater long-term significance has been the government's accompanying initiative to encourage the voluntary reporting of all archaeological finds for public benefit – the Portable Antiquities Scheme. Six posts were established in 1997 and a further six in 1999. A lottery bid for three-year funding for a national scheme of 46 posts has recently been approved and will start in 2003. The paper summarises the work of the finds liaison officers to date as a case study in developing public archaeology in England and Wales.

The common law of Treasure Trove

Until the Treasure Act came into force in 1997, the common law of Treasure Trove provided effectively the only legal protection afforded antiquities found in England and Wales. The doctrine of Treasure Trove is thought to date back to Anglo-Saxon times and it would seem to have derived originally from the principle that all ownerless objects should belong to the king (Hill 1936). The law first became formulated in the twelfth and thirteenth centuries AD and changed little from the account given by Henry de Bracton in his law book of c.1250 (*De legibus et consuetudinibus Angliae*).

The essence of the English law was that only objects of gold or silver that had been deliberately hidden with the intention of recovery qualified as Treasure Trove and became the property of the Crown. In practice the Crown offered museums the opportunity to acquire Treasure Trove finds, the finder receiving the full market value. The main difficulties with the old law stemmed from the fact that it was never intended as an antiquities law: it was extremely restricted in scope and was riddled with anomalies with the result that it was legally unenforceable (Palmer 1993; Bland 1996). The main aims of the Treasure Act were to replace the old subjective test of what was Treasure Trove with a new objective one[1] and to make the law enforceable by introducing a new criminal offence of failure to report treasure (DNH 1997). However, the Act did not extend legal protection to all antiquities and it is worth examining why this was so.

In the nineteenth century it came to be realised by antiquarians that the old law of Treasure Trove had a significance over and above simply adding to the royal revenues. In 1858 Lord Talbot de Malahide introduced a Private Member's Bill to reform Treasure Trove (Hill 1936: 239–40).[2] Lord Talbot's main concern was to ensure that finds of treasure were reported: so long as Treasure Trove simply served as a mechanism to increase royal revenues, with the objects claimed as Treasure Trove destined to be melted down into bullion, there was clearly no incentive for finders to report their finds. However, as it came to be appreciated that these objects had an antiquarian value much greater than their bullion value, so the movement developed to give finders an incentive to report finds by paying them rewards. Although Lord Talbot's Bill was unsuccessful it did lead, 28 years later in 1886, to the government announcing a new policy whereby finds claimed as Treasure Trove were offered to museums and finders were paid a reward for them (Hill 1936: 240–1). This practice of paying rewards for finds claimed by museums is an important factor in encouraging the reporting of finds.

Although archaeologists had succeeded in one of their aims, that of providing an incentive for finders to report their finds, they were still aware that many problems remained with the law, most especially its very restricted scope. The movement for reform started in earnest after the war. In 1944 one of the aims of the newly established Council for British Archaeology was to reform the law of Treasure Trove, but no progress was made mainly because of the difficulty of securing an archaeological consensus as to what needed to be done and then of persuading the government to take action (Cleere 1994).

Metal detecting

What transformed the whole issue was the widespread use of metal detectors. These machines became widely available in the 1970s and at their peak, in around 1980, it is thought that there may have been as many as 180,000 metal detector users in this country (Dobinson and Denison 1995: 6). One obvious consequence of this was an enormous increase in the quantity of objects being found, the great majority of which fell outside the law of Treasure Trove.

In its early days metal detecting was a very anarchic activity, as is apparent from issues of *Treasure Hunting* magazine of the time. Many detector users felt that they had the right to take their machines anywhere they chose, whether on private or public land, and keep what they found. Equally many archaeological sites suffered damage from rogue detector users (as they still do: see Dobinson and Denison 1995: 84–94). In the late 1970s detector users started to organise themselves into clubs and so came to adopt a more responsible attitude. Now they are represented by organisations such as the National Council for Metal Detecting which clearly condemns trespass and has its own Code of Conduct which has recently been revised to take account of the Treasure Act and the Portable Antiquities scheme (National Council for Metal Detecting 1992; the revised version of the Code is published in the May 2000 issues of *The Searcher* and *Treasure Hunting*, p. 54).

The initial archaeological response to metal detecting was to seek to ban or restrict the use of metal detectors and this is the approach that has been followed in most European countries (Council of Europe 1981; Bland 1998: 14–17). In Britain, however, the government was not persuaded, although archaeologists did win one significant success which was a clause in the 1979 Ancient Monuments Act that made it a criminal offence to use a metal detector on a scheduled monument without the permission of English Heritage. At about the same time the Council for British Archaeology launched a campaign, the so-called STOP (Stop Taking Our Past) campaign, to draw attention to the damage done by uncontrolled detecting, the net effect of which was to ensure that most detector users remained very distrustful of archaeologists (Cleere 1979: 26–7). Equally, attempts by the Council for British Archaeology to sponsor a Bill to reform the Treasure Trove law, which Lord Abinger introduced into the House of Lords in 1979 and again in 1982, failed because the government was unwilling to support it (Palmer 1993; Bland 1996).

In the battle of public opinion, so essential if politicians are to be persuaded to take action, it would seem that detector users had more success than archaeologists, as is reflected in the exasperated reference of Henry Cleere, the then Director of the Council for British Archaeology, to 'the excesses of the treasure hunters, who until then were viewed as harmless hobbyists in official circles' (Cleere 1982: 8). However, there were exceptions to the general atmosphere of mistrust that prevailed between archaeologists and detector users in the 1970s, most notably in Norfolk where, starting in 1977, the late Tony Gregory and colleagues systematically encouraged detector users in the county to report their finds (Fletcher 1977; Green and Gregory 1978). This initiative proved so successful that by 1995 some 24,000 objects a year were being recorded from this county, with detector finds accounting for about a third of all Sites and Monuments Record entries (Dobinson and Denison 1995: 20–1 and fig. 19 on p. 30), and this work took up the time of two and a half members of staff. The Norfolk scheme was to provide the model for the government's Portable Antiquities Scheme.

In 1994 the Council for British Archaeology carried out a survey which estimated that several hundred thousand archaeological objects are being found each year, maybe around 400,000 in England alone (Dobinson and Denison 1995). The survey also estimated that the number of detector users was about 30,000, considerably down from its peak at the end of the 1970s.[3] However, it seems that the overall number of objects being found might not be much lower than fifteen years previously, as a large minority of these detector users were finding very significant numbers of objects. Of the estimated 400,000 detector finds, only a very small percentage were reported to archaeologists or museums, perhaps five to ten per cent, and fewer finds still were declared Treasure Trove. The main reason for this is it has never been one of the core responsibilities of any museum or archaeological body to record detector users' finds so that the effort devoted to this work has been very patchy and dependent on committed individuals. The other reason is the deep distrust that existed between detector users and archaeologists.

Treasure Act

Clearly the problem was not going to go away and so towards the end of the 1980s another attempt to reform the law began, this time through an initiative of the Surrey Archaeological Society, working with Lord Perth and the British Museum (Palmer 1993; Bland 1996). A new Bill was drafted after extensive consultation. One factor that helped their efforts was the creation in 1992 of a new government department, initially named the Department of National Heritage (DNH), with the result that for the first time government policy on archaeology and portable antiquities was all dealt with in one place. It was difficult for a government department with such a name to deny responsibility for this issue.

In March 1994 Lord Perth introduced the Treasure Bill into parliament. As a Private Member's Bill it stood little chance of success without government support and at first this seemed unlikely. The government had blocked all previous attempts at reform. This time, however, Lord Perth assembled a powerful coalition of peers to speak in favour of his Bill, together with both the opposition parties, and the result was that the government was forced to change its attitude to one of support. Although that support was not enough to ensure the success of the Bill in 1994, it was reintroduced two years later by an MP, Sir Anthony Grant, who successfully piloted it through the House of Commons. The Act itself came into force in September 1997 after a Code of Practice setting out the details of how the Act should work had been drafted and passed by parliament (Bland 1997; DNH 1997).

Objections to the Treasure Act

It is instructive to look at the opposition that the Act faced, because it is the nature of the opposition that actually explains why the Act looks like it does. The one major group to oppose the Act were the metal detector users. They objected not so much because it contained anything harmful towards responsible detecting – it did not – but because many resented the fact that the state should have any claim on their finds at all. In addition many detectorists believed that the Bill represented the thin end of the wedge – that it would be the first step towards much more comprehensive legislation – and because they felt that anything supported by the archaeological community must be hostile to their interests. This has to be seen against the background of the long history of distrust between archaeologists and metal detectorists and was probably not helped by the fact that the Bill was originally an initiative of the Surrey Archaeological Society as a result of the failure of prosecutions of detector users caught looting at the site at Wanborough (Bland 1996: 18–19; O'Connell and Bird 1994; Ward 1992). It is also true that the media coverage of the Treasure Bill generally presented it as an attempt to clamp down on detecting. Thus, for example, the headline on a report in *The Times* on Lord Perth's Bill was 'Peer aims to save heritage from metal detectors' (2 March 1994) even though Lord Perth had been at pains to point out that his Bill was not anti-detecting.

In addition, elements of the metal detecting world deliberately sought to whip up opposition to the Bill by spreading exaggerated and misleading accounts of it (for some examples see *Treasure Hunting* June 1994: 32–4; July 1994: 45; August 1996: 24–7; September 1996; 18–20). It was a frustrating experience for the Bill's sponsors that not once during the two-year period when the Treasure Bill was being considered did either of the two metal detecting magazines publish a factual account of it. It is therefore hardly surprising that detector users should have protested to their members of parliament when they read such partial and exaggerated references to it in their magazines.

As a result, detector users were very active in lobbying their members of parliament against the Bill when it was before parliament in 1994 and again in 1996 and then against the Code of Practice in 1997, but it is notable that they did not persuade a single MP or peer to speak against the Bill either in 1994 or in 1996 (although some of the objections to the Bill in the Commons in 1994 may have been at the behest of detector users).

The detecting lobby was nothing if not ingenious in devising new objections to the Bill, at various times trying to mobilise landowners' support for their cause; portraying the Bill as unconstitutional on the grounds that it was a money Bill (that is one intended to raise revenues for the government), which could not be introduced as a Private Member's Bill; or even portraying it as a 'grave robber's charter' on the grounds that precious-metal objects found in graves would henceforth qualify as treasure.

The Department of National Heritage had a number of discussions with representatives of the National Council for Metal Detecting (NCMD) in 1994–96 and in the spring of 1995 the NCMD produced a considered response outlining their objections to the Bill. As a result the Bill's sponsors made five amendments to meet their concerns (Bland 1996: 23n). In addition, Ministers stated during the debates on the Bill in parliament that the government had no intention of banning or otherwise restricting responsible metal detecting, nor was it the first step down a road which would eventually result in compulsory reporting of all finds or the licensing of all detector users.

Although the Bill's sponsors and the government were able to have a dialogue with the NCMD, other detecting interests, such as the Federation of Independent Detectorists (FID), made much more violent criticisms against the Bill and indeed split away from the NCMD because they opposed the NCMD's policy of having discussions with the government. Another group set up to oppose the Bill, the Finders and Collectors Action Group, was established by an antiquities dealer. *Treasure Hunting* magazine provided a forum for these views; *The Searcher* magazine for the NCMD's views.

The view has also been expressed that giving legal protection to additional categories of objects is tantamount to nationalisation by the state and represents an attack on private property rights (Selkirk 1997). In fact, though, the Bill was supported by the two main landowners' organisations, the Country Landowners' Association and the National Farmers' Union, because in return for widening the scope of treasure in a modest way it gives them an important benefit that they did not previously enjoy, which was that for the first time it made them eligible for rewards (under the old Treasure Trove system landowners had not been eligible for Treasure Trove rewards under any circumstances). It is also of course the case that even after the new Act has come into force the state lays claim to a far more restricted range of archaeological objects than do other countries of Europe (Bland 1998: 14–17). The original proponent of this criticism has more recently held up the Treasure Act as an example of moderate reform which other countries should emulate (Selkirk 1999).

Lastly, at the opposite end of the spectrum, some archaeologists have condemned the Bill as an unhappy compromise which is far too limited in its scope, arguing that its enactment will make it harder to secure what they believe is really needed, which is full-scale portable antiquities legislation (Schadla-Hall 1994, 1995a, b). It is undoubtedly true that the Act was a compromise and it is always easy to criticise compromises, but more comprehensive legislation would have required substantial new resources and would not have

obtained government support. Furthermore, legislation extending state ownership to all archaeological finds would have run into very severe opposition not
just from several thousand metal detectorists, but also from those who object
to any extension of state ownership.

The Treasure Act was in fact the best that could be achieved within the very
tight constraints that have been imposed on it, the main one being that it
should have no resource implications. Most archaeologists have now taken a
more pragmatic line and in May 1995 the Council for British Archaeology's
Standing Conference on Portable Antiquities, which brings together all leading
archaeological and museum organisations, unanimously approved a motion
endorsing the Treasure Bill (Bland 1996: 25).

Portable antiquities discussion document

Archaeologists' reservations about the Treasure Act were to a large extent
answered by the publication by the Government of a discussion document
on portable antiquities in March 1996 (DNH 1996). This paper made
a distinction between the public acquisition of finds, which the Treasure
Act addresses, and the recording of finds, which it attempted to tackle. It noted
that only a small percentage of objects found by the public are recorded by
museums and confirmed that in the government's opinion

> this represents a considerable loss to the nation's heritage. Once an
> object has left the ground and lost its provenance, a large part of its
> archaeological value is lost. The result is a loss of information about
> the past which is irreplaceable.
>
> (DNH 1996: 4)

The document went on to state that the government accepted that there was
an urgent need for action and it set out proposals for voluntary and compulsory
schemes for the reporting of finds that fall outside the scope of the Treasure
Act and sought views on their relative merits.

A total of 174 responses was received, roughly equally divided between
archaeological and metal detecting interests. They all agreed that the recording
of all archaeological finds was important and that there was a need to improve
the current arrangements and they stressed that this could not be done without
additional resources. The responses showed that for the first time there was
a consensus among both archaeologists and detector users that a voluntary
scheme, along the lines of the Norfolk approach, offered the best way forward.
As noted above, it is completely legal for anyone to search with a metal detector
in England and Wales, provided they have the permission of the landowner,
except on scheduled ancient monuments.

Scotland and Northern Ireland

Before examining the results of these two initiatives it is worth looking at the different systems that obtain in different parts of the UK. Both Scotland and Northern Ireland have their own legal frameworks governing portable antiquities. In Scotland all newly discovered archaeological objects, whether they are of precious metal or not and regardless of whether they were hidden or lost, belong to the Crown under the legal principle of *bona vacantia*. Although the Crown only chooses to exercise its claim in certain cases, this does mean that in Scotland there is in effect a legal requirement to report all archaeological objects and so the Treasure Act did not take effect in Scotland (Sheridan 1991, 1994, 1995; Carey Miller and Sheridan 1996).

In Northern Ireland the old common law of Treasure Trove applied and so the Treasure Act has effect in the province (with, however, its own Code of Practice). However, there is also in Northern Ireland a statutory duty to report all finds of archaeological objects, as well as legal controls over archaeological excavations, neither of which exists in England or Wales. The 1995 Historic Monuments and Archaeological Objects (Northern Ireland) Order includes a statutory requirement under Article 42 for the finder of any archaeological object to report the circumstances of its finding and the nature of the object within fourteen days. The object should be reported to the Ulster Museum, the police or the Department of the Environment for Northern Ireland, who may retain it for up to three months. In addition the Order makes it an offence to excavate any land while searching for archaeological objects without a licence, which means that metal detecting is at best a dubious activity. The Order also contains provisions, under Article 29, for archaeological objects found on scheduled monuments. Archaeologists in both Scotland and Northern Ireland believe that legal requirements to report all portable antiquities are workable in their countries, because of the much smaller numbers of objects being found, whereas they almost certainly would not be in England.

Results of the Treasure Act

Some detector users claimed before the Act came into force that it would deter finders from reporting their finds while others said that there would be so many finds that the system would be swamped. In fact neither has happened. The total number of cases of treasure reported in 1998, the first full year of the Act, was 191; in 1999 this rose to 223 and in 2000 the figure was 221. This compares well with the prediction that there might be between 100 and 200 cases a year (DCMS 2002a) and is about nine times as many as the 25 finds a year that were being declared Treasure Trove. The Act has, therefore, passed its first hurdle of ensuring that more finds are reported. Although there have been a number of reports of undeclared treasure, there is no evidence that the incidence is any higher than before.[4]

All but 34 of the 737 treasure cases reported in the first three annual reports (DCMS 2000a, 2001a, 2002a) are finds of gold and silver objects that should have been reported under the old law, so the Act does in fact seem to have encouraged finders to report more of their finds. The great majority of the finds came from England (699), the remainder coming from Wales (36) and Northern Ireland (two).

These finds fall into the following categories:

Artefacts

Prehistoric	27
Roman	63 (includes six finds of both coins and artefacts)
Early medieval	106 (includes one find containing both coins and artefacts)
Medieval	165
Post-medieval	147
Total	508

Coins

Prehistoric	43
Roman	104
Early medieval	11
Medieval	41
Post-medieval	30
Total	229

Ninety-two per cent of all finds were recovered with metal detectors, 3 per cent were chance finds and 5 per cent archaeological finds.

One of the most significant benefits of the Act is the requirement that objects found in association with treasure should be reported as this is producing new archaeological insights. An example is provided by a find reported from Hamstead Marshall in Berkshire which included 84 Roman silver *denarii*, 13 bronze coins of the same period together with Roman copper brooches and other objects (DCMS 2002a: no. 123). Under the old law there was no requirement to report the base metal objects, but at the inquest the coroner decided that they were treasure because they were deemed to be from the same find. This in turn raised the question of whether the brooches are likely to have been part of the same find as the coins: very few records exist of such finds from this period but this may simply be because they were not reported in the past. Another important find was a Roman gold ring from Poringland, Norfolk, set with a gold aureus of Postumus (AD 260–9) (DCMS 2002a: no. 8). This is only the second piece of Roman coin jewellery and the second aureus of Postumus ever to have been recorded from Britain; it would probably not have been Treasure Trove under the old law, since it is unlikely that the coroner's inquest would have decided that the object had been deliberately buried. Under the Treasure Act it qualified as treasure and has been acquired by the British Museum.

About half of all finds reported as treasure are acquired by museums and the remainder are disclaimed without the need for the coroner to hold an inquest and have been returned to the finders. The great majority of the treasure finds that have been retained were acquired by regional museums.

The new arrangements include new measures to reassure finders that the rewards that they receive for finds which are claimed by museums are based on a fair market value, as determined by an independent committee. These rewards are now shared between the finder and the landowner. It is crucial that finders should receive an adequate incentive to report their finds. It is also the case that not all finds being reported as treasure are being acquired by museums: over half are recorded and then returned to the finders.

One of the features of the Treasure Act was to introduce a new criminal offence for failure to report treasure. This has also played a part in ensuring that finds are reported. Although no prosecutions have been made so far, the threat of prosecution has proved effective in a number of cases. It is a priority to ensure that the antiquities and coin trade is now aware of the penalties for selling undeclared treasure (for a revealing account of how the antiquities trade operates in England see Stead (1998); for other examples see Bland (1996: 18–19)).

There have been a few teething problems with the new system, as the museums and coroners responsible for administering the system get used to the new arrangements. Finding the money to pay for the acquisition of treasure has proved a problem for museums and many finds that should be in a museum are being disclaimed. However, there are sources of acquisition grants available to museums and no major finds have been disclaimed. There is also a continuing need to ensure that all concerned deal with cases as expeditiously as possible, as the Treasure Act Code of Practice states that it should not normally take more than a year between a finder handing in a find and the museum paying the reward (DNH 1997), but by and large the Treasure Act has more than fulfilled the expectations of those who promoted it. However, perhaps the greatest significance of the Act is that it has paved the way for the accompanying Portable Antiquities Scheme.

In September 2000, after the Act had been in force for three years, the government announced a review of the Act, as was required under the Code of Practice. The review focused on (a) the definition of Treasure in the Act, as section 2 of the Act gives the Secretary of State powers to alter the definition by order, and (b) the administration of treasure cases. An independent consultant was commissioned to carry this out and a consultation paper was published in December 2000 (DCMS 2000c). The *Report on the Operation of the Treasure Act: Review and Recommendations*, was published in October 2001 (DCMS 2001c). Both documents were widely circulated to interested parties.

The Report contained 52 individual recommendations in all. The government has agreed to implement the two principal recommendations: to extend the definition of treasure to include deposits of prehistoric base-metal objects; and to revise the Code of Practice on the Act (DCMS News Release 288/01, 8 November 2001). At the time of writing (May 2002), the draft Order altering the definition of Treasure and the revised Code of Practice are about to be laid before parliament for approval and it is hoped that the new measures will come into effect from the beginning of 2003. This will represent a significant extension of the Act – and an important move away from the current scope of treasure which is essentially limited to precious-metal objects – and it has been welcomed by archaeologists.

The Portable Antiquities Scheme

As a result of the responses to the portable antiquities discussion document (see above), the government announced that it would fund a programme of pilot schemes to promote the voluntary recording of all archaeological finds in up to five regions of England from September 1997 (DNH 1997: 40–1; the British Museum funded a sixth post for two years). From 1997 to 2003 these posts were funded by the government on an annual basis with Resource (The Council for Museums, Archives and Libraries) acting as the channel for the funding. Since spring 1999 the Heritage Lottery Fund has been funding a second tranche of six posts and so twelve finds liaison officers are currently (2002) in post covering about half of England and Wales, together with a co-ordinator and an outreach officer.

The aims of the pilot schemes are:

- to advance our knowledge of the history and archaeology of England and Wales (see, for example, Figure 15.1);
- to initiate a system for recording of archaeological finds and to encourage and promote better recording practice by finders;
- to strengthen links between the detector users and archaeologists;
- to estimate how many objects are being found across England and Wales and what resources would be needed to record them.

A second bid to the Heritage Lottery Fund for three-year funding for a national scheme was originally submitted in May 2000 and was finally approved in

---

Figure 15.1 Finds of Anglo-Saxon metalwork in Lincolnshire. The results of systematic recording of chance metal-detected finds are beginning to have some dramatic effects on the way in which we are able to interpret the historic landscape. This map shows metal-detected finds of Anglo-Saxon metalwork of the fifth to tenth centuries. Data were collected by the North Lincolnshire Museum and the Lincolnshire Sites and Monuments Record prior to the start of the Portable Antiquities Scheme, but the project has allowed the large-scale recording of finds which is in turn allowing us to see settlement patterns. Already we can see that the three parts of Lincolnshire have differing patterns of finds. Lindsey, to the north, has many finds and some large sites.

Finds of Anglo-Saxon metalwork in Lincolnshire

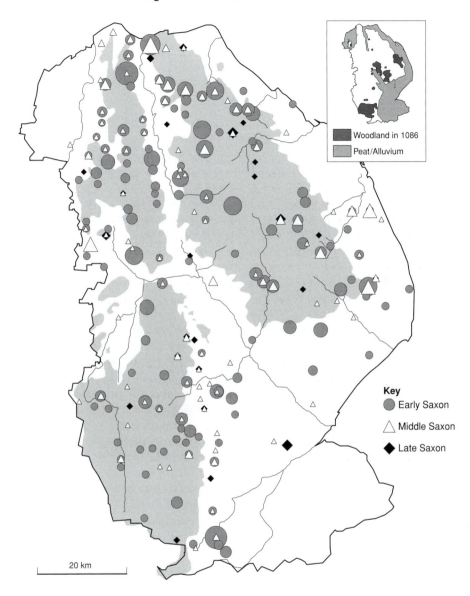

Kesteven, in the southwest, lacks the large sites and Holland, to the southeast, has produced few finds. The lack of finds from some areas can be explained by the Domesday survey, which records these areas as marsh or woodland in 1086. The digital mapping was completed by Mike Hemblade, North Lincolnshire Museum (DCMS 2001b: fig. 32).

April 2002. The bid is for 46 posts in all: 37 finds liaison officers based in museums and archaeological services around the country, a small central co-ordinating unit (based at the British Museum) of five, and four finds specialists who will be based in universities and will have a role in training the liaison officers and in assuring the quality of data being gathered. The new posts will start in 2003 and the funding will run until 31 March 2006. A national scheme will have the following aims:

- to increase opportunities for active public involvement in archaeology;
- to significantly raise awareness, among the public and across the educational spectrum, of the educational potential of archaeological finds;
- to arrest the large level of archaeological information lost every year by actively recording this material on a systematic basis for public benefit;
- to change public attitudes so that those who make finds accept that it is normal practice to make them available for recording;
- to test the appropriateness and effectiveness of the Portable Antiquities Scheme over the whole of England and Wales, rather than just half of that area (the current pilot project);
- to define the nature and scope of a scheme for recording portable antiquities in the longer term, to assess the likely costs, and to identify resources to enable it to be put in place.

The results of the first four years of the pilot schemes are set out in four annual reports (DCMS 1999, 2000b, 2001b, 2002b); there is also a leaflet, *Finding our Past*, which explains the scheme to finders, two national newsletters (Museums and Galleries Commission 1999; Resource 2000) and Welsh newsletters. The liaison officers have rapidly succeeded in gaining the trust of hundreds of detector users, convinced for the first time that this is a genuine attempt to turn over a new leaf, and as a result were able to record some 13,500 objects from some 1,000 finders in the first year, 20,700 objects from 1,900 finders in the second year, 31,783 objects from 1,788 finders in the third year, and 37,518 objects from 1,764 finders in the fourth year. Where statistics were kept on the numbers of finds recorded before the liaison officers took up their posts, they have generally at least doubled the number of finds being recorded and have often achieved much higher increases: for example, an average of 14 finds a year were recorded by the Cheshire Sites and Monuments Record during the five years between 1988 and 1993, whereas the finds liaison officer for the northwest has recorded ten times as many objects (DCMS 2000b: 25).

The liaison officers' main efforts, therefore, have been directed at those who make finds, principally detector users: between 90 and 99 per cent of all objects recorded by the finds liaison officers in their first year were metal detector finds (DCMS 1999: 11); in the second year this proportion fell to 87 per cent and in the third year it fell further to 79 per cent (demonstrating the success the liaison officers have had in reaching out beyond metal detector users). So their primary task is to establish contact with detector users (whether or not they are members of clubs) in their area. They attend detecting club meetings to explain the project and to record finds; encourage clubs and finders to record their finds themselves where appropriate; produce regular newsletters in order to keep finders in touch with their work and to highlight important finds; organise museum displays of objects found by detector users and others; develop finds recording forms and attend other museums in their area on a regular basis to record finds deposited there.

The purpose of these contacts is to foster a spirit of co-operation between detector users and archaeologists and to educate detector users on best practice. One very tangible way in which this can be achieved is through inviting detector users to participate in archaeological survey work (see Figure 15.2). All the liaison officers have become involved in creating opportunities for detector users to participate in archaeological investigations as these mean that archaeologists will naturally build up trust with local detector users and can benefit from their local knowledge, while detector users benefit from learning how archaeological investigations are conducted and in particular learn the importance of recording the precise context of their finds (for more examples see DCMS 2000b: 10–14; 2001b: 12–14).

Figure 15.2 Catherine Read, Kent Finds Liaison Officer, examining an object found during a metal detecting survey at Ashford. Catherine organised the metal detecting survey on a Roman site that was being excavated by the Oxford Archaeological Unit in advance of development. Twelve detector users recovered 300 objects, each carefully plotted, that would otherwise have been lost to the archaeological record (see DCMS 1999: 14–15; 2000b: 10–11). Department for Culture, Media and Sport.

The liaison officers also seek to record objects made by any member of the public. They encourage contacts from non-detector users by generating local publicity for their work, for example in the local press and radio. They also give talks to local archaeological and historical societies and schools, as well as holding finds identification days in museums (DCMS 1999: 9–18; 2000b: 9–24; 2001b: 10–23).

The liaison officers also record all archaeological objects, not just those made of metal, and in their first four years they recorded 12,000 stone and some 20,000 pottery objects (DCMS 1999: 23; 2000b: 38; 2001b: 39; 2002b). The liaison officers have an important role in ensuring the effective working of the treasure system by educating finders about their new obligations and by acting as a convenient channel for finders to report their finds, and their work has led to several treasure finds being reported which would otherwise not have been (DCMS 1999: 19; 2000b: 22–3).

The systematic recording of portable antiquities is also having a very positive impact on our understanding of the historic environment. Many new sites have come to light through the scheme (DCMS 2000b: 34; 2001b: 34–5) and the data will significantly enhance Sites and Monuments Records.

All the information about finds gathered by the liaison officers is passed on to the relevant Sites and Monuments Record to ensure that it can play its full part in the local planning control process, as well as being made available for educational purposes and archaeological research. However, the Sites and Monuments Record is not the only target of the data being gathered. The Portable Antiquities Scheme is making the data directly accessible by placing it on the Internet and in order to do this it has been necessary to develop a new database program for recording finds. It became clear at an early stage in the project that common standards for recording many types of find did not exist at present (traditionally monuments rather than finds have been the main focus of Sites and Monuments Records, which in any case do not all follow the same standards and use different programs). Therefore it was necessary to develop a standard that the liaison officers could adopt as quickly as possible. The best way to do this was to produce a common software program for them to use. Developing the program and the standards that accompany it has in fact been a major focus of the first two years of the scheme. The first working version of the Portable Antiquities Program was distributed to the liaison officers in May 1998 and a revised version, with the capacity to include images, was distributed in July 1999. The website (http://www.finds.org.uk) was launched in March 1999 and the number of page requests received each month has risen from 20,000 to nearly 100,000. In spring 2002 the data available on the website were relaunched with records of some 45,000 objects, images of over 7,000 of them and locational information about the findspots of the objects down to parish level. The database is therefore starting to become an important academic and educational resource.

One issue that the website has raised is the question of exactly how much of the data should be made available on it. The aim is to make as much information available as is consistent with the need to protect sites from damage and to protect the personal details of those supplying the information. Thus the personal details of finders and others are omitted and in the first launch of the data on the website the findspots of objects were only identified by county. This was because of concern expressed by finders about the publication of details of the locations where they made their finds. In fact obtaining accurate findspots has proved to be one of the most difficult tasks for some of the liaison officers. For historical reasons detector users and landowners have often been reluctant to reveal precise findspots to archaeologists, who would agree on the importance of keeping the precise locations of new sites or finds confidential, at least initially, in order to protect them from being attacked. In areas where there has been less tradition in recording finds, the liaison officers have found that finders are sometimes only willing or able to give four-figure grid references or a parish name at present, whereas in areas such as Norfolk, where there has been a long tradition of co-operation, finders routinely give precise findspots without demur. It has been a priority to improve the quality of locational information in the second year of the scheme and every pilot area showed an improvement in the second year. Overall in the first year 49 per cent of all findspots were recorded to at least a six-figure grid reference (equivalent to a hundred square metres), while by the fourth year this figure rose to 68 per cent (DCMS 2001b: 43; 2002b).

It was therefore felt that it was best not to identify findspots more precisely than by county in the initial version of the data made available on the website. However, since 2000 parish references have been included for all except the most sensitive finds.

Once the information can be made available in this way, it will be possible to start exploiting the educational benefits of the scheme and for this purpose the scheme now has an outreach officer, appointed in spring 1999. Interested individuals and educational bodies such as schools will be able to download information about finds from their area and this will, for example, enable teachers covering the Romans at Key Stage 2 to be able to give the subject a local context. The lottery bid for the expansion of the scheme (see below) contains a detailed plan for developing its educational potential. In particular the following goals have been set for the next phase:

- to ensure that the website is integrated into the National Grid for Learning;
- to develop teaching resources for primary and secondary schools and work with local education authorities and museum education departments to publicise these;
- to develop teaching resources and pilot their use for A-level archaeology;
- to promote the use of the resources available through the scheme in universities and colleges;

- to encourage adult learners to use our on-line resources and materials available through their local museums and the Portable Antiquities Scheme.

Conclusions

To conclude, the approach that has been adopted to the difficult question of how best to protect portable antiquities found in England and Wales has been dictated by pragmatic considerations. If effective controls on the use of metal detectors had been introduced at the beginning of the 1970s, then a legal requirement to report all portable antiquities might have been workable. As it was, controls were not introduced and instead metal detecting was allowed to develop into a widespread, and legal, activity. Under such circumstances a mandatory requirement to report all finds would be unworkable: no compulsory reporting system could cope with 400,000 finds a year, most of which would be of very little commercial value. The only option would be to introduce strict controls on metal detecting such as exist in most other countries in Europe, but the experience of the Treasure Bill shows that this would not be politically acceptable. This might be regrettable, but it is the case.

Some archaeologists fear that the Portable Antiquities Scheme is effectively legitimising metal detecting. This is to misunderstand its purpose: our message to metal detectorists is not 'we think what you are doing is a good thing' but rather 'we recognise that what you do is legal and we would like to record your finds for public benefit and also educate you about good practice'. Of course there will always be some detector users who will refuse to report their finds under a voluntary scheme, but such people are unlikely to heed a legal requirement to report. Many will already be breaking the law by searching without the permission of the landowner (as in the case of the Salisbury hoard: see Stead 1998) or on scheduled ancient monuments (see Dobinson and Denison (1995: 84–94) for a summary of the damage done to scheduled ancient monuments by illicit detecting).

Another factor is that the great majority of detector finds are recovered from cultivated land, from the disturbed layer of the ploughsoil. The Portable Antiquities Program includes provision for recording the type of land in which objects are found and 91 per cent of objects of which the landuse has been recorded were found on cultivated land (DCMS 2000b: 43–4). English Heritage's Monuments at Risk survey (Darvill and Fulton 1998) has shown that the principal cause of the piecemeal destruction of sites is agricultural activity, largely a consequence of the European Union's Common Agricultural Policy. Once metal objects get into the disturbed layer of the ploughsoil not only have they normally lost their immediate archaeological context (for example hoards of coins are frequently found scattered over a wide area in ploughed fields), but they are also extremely vulnerable to further damage, either from repeated ploughing, or else to degradation caused by the chemicals farmers put on fields. Archaeologists are increasingly prepared to admit that the recovery of objects in such circumstances – provided they are properly recorded – is a good thing.

I think it is both interesting and depressing to reflect why the very modest degree of reform embodied in the Treasure Act took so long to achieve in this country. One reason is that the nationalistic feeling that the heritage is something that should be preserved at all costs seems to be weaker in England than in other parts of Britain or Ireland. But most importantly archaeologists have more to do to persuade the public that the protection of the archaeological heritage should transcend private property rights. The success of the lottery bid will mean that the Portable Antiquities Scheme can be extended across the whole of England and Wales from 2003 and this will result in a major effort of public education to ensure that finders in all parts of the country are aware of the importance of recording their finds and of behaving responsibly. The pragmatic approach represented by the Treasure Act and the Portable Antiquities Scheme must be judged by the results that they obtain.

Notes

1 The Treasure Act defines treasure as (a) all objects other than coins that have at least ten per cent of gold or silver and that are at least 300 years old; (b) all groups of coins from the same find that are at least 300 years old; and (c) all objects found in association with treasure. From 1 January 2003 the definition has been extended to include deposits of prehistoric base-metal objects (pp. 281–2).

2 Lord Talbot's Bill was in fact the first attempt to introduce any kind of legislation to protect the archaeological heritage in this country and it paved the way for the Ancient Monuments Act which was passed in 1882 (Carman 1996: 49–55, 67–70).

3 In fact it now seems that this number was an over-estimate and that the true number of metal detector users is likely to be around 10,000.

4 Supplementary note (February 2004). Since this was written the number of Treasure cases has continued to rise and has doubled in the last two years, from 214 in 2001 to 414 in 2003. This is largely due to the impact of liaison officers, whose presence can lead to a five-fold increase in the reporting of Treasure.

The Dealing in Cultural Objects (Offences) Act, which came into force on 30 December 2003, creating a new offence of dealing in illegally-removed cultural objects, should make it harder for illicit detector-users to sell thier finds to dealers.

In January 2004 the Headley Trust established a new fund to help regional museums to acquire treasure finds.

Bibliography

Bland, R. 1996. Treasure trove and the case for reform. *Art, Antiquity and Law* I (1): 11–26.

Bland, R. 1997. The implementation of the Treasure Act. *Museum Archaeologists News* 25 (Autumn/Winter): 4–6.

Bland, R. 1998. The Treasure Act and the proposal for the voluntary recording of all archaeological finds. In Denford, G. (ed.) *Museums in the Landscape: Bridging the Gap*. Society of Museum Archaeologists. The Museum Archaeologist Volume 23. Conference Proceedings, St Albans 1996: 3–19.

Carey Miller, D. L. and Sheridan, A. 1996. Treasure trove in Scots law. *Art, Antiquity and Law* I (4): 393–406.

Carman, J. 1996. *Valuing Ancient Things*. Leicester: Leicester University Press.

Cleere, H. 1979. *Archaeology in Britain 1978*. London: Council for British Archaeology.

Cleere, H. 1982. *Archaeology in Britain 1981*. London: Council for British Archaeology.

Cleere, H. 1994. The CBA: the first fifty years. In *Council for British Archaeology Report No. 44*. London: Council for British Archaeology.

Council of Europe, 1981. *Metal Detectors and Archaeology. Report of the Committee on Culture and Education*. Strasbourg: Council of Europe, Parliamentary Assembly, Doc. 4741.

Darvill, T. and Fulton, A. K. 1998. *MARS: The Monuments at Risk Survey of England, 1995. Main Report*. Bournemouth University and English Heritage.

DCMS (Department for Culture, Media and Sport). 1999. *Portable Antiquities. Annual Report 1997–98*. London: DCMS.

DCMS. 2000a. *Report on the Operation of the Treasure Act 24 September 1997 – 23 September 1998*. London: DCMS.

DCMS. 2000b. *Portable Antiquities. Annual Report 1998–99*. London: DCMS.

DCMS. 2000c. *Treasure Act 1996: Review. Consultation Paper*. London: DCMS.

DCMS. 2001a. *Report on the Operation of the Treasure Act 24 September 1998 – 31 December 1999*. London: DCMS.

DCMS. 2001b. *Portable Antiquities. Annual Report 1999–2000*. London: DCMS.

DCMS. 2001c. *Report on the Operation of the Treasure Act: Review and Recommendations*. Available at: www.culture.gov.uk/heritage/index.html

DCMS. 2002a. *Report on the Operation of the Treasure Act 1 January – 31 December 2000*. London: DCMS.

DCMS. 2002b. *Portable Antiquities. Annual Report 2000/2001*. London: DCMS.

DNH (Department of National Heritage). 1996. *Portable Antiquities. A discussion document*. London: DNH.

DNH. 1997. *The Treasure Act 1996. Code of Practice (England and Wales)*. London: DNH.

Dobinson, C. and Denison, S. 1995. *Metal Detecting and Archaeology in England*. London: English Heritage/Council for British Archaeology.

Fletcher, E. 1977. Archaeology v. Treasure Hunting – the beginning of the end of the war? *Treasure Hunting* September: 9–10.

Green, B. and Gregory, T. 1978. An initiative on the use of metal detectors in Norfolk. *Museums Journal* 77(4): 161–2.

Hill, G. F. 1936. *Treasure Trove in Law and Practice*. Oxford: Clarendon Press.

Museums and Galleries Commission. 1999. *The Portable Antiquities Scheme. Finding our Past. Newsletter* 1, November 1999.

National Council for Metal Detecting. 1992. *A Shared Heritage*. London: NCMD.

O'Connell, M. G. and Bird, J. 1994. The Roman temple at Wanborough, excavation 1985–1986. *Surrey Archaeological Collections* 82: 1–168.

Palmer, N. 1993. Treasure Trove and Title to Discovered Antiquities. *International Journal of Cultural Property* 2(2): 275–318.

Pugh-Smith, J. and Samuels, J. 1996. *Archaeology in Law*. London: Sweet and Maxwell.

Resource. 2000. *The Portable Antiquities Scheme. Finding our Past. Newsletter* 2, Summer 2000.

Schadla-Hall, T. 1994. Antiquities legislation: A proper basis? *The Museum Archaeologist* 21: 12–16.

Schadla-Hall, T. 1995a. Letter in *Museums Journal*, September 1995: 18.

Schadla-Hall, T. 1995b. Letter in *Museums Journal*, December 1995: 16.

Selkirk, A. 1997. *Who Owns the Past?* London: Adam Smith Institute.

Selkirk, A. 1999. Portable antiquities. *Current Archaeology* 162: 162.

Sheridan, A. 1991. What's mine is Her Majesty's – The law in Scotland. *The Museum Archaeologist* 16: 35–40.

Sheridan, A. 1994. The Scottish 'Treasure Trove' system: A suitable case for emulation? *The Museum Archaeologist* 21: 4–11.

Sheridan, A. 1995. Portable antiquities legislation in Scotland: what is it, and how well does it work? In K. Tubb (ed.) *Antiquities, Trade or Betrayed*. London: Archetype Press: 193–204.

Stead, I. M. 1998. *The Salisbury Hoard*. Stroud: Tempus.

Ward, A. 1992. Treasure Trove and the law of theft. *International Journal of Cultural Property* 1: 195.

16

THE EFFECTS OF THE ANTIQUITIES MARKET ON ARCHAEOLOGICAL DEVELOPMENT IN CHINA

Dashu Qin

When considering the influence of the antiquities market on the development of archaeology in China, we have to take a historical point of view, as the effects have been different in different periods. In other words, the damage to ancient remains and artifacts that has ensued as a result of the trade in antiquities and the negative effects of this trade for archaeology can be shown to have occurred on different scales. The antiquities market I refer to here is the international trade in antiquities, especially for people in Western countries (and other developed countries such as Japan). For customers in these developed countries the desire to possess cultural relics from ancient civilisations has led to the creation of a large, well developed antiquities market.

Most centres of ancient civilisation in the world are located in developing countries, including China, Egypt, Mesopotamia and India. But initiatives and development in the field of modern archaeology in these areas lag behind those in most Western countries. Archaeologists and collectors in developed countries often acquire antiquities from the market in order to carry out archaeological research or for their own collection. Therefore, the development of archaeology in the centres of ancient civilisations is closely associated with the antiquities market. The development of this relationship can be divided into three stages.

The early stage: the beginnings of archaeological research

In the early stage, actions by people from developed countries who sought ancient cultural relics had the effect to a certain extent of promoting the initiation and development of archaeology. For example, in Egypt, early excavations were often associated with the quest for antiquities (Bierbrier 1995).

In China, approximately before the 1930s, some foreign scholars undertook a number of valuable surveys and excavations, with the purpose of discovering Chinese antiquities. But as a result of their work, large quantities of valuable cultural artifacts and relics were taken to the West. Paul Pelliot from France and Aurel Stein from Britain, for example, conducted many expeditions to remote areas in northwest and north China during the early part of the twentieth century. They investigated dozens of important sites, and made valuable records of many ancient remains (Thote 1995; Walker 1995). In fact, these Western scholars can be said to have initiated archaeological work in these regions, and their records still serve as important references for researchers. However, they also removed large numbers of relics to the West, some of them bought from local people, without the permission or knowledge of the Chinese government.

Let us take ceramics as an example, which are undoubtedly one of the main interests pursued by Western collectors. In China, people collected ceramics as antiques from very early times (beginning around the tenth century AD), and they classified them according to the few ancient textual records. When Westerners began to collect ceramics, they paid a great deal of attention to the site of production, dating and production techniques. Partly due to the research undertaken on these items, Chinese people realised the importance of ancient kiln sites and began to investigate them. In 1918, Ju Lu City, which was buried by a flood in the latter part of the Northern Song Dynasty (1108), was discovered and many antiquities were dug up by local people (National Museum of Chinese History 1927; Lovell 1970). Spurred by their unrestricted ability to purchase these objects, Western collectors began to investigate where exactly they had been made and the range of objects produced at the Ju Lu site, by comparing the unearthed objects with sherds from the kiln sites. As a result, the importance of ancient kiln sites began to be realised. Subsequently, Chinese scholars began to investigate such sites themselves, and this is held to mark the beginning of ceramic archaeology in China (Qin 1990).

As can be seen from the above, in the early stage, the antiquities market played a dual role: on the one hand, it caused serious damage to ancient remains; and on the other hand, it brought modern archaeology in some degree to developing countries. This kind of relationship between the antiquities market and archaeology at this stage resulted from the fact that most centres of civilisation were under the rule of colonial powers or indirectly controlled by them. Local people had no power or right to protect their ancient property. Foreign scholars and others were able to discover antiquities and take them away by undertaking archaeological investigations and excavations. Therefore, the acquisition of relics was always associated with formal archaeological work.

Second stage: archaeology and the market move apart

In the following stage, archaeology developed in each of the centres of ancient civilizations, without much influence from the antiquities trade. The main reason for this was that countries which had sophisticated ancient civilisations at their heart gradually achieved independence and came to control their own sovereignty. As a result, each of these countries established their own laws and policies relating to cultural property.

In Egypt, foreign agencies were instructed to obtain permits from the Egyptian authorities, who would examine and verify their qualifications and *bona fides*. Only then would they be able to proceed with an excavation, under the inspection of Egyptian experts. The excavators were made responsible for protecting the site after the excavation, and the excavated antiquities were mainly retained in Egypt.

In China, after 1949 foreign agencies were forbidden from taking part in excavations, and antiquities were restricted from export. These policies were implemented and well enforced for quite a long time, and seem to have been relatively effective at preventing antiquities from leaving the country.

During the second stage, the antiquities sold in the market were mainly those which had been taken out of the original countries in the first stage, and only relatively small quantities of objects were newly discovered and smuggled out. During this stage, smuggled objects did not necessarily come from important ancient sites and were not always dug up with a clear purpose. As a result, relatively few objects of high value were being sold through the antiquities market. In sum, during the second stage, archaeology and the antiquities market developed relatively independently of each other.

The third stage: archaeology and the antiquities market today

The third stage, which covers the most recent two decades, is characterised by different situations in different countries depending on their laws and policies. In Egypt and some other countries, because of consistent implementation of the law, there has been a reasonably effective restriction on the expansion of the antiquities market. The amount of damage to ancient remains is not as serious as it is in China.

Over the last two decades, Chinese archaeology has undergone significant progress. Large numbers of archaeological surveys and excavations have been carried out, and some highly significant discoveries made. Meanwhile, the antiquities market has also developed rapidly and extended its reach, for two main reasons.

The first is that, following the economic boom, particularly in East and Southeast Asia, many people developed the economic capacity to purchase even quite expensive antiquities. This caused the number of collectors to increase greatly, and the demand for collectable objects increased with the same speed. In general, before the 1970s, the most numerous and important collectors were from Europe, America and Japan. However, after the economic boom in Asia, people from Southeast Asia, Hong Kong, Taiwan and Korea began to purchase Chinese antiquities in large quantities. Compared to the West, people in these regions feel a closer attachment to ancient Chinese culture and there is a strong demand for antiquities. Some people collect because of their own interest, some collect in order to display their wealth or to enhance their dignity, and some others collect for purposes of investment. People often tell one successful story: in 1974, following the stock market crash in London, the British Rail Pension Fund decided to invest its funds in (amongst other things) Chinese antiquities, and over a period of more than ten years, successfully increased its assets (Thompson 1993).

A similar situation has developed in China over the last decade. Wealthy individuals and large companies have begun to purchase relics through the antiquities market in order to demonstrate their wealth and dignity. This demand has caused auction houses to spring up in large numbers (Phillips 1998). China has also experienced serious inflation, and some media stories have strongly suggested that ordinary people have bought antiquities as investments or to preserve the value of their currency.

The number of collectors both inside and outside China increased rapidly and collectors became more experienced in buying in the market; this led to a corresponding increase in the demand for antiquities. Buyers not only began to request more objects to collect, but also began to place a premium on complete and more valuable objects. These nearly always come from important ancient sites, such as mausolea and pagodas. The desire for such objects therefore represented a serious threat to these sites through looting and destruction.

A further reason for the expansion of the antiquities market is the success of archaeology itself. As excavation and research have systematically improved, knowledge of many ancient sites and cultural artifacts has become much more developed. For example, some of the objects found in recent years were previously unknown, to the astonishment of scholars and the admiration of collectors;[1] other objects that were ignored in the past began to gain more attention. People began to value antiquities not only for their beauty, but also for their academic significance; therefore, museums and research agencies outside China no longer felt content with collecting at the same level as before. The requirement for objects of high academic value increased as archaeological research intensified. Objects from special places and periods became particularly sought-after. In this respect, many Western museums played a negative role, by collecting artifacts of high quality and academic value, by collecting material from ancient sites, and by collecting the kinds of objects that could not easily be collected by individuals, such as monumental sculpture.

While robbing tombs to acquire antiquities has been occurring in China for centuries, the pace and nature of looting has changed greatly in recent years.

For example, even tombs plundered of their grave goods a long time ago have become attractive to a new kind of tomb robber who, following the further development of academic research, has found it lucrative to remove wall paintings, stone carvings and brick reliefs from tombs. As museums outside China have paid high prices for these kinds of antiquities, tomb sites have become renewed targets for plunder. This has caused serious damage or even total destruction to many ancient remains, and has in turn brought the local cultural relics administration agencies under a great deal of pressure in trying to deal with the problem.

In recent years, certain museums in the USA have acquired many large and important antiquities from China, such as a very heavy Northern Wei Dynasty (386–534) stone coffin covered with stone carvings in different designs, and a four metre square Liao Dynasty (907–1125) outer coffin board painted with a hunting picture. Both are very important for research and have a high academic value, and are unlikely to have been collected by an individual person. The implication is that museums' willingness to acquire such material is fuelling looting on the ground in China.

Another example of how academia and museums can fuel destruction can be taken from the development of ceramic archaeology. As interest in Chinese ceramics has grown, many Western museums have begun to collect more of them. In some cases, complete objects are very rare, so museums began to collect shards. As a result of this interest, kiln sites have been plundered by local people in order to acquire different ranges of material, for example, with different glazes, designs or techniques of decoration. There has also been a demand for provenanced shards in order to demonstrate the place of production of complete vessels. These demands have caused different degrees of destruction to many ancient kiln sites. For instance, when the imperial kiln site of the Southern Song Dynasty (1127–1286) was discovered a few years ago, local people tried to loot the site because museums outside China were prepared to pay a high price for this relatively rare pottery. As a result, the local cultural relics administration agency had to hire security staff to protect the site day and night, which became a heavy drain on its resources.

For the reasons mentioned above, the market in Chinese antiquities has become widespread and lucrative. Over recent years, the antiquities market has become a strongly negative force in archaeological development, as the number of looters has greatly increased. Looters have formed themselves into small well-funded cliques equipped with high technology, and sometimes supported by dealers outside China. The impact of this situation has been twofold.

First, because the demand for antiquities is intense and sustained, many looters have become full-time professionals, searching for ancient sites all over China. This has meant that many important ancient sites have been discovered and destroyed before archaeologists could undertake any recording, resulting in the total loss of some extremely important research material. In total, looters have been first to find – and loot – over half of the important archaeological discoveries made in recent years. Some of the sites were excavated by archaeologists after the looters had been there, and some records were able to be made of what remained. But in most cases, the sites have been destroyed without any record. The losses are beyond remedy.

Second, the looters and art dealers have targeted ongoing archaeological investigations, with the result that some important sites have been seriously damaged. For example, the Tianma-Qucun site was the Jin Marquisate capital in the Bronze Age, and was one of the largest sites of this period in China. Ancient Chinese texts recorded the Jin Marquisate capital as located in Tai Yuan, which is hundreds of kilometres north of the Tianma-Qucun site. Because of this, for a long time no attention was paid to this area and the site was well maintained. In 1979, Professor Zou Heng of the Department of Archaeology, Peking University, found the site and showed it to be the capital of the Jin Marquisate. The discovery caused a sensation in academic circles, and the Department has been excavating there continuously ever since. However, the discovery also alerted the looters, who began to target the large unexcavated area of the site from 1986, and increased their activity from 1987 to 1990. The looters dug the site day and night, with up to several hundred people involved in a single day. According to incomplete statistics, during these three years more than a thousand graves were opened up, and several thousand bronze and jade objects were dug up, most of which were smuggled out of China.

Furthermore, in 1991 and 1992, looters began to dig the Jin Marquis and Marquise tombs. Seventeen unexcavated tombs were known to exist, containing eight Marquis and nine Marquises, generation by generation. The tomb robbers ransacked seven large tombs (four Marquis, three Marquises) and the antiquities were removed to Hong Kong within a month. Some antiquities were bought on the market by the Shanghai Museum in order to bring them back to China, but the whereabouts of others are unknown, and the names of two Marquis are therefore lost (Zou 1998).

The Department of Archaeology at Peking University has also excavated a Neolithic site in Gansu Province, during which local villagers were hired as workers and taught how to recognise different kinds of earth. After the work was finished, local people began to dig graves on a large scale on their own initiative. Thousands of coloured pots were dug up and carried out of China by truck, causing a steep decline in the price of coloured pottery on the market. When the cultural relics administration agencies took steps to prevent this looting, the local governor complained that the Department of Archaeology had trained the tomb robbers!

Conclusion

Looting of antiquities in China has an old history, but has increased greatly in scale in recent years. Part of the reason for this increase is the demand for Chinese antiquities in the West and in the more developed Asian countries, amongst both private collectors and museums. At present, archaeology as an academic discipline, and museums as places of exhibition, are – innocently or not – fuelling looting at Chinese sites. Unfortunately, archaeologists within China are even themselves seen as making the situation worse by drawing attention to important sites. Ultimately, though, it is the market for antiquities which is fuelling the destruction. What must be done urgently, therefore, is for the practices of the antiquities market to be addressed seriously.

The governments of 'resource countries' – those with the cultural relics – should pay much greater attention to the protection of their ancient remains and hinder the looting that takes place. However, it will always be difficult to stamp out all looting because of the size of the countries and the limited resources available for policing.

The real way forward must be for a concerted effort to be made in the West and in the Asian countries that purchase antiquities, to prevent collecting of looted artifacts through a combination of legislation, education and public opinion. Recent studies such as that by Brodie *et al.* (2000) have shown the complexity of the situation world-wide. It is clear that as long as a market exists, local people will generally try to supplement their income by looting poorly protected sites unless they can be persuaded through education and the development of alternative sources of income (such as tourism) to do otherwise. The answer then must lie in ensuring that the antiquities trade becomes open and transparent, so that legally obtained items can be traded freely, while looted material becomes unpurchaseable.

Note

1 This situation is summarised well in the following extract:

> Chinese art-history books are going to have to be rewritten,' says dealer Carol Conover of New York's Kaikodo, noting that many unusual pieces in the recent 'China: 5,000 Years' exhibition at the Guggenheim Museum in New York were found in the past ten years. 'If I'd seen that show 20 years ago,' she says, 'I would have said, "You're kidding."'
>
> (Harrington 1998: 135)

Bibliography

Bierbrier, M. L. (ed.) 1995. *Who Was Who in Egyptology* (third edition). London: The Egypt Exploration Society.

Brodie, N., Doole, J. and Watson, P. 2000. *Stealing History: The Illicit Trade in Cultural Material.* Cambridge: McDonald Institute for Archaeological Research.

Harrington, S. P. M. 1998. The China Syndrome, *Art News* October: 135.

Lovell, H-C. 1970. Notes on Chu-Lu Hsien. *Oriental Art* 16(3).

National Museum of Chinese History 1927. *Bulletin of the National Museum of Chinese History* 1(1).

Phillips, F. 1998. Auction Houses in Beijing. *Asian Art*, February.

Qin, D. 1990. History of the study of Cizhou type wares, *Wenwu Chunqiu* 4.

Ronghua, J. 1993. *Studies on the Critical Persons Engaged in Bringing Dun Huang Artifacts Abroad*. Taipei: Xin Wen Feng Publishing Inc.

Thompson, J. 1993. Sotheby's Hong Kong – Twenty Years. In Sotheby's (ed.) *Sotheby's Hong Kong – Twenty Years*. Hong Kong: Tai Yip Company.

Thote, A. 1995. Paul Pelliot: A Bridge Between Western Sinology and Chinese Scholarship. *Orientations* 26: 6.

Walker, A. 1995. *Aurel Stein – Pioneer of the Silk Road*. London: John Murray.

Zou, H. 1998. The looting of the Bronze Age Cemetery Site at Tianma-Qucun, China. Paper presented at the international conference, Art, Antiquity, and Law: Preserving Our Global Cultural Heritage, Rutgers University, New Jersey, USA, October 1998.

INDEX

INDEX

archaeological sites *see* sites
archaeologists distrusted by metal
detectorists 274, 275; educational
role *vis-à-vis* public 132; impact on
local economies 227–8; media skills
156–7; relations with local
communities 227–9, 230–1, 233
archaeology alternative *see* alternative
archeology; art and imagery inspired
by 53–4, 98–100; beneficiaries of 11;
benefits to local people 211–23;
changing attitudes in 3–4;
communication with public 8–12;
democratic discourse in 159–87;
focus group views on 124–6; and
Internet 159–87; media
representations 145–58 *see also*
media representations;
professionalisation 3; public
awareness 212; public interest 3, 6,
133, 154; retreat from scientific
objectivism 267, 269; social
engagement of 205
artefacts curation and storage 41;
looting 24, 38–40, 61, 295–8
artistic/creative projects run by
archaeologists 53–4, 98–100
Australia European territorial expansion
241; *see also* Aboriginal people in
New South Wales
authority of state ancient monuments
protection 191–3; diminution of
193; and market forces 193; rejection
of 194

'beats' Aboriginal networks of
movement 244
Beneath These Waters 35, 53
Black cultures Brazil 205, 206, 207
Black Egyptologists 113
Brazil audience for archaeology 204–7;
exclusion of black and indigenous
cultures 205; heritage of the elite
206; nature of society 202–4; state of
archaeology 13, 204–7
British Museum attitudinal surveys
8–10; communication with public
8–12

Canada lack of federal heritage
protection laws 65
Canadian Archaeological Association
65
ceramics damage to kiln sites 296;
research in China 293, 296
China demand for artefacts by collectors
and museums 292–3, 294–6; early
research phase 292–3; economic
factors in collecting 294, 296; effect
of antiquities market on archaeology
13, 292–9; looting 295–8;
protection of antiquities 294; recent
archaeology 294, 297; removal of
antiquities to West 293
choice in society 193 rejection of official
versions of the past 191, 193–4, 195,
197, 199 *see also* alternative
archaeology
collections digital access to 90–1;
human remains in 247, 248; in
museums *see* museum collections
colonial expansion and Aboriginal
people 241; methods of
disempowerment used 251
colonial history indigenous
communities and 225, 226, 235
Colonial Williamsburg 43, 75
colonised landscape visibility of
Aboriginal people in 248
community museum movement 88;
mobile museums 96
compliance-related archaeology 36–7
conservation 91–3; on public display 92
construction of meaning expert v.
public 135; by on-site visitors
139–40
constructivism radical 134; social 134
constructivist site needs of visitors
140–2
Council for British Archaeology 273,
274, 275
Cramond Lioness 148, 150, 151
creationism 266, 268
critical theory approach to archaeology
37
cultural diversity alienation of ethnic
minorities 97 of London 97–8

301